FUNCTIONS
AND
POLICIES
OF
**AMERICAN
GOVERNMENT**

Edited by

JACK W. PELTASON
University of Illinois

JAMES M. BURNS
Williams College

Co-authors

RICHARD W. TAYLOR
Coe College

JAMES N. MURRAY, JR.
The State University of Iowa

ROBERT SALISBURY
Washington University

LAWRENCE J. R. HERSON
Ohio State University

Englewood Cliffs, N.J.

PRENTICE-HALL, INC.

FUNCTIONS
AND
POLICIES
OF
AMERICAN

GOVERNMENT
Big Democracy in Action

FUNCTIONS AND POLICIES OF AMERICAN GOVERNMENT
Big Democracy in Action

Edited by
Jack W. Peltason and James M. Burns

Co-authors
Richard W. Taylor
James N. Murray, Jr.
Robert Salisbury
Lawrence J. R. Herson

© 1958 BY
PRENTICE-HALL, INC.
ENGLEWOOD CLIFFS, N.J.

LIBRARY OF CONGRESS
CATALOG CARD NO.: 58-9307

Third printing, June, 1960

PRINTED IN THE UNITED STATES OF AMERICA
33163—C

Preface

THIS volume is a presentation of governmental policies, functions, and programs, discussed in greater detail than is possible in standard introductory American government texts. In a context as complete as space permits, specific policies are described against a background of history, politics, and government. The emphasis is on functions, policies, and programs of the national government; but since much of what the national government does is closely intertwined with state activities, there is a good deal of treatment of the latter.

The book is a joint effort in both the full and limited meaning of the words. The authors agreed in advance on the general approach, emphasis, and subject matter; but in the light of the great diversity of the subject, we have not tried to fit each chapter into a narrow, cramping mold. The reader will find, consequently, that the chapters are roughly similar in problems raised and concepts discussed; but the organization, emphasis, and viewpoint may vary somewhat from chapter to chapter.

We wish to thank our colleagues for their suggestions and our students for allowing themselves to be exposed somewhat experimentally to much of the material. Special thanks are due Professor John R. Schmidhauser of The State University of Iowa for reading the drafts of the chapters on foreign and military policy.

THE AUTHORS

Contents

6.

Robert H. Salisbury

AGRICULTURE AND NATURAL RESOURCES, 195

7.

Richard W. Taylor

GOVERNMENT AND BUSINESS, 241

8.

James M. Burns

GOVERNMENT AND LABOR, 290

11.

James M. Burns

SOME CONCLUSIONS ON THE STUDY OF PUBLIC POLICY, 418

FUNCTIONS
AND
POLICIES
OF
AMERICAN
GOVERNMENT

1. JACK W. PELTASON

An Approach to the Study of Public Policy

SINCE readers often ignore the preface—undoubtedly they are in a hurry to get on with the business of learning—this introduction includes comments ordinarily found in prefaces. The chapters that follow might be misunderstood if our purposes and terms of reference are not clear.

This book is designed for the reader who is acquainted—or is becoming acquainted—with the general organization of American Government as it is taught in the standard introductory course. In most such courses limitations of time preclude any extended study of programs and policies: the functions of government, if discussed at all, are given only cursory treatment. Here the emphasis is reversed. The focus is on what American governments do.

The purposes of this book are to provide historical background for each major policy area, to describe the broad outlines of existing programs, to identify the interest groups and organizations most immediately concerned, to bring to the fore the values that are in conflict, to point to the interrelations between process and policy, and to suggest the possible consequences of various choices.

A study of the functions of government is inevitably a study of politics and administration. Questions about what our governments

1

should do and how they should do it are resolved not through the application of abstract scientific principles but through the policy-making process, in which we all participate.

THE POLICY PROCESS

To some, politics is a struggle between heroes and villains—the good guys against the bad guys. Others divide the political world into two parts, the "government" and the "people." To others the government is a group of statesmen standing above the clamour of politics and applying predetermined scientific rules to protect the "people" against the "special interests." But the good-guys-versus-the-bad-guys approach is an exercise in conclusions, not in description, nor does it give us precise analytic tools. Similarly, to organize all the "booming-buzzing-confusion" of politics into such broad gauge moulds as "government" and "people" is an obvious oversimplification. "Government" and "people" are terms of such wide scope that they conceal more than they reveal. Government consists of people, many different kinds of people who have many different kinds of values. And the "people" are not a homogeneous unit, internally united and uniformly hostile to all public officials. We need categories of description more restrictive in their focus.

Politics as interest group conflict

Government programs and politics are fundamentally the products of contests among citizens, both private and official. Within the context of widely shared and deeply held common values, Americans have conflicting political goals—differing ideas about which policies are "in the public interest." Each of us is likely to erect a system of thinking or an ideology in which our own role—manager, professor, inventor, housewife—is the axis on which the world turns. From our differing perspectives we view the world differently. The miner who goes into the earth to dig for coal thinks that he is performing the most essential economic task and his perspective toward government programs that boost wages is likely to be different from that of the harried company treasurer who is worried about meeting the company payrolls.

As a result of their varying perspectives, Americans differ concerning the desirability of many public programs. They make various claims on and through the instruments of government. One way to describe this political activity is in terms of *interest groups*. All the kinds of activity—writing, speaking, voting, lobbying, forming organizations—designed to secure a particular political goal may be related to an interest; those engaged in like activities make up a group. It is theoretically possible for a particular interest to consist of the action of only one man. For the most part, however, it is only those programs supported by more than one person that take on enough significance to be of concern to a study of policy-making. We shall consider public policies as essentially the products of interest groups.

The term "interest group" is merely a descriptive category that the observer creates in order to relate diverse events. The term "interest" has the disadvantage of carrying overtones of selfishness, of material and personal gain. No such suggestion is intended here. Differing concepts of ultimate good bring about conflicts of interest as often as do struggles over the distribution of material rewards. As used here, "interest group" is *not* an evaluating term. There is no implication of either criticism or approval, for example, when it is pointed out that producers of natural gas were an important part of the interest group working to secure passage of a law to free their businesses from regulation by the Federal Power Commission.

People who share common roles and characteristics often have common interests, and they often organize. But an interest group should not be confused either with an organization or with groups of people having certain attributes in common. Workers, farmers, veterans, fathers, and Negroes, for example, are various ways to group people by characteristics they share or by roles they perform. The United Mine Workers, General Motors, and National Association for Advancement of Calendar Reform are organizations. Proponents of compulsory health insurance and opponents of federal civil rights legislation, for example, are interest groups. Although organization is, as we shall presently note, a characteristic activity of an interest group, the organization and interest group should be kept distinct. Not all members of the American Legion, for example, belong to the interest group working for pensions for veterans. On the other hand, some who are not members of the American Legion do work for veterans' pensions.

The role of government in the policy process

Government consists of public officials. In a democracy what they do is related to what those who are not public officials want done. These officials are not outside the group struggle, they are very much in it. When a congressman votes, a President vetoes, a judge decides, or a civil servant issues an order, these actions are interest group activity and the official becomes a member of an interest group. A congressman may resent our description of his votes as interest activity: he may insist that he is supporting the "public interest." We do not deny that the vote may be in the "public interest"—but that is a conclusion, not a description. Some people think, for example, that civil rights legislation is in "the public interest," others deny this. When a congressman casts his vote he supports one view and rejects the other. The very function of public officials makes them participants in the group struggles. In fact, victory in our democracy goes to the group able to recruit the support of the largest number of public officials.

To describe the action of public officials as interest activity is not to suggest that they have "sold out to the special interests." Rather it is an attempt to give a three dimensional scope to our study of public policy so that what public officials do can be seen in relation to the political community of which they are part. Hence, the debating, voting, decision-making, speech making, and conflicts in Congress, the White House, the courts, and the state agencies may be seen not as isolated events, but as part of the competition among the overlapping interest groups which these officials reflect and represent.

Politicians—the vital link

Even in nondemocratic countries it is likely that the government, through force and suppression, does gain some support among the citizenry. But in a democracy, where all interest groups are allowed to use peaceful procedures to secure their goals, the connections between public programs and private wishes is more direct and immediate.

Frequently pleas are made to "keep politics" out of policy-making. If by keeping politics out of governmental decision-making and administration is meant the restricting of political-party partisan advantage, conceivably this could be done in some areas without undermining democratic procedures. But to suppress interest conflict is to suppress democracy. In a police state a small group of rulers can make policy and throw in jail all who would oppose it. The policy reflects only the claims and concepts of the rulers. But in a democracy the dependence of public officials on approval at the polls is the ultimate insurance that they will be responsive to the largest rather than the least part of the community.

Voters do not directly determine the nature of governmental programs and do not administer them. Government is always the special responsibility of a few. But the voters select the officials who make the decisions, and the officials are subject to criticism and possible defeat at the polls. Moreover, voters do not mark their ballots and then retire abjectly to their homes unconcerned and uninterested. Some of them, the group leaders, have many devices to influence policy. Congressmen, Presidents, Governors, civil servants, and judges make decisions, but in a free society these decisions reflect and are part of the group struggle.

It is the politicians who provide the vital link. And "politicians" is used here in the broadest sense to include all those who are active in making and applying policies. They sponsor programs and provide the means of access to the decision-making arenas. Because they desire and need to win votes, the political system operates in a democratic fashion and public officials promote the interests of majority groups. Unless they please more voters than they displease, they will be replaced by other politicians.

Our political system, like our economic system, harnesses private goals. It is not necessary for either the politicians or the businessmen to be angels, willing to sacrifice their own aims for those of others. Both are expected to work within accepted channels, and they have other roles and values besides business and politics. But their own private goals can be satisfied by providing the goods that the voters or customers will buy; in short, their desires to win votes and make money are put to social use.

The socially useful role of the businessman's desire for profit is widely recognized. Not much energy is spent in determining whether a businessman is "sincere." Seldom is he condemned because he sells his customers the kind of shoes they ask for rather than those he feels are best for them. No one is disturbed by the fact that the businessman's personal motive may be to make money rather than to provide people with shoes. And few would argue that profit-making should be "kept out of business."

But the indispensable and socially useful role of the politician is less widely recognized. Often he is accused of not really being interested in farmers when he votes for farm supports but rather of playing politics in order to get votes. (This is about as profound as saying that a businessman is playing business in order to make money.) The politician is criticized because he lacks courage to support programs the voters do not like, and he is urged to operate without regard to the political repercussions of his actions.

This democratic fusion of politics and policy growing out of the dependence of decision-makers on popular approval, does not turn politicians into mere puppets responding to the commands of the electorate. The electorate speaks with many voices. The voters are not a unit but represent many interests. Even if the politician were content to do what his constituents wanted done, he would not find his constituents in agreement. On many issues most of the voters would be unconcerned and content to leave the choice to others, subject only to approval of the ultimate consequences. The criss-cross and push-pull of the interest struggle give policy-makers ample room for maneuver and for playing a dominant role. They are leaders as well as followers. They do what a majority of their constituents want done, but in part, the constituents want what their political leaders tell them they should want.[1]

The ground rules of policy-making in a democracy

So far we have stressed the element of conflict, but we must remember that these conflicts take place within the context of agreement on fundamental questions. Despite their many differences over immediate issues, Americans are strongly committed to basic values. In a sense, there is an interest group supporting our constitutional and democratic system, and this interest group includes almost all Americans. All unite in believing that the preservation of our free system and the use of democratic procedures is more important than the winning of any political victory.

Without this basic agreement it would be impossible for political conflicts to be resolved by peaceful procedure. If any group of significant size were to become convinced that attaining its goals was more important than abiding by the ground rules, we would have a civil war or would cease to be a single political community. This is not likely to happen, however, because Americans have so many overlapping

[1] The analogy between customers and voters breaks down in at least one major respect. When one man wants brown shoes, he can achieve his desires without denying his neighbor the chance to buy black shoes. But all the voters cannot be pleased. Some wanted Eisenhower to be President and some wanted Stevenson. Through politics we decide which group will be disappointed. Because ours is democratic politics, this group is ordinarily the group with the least votes.

and conflicting interests that no single dominant conflict divides the public into permanent camps. Today's political allies are tomorrow's enemies. A businessman, besides belonging to that large and indefinable grouping of consumers, may also be a member of a church, a fraternal society, the American Legion, and a trade association. One of his employees may belong to the same church and American Legion post, but may be associated with a trade union and a different political party. On some issues, the worker and his boss may belong to the same interest group, on others to a different group. A single individual may even participate in conflicting interest groups. As a veteran, he may write to his Senator urging support for a bonus bill, but as a businessman he may contribute to an organization that is writing to the same Senator urging him to vote against the bonus bill.

This pluralism of American society with its overlapping allegiances —this basic social check and balance—tempers and moderates the intensity of interest conflicts. It makes public decisions highly tentative. Few laws, court decisions, regulatory orders, or elections make any drastic alteration in governmental policy. Rather there is a continuous stream of action in which the group that gains a small advantage at one moment will lose the next round. No one group feels that it has been forced to sacrifice basic values; hence groups are willing to accept their defeats gracefully and hope for a victory tomorrow.

Tactics

Our political battles thus take place according to the rules of the game upon which all agree. Everybody is free to argue, cajole, propagandize, nominate candidates, and campaign. Nobody may use bribery, intimidation, suppression, or violence to achieve his goals. Those who get the most support through peaceful persuasion get their way, for the moment. Those disappointed by the immediate decision must abide by it, but they are free to work for its reversal, provided they work through democratic and legal channels.

Some people are more active than others. But even those who do nothing participate in the battle because their apathy aids the group which at the moment is strongest. Participation includes more than merely marking a ballot. As Paul H. Appleby has pointed out, "Citizens vote by adding their names and energies to membership rolls. They vote by swelling, or failing to swell, the circulations of particular newspapers or periodicals. They vote by contributing to the popularity of particular radio or newspaper commentators. They vote by writing 'letters to the editor.' They vote in every contribution they make to the climate of opinion in a thoroughly political society." [2]

Here are some characteristic kinds of political action:

Organization. A small number of well-organized persons who work hard may be victorious over a large number of unorganized people whose political action is passive and undirected. As a result, persons who share a common interest or set of interests frequently create an organization to promote their goals or work through existing ones.

Lobbying. A direct approach to public officials is of course an ancient and important political tactic. Lobbying is not restricted to pressures on legislators. Interest groups also attempt to influence judges, administrators, political leaders, in fact any person who makes decisions in which they are interested. The procedures vary. Legislators may be appealed to by promises of help in the next election, or by threats of opposition. Evidence may be presented to them to persuade them that a certain position is sound. Judges are approached through lawyers' briefs and appeals to law and logic.

Propaganda (or Persuasion). As the word is used here, "propaganda" refers to the use of symbols to secure a desired response and reaction from certain persons or groups. One interest-group leader has asked: "In the long run isn't it better and surer to lay a groundwork with the people back home who have the votes, so that proposals of this character [hostile to this particular interest group] are not popular with them, rather than depend upon stopping such proposals when they get up to the legislature or commission?" [3]

Interest groups attempt to persuade those who count, and in the United States those who count amount to millions of people. These groups try, however, to make a special appeal to opinion leaders. With the development of public relations experts, considerable skill and even science has been marshalled to mould opinion. Voters are approached through a variety of media and with a variety of arguments, which are channelled through many organizations and tied into existing loyalties. Interest groups and organization leaders insist that they are carrying on "an educational campaign," but they are just as sure that their opponents are engaging in "propaganda." Organizations often develop ideologies that by their abstractness and generality

---

[2] Paul H. Appleby, *Policy and Administration* (University, Ala.: University of Alabama Press, 1949), p. 168.

[3] B. J. Mullaney, Senate Document 92, 70th Congress, 1st Session, p. 17 quoted by Stankley Kelley, Jr., *Professional Public Relations and Political Power* (Baltimore: The Johns Hopkins Press, 1956), p. 13.

seek to appeal beyond the goals of one group and provide a broader basis for support.

Electioneering. Interest groups not only are active in campaigns for the selection of elected officials but also attempt to influence the selection of *appointed* officials as well. Groups subject to governmental regulation are especially concerned with the administrators who regulate them, and they can be expected to work for the appointment of men whose concepts of policy jibe with their own.

These several tactics are obviously interrelated. Interest groups are much more likely to be successful in winning the support of a congressman if they have persuaded a large number of voters to join their cause. And if they have the support of a large number of voters, they will have more influence over the selection of public officials. Nevertheless, groups stress those tactics that are most suitable to their nature. Large membership organizations such as trade unions are likely to promote their interests through electioneering for candidates, and they devote most of their political energies to mobilizing the political strength of their own members. On the other hand, the American Medical Association, which has relatively few members but which enjoys prestige and influence, is not likely to endorse candidates or to ring doorbells but is likely to use propaganda and lobbying tactics.

Interest groups are active in all branches, and at all levels, of government. Watching the American political process is harder than keeping an eye on all rings of a big circus. Congress may enact a law, but opponents of the measure may nullify it by blocking the necessary appropriations to carry out the program. Or they may alter its nature by securing the appointment of men to administer the program whose concepts of policy are favorable to their position. Policy-conflicts suffuse the entire stream of governmental activity. Politics is everywhere.

THE POLICY CONSEQUENCES OF ORGANIZATION

The emphasis in this volume is on substance rather than instruments; nevertheless, the shape of the machinery of government cannot be ignored. Congressional procedures, the role of judges, relations between national and state agencies are features of the governmental system that set the frame, establish the rules, and provide the arenas for political battles.

The basic principles of democratic government—freedom of communication, right to organize, acquiescence in the decisions of the majority, avoidance of violence—do not change. And although procedures are stable, they are stable only in relative terms. Disputes over the organization and procedures of government machinery are not uncommon and these disputes are closely related to policy and programs. To change the procedures of government is to affect the kinds of policies that will be adopted and the services that will be performed. Changing the procedures alters the accessibility of the decision-makers to the influence of various groups. Decisions about the forms of government have an impact on which policies get adopted and whose values are represented.

The merits and demerits of organization are sometimes judged by what purport to be nonpolitical scientific standards divorced from considerations of immediate group advantage. There are, of course, standards for measuring procedures other than their impact upon the strengthening or weakening of particular interests. However, procedure and policy are interrelated, as many of the ensuing chapters will demonstrate.

Groups with different values and different assessments of the policy consequences that may flow from a particular change come to different conclusions about its desirability. Judgments, for example, about changing the electoral college, limiting the jurisdiction of the courts, shortening the ballot, and adopting the manager form of government are influenced by expectations about how these changes will enhance or diminish the strength of particular interests. Perhaps we can see the relation between process and policy by considering the politics of some recent organizational discussions.

National-state relations

In 1953 President Eisenhower sponsored the establishment of a Commission on Intergovernmental Relations. This Commission, composed of members of both political parties, was instructed to make an impartial and objective study and to come forward with recommendations about the "proper" distribution of functions between the national and state governments. (Incidentally, it is worth noting that this device of appointing "high level commissions" has been adopted frequently in an attempt to take issues "out of politics.") Apparently it was thought that the Commission on Intergovernmental Relations could find some non-political standards to determine which functions are "proper" for each level. But the Commission, like others of its kind, was not long in operation before it realized that the criteria to determine the "propriety" of vesting a function in the national government rather than the states are, whoever applies them, *political* judgments.

Those who anticipate that they will have influence with state officials and who believe that state agencies are likely to adopt programs in accord with their own values, are the groups who defend "states' rights." On the other hand, those who believe that a state legislature may not support programs they want and who anticipate that they will find national officials representative of their values champion national action. For example, segregationists have rightly recognized that their values are likely to be the values of those who dominate southern state and local governments. They fear that national officials, responsive to different political majorities, are likely to oppose segregation. Naturally, segregationists sing of the virtues of local government close to the "people," they talk of the dangers of "overcentralization," and they do not believe that the protection of civil rights is a "proper" function of the national government.

In recent decades, employers have discovered that state legislatures and state courts are more likely than their national counterparts to make decisions favored by employers. They recognize that pressures for regulation of employer activity are more apt to be felt through national rather than state agencies. On the other hand, labor leaders find national agencies more responsive to their claims. It is not surprising, therefore, to find that businessmen's organizations are quick to defend the states against what they characterize as the "federal octopus," while labor leaders emphasize the need for national action and charge the states with being dominated by "special interests." Although the debates over national-state relations are couched in constitutional language, and appeals are made to general principles, the words are symbols used to debate more immediate and specific policy goals.

The policy consequences of congressional reform

Attitudes toward reforming congressional procedures furnish another example of the "seamless web" between procedure and policy. Chairmen of congressional committees are important: they have much to say about what kinds of laws Congress enacts. Under the rule of seniority these positions go to the member of the majority party (in the chamber) with the longest continuous service on the committee.

This means that congressmen from one-party states and districts, which tend to be rural areas, dominate Congress.

Proposals to abolish the rule of seniority are debated in terms of experience versus competence, accountability to the congressional majority versus accountability to local constituents. Those whose influence in Congress would be decreased by abolishing the rule—southern states and rural and small town regions in the North—generally support the rule. Groups whose geographic strength is in areas where congressmen are less likely to acquire seniority, favor new techniques of selection.

The "proper" scope of judicial review

Until recent decades federal judges usually made decisions more apt to win the applause of political conservatives and employers than of liberals and union leaders. The courts frequently struck down as unconstitutional social legislation supported by trade union and liberal organizations and opposed by businessmen and conservative groups. They interpreted laws regulating business narrowly, and closely supervised the establishment of rates and other regulations imposed by administrative agencies.

Those who did not like the decisions charged the judges with being biased and usurping authority. They argued that the scope of judicial review should be narrowed since administrators were trained experts dealing with technical issues and should be allowed some measure of flexibility in the procedures they used. Liberal lawyers, of whom there were a few, and liberal political scientists and historians, of whom there were many, wrote articles and books emphasizing the policy-making role of the judiciary, the significance of the judge's personal values, and the desirability of imposing political checks upon the judiciary. They emphasized the undemocratic connotations of judicial review as a check on the people's elected representatives.

On the other hand, those who liked the decisions argued that judicial review of administrative regulation of business was an essential check on biased administrators who used unfair procedures. Conservative lawyers, of whom there were many, and conservative political scientists and historians, of whom there were a few, wrote articles and books denying that the judges made policy or that their own values had anything to do with the decisions they made. Judges, they insisted, merely *discovered* the law by applying the established rules to the facts. They emphasized the value of checks and balances and insisted that critics of the courts were really attacking the Constitution and the rule of law.

Then, perhaps for the first time in American history—beginning in 1937 and especially in the 1950's—the Supreme Court was more "liberal" than the Congress. The Court supported generous construction of national laws regulating business and protecting labor, championed the civil rights of Negroes, struck down state laws regulating civil liberties, and gave narrow interpretations to federal legislation touching on the First Amendment.

Coincident with this liberal domination of the Supreme Court was a shift in the nature of old as well as new regulatory agencies. Administrative agencies responsible for the regulation of businessmen came to be headed by men less inclined to vigorous action than their predecessors had been during the early days of the agencies. But perhaps even more significant, whereas administrators had in the past regulated only businessmen, by the 1940's they were being given discretion to determine which government employees were loyal, which books were "obscene," which immigrants were "deportable," and other matters affecting civil rather than property rights.

In this new situation, many who had previously insisted on broad judicial review of administrative decisions began to argue that determinations of loyalty, obscenity, and deportability required administrative expertness and special procedures and that judges should not interfere or require the use of established legal procedures. Conservatives began to write articles and publish books accusing the judges of being "biased." They began to agitate for legislation to curb "judicial usurpations." On the other hand, liberals began to use the arguments of their former opponents. They began to find new virtues in the doctrine of separation of powers and checks and balances. They insisted that the judges were merely applying the clear commands of the Constitution.

What then is the "proper" role of judges? In part it depends upon whose values the judges are supporting. Here we have another illustration of how organizational issues are related to policy conflicts.

TECHNIQUES OF GOVERNMENTAL ACTION

Conflicts over *how* the government, that is how public officials, should do something are frequently as serious as controversies over whether the government should do anything at all. In the chapters that follow we shall describe various kinds of governmental programs. We shall see that all the following techniques are used:

Public ownership and operation. Our governments directly provide police and fire protection; recruit, operate, equip and direct the military services; carry the mails, build some dams, build highways either through public employees or private contractors; build and operate many hospitals, and in many other fields directly provide the services that are paid for out of taxes or from fees charged. Many of these "socialized" activities are old and widely supported. Others such as building dams, generating and selling electricity, are hotly opposed by certain groups. These programs are authorized by the legislatures, and the actual tasks are carried out by administrators.

Imposition of criminal sanctions. The legislature makes certain kinds of conduct illegal and provides for punishment of those who commit these acts. The police are charged with apprehending the law-breakers, and public officials prosecute them before the judges. The function of protecting life, liberty, and property is largely effected by the government through the imposition of criminal sanctions.

Imposition of civil sanctions. The legislature, by statute, and judges, through the common law, define the rules governing many areas of human relations. But the government merely provides the courts to adjudicate disputes and establishes sheriffs and others to help carry the courts' decisions into effect. It is up to the aggrieved persons to invoke judicial authority to defend their rights.

Taxation. Governments do not exist to collect taxes, but they collect taxes in order to exist. However, through taxation the flow of money from some people to others can be affected, and in these days of large-scale budgets the kinds and amounts of taxes influence the general level of economic activity, as later pages will show. Moreover, by imposing heavy taxes on some goods and some kinds of activity, the government can discourage or even prohibit them.

Expenditures. Governments may give money in order to encourage certain activities. For example, in the nineteenth century railroad builders were given subsidies; today airlines are subsidized. Governments also spend money to provide pensions for veterans and relief for the needy.

A very important technique is the intergovernmental grant by which the Congress grants money to the states and the state legislature grants it to municipalities. These grants are usually conditional, the "giving government" requiring that the "receiving government" do certain things and do them in certain ways.

In addition to capital grants, governments make loans and use their control over credit institutions to encourage them to make loans for certain purposes.

Publicity and investigations. In these days of mass communication this technique has become increasingly significant. It is used by congressional committees and administrative agencies. In the 1930's a Senate subcommittee investigated and publicized certain sabotage practices used by some employers against unions; in 1957 a Senate Committee investigated and exposed the unethical use of labor union funds by certain prominent labor leaders. Both these investigations resulted in corrective action. The impact of adverse publicity is often so great and has such a punitive effect that there are growing demands for procedural safeguards for those who stand "accused."

Licenses and franchises. Individuals and corporations are permitted to do certain things only with a license or franchise. The corporate charter is a franchise, as are permits to corporations to lay tracks on streets or to run gas, water, electricity, or telephone lines under, by, or over streets. By requiring a license for engaging in certain activities —operating a utility, practicing medicine, selling eye glasses, and selling alcoholic beverages—public agencies exercise regulatory supervision.

Inspection. An old technique dating back to medieval times is the municipal inspection to insure the quality, price, and weight of commodities sold on local markets. Modern uses are to insure safety of working conditions, sanitation of food, protection against fire. Inspection is supported by a variety of sanctions for violations such as revocation of licenses, fines, imprisonment, publicity.

CONCLUSION

The chapters that follow describe the policies and programs of our governments in important fields. The authors know that complete objectivity is impossible. As citizens each of us has strong convictions. Certainly our commitment to democratic procedures is evident. But it is our intention to be as objective as possible and to attempt to correct for our own biases. It is not our purpose to take sides, instruct the reader as to merits or demerits of particular programs, or to pronounce judgments about which programs we believe are, or are not, in the national interest.

In a democracy no group has any special claim to having the purest insights into what programs should be adopted. Political scientists are no exception, and our functions should not be confused with those of politicians, partisans, or public officials. True, as citizens we participate in politics. And it may be that some give special weight to our pronouncements, but such pronouncements are more likely to reflect our values as men rather than the dictates of our discipline.

2. RICHARD W. TAYLOR

Public Fiscal and Monetary Policy

OF every dollar spent in the United States, 25 cents is spent by government. Although most of this spending is by the national government, and for the costs of past and future wars, non-military expenditures equal the costs of state government; they also equal the costs of combined local government activity. Moreover, when the national government spends annually close to 70 billion dollars, these expenditures have a significant impact on the total economic activity of the nation. The taxing, borrowing, and spending activities of the national government are important devices by which the flow of total economic activity can be affected. Furthermore, the national government controls the money and credit supply of the nation.

For these reasons public finance involves far more complex activities than does private finance. The issues of government revenues and expenditures involve many factors in addition to those faced by private individuals or even by large corporations. Individuals usually need consider only their family needs in terms of their income and outgo. Corporations consider in addition the purchase of labor and the maintainance of a flow of capital and material to produce for an unpredictable market. But the national government controls many of the conditions under which individuals and corporations can operate and is responsible under the Constitution and present legislation for maintaining a high level of employment and conditions for economic

17

growth and stability. Hence this chapter will consider fiscal policy both in terms of national, state and local spending and raising of money, and also in terms of the impact of the national government's fiscal and monetary policy on interest groups and the whole economy.

Public finance is the name given to the study of all issues relating to governmental taxing, borrowing, lending and spending policies as well as issues relating to the manipulation of currency and credit. Money is the central focus. In addition, authorities frequently also distinguish between *fiscal* and *monetary* policy in a technical sense. Fiscal policy is usually confined to the first group above, while monetary policy relates to the manipulation of credit, currency and banking. A chapter on public finance must deal briefly with all of these as well as examine the methods by which governments budget their income and expenses.

THE PROCESS OF PUBLIC BUDGETING

The method whereby governments plan their raising and spending of money is the budget. Only an imperfect instrument of financial planning since situations often arise that have not been foreseen, the budget is, nevertheless, the crucial instrument for trying to keep the fiscal house in order. The three recognized steps in public budgeting are (1) the preparation of the budget; (2) its acceptance into law; and (3) its administration. In the United States the responsibility for formulating the budget is generally lodged in the executive branch: the President for the national government; the governor for the states; and the mayor for cities. Responsibility for enacting the budget into law is vested in the legislative branches following parliamentary practices adapted from Europe. Constitutional theory here (although occasionally violated) requires that no money be spent by the national government without Congressional authorization. Administration of the budget is again an executive responsibility, although here as at every other stage there is occasional and even significant participation by the other branches of government.

National budgeting in the modern sense is relatively new, dating from the creation of the Bureau of the Budget under the Budget and Accounting Act of 1921. By that time Britain had already two centuries of experience and France at least one century, and many municipalities had already adopted this tested method of financial planning. Except during Alexander Hamilton's administration of the Treasury, there was until 1921 no coordination of executive requests for appropriations. Appropriations were not gathered together in a single bill by Congress, nor were revenue measures integrated with proposed expenditures, except in a most haphazard way by the separate Congressional committees.

The creation of the Bureau of the Budget provided the President for the first time with an agency that could to some extent integrate the requests of the several government departments with the Presidential program and with the anticipated government income in a neat though bulky package that could be presented to Congress. The Bureau was also given extensive responsibility to administer the Budget which Congress adopted.

Preparing the national budget

Under the Budget and Accounting Act, the President of the United States is responsible for preparing the budget of the national government. At the preparatory stage his most important assistance comes from the Bureau of the Budget, which has administrative control over the process of receiving departmental estimates and disposing of them through budget hearings. Additional official advice may flow through the Cabinet; and economic advice and prognostications come from the Council of Economic Advisors, the Treasury, and the Federal Reserve Board. It should be noted that the major portion of this assistance is immediately under the control of the Chief Executive. In 1939, the Bureau of the Budget was transferred from the Treasury to the Executive Office of the President. The Cabinet, of course, has always been under the formal authority of the President; and the Council of Economic Advisors, created by the Employment Act of 1946, was put by Congress into the Executive Office.

The Bureau of the Budget has the authority to "assemble, correlate, revise, reduce, or increase the estimates of the several departments and establishments," including the wholly owned semi-independent government corporations. To carry out these tasks the Director of the Bureau is assisted by four offices: Budget Review, Legislative Reference, Management and Organization, and Statistical Standards. An Executive Order specifically charges the Bureau with the following:

1. Assist the President in preparation of the Budget.
2. Assist the President by clearing and coordinating departmental advice on proposed legislation and Executive Orders by making recommendations with respect to Presidential action on the basis of past practice.

3. Supervise and control the administration of the budget.

4. ". . . keep the President informed of the progress of activities by agencies of the Government with respect to work proposed, work actually initiated, and work completed, together with the relative timing of work between the several agencies of the Government; all to the end that the work programs of the several agencies of the executive branch of the Government may be coordinated and that the moneys appropriated by the Congress may be expended in the most economical manner possible with least possible overlapping and duplication of effort."

To carry out these functions the Bureau is further subdivided into five divisions, each concerned with a broad segment of the Government's program. These divisions are Commerce and Finance, International, Labor and Welfare, Military, and Resources and Civil Works.

Two things should be noted at the outset about the organization and purposes of the Bureau of the Budget. First the Bureau has come to be the chief arm by which the President can control the specific day-to-day activities of the executive branch of government. Second, a key reason for setting up the Bureau—and still a major goal—is to cut the costs of government. How successful the Bureau has been in these matters can better be determined after an examination of the whole budget process, including its political ramifications.

July 1 has come to be a most important date in our government's budgetary operations. This date is the beginning of the new national fiscal year which ends on the subsequent June 30; this date is also the time when the Bureau of the Budget makes its call for agency estimates from the several departments for the *next* fiscal year. In other words the time for one year's budget to go into effect is precisely the time for departmental planning to begin for *next* year's budget. Thus the Bureau keeps a year ahead in its budgetary planning.

Actually, next year's budget has already been carefully discussed in the Bureau of the Budget. Under the guidance of the President and his advisors the office of Budget Review has already developed general budget policies and assumptions which have been incorporated in the form of directives to the various agencies. These policies are incorporated in the Budget Director's Policy Letter which is included with the call for agency estimates. This document includes proposed ceilings on governmental and agency expenditures.

Using the Policy Letter as a general guide, each department's own budget officer prepares the departmental (or agency) financial requests. The departmental budgets are highly detailed, and besides financial requirements they must include estimates on anticipated needs for personnel, supplies, office space, and the like (often for 18 or 20 months in advance). These departmental budgets are then submitted to the Budget Bureau where the appropriate functional division reviews them. During September and October, department and other agency heads make detailed justifications of new and existing programs at a series of budget "hearings." Between October and November examiners in the Budget Bureau make their recommendations to the director, and the director makes his own review in terms of likely Presidential policy for the ensuing year. At this time the director works in close consultation with the President and his advisors, and in late November or early December the President spends a few days reviewing the budget. Agencies are then notified as to what they can anticipate; possibly they will be asked for additional revised estimates.

This long process is all in preparation for the final Budget and the President's Budget Message. This latter message will be worked out between the President and the director, possibly in consultation with the President's political lieutenants on Capitol Hill. The message is presented in January to Congress where, of course, it must undergo lengthy scrutiny by the lawmakers. If Congress acts according to schedule, at least the appropriations phase of the budget is disposed of by July 1; if not, Congress must pass special legislation authorizing agencies to continue their activities until such time as Congress has completed its work.

Is the Bureau's control over agency estimates as absolute as the foregoing summary suggests? The answer depends on the general political climate and the specific power of different agencies. One President may be especially favorable to welfare projects; another may be more responsive to budget requests of the Department of Defense. The Chief Executive must always keep in mind the popularity of the agencies with Congress; the FBI and the Army Corps of Engineers, for example, can resist Budget Bureau and even presidential directives. The Defense Department, as a whole, when it is seriously anxious to proceed with a project that the Bureau thinks unwise is likely to have its way. On the other hand, agencies such as the Departments of Labor and Interior are not likely to have their way against the views of the Bureau. Budget-making must always be seen as part of the political decision-making process.

Acceptance of the national budget

The formal responsibility for enacting the budget into law is vested in the Congress. Congress receives the Budget Message and the elephantine seven-pound budget in January. The Budget and Accounting Act of 1921 originally sought to integrate congressional consideration of financial problems by providing that appropriations should be considered by only one committee in each chamber and that revenues should be considered by only one committee in each chamber. Consequently, each house has an Appropriations Committee and tax laws are written by the House Committee on Ways and Means and the Senate Finance Committee. The Congressional Reorganization Act of 1946 endeavored to create additional coordination by providing that these four committees should sit jointly for the purpose of creating a legislative budget. This experiment proved unavailing, and although the earlier experiment provided little coordination Congress continues to operate under the organization it established. In addition, the committees in each house on Banking and Currency exercise important jurisdictions with respect to the borrowing, lending, and currency policies of government, and these functions have important budgetary implications. Finally, the Joint Committee on the Economic Report examines the Presidential economic reports in accordance with the Employment Act and can provide Congress with an economic overview of the nation, but it has little influence in the short run in disposing of executive budget recommendations.

The first six committees are politically potent; they are among the most desirable committee assignments of the Congress. But not one of these committees is organized to treat the governmental financial plan as an integrated whole. In fact, the Appropriation Committees further seriously subdivide their work into small three-member subcommittees organized to parallel the structure of the executive branch. The hearings of these subcommittees often provide the most important occasion for examination of specific departmental organization and intradepartmental politics. At such hearings political cross-currents may be evident. Bureau chiefs and department heads sometimes testify against the budget recommendations of the Bureau of the Budget; occasionally chiefs of bureaus within departments undermine the political front loyally adopted by the department head in support of the President. Occasionally, evidences of misadministration and misappropriation are discovered at this level, and this sort of thing provides fuel for the traditional political battle between Congress and the Executive. However, the review provided at the subcommittee level is piecemeal; no evaluation is made of the relative merits of one departmental program against a similar program of another department. Congressional oversight of the appropriations process consequently is sporadic and disintegrated—as perhaps it must be, given our present institutions of government.

One curious feature of the appropriations process is that Congressmen are loud in their proclamations of economy but usually end up by appropriating more than the President asks for. The cartoonist's version of the battle for economy is not entirely accurate because Congressmen have their own pet projects which they support at the legislative stage and which increase the work and expense of government. Furthermore, Congressmen find it impossible to examine intelligently many proposed budget items because they lack both information on the matter and the staff to do research. Consequently, Congressional attention is likely to be confined to occasional items that some lawmaker may be concerned about. On these items, especially, appropriations subcommittees are likely to instruct bureaucrats as to how they wish the money spent. Sometimes, these instructions are incorporated into appropriations acts, but in any event, they carry great weight. In addition, the House Appropriations Committee is more likely to concentrate on economizing because members of the House come up for election every two years. Sometimes the bureaucrats then go before the Senate Appropriations Committee to complain of House cuts, and the Senate exercises a not inconsiderable review function here.

In short, despite the very considerable influence in the matter of specific appropriations, Congressional action on appropriations as a whole is largely a matter of reviewing what the executive has initiated. Although it retains ultimate constitutional authority, Congress is simply not organized to provide the initiating or controlling guidance in the budgetary process. Legislative control is exercised in a hit-or-miss fashion by interested lawmakers over individual items.

Administration of the national budget

As the last two paragraphs suggest, Congress and the Executive exercise intermingled jurisdiction in administering the budget, although here again most of the cards are in the hands of the President. President Truman showed that the Chief Executive requires no *item veto* to prevent the expenditure of funds that he thinks should be left unspent. When Congress appropriated money for a larger Air Force than he requested, Mr. Truman simply forbade the Air Force to spend more money than it was his policy to spend.

The President's principal means of exercising administrative budgetary control is again through the Bureau of the Budget. This agency may require periodic reports from the agencies, and it has the power to order the agencies to keep within their allotted appropriations. One means by which Congress exercises some control in addition to the hearings of the appropriations committees is through the General Accounting Office, an agency of Congress. Created by the Budget and Accounting Act of 1921, this office is headed by the Comptroller General. Its primary function is the postaudit, designed to guarantee that all funds have been spent in accordance with legislative intent and that they have been properly accounted for. The Comptroller is appointed for fifteen years; he is required to report to Congress and he may be removed either by joint resolution or by impeachment.

Some aspects of national budgeting

The budget process must be closely related to the political process and the issues of national budgeting should be distinguished from those of state and local budget-making.

The apparent formality and the manifest rationality of the national budget-making process should not obscure the political context in which it takes place. In a sense the father of the Bureau of the Budget is the political desire to cut government expenses to a minimum, especially on the part of the "economy bloc" in Congress. The mother of the Bureau is the political desire of the President to achieve a better control of administration and finance in the executive branch, which previously had an even greater tendency toward insubordination and disintegration. Hence the Bureau of the Budget becomes a kind of "executive legislature" with diplomatic outposts in the several departments of administration and an Office of Legislative Reference to handle the frequently delicate issues of "foreign relations," namely negotiations with members and committees of Congress. This latter office clears, for conformity with the Presidential program, all the enrolled bills of Congress and the proposed legislation by the departments of the Executive. Congress, therefore, has a type of preview of what bills the President will *veto,* and this sometimes has a moderating impact on the action of Congress.

The legislative disposal of the President's budget is no less political; it is in this way that a democracy arrives at its decisions of policy, and this should not be clouded by the appearance of scientific administrative management. The fact is that the President must secure sufficient political support from the voters and from Congress to get his budget adopted more or less intact, or else the administrative wheels of government will be thrown out of adjustment. Occasionally Congress can frustrate some pet Presidential project; and, even more rarely, Congress may impose some moderately important project on an unwilling President, but in this political game the President usually has most of the trump cards.

It is important to note some fundamental distinctions between national financial management on the one hand and private, state, and local financial planning on the other. One distinction rests on the unique *monetary* powers of the national government; the second rests on the important place of the national government in the economic transactions of the nation. The fiscal capacity of the national government includes the powers to tax, spend, borrow, lend, buy, and sell, and in these respects the national government differs in only minor ways from state and subordinate governmental units. The unique legal position of the national government lies in its monetary powers to control credit and coin money. Although the states had some monetary powers with respect to credit at one time, Congress has effectively occupied this field and made it the exclusive province of the national government. Through these monetary powers the national government can substantially influence economic development, cause or moderate inflationary movements, fix interest rates of banking institutions, and ensure an adequate market for its own bonds. The states, local governments, and private parties are much more limited in their control over the marketing of their own securities, and they have little capacity to control the basic monetary conditions under which they may borrow or lend.[1]

The pre-eminent position of the national government in our economic system is a second major distinction between national economic power and that of the states and local governments. This position of economic importance rests firmly on clear constitutional authority, such as the powers to conduct war, to carry on foreign relations, and to regulate commerce among the states and with foreign nations;

---

[1] Private persons are without taxing powers which, of course, differentiates them from governmental bodies in a significant way.

naturally the fiscal powers already described are strong supports for the national government's financial pre-eminence.

These two factors make that traditional view of budgeting which led to the creation of the Bureau of the Budget in 1921 somewhat antiquated in terms of actual economic impact of the national government. The traditional budget concept developed from the days of financial management of the King's household, and the chief problem of budgeting was to balance income against expenditure so that the King would not spend beyond his means. This view of budgeting continues as a major influence in family budgeting when borrowing is viewed as legitimate only at a time of emergency or in the purchase of something of lasting value, such as a home. Constitutional restrictions largely require the states and local governments to operate in this old framework. The situation of the national government is different. The responsibilities of national defense and of maintaining a high level of employment are often regarded as being much more important than the responsibility of maintaining a formal balance of the budget.

These additional and often competing responsibilities lead to a paradox. In times of economic distress, for example, individuals as well as state and local governments endeavor to cut their expenditures in order to balance their budgets at a lower level to conform with their lower income expectations. At the same time the national government since the New Deal has generally felt obliged to raise its expenditures and balance its budget at a higher level, making up the difference between income and expenditure by borrowing. This paradox goes even further. Many economists believe that in bad times the government should reduce taxes and increase spending, while in good times it should raise taxes and reduce expenditures. Many businessmen as well as some economists, of course, disagree with this point of view, arguing that the government should always cut taxes and cut out most expenditures (except, perhaps, those specifically designed to help business). Although clothed in the argument of "economy" or "welfare," these arguments are fundamentally positions taken by a variety of opposing groups seeking to achieve a variety of ends that are not mutually consistent and reconcilable. These issues must be fought out in the political scramble.

The national government, in short, is not limited by the same budgetary considerations as are other governments or individuals, because of its constitutional and economic position and because of decisions made by Congress and the Executive in times past as a consequence of political pressures and popular expectations.

State and local budgeting

In the states, as in Washington, the executive generally proposes, while legislatures dispose of, budgets. The legislatures are more restricted in this process than our national Congress in two respects. A large number of state legislatures meet only once every two years, and the governor in 38 states has the *item veto*. The enforcement of the budget is again in the hands of the executive branch, without as intensive legislative supervision. State courts also have a larger role in financial planning and administration than the national courts, which have no powers of interference at this point.

Among lower units of government (especially in counties) budgetary responsibility is often dispersed among a large number of elective officials, although many municipalities have this process firmly centralized in the office of the mayor or city manager. In "strong-mayor" cities the responsibility for presenting the budget belongs to the mayor, who often has also an *item veto* over council appropriations. In many cities, the council is not permitted to add to the appropriations requests of the mayor; here its responsibility is largely review, although it must give final approval before expenditures may be made. In the council-manager plan, the city manager frequently acts as a director of the local budget, although he must maintain good political relations with his council. Under the commission plan of municipal government there is always a commissioner of finance who has formal authority, but this authority depends frequently on how willing the commissioner of finance is to listen and act on the requests of his fellow commissioners.

In "weak-mayor" cities, annual budgets, insofar as they are orderly plans, are generally the product of efforts of the council finance committees; however, financial planning in this type of city is most likely to resemble national budgetary practice prior to 1921. County government in the United States has been labled the "dark continent" of our political institutions; the multitude of elective officers who are not responsible to any central authority reflects itself in unintegrated budgetary practice. The fact that counties are primarily administrative subdivisions of the state, are confined to administering laws, and are without legislative authority of their own suggests that coordination of budgetary practice in counties is largely the work of state legislation and not of local planning. The county-manager plan is in part an effort to alter this legal and budgetary situation by reposing more authority in one county official. But this form of county government has not been extensively adopted.

As in the case of the national government, in both state and municipal governments budgeting is an important instrument of executive control over policies and administration; and budgeting has been instituted in order to curtail public expenditures by increasing the effectiveness of administration.

Some issues presented by authorities on budgeting

Studies of budgeting have often leveled the criticism against United States budgets that they do not present a complete financial picture. Often budgets take only incidental notice of the revenues, and they occasionally omit important aspects on the expenditure side. At the national level the defense and foreign-aid programs have been particularly criticized because of the use of carry-over funds from previous appropriations. Another and related criticism involves the segregation of specific revenues for special purposes. For example, automobile gasoline taxes are typically assigned to the specific task of highway improvement. This segregation of specific revenues and assigning them to special purposes has been condemned by "budgeters" because this eliminates one element of financial control. Budget officials in maintaining this position reflect some well-defined interests. These interests include the executive branch and the chief executive who is usually concerned with securing integrated control over his administration. Others include the economy in government interest. The opposition is generally concerned with protecting a special governmental benefit that they enjoy. For example, trucking and automobile associations are anxious to maintain the principle that the gasoline tax should be used to support and improve roads.

At the national level, budget experts were pleased with the recommendation of the Hoover Commission that "the whole budgetary concept of the federal government be refashioned by the adoption of a budget based upon functions, activities, and projects: this we designate as a performance budget." [2] This recommendation has become, in the interest of intelligibility, the general practice of the national government. This involves simply the focusing of budgetary attention on the

[2] *Hoover Commission Report* (New York: McGraw-Hill Book Co., Inc., 1949), pp. 36-37.

performance of tasks or functions rather than segregated allocations by agencies. For example, instead of allotting an army hospital money from several different Defense Department appropriations, the performance budget would group all the costs of the hospital in such a way that they could be compared with those of previous years and those of comparable hospitals. The performance budget also calls attention to the fact that there is work to be done by the government, the cost of which will incidentally be footed by the taxpayer. The previous national budgets appeared to concentrate on the fact that there were agencies that were spending taxpayers' money without any clear view as to what the money was doing. Some agencies with vested interests and some congressmen resisted the change-over to the performance budget, and its proponents were not altogether clear about all the interests that would be served by this change.

SOURCES OF GOVERNMENT REVENUE

In order to spend, the government must first have means of getting money. As we have mentioned, the Constitution of the United States gives the national government the power to tax, to borrow, and to coin money. This is only a partial catalogue of governmental revenue sources; other sources—such as fines, rents, interest, and income from public businesses—although important in certain localities, are not included in this discussion, since they are rarely a major revenue source.

Before dealing with governmental revenues, two points should be repeated: (1) the exercise of these constitutional powers not only brings income but also may have important effects on the whole economy, and (2) the differences between the central government and the state and local governments must be kept in mind. The national government has important fiscal powers denied the states; and until now there has been a notable lack of coordination in the use of fiscal powers between these several levels of government. The following discussion will separate the question of taxation from the issues of general monetary policy.

Types of taxes

The imagination of legislatures has been fertile in devising means for taxation, and this, in addition to the pressure of a multitude of interests searching for economic advantage over other interests, accounts for the

bewildering variety of taxes levied in the United States. This variety
often obscures the fact that in one sense taxes are simply compulsory
contributions made by persons or corporations from their wealth to be
used for public purposes. It also frequently renders indistinct the
economic impact of taxation, although it is undoubtedly this impact
that makes the political and legislative mind so fecund when this sensitive topic must be dealt with. Grievances over taxes can quickly be
converted into votes. Perhaps an ideal tax system would focus on income and real property alone. By manipulating taxes on each, needed
revenues would be secured with the desired regulatory effect in such a
way that the voters could be sure precisely what the taxes were doing
for and to them. However, the citizen is not always interested in having
these unpleasant matters made clear to him, and the politician who
dwells on them overlong may not be reelected. Public desire to avoid
the distasteful makes taxation a complicated and painful topic.

The variety of revenue sources and the extent to which each source
is used by each level of government is partially suggested by Figure 2.1.

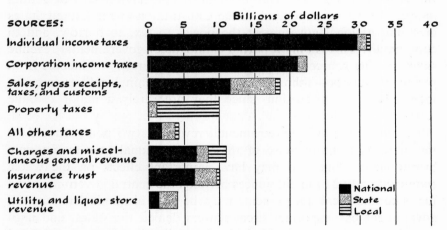

Source: Dept. of Commerce, Bureau of the Census, as reported in STATISTICAL ABSTRACTS OF THE
UNITED STATES, 1956, p. 394.

Fig. 2.1. Governmental revenue by source: 1954

These figures indicate that the major sources of national revenue are
the personal and corporate income taxes, various excise taxes, and the
tariff; the major sources of state revenues are the general sales tax,
motor vehicle fuel tax and licenses, individual and corporate income
taxes, and unemployment compensation; for local governments, the
property taxes are the primary sources while licenses, fees, and fran-

chises provide some additional revenues. In other words, what the taxpayer *earned* largely determined his national tax bill through the income tax; what he *spent* probably determined his major state tax bill through the sales tax; and what he *owned* determined his local tax bill through the property tax.

The conventional approach to judging the adequacy of particular taxes has its reputable source in Adam Smith's *Wealth of Nations* (1776). According to Smith, taxes should meet the following four criteria: (1) They should be *equitable*—they should fall upon individuals in accordance with their economic capacity; (2) they should be *certain and not arbitrary*—the taxpayer should be aware of the fact that he is paying a tax or he may be subject to excessive levies; (3) they should be *convenient*—they should not require the taxpayer to make inappropriate payments at seasons when he is unprepared to make them; and (4) they should be *economical*—they should be inexpensive to collect. To these four criteria is usually added a fifth, namely that taxes should be *adequate* to support the government. The standards established by Smith are still very useful. But they tend to overemphasize the revenue aspect of taxation and to underemphasize the fiscal policy aspect of taxation. Adam Smith's standards do suggest, however, the important fact that there would be no taxation if the government did not require revenue. The following description of different taxes will embrace an examination of both the revenue and public policy implications of each type of tax.

Income tax. The national income tax, authorized by the Sixteenth Amendment in 1913, quickly became the prime revenue producer for the national government. Under the personal income tax the national government secures annually over 30 billion dollars, while the corporate form brings in an additional 20 billion dollars. This form of tax is convenient in the sense that it falls upon the taxpayer at a time when he is most able to pay, recognizing as it does that all tax payments must be derived from some type of income. This tax is both equitable and certain in the sense that payment is determined in accordance with the income that is received and is easily calculable. It also has a reputation for being an economical tax, for the administrative costs of collection are relatively low.

Nevertheless the income tax is a highly controversial tax. Indeed, the national income tax was born out of controversy. The Supreme Court in the case of *Pollock v. Farmers' Loan and Trust Co.*[3] had held

[3] 158 U.S. 601 (1895).

a national income tax law unconstitutional because it was a direct tax which should be apportioned among the states. The majority opinion in this case expressed fear that the establishment of this tax would destroy the capitalistic economic system, an opinion that continues to be held by some important economic groups today. In 1953 the Organization to Repeal Federal Income Taxes was incorporated to marshal these groups in a campaign to limit the effect of the federal income tax. With the petition by the Indiana legislature of March 8, 1957, 27 states had requested Congress to call a Constitutional Convention to introduce an amendment putting a 25 per cent ceiling on income taxes. However, by this time the ORFIT had changed its tactics, and efforts are being directed to the repeal of the Sixteenth Amendment. Whatever the tactic, the arguments advanced in the income tax controversy by this group are the same: (1) the present system of graduation is "socialistic" because it amounts to a redistribution of income, and (2) the excessive taxation of a man's earnings is confiscatory and destroys incentive. Among the arguments advanced in opposition to a constitutional limitation on the power of Congress to tax incomes are the following: (1) the income tax is an efficient and equitable revenue producer; (2) it has not destroyed the capitalistic system in the past and therefore will not destroy it in the future; and (3) Congress should have the power in any emergency to call upon all the resources of the nation. Supporters of the income tax contend further that the proposed limitation on income taxation is designed to protect the wealth of large income earners and to shift the burden of government costs to the people with smaller incomes. The efforts to partially repeal the Sixteenth Amendment have until now been unsuccessful, but this campaign has generated much steam and confusion. It would be worthwhile to determine through political research just why so many state legislatures can be persuaded to petition Congress to call a Constitutional Convention on this question when all efforts in Congress to propose such an amendment or call a convention are unsuccessful.

Not only is income tax itself still controversial, but there is also much economic and political discussion of various individual features of the national income tax law. One controversy revolves about the question of double taxation involved in the corporate income tax. Some hold that since individuals are taxed on their incomes, there is a special bias against the owners of corporate wealth when corporate income is also taxed. In opposition, it is argued that this source of revenue affects those who can most likely afford it. A second argument relates to the question of exemptions for dependents. These are justified on the grounds that a man's ability to pay decreases as his family increases. Election years are particularly opportune for raising the question of increasing the exemptions, since such an increase will benefit most taxpayers. If the President does not raise this issue, the Ways and Means Committee of the House of Representatives is sure to do so in an effort to get members of the House of Representatives on the right side. Two arguments are usually advanced in opposition to raising exemptions. The first is that this will substantially reduce government income at a time when government expenses are increasing, with possible inflationary effects. The second is that by raising exemptions fewer people will be required to share directly in the burdens of supporting the activities of the national government.

Probably of greater economic importance are the advantages given to certain industries such as the oil and defense industries which are permitted to write off capital investments quickly under depletion allowances or speedy amortization. The depletion allowances permitted the oil industry are justified as encouraging exploration of resources in this "new" industry and have made possible the development of some extraordinary fortunes, particularly in Texas, for those with oil and gas investments. Speedy amortizations of capital investment in defense industries have been justified as emergency measures, although they have been extended to relatively established industries such as private electric utilities.[4] Opponents of depletion allowances and quick tax write-offs contend that if these industries need subsidies, they should be handled as subsidies through regular legislative and administrative procedures which would provide more careful scrutiny of the claimed needs of these industries. They further argue that the income tax laws should not be burdened by numerous exceptions and exemptions such as these.

Each of these facets of the income tax laws may be described in moralistic terms as tax avoidance. They are viewed here in political terms as the competition of interests seeking special treatment for their special problems. Given the inescapable duties of modern government, the main question of taxation is "who should pay" rather than "how much should be raised"; hence the basic struggle over taxation is to shift the tax burden from one group of taxpayers to another. The 25 per cent constitutional limit proposal is an attempt to shift the burdens

[4] See discussion of the Hells Canyon controversy, pp. 281-82.

of national taxation toward the middle and low income groups; the corporate income tax is a successful attempt on the part of nonparticipants in this form of wealth to tap that rich source for public purposes; and each of the numerous special appeals by interested groups for exceptional treatment in handling deductions, depreciation, amortization, depletion, interest, and capital gains is an effort by one group to shift the burdens onto some other group. In theory the income tax is a simple device by which the government may collect needed revenues. It is made complex by virtue of the multitude of social and political purposes which Congress feels necessary to accomplish while it is trying to raise money. One should not be deceived into believing, however, that there is an absolutely scientific, nonpolitical income tax, since the amount or the lack of graduation is itself a reflection of social policy, whether it be to "soak the rich" or to "equalize" the burdens on all incomes.

Over three-fourths of the national revenues but only a small part of state revenue come from personal and corporate income taxes. Although 31 states have personal income taxes and 33 have corporate income taxes this is the source of only 15 per cent of all state revenues. Some cities, such as Philadelphia, have been given permission by states to levy payroll taxes. This is one way that cities can make the suburbanites who live off the city pay for a portion of the public services that the city otherwise provides *gratis*.

If the income tax is relatively easy to collect, why is it not more extensively used in local and state government finance? There are several reasons: (1) Many states, including some of the wealthiest, have constitutional barriers to income taxation. (2) Agricultural states, such as North Dakota, have populations which do not receive high incomes. Furthermore, agricultural income is notoriously hard to calculate and lends itself to evasion. (3) The income tax is notoriously a "fair-weather tax." When economic conditions are good, revenues are high; when economic conditions are bad and government needs increase, the yield is lower. States and municipalities are likely to find this a source of embarrassment because of the constitutional limitations on borrowing and their political incapacity for planning in good times for lean years. (4) The national government already occupies this field; an additional income tax has a tendency to harass businesses and individuals who must make their plans in accordance with the much more important national income-tax law. Conflicting economic interests vying for special treatment under the tax laws would make it politically difficult and often economically impractical for states to standardize their income tax procedures to accord with the more important national tax laws.

Consumption taxes. Harold M. Groves lists a considerable variety of consumption taxes: [5]

1. Special excise tax: on individual goods and services.
2. Selective sales tax: (British Purchase Tax) like (1) above but broader.
3. Gross income tax: (Indiana) covers all exchanges with no distinction as to levels (retail, wholesale) or as to commodities and services.
4. Turnover tax: (Germany) much like (3) though less inclusive as to services.
5. Transactions tax: extends beyond exchanges to cover such transactions as bank deposits.
6. Manufacturers sales tax: (Canada) confined to sales of commodities at the manufacturers' level.
7. Retail sales tax: (Michigan) confined to sales at retail; may include some services; does include final sale of some capital goods (cash register to merchant).
8. Value-added tax: (scheduled in Japan) like a gross income tax except that an effort is made to eliminate duplication (cost of goods sold deductible).
9. Over-all spending tax: like a net income tax except that the levy is on total annual spending (saving and investment exempt).
10. Use tax: a supplementary levy on the use or possession of a commodity specially immune to taxation on its acquisition.
11. Net income tax without personal exemptions: (Philadelphia) frequently labeled a gross income tax though really on net income. [This tax was briefly mentioned above in the discussion of income taxes.]
12. Tariff or customs: on goods bought or sold in foreign trade.

This list of consumption taxes suggests the inventive capacity of governments to devise methods to secure money. It also illustrates the fact that the classification of taxes is most difficult, and this in turn explains why the subsequent discussion of excise and sales taxes and tariffs does not exhaust the possibility of consumption taxes.

Consumption taxes are important to every level of government. In 1957, for example, the sales taxes constituted close to 60 per cent of all state revenues and 7 per cent of local government income. During the same year the national government received approximately 16 per cent of its income from excises and tariffs.

The national excise taxes on liquor, tobacco, and luxuries constitute

[5] Harold M. Groves, *Financing Government* (New York: Henry Holt, Inc., 1955), p. 253. Quoted with the permission of the publisher.

a major source of revenue. The excise taxes are designed mainly for the purpose of securing money from special classes of consumers, but occasionally excise taxes have been used to prevent the sale of certain products. A 1911 tax on phosphorous matches destroyed a dangerous business and had no revenue intent; on the other hand, periodic efforts by the national and many state governments to protect the butter industry by taxing the sale of oleomargarine has often been a fruitful source of revenue while quite ineffective in preventing competition of margarine to butter.

More often the excise tax is used because it is an effective money producer. One should carefully examine the moralistic arguments frequently advanced in favor of liquor and tobacco taxes. It is interesting to note that the advocates of prohibition, for example, are generally opposed to liquor taxes because they do not wish governments to become dependent on this lucrative source of revenue. Most excises are designed not to reduce consumption but to gain as much revenue as possible from low income groups. As Professor Simons explains:

> The plain fact to one not confused by moralistic distinctions between necessities and luxuries, is simply that taxes like the tobacco taxes are the most effective means available for draining government revenues out from the very bottom of the income scale. The usual textbook discussions on these points hardly deserve less lampooning than their implied definition of luxuries (and semi-luxuries!) as commodities which poor people ought to do without but won't.[6]

Hence excises on both tobacco and liquor are generally placed at a level thought to produce the highest revenue and not with a view toward reducing consumption (which would certainly reduce government income). Another consideration usually affecting liquor taxes is that they must not be placed at such a high level as to encourage bootlegging.

The virtues of these excises may be seen by turning to tobacco taxes. This national tax is highly productive of income, provides few administrative difficulties, and is very inexpensive since it is collected from the manufacturer. Furthermore, the demand for tobacco is relatively inelastic, thus permitting taxing authorities to hang high taxes on an otherwise cheap product. Curiously, the tax on pipe tobacco and chewing tobacco of the national government is only half that on cigarettes. Under state laws there is also usually a considerable discrimination in

---

[6] Henry C. Simons, *Personal Income Taxation* (Chicago: University of Chicago Press, 1938), p. 40. Quoted with the permission of the publisher.

favor of cigar smokers. Another virtue of this excise (true of liquor as well) is that income from this source shows only a slight tendency to fall during depressions. Although falling hardest on low income groups, these taxes are steady revenue producers.

Until the passage of the Income Tax Amendment, the tariff was the primary producer of national revenues. Today virtually its sole purpose is to prevent foreign goods of many types from entering the United States. In the fiscal year of 1958 the national government received only 800 million dollars or a little more than 1 per cent of its income from this source. Studies of tariff legislation suggest that the revenue potentialities are a negligible consideration in the establishment of this type of consumption tax. Manufacturers and their employees who are subject to effective foreign competition often request Congressmen to raise tariffs on individual commodities. Congressmen oblige because foreign producers have no votes, and importers may be discounted as somehow foreign representatives. Consumers can be generally ignored since they are not sufficiently organized as such to be a force. Economists and the State Department (especially during the administration of Secretary of State Cordell Hull) may wring their hands in anguish, but the consumer hardly knows what he may be missing. Local interests in this context are most effective in promoting a property in their market behind the high tariff walls erected about the United States. Efforts by succeeding administrations to encourage the expansion of international trade have had some minor successes under the Reciprocal Trade Agreements Acts, and efforts have been made to improve the administration of the Customs Service so that foreign businessmen will not be unduly hindered from entering the United States market.

The tariff is a tax that the consumer pays indirectly. It may be in high prices on protected domestically produced goods; or it may be in the augmented purchase price of an imported product such as a Swiss watch on which the importer has already paid a heavy duty. The consumer may wax indignant, but he has not effectively organized himself to encourage a competitive market in this field. Although there is considerable reason to believe that substantial reductions on the tariff on the mentioned products would provide the government with a good income source, proponents of these tariffs argue that their businesses should be protected from unfair foreign competition; foreign producers, they contend, can produce at lower cost because of cheap labor and better access to raw materials. They also argue that tariffs are good revenue producers and that their industries are essential for national defense.

The sales tax is a complicated and expensive tax to administer, but it is being increasingly used by the states, and occasionally by cities, because of its relative painlessness to the consumer and because of its broad incidence. Two sources of complication may be mentioned: What items should be taxed? Who is to determine whether a particular item is taxable or not?

The problems surrounding the first question are most difficult. Should food and medications be excluded? If they are, low income groups are to a large degree freed from the burdens of the sales tax and government revenues are likewise seriously reduced. Should taxes be levied only on the last stage of sale, or should every sale be taxed? If only the last stage is taxed, inequity may result; for example, in the production of automobiles the sale of steel to the manufacturer might not be taxed, but the coal used to fuel the blast furnace might be. If one taxes at every sale, then vertical combinations are benefitted over independent firms because vertical combinations would not be required to pay taxes on the steel and coal that are mined and shipped to the factory when these resources are under their control. Independent producers, on the other hand would be discriminated against, since they would pay tax on everything they bought. These questions raise the second and administrative question, namely, who is to decide which item is to be taxed? Furthermore, there is another closely related issue involving the problem of interstate sales. How does one state collect for products produced and sold in another state but used in the sales-taxing state? Attempts to apply "use taxes" on large goods such as automobiles have proven feasible; but the administrative difficulties of applying similar taxes on small items such as cigarettes, liquor, oleomargarine, and groceries have proven almost insuperable.

These problems do not begin to catalogue the complications of sales taxation. The listing of them does suggest again conflicts of interest between wealthy and poor, between retail merchant and artisan, between states, and between retailer and consumer. For example, a retailer may especially favor a manufacturer's excise, for this tax is entirely hidden from the consumer, the retailer does not have to account for and collect the tax, and the retailer generally marks the price of his product up on his cost by a certain per cent, which means that his profit includes a per cent mark-up on the included tax as well as the cost of the product. The consumer may well object to this type of tax because it results in even greater cost to him on purchases. To repeat, any sales tax is the product of an effort by some form of wealth to shift the burden of taxation to some other form; generally the sales tax has been viewed as a means of relieving the property taxpayers of additional costs of state government.

Although the sales tax may be expensive to administer, easy to avoid, and lend itself to petty corruption, it is a relatively painless tax in one sense. The consumer pays every time he purchases in small and momentarily insignificant amounts. The politicians appreciate this virtue because the taxpayers are less likely to shout. Furthermore, since all people—rich and poor alike—are consumers, these insignificant amounts cumulate to respectable totals of state revenue. Hence the sales tax is often looked upon as the remedy for the trials and tribulations of property owners who feel that ownership of real estate is again no index of ability to pay.

One reason why states are depending largely on the sales tax is that the national government has been increasing its reliance on the income tax, thus further pre-empting this revenue source. A second reason is that there is great competition between states to attract new business; this competition has served as an effective argument in many states against the graduated personal and corporate income tax. In these two ways the federal system apparently serves as the argument for states applying the sales tax in preference to the income tax. To make the sales tax politically palatable, despite its regressive features, the revenues may be pledged for educational purposes, thereby ensuring the support of many property owners as well as many educational authorities. However, cities are unlikely to depend on the sales tax very heavily because of the possibility of consumer evasion by purchasing across city boundaries in suburbs.

Property taxes. Property taxes are the source of 87 per cent of local government tax revenues and provide almost the only source of tax revenue for the special school districts in the United States. Some states continue to use the property tax as a minor source of their revenues, but the national government raises no revenue from this source. The emphasis on this tax for securing local revenue cannot be explained on the basis of any inherent virtue; the units of local government have been creatures of a rural culture and the property tax in part is a carry-over from early rural conditions. Furthermore, as other governmental units—such as the states and the nation—have become aware of the political and administrative difficulties of this type of tax, local government has increasingly been allowed to occupy this field; hence cities, villages, counties, townships, and school districts have a major source of otherwise untapped revenue that is at least relatively flexible and sure.

A major problem of the property tax is the natural rights tradition of identifying property with things. This results in its major theoretical and administrative difficulties. The general property taxes have usually been applied indiscriminately to physical property such as land and improvements, tangible personal property such as furniture, automobiles, livestock, and jewelry, and to intangible property such as stocks, bonds, mortgages, and patents. This has resulted in some curious double taxation and all kinds of administrative complications.

For example, under a general property tax a person who owns his land and home clear of any mortgage will probably pay less taxes in effect than a person who "owns" a property of equal value but with a mortgage worth one-half of the assets. This is because the owner of the mortgage must pay a property tax on his intangible property; and he is likely to try to shift the tax on the mortgage to the owner of the property in the form of higher interest rates than would be justified if there were no tax on intangibles. Another administrative complication of this tax results from the difficulties of securing an honest and/or fair appraisal of the worth of various items of property and of locating all elements of property. Some people have quipped that the general property tax in a modern industrial society is indefensible in theory, and the only thing that makes such a tax bearable is the administrative difficulty in applying it.

Much of the present tax controversy in the states concerns the question of whether or not they should retreat from property taxes to sales or income taxes. During this century some states have met this issue by shifting some of their fiscal burden exclusively from property to sales or income taxes, and some have compromised and tried both (or all three). More generally, the states have shifted substantial burdens particularly in the welfare field to the national taxpayer because the federal income tax has proven such an excellent source of revenue for the national government. It may be presumed that efforts by the President of the United States (for example at the 1957 Governors Conference at Williamsburg, Virginia) and the talk by many vocal governors of returning functions to the states will come to naught because the state and local governments will prove politically incapable of shouldering the heavier burden. Furthermore, these efforts usually neglect to account for the unequal economic capacity of the various states to finance their own governmental responsibilities.

Another issue involves the twin problems of making the property taxes both financially bearable and administratively fair. The gradual exclusion of intangibles and personal property from the tax rolls either through administrative lethargy or by explicit law has tended to throw the burden of this tax on land and improvements. This has simplified some problems of administration, but ownership of land has not been found to be a sure guide to ability to pay. In the first place, such a focus (unless it provides exceptions—for example, forest lands) tends to encourage the exhaustion of natural resources. Secondly, agricultural properties around cities have a tendency to rise in price and force farmers off the land prematurely, thereby encouraging land speculation. Finally, assessors usually under-assess large land holdings and valuable improvements to the disadvantage of small land holders. States have sometimes tried to provide for equalization of assessments between districts and within districts by providing state boards of equalization and by increasing the professional qualifications of the assessor, a job traditionally subject to local election. These efforts, besides improving revenue potentialities of the property tax, have run into obstructions because again they inevitably result in shifting tax burdens from one class of property holder to another.

Despite all these difficulties, the property tax is an important tool for local land-use planning if it is applied merely to land. Although in the United States this tax has not been used extensively as a tool for community planning, it remains a fruitful steady source of income for local units of government.

Other taxes. A large variety of other types of taxes render a substantial amount of revenue to national, state, and local government treasuries. Licenses, franchises, and private utility taxes are one form. Revenues derived from these sources are in exchange for permission to exercise some kind of profession, or to use the public right of way, and may even involve the right of eminent domain or to occupy some monopolistic position under explicit state grant.[7] Another form of tax is represented by the motor vehicle fuel taxes, which are generally segregated as revenue for purely highway purposes under the pressure of the automotive industry, trucking interests, and automobile clubs. Tax authorities generally frown on this type of segregation of revenues; some claim that it simply uses the tax laws to subsidize a particular

[7] See pp. 253-54.

group of interests to the disadvantage of good budgetary and administrative control. The alliance of road-using pressure groups claim that this segregation is justified as a fee for highway use.[8] A third form of tax is exemplified by the social security taxes that are intended to pay for Old Age and Survivors Insurance and Unemployment Compensation. Since this type of tax has a specific nonrevenue purpose, it is explained in the chapter on social insurance in this volume.[9]

Taxes conclusions

The system of taxation that has been devised in the United States reflects the institutions of government, the political process, and the ideas and interests that find expression in that process. The system of national taxation is much more a mirror of tax politics and tax-writing processes in Congress than a realization of the criteria according to which Adam Smith thought taxes should be levied. Consequently, one should not be surprised that the tax system is only partially designed to help the government pay its bills; in recent years there have been few occasions when the budget has in fact been balanced. Taxes are likely to be applied where political repercussions are the least hostile. Once applied, a tax is unlikely to be lifted when it has proved a fruitful source of revenue. Hidden and uncertain taxes have not been unknown, and much effort has been applied to the question of making taxes more tolerable by such methods as grafting the installment feature of the withholding tax on to the income tax. These factors make the study of taxation difficult; they make our revenue measures more complicated than theoretically would be necessary; and they conceal from the voter the significance of a wide variety of tax measures.

PUBLIC POLICY ISSUES OF TAXATION

Two questions of fiscal policy deserving further examination are the use of taxation to promote economic growth and the issue of intergovernmental fiscal relations. Both these questions have been given serious consideration by economists, Treasury officials, and members of committees of Congress. State officials have lobbied extensively at the national capital in an effort to secure new and more palatable sources of revenue by winning an agreement from the national government to relinquish some of its tax sources. Furthermore, President Eisenhower appointed a Commission on Intergovernmental Relations

[8] For the view of budgeters and administrators, see p. 28.
[9] See Chapter 9.

and National-State Fiscal Relations to implement a Republican campaign promise to study methods for reduction of the scope of national government activity.

"Federal Tax Policy for Economic Growth and Stability"

Under the above title the Joint Committee on the Economic Report issued in 1955 two important documents dealing with the question of how national tax policies affected the economy. The responsibility of this joint committee under the Employment Act of 1946 is to provide Congress with advice as to methods for achieving economic stability and a high level of employment. One of the volumes includes the reports and papers of a large number of tax experts, economists, accountants, and lawyers, while the other includes panel discussions of the various papers by these different authorities.

It was the committee's unanimous judgment that the tax writing committees of Congress should be more careful to assess the economic implications of present fiscal policies. The committee complained that the Ways and Means Committee of the House and the Senate Finance Committee frequently lacked satisfactory data in dealing with their responsibilities. The Committee further recommended that these committees and the Executive Branch should "recognize that the level of tax revenues in relation to the amount of government expenditures has an important bearing on the level of economic activity. This should tend to result in Federal surpluses and debt retirement during prosperous and boom periods and deficits during recessions and depressions." [10]

The fact that there has been no substantial revision of the national revenue system since the writing of this committee report suggests that either the tax writing committees or the Eisenhower administration are resisting any substantial alteration of the present national revenue system, or perhaps that these committees or the administration feel that the present system achieves the ends that the Joint Committee feels it does not. To be sure, the question of national revenue reform is most controversial. On one side, as noted previously, there are efforts to destroy the principle of graduation in the income tax system by placing a 25 per cent constitutional limitation on income taxes and replacing the income tax by a manufacturers' excise. On the other side,

[10] Joint Committee on the Economic Report, *Report 1310,* 84th Congress. 2d Sess. (Jan. 5, 1956).

there are somewhat feeble efforts, unsupported by the administration, to improve the principle of graduated income taxation by eliminating various loopholes by which particular interests achieve preferential treatment. Here again we have the effort of various interests anxious to shift the incidence of the tax burden, with various groups competing against one another for special advantages. It seems clear that in this context actual tax writing is directed less toward achieving the economic purposes proclaimed in the Employment Act than toward placating various forceful and well-organized interests.

Intergovernmental fiscal relations

Another aspect of the 1956 Report of the Joint Economic Committee was its opposition to the groups seeking to undermine the welfare programs of the national government by returning them to the states. The new administration inaugurated in 1953 was partially authorized by platform commitments to cease the trend toward centralization of governmental functions in the nation's Capitol and to find means for decentralizing some of the vast responsibilities in the states. To this end President Eisenhower was authorized to appoint a commission.[11] Under the chairmanship of Meyer Kestnbaum this commission authorized a number of valuable studies in intergovernmental fiscal relations and other national-state issues. The Commission was unable to agree upon any substantial return of functions to the states or on a different division of revenue system. It merely piously recommended that the national government should not assume any additional burdens such as Federal Aid to Schools. It also opposed the replacement of the national grants-in-aid program by the adoption of a system of unrestricted national subventions to the states, such as is practiced in Canada, on the grounds that this would put the states under greater control by the national government. Instead, they recommended, for example, that the highway grants-in-aid to states should be under less national supervision.

The factors behind this controversy are: (1) the continued complaints of the states that they have inadequate revenue sources to carry on their many governmental jobs; (2) the reluctance of the more wealthy states to supply funds to poorer states; and (3) the continued effort of those groups opposed to the welfare state, or aspects of it,

[11] The authorizing legislation enacted by Congress to establish the Kestnbaum Commission provided that the President should appoint 15 members, and the Vice-President and Speaker of the House should appoint five members each.

to relieve the national government of its responsibility in the welfare field. This latter group has been aided by other groups that are seeking mainly to reduce taxes or to shift the burden of taxation. By giving the states the responsibility for these welfare functions, either the states would be unable to continue the programs or the programs would be paid for in effect by different people, for the reason, as we have seen, that the national fiscal system depends largely on the income tax while the state systems generally depend on the sales tax and local property taxes.

This issue is reflected in a significant supplement appended by Senator Paul Douglas to the aforementioned Report of the Joint Economic Committee. Senator Douglas tries to show on the basis of evidence collected by the committee that the 28 billion dollars collected by state and local governments is significantly regressive (that it hits lower-income people harder). While state governments "derive about two-thirds of their revenue from some form of sales taxation, whether this be general sales taxes or specific excises such as a gasoline tax, a liquor or cigarette tax, or a motor vehicle tax," local revenues are seven-eighths dependent on the property tax. Douglas argues that both types of taxes are regressive, the latter because properties of low value are assessed more nearly at their true value than high value property.

That this controversy is not simply between Congress and the Executive may be gleaned from two important facts. President Eisenhower has recommended the establishment of a program of national aid to education, following the recommendations of the White House Conference on Education instead of the opposing views of the Kestnbaum Commission. Furthermore, in July 1957, the President challenged the governors of the states to present a plan whereby some national government functions might be decentralized to the states. He suggested that the states might take over a program of disaster insurance, a proposal somewhat frigidly received by the states. One notes a coolness by the states to programs that might involve additional expenditures on their part, and a warmth on their part to any proposal that might increase their income, either through additional sources of taxes or through additional grants-in-aid. In the South there is an additional controversy regarding the integration of schools, which gets mixed up in this situation but is dealt with elsewhere in this volume.[12]

[12] See chapters 1, 2, and 10.

Tax agencies

The agencies of the national government in the middle of these controversies of interest include, on the Executive side, the Treasury Department and, on the congressional side, the Senate Finance Committee and the House Ways and Means Committee. While these agencies are supposed to give careful thought to the problem of taxation, they are mainly concerned with the practical development and administration of our internal revenue system.

Although the Treasury has been given a number of not altogether related functions, its primary obligation is to superintend and manage the national finances. The Office of the Secretary of the Treasury (who has Cabinet status) includes the Analysis Staff, which has the responsibility for coordinating the analytical activities in the department relating to taxation, financing, and debt management. Its primary responsibility is to prepare economic and statistical materials for use by Treasury officials in the formulation of tax and debt policies. To this end the staff is divided according to function into two divisions: the Tax Division and the Debt Division. Our present concern is with the Tax Division, which prepares analyses of tax proposals and assembles the materials necessary to justify and explain tax policies in the light of economic and budgetary requirements. It helps supply information to the President, the tax writing committees of Congress, and individual Congressmen when requested. More significantly, it helps prepare the official estimates of the Government receipts that are incorporated in the President's annual budget message and explains the economic and revenue impacts of proposed new taxes or revisions of the present tax laws. The Analysis Staff is a young agency, created on March 1, 1953, to replace the Tax Advisory Staff and the Office of Technical Staff which previously performed some of these functions.

The Bureau of Customs and the Bureau of Internal Revenue have the key role in the collection of taxes. The Bureau of Customs' principal task is the assessment and collection of import duties and, incident to this, the prevention of smuggling, including the smuggling of contraband such as narcotics. The Internal Revenue Service is responsible for the collection of most other tax revenues. The actual taking in of taxes is decentralized in nine regions throughout the United States and its possessions. The headquarters organization has the responsibility for coordinating the field service and for developing nation-wide policies and programs for the administration of the revenue laws.

As with appropriations measures, the Executive exercises considerable initiative with proposals to revise and extend the tax laws of the nation. Much of the staff work that supports Executive proposals is done in the Treasury. However, Article I, Section 7, of the Constitution specifies that all bills for raising revenue shall originate in the House of Representatives. The Senate is not barred from proposing amendments to revenue bills, but the responsibility for revenue measure initiation is in the House, which takes pride in its special function. The House Ways and Means Committee is in a key position to influence the tax laws, and it is all the stronger because the Democratic members of this committee constitute also the Committee on Committees for the Democratic Caucus and are responsible for making Democratic committee assignments in the House. As the Democratic party has controlled the House in every Congress but two since 1931, the political influence of this committee should not be underestimated. On both Senate and House committees local interests are likely to prevail and Congressmen will tend to be more concerned with protecting the particular interests of their constituents than with the theoretical integrity of the national tax system. Tax policy is, consequently, always controversial, always in flux.

MONETARY POLICY

The Constitution grants the national government substantial monetary powers including the authority to borrow, lend, and coin money and to control credit. The states have many of these powers too, except they no longer control either credit or currency; they never had power under the present Constitution to coin money. The borrowing power is used at every level of government to pay public expenses that are not being paid by current taxes; the lending function is used also to support and subsidize numerous business activities that legislatures feel the government should support; and the coinage of money provides the lubricant for a dollar economy in place of its barter alternative. The governmental monetary policies naturally have a large impact on the total economy. They are devised, therefore, not only for the purpose of achieving specific results but also to maintain the economic conditions that seem likely to promote economic growth and stability.

Throughout our history monetary policy has been highly controversial. One of the chief issues between the Hamiltonians and the

Republicans at the outset involved the creation of the first National Bank. Taking over the earlier Jeffersonian Republican policy of opposition to the National Bank, the Jacksonian Democrats encouraged the development of state banking. In the latter part of the 19th century the Populists, Greenbackers, and the Bryan free-silverites all developed in opposition to the hard money policy followed by both Republican and Democratic administrations of this period. During the Wilson administration the Federal Reserve System was created in order to provide a more flexible monetary policy.

Monetary institutions of the national government

The chief monetary institutions of the national government are the Treasury Department and the Federal Reserve System. The Treasury Department especially through its Bureau of Public Debt is responsible for the issues of securities which constitute a major portion of the public debt. The Federal Reserve System, through its control of the reserve requirements of the national banks, can regulate many of the conditions under which the Treasury will issue its bonds. It is curious that these public bodies since World War II have often failed to cooperate with each other, and occasionally Treasury policy has been diametrically opposed to the policy of the Federal Reserve Banks. One reason why conflict is possible between these two agencies lies in the way that they are organized and the divergent interests that they reflect. The Department of the Treasury is directly under the control of the President, and the Secretary of the Treasury is a political appointee of the President. The Treasury is consequently more likely to reflect the points of view of the dominant interest groups which have influential access to the President.

The Board of Governors of the Federal Reserve System is also appointed by the President but with due regard to a fair representation of financial, agricultural, industrial, and commercial interests, and the geographic regions of the country. The seven members are appointed for overlapping terms of 14 years each, which means that the incumbent president is not likely to have substantial political control over this agency. Furthermore, the Federal Reserve Banks are owned by privately controlled member banks which elect six out of nine directors for each of the 12 District Federal Reserve Banks; the other three are appointed by the Board of Governors and all the officers of the District Reserve Banks must be approved by this Federal Reserve Board. These two differences in manner of appointment and constituency go

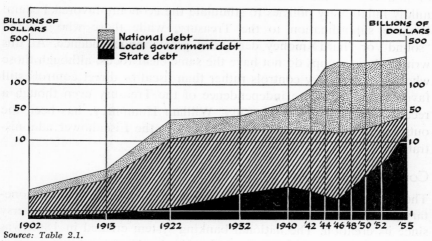

Source: Table 2.1.

Fig. 2.2 Total public debt by level of government for selected years (logarithmic scale)

TABLE 2.1

TOTAL PUBLIC DEBT BY LEVEL OF GOVERNMENT
FOR SELECTED YEARS, 1902–1955 *

	All Govern-				Per Capita Debt All Govern-			
Year	ments	National	State	Local	ments	National	State	Local
	—(Amount in millions of dollars)—				—(Amount in dollars)—			
1902	3,285	1,178	230	1,877	41	15	3	24
1913	5,607	1,193	379	4,035	58	12	4	42
1922	33,072	22,963	1,131	8,978	301	209	10	82
1932	38,692	19,487	2,832	16,373	310	156	23	131
1940	63,251	42,968	3,590	16,693	479	325	27	126
1942	92,128	72,422	3,257	16,449	683	537	24	122
1944	218,482	201,003	2,776	14,703	1579	1452	20	106
1946	285,339	269,422	2,353	13,564	2018	1905	17	96
1948	270,948	252,292	3,676	14,980	1848	1721	25	102
1950	281,472	257,357	5,285	18,830	1856	1697	35	124
1952	289,205	259,105	6,874	23,226	1842	1650	44	148
1953	299,852	266,071	7,824	25,957	1878	1667	49	163
1954	310,190	271,260	9,600	29,331	1910	1670	59	181
1955	318,641	274,374	11,198	33,069	1928	1660	68	200

* Statistical Abstract of the United States, 1957, Table 486, p. 406.

far to explain differences of policy between the Treasury and the Federal Reserve System. Obviously, some of the controversy which we shall discuss expresses itself in terms of whether the relationship between the Federal Reserve System and the Treasury should be closer or not. During the Truman administration those who approved of mildly inflationary policies to stimulate the economy favored Federal Reserve subordination to the Treasury, while those who favored "sound" or "hard" money demanded greater independence. At this writing these groups do not have the same clear focus, although those who favor monetary controls rather than fiscal or direct controls still favor Federal Reserve independence of the Treasury even though a recent Secretary of the Treasury, William Humphrey, has been the outstanding exponent of "sound" money in the Eisenhower administration.

Conflict over monetary policy

The Federal Reserve System arose out of political conflict over monetary policy, and has been the center of continued political controversy since its creation. The national banking system created in 1863 was designed to stabilize currency and assist in the sale of government bonds. To this end the paper money issued by state banks was taxed out of existence, and national banks enjoyed a monopoly over the issuance of paper currency. The national banks were limited in this regard only by the requirement that note currency could be issued only to the extent that the national banks were holders of national government bonds. A gradual reduction of the national debt during the late Nineteenth and early Twentieth centuries resulted in a reduction of currency that severely hampered small business transactions. Part of the political cry for free coinage of silver was an effort to expand the currency to meet the needs of small and new business establishments as well as agriculture. Senator Carter Glass, the author of the Federal Reserve legislation of 1913, described in forceful terms the national banking system that his legislation replaced as "the Siamese twins" of an "inelastic currency and a fictitious reserve system."

The monetary powers given to the new reserve system were quite extensive although only gradually and cautiously explored. These powers are derived from Federal Reserve's influence over bank credit, the chief source of money supply. Commercial banks—including all the banks chartered by the national government and holding over 85 per cent of all bank deposits—are required to carry reserves equal to a specific portion of their deposits. The amount of credit that these banks may extend is determined by the level of reserves. The Federal Reserve Board has the power to increase or decrease the reserve base, thereby contracting or expanding the available credit. When reserve requirements are increased, money is said to be "tight"; when contracted, money is "easier." There are two additional ways in which the Federal Reserve System can ease or tighten credit. One way is by changing the discount rate on temporary borrowing by member banks; as the discount rate increases, credit is tightened because borrowing becomes more expensive; decreasing the discount rate makes credit become cheaper. The second way that the Federal Reserve System affects credit is through buying government securities on the open market which has the effect of expanding the currency, or by selling government securities which tends to make credit "tight."

These manipulations have a notable effect on the cost of Treasury security issues and the national debt, and consequently the policies of the Treasury are directly affected by the policies of the Federal Reserve System. Tight money and high interest rates increase the cost of Treasury borrowing and hence increase the cost to the tax payer of servicing the national debt. Cheap money reduces the cost of servicing the debt. Each of these policies also has the effect respectively of increasing or lowering the cost of state and local debts. The Federal Reserve can support Treasury financing by buying securities to ensure their market, or it can refuse to do this. However, if the Federal Reserve buys and supports government security issues, its capacity to manage the money supply is severely limited. These factors have been at the center of the controversy about what position the Federal Reserve System should take during both the Truman and Eisenhower administrations. In this controversy the Truman administration generally went against the advice of the Federal Reserve Board, and the Democratic-controlled Joint Committee on Economic Report usually supported the President's reliance on fiscal measures as opposed to the FRB's monetary proposals. During the subsequent Eisenhower administration, reliance has been placed largely on monetary policies and in support of the views that the Federal Reserve Board has defended. Interestingly, the Eisenhower preoccupation with monetary policies has come under some criticism by both the Republican- (during the 83rd Congress) and Democratic- (during the 84th Congress) controlled Joint Committees.

What have these controversies been about? During World War II the Federal Reserve System loyally supported national government security issues in the paramount interest of winning the war. This resulted in a tremendous expansion of credit and money, which was partially sopped up by high taxes and enforced savings through compulsory purchases of war bonds. It also resulted, however, in tremendous inflationary pressures because such a great portion of the national production was devoted to war purposes. This inflationary pressure was partially controlled through a system of direct price controls and rationing. The quick elimination of price controls and rationing following the war resulted in a rapid inflation of prices in spite of the miraculously speedy conversion of industry from war to peacetime production. Advocates of monetary policy for control urged (and were hesitatingly supported by the Federal Reserve Board) that this was a time to tighten credit using all the weapons at the disposal of the Federal Reserve System. Advocates of the opposite approach urged that this would be inefficient; that the same ends could be achieved more economically and efficiently through manipulation of the fiscal system and the reintroduction of direct controls. Congress was unwilling to reintroduce direct controls and remained anxious to reduce both national taxes and spending, until the Korean War in 1950. During this previous period the Federal Reserve Board reluctantly supported Treasury securities, which suggests that neither monetary nor fiscal nor direct control advocates had their way. During most of these years inflationary pressures mounted in spite of government surpluses and a "favorable" balance of the budget.

In March, 1951, the Truman administration partially yielded to the position of the Federal Reserve Board, resulting in an accord on a new money-debt policy. The main feature of this accord was that the Federal Reserve Board would permit some rise in the yield of government securities if necessary as a part of a more restrictive monetary policy. This accord had already been recommended in principle in a report by the Douglas Subcommittee on Monetary, Credit and Fiscal Policies in 1949. This subcommittee had unanimously subscribed to the monetary approach in the following words:

> We recommend not only that appropriate, vigorous, and coordinated monetary, credit, and fiscal policies be employed to promote . . . [economic growth and stability, and full employment] but also that such policies constitute the government's primary and principal method of promoting those purposes.[13]

Judging from the practice of the national government, its policy since this time has been to rely primarily on monetary instruments to

[13] *Report,* Monetary, Credit and Fiscal Policies Subcommittee, Joint Committee on the Economic Report, Senate Document 129 (January, 1950).

influence the economy (the Korean War period being a partial exception). The issues involved here are not merely economic. They reflect both conflicts of interest within the economy and the ideologies of individuals reflecting these conflicts of interest. One extreme statement of the position favorable to monetary techniques and the recommendations of the Federal Reserve Board was made by a former Board member, E. A. Goldenweiser, who wrote:

> The Committee favors the more impersonal and democratic approach through money flow over more dictatorial approaches through direct intervention in the economic behavior of individuals.[14]

Others are more disposed to utilize the tax system, government spending and, if necessary, direct controls. Professor Harris, while oversimplifying party differences, explains the alternatives as follows:

> Though this is no black and white matter, Democrats tend to stress fiscal policy more and monetary policy less; the administration, monetary policy more and fiscal policy less. In part, *this difference of emphasis is based on the theory that fiscal policy means Government activity and intervention through debt policy, through variations of the amount and structure of taxes and expenditures.* Hence Republicans tend to look with disfavor on the use of these weapons. *They prefer monetary policy because to them this reflects the operations of the free market.*[15]

Another important issue involved in the controversy between the Executive and the Federal Reserve System (and to a lesser extent, Congress) is what agencies should control and be responsible for fiscal and monetary policies. Should this be the obligation of a politically accountable President and Congress? Or should a sheltered *quasi*-political administrative agency such as the Federal Reserve Board be permitted to determine policy? In the political melée this question is rarely faced.

Practically speaking, the issue is not whether to control the economy or not, or what agency is to be responsible, but rather to *whose advantage* the economy should be controlled. That this is the case may be illustrated from the consequences of the tight money policy inaugurated by the Eisenhower administration, which has raised the interest rate on government securities to 4 per cent. On the political level one con-

[14] Goldenweiser, "Douglas Committee Report," *American Economic Review,* Vol. 40 (June, 1950), p. 389.

[15] Seymour E. Harris, "Effectiveness and Relationship of Fiscal and Monetary Policy," *Hearings* on the January, 1957, Economic Report of the President, Joint Committee on the Economic Report, 85th Cong. 1st Sess. (1957), pp. 484 ff. Italics ours.

sequence was an illustration of why Senators Eastland and Humphrey can continue to live together in the same Democratic party. A debate on the floor of the Senate in the summer of 1953 showed how both of these gentlemen represent constituencies appearing to be adversely affected by the tight money policy that had just been brought into being. Small business and agriculture, which predominate in both Mississippi and Minnesota, had difficulty securing financing to carry on their operations. On the other hand, bank interest has increased, as have the dividends from stock ownership. Large corporations have no difficulty securing financing, for they depend largely on undistributed profits and can increase the level of profits because they are sufficiently powerful to control prices.

In addition, although it has been the policy of the Republicans to encourage highway construction by the states and additional school construction by local governments, these policies have been effectively negated by national monetary policies. State governments must pay much higher interest on their security issues, and are occasionally prevented by state laws from doing this; school districts are under even greater limitations. Not only are school districts limited by restrictive state laws in accumulating debts, but they are also handicapped by the limitations of the property tax base on which they depend for income. The argument against monetary policy is that this policy puts control of economic development in the hands of the bankers through their control of the Federal Reserve System; this control is used to the advantage of banking interests and large business and to the disadvantage of small business and certain other public purposes. Those who favor continued monetary controls argue that these promote economic stability and business confidence.

It seems clear, in short, that who gets control, and the methods used to exercise this control, helps to determine the political question of "who gets what and when?"

Meeting the 1958 economic emergency

The 1959 budget proposals of President Eisenhower exemplify the means by which the Republican administration proposed to deal with the four major financial problems of 1958. First it was necessary to find additional money to pay for the administration's augmented space age defense program to meet the challenge of the Soviet Sputnik. Secondly, the budget had to cope with increasing signs of a depression which was evidenced by declines in production, national income, and on the stock market, as well as increases in unemployment threatening to exceed 5,000,000 jobless. Third, in spite of business decline, the administration also faced a continued inflation in prices. And finally, it was under severe pressure from Republican congressmen to provide a program which would enhance their chances of reelection. This last pressure was particularly urgent since the success of the Eisenhower proposals depended so much on possible Republican congressional support.

To cope with the defense, economic, and political difficulties the President submitted a $73.9 billion budget, major aspects of which are presented in Table 2.2. To meet the immediate military problem

TABLE 2.2

BUDGET EXPENDITURES AND AUTHORIZATIONS BY PURPOSE
IN BILLIONS OF DOLLARS *

	1957 (Actual)	1958 (Estimated)	1959 (Estimated)
Defense	$45.2	$46.3	$47.1
Civil benefits	15.1	17.0	16.4
Interest on debt	7.3	7.9	7.9
General government	1.8	1.4	1.4
allowance for proposed legislation and contingencies	—	0.2	1.1
TOTAL	$69.4	$72.8	$73.9

* Budget Message of the President (January 13, 1958).

this budget included $3.8 billion additional for missile development and one billion for educational assistance, primarily for the training of scientists and engineers. To cope with a possible depression the administration eliminated many previously proposed plans to retrench its civilian projects. In fact, the budget provided for advance planning for public works to the amount of approximately $8 billion in case some of its other policies did not succeed in stopping the business decline. To pay for the billion-dollar increase over the 1958 budget, the government would depend largely on increased revenues from present taxes and changes of allocations of funds within the military establishment. A surplus of $466 million was budgeted, but this surplus depended on improved business conditions in addition to increases in postal rates and taxes on aviation fuel. In a press conference the President announced that he would approve of a return to deficit financing if tax reductions were necessary to bolster the economy. His budget message proposed an increase of $5 billion in the national debt limit to $280 billion in order to "give the Treasury some much-needed flexibility in conducting its financing during this coming period."

Significantly, the administration relied primarily on the monetary approach to deal with the "recession." The Federal Reserve Board changed its policies which had been designed to prevent overexpansion of business and inflation. The new policy was designed to ease the supply of credit to support the capital market, home building, and the stock market. In November, 1957, the discount rate was reduced from 3.5 to 3 per cent, in January to 2.75, and in March to 2.25 per cent. This permitted banks to lower interest rates on their loans, making money easier to borrow. In January the Federal Reserve Board also reduced stock margin requirements from 70 per cent to 50 per cent, hoping thereby to encourage investment in stocks and to bolster the sagging stock market. Finally, the Treasury announced a 32 year 3.5 per cent bond issue as part of a program to refund $16.8 billion of government securities coming due in February. This was a retreat from the previous Treasury policy of issuing 4 per cent securities.

These programs suggest that a Republican administration is willing to use most of the tools that fiscal and monetary experts regard as useful to support a flagging economy in a time of emergency. They are willing to consider deficit financing—that is, the increase of public expenditure at a time when government income will probably decline. They are also willing to retreat from a policy of high interest rates and "sound" money to increase the circulation of money, investment, and consumer buying. Although the Republicans concentrated on increased military spending to deal with the immediate defense emergency, they also appear willing to plan for public works projects in case these methods prove insufficient. They continue to rely primarily on monetary approaches and have shown no interest at this writing in the possibilities of direct controls over prices or labor in order to deal with the inflation issue. Nevertheless, the President has repeatedly asked both businessmen and workers to show restraint, an appeal that has been generally ignored.

Willingness to use the fiscal and monetary powers of the government to promote a sound economy does not mean automatically that these powers will be used wisely. Different people will have a variety of views on which financial tools the government should use. Congressmen who depend on a "balance the budget" and "cut government costs" philosophy may be disappointed and oppose the President's program. Those who favor financial manipulations may still disagree with the precise policies the administration has advanced.

And those who feel that more direct controls over price or labor are necessary will fear that the Republican program for 1958–1959 is inadequate. It is most significant that the administration allowed itself a great deal of room for flexible adjustment of policy to meet possible political and economic contingencies.

BIBLIOGRAPHICAL NOTE

Arthur Smithies, *The Budgetary Process in the United States,* 1955, is an extensive survey of the role of the federal budget by a well known economist. A. E. Buck, *The Budget in Governments of Today,* 1934, is old but provides the still standard and useful source for state and national budgetary matters. *The Federal Budget in Brief,* published annually by the Bureau of the Budget, provides a well illustrated summary of the national budget.

J. Roy Blough, *The Federal Taxing Process,* 1952, is an authoritative presentation of the forces at work and the institutions involved in the taxing process. Randolph E. Paul, *Taxation in the United States,* 1954, gives a realistic treatment of this subject from the point of view of a former high official in the Treasury.

E. W. and D. L. Kemmerer, *The ABC of the Federal Reserve System,* rev. ed., 1950, is a clear and reliable account of the operations of the Federal Reserve system. George L. Bach, *Federal Reserve Policy Making,* 1950, emphasizes the process and political aspect of the Federal Reserve system.

Arthur W. MacMahon, "Congressional Oversight of Administration: The Power of the Purse," *Political Science Quarterly,* Vol. 58, pp. 161, 380 (1943), provides a brilliant view of the political and process aspects of legislative scrutiny of the budget. H. C. Simons, *Personal Income Taxation,* 1938, provides a careful examination of the theory of income taxation by a strong defender of *laissez faire.* A. P. Lerner, *The Economics of Control,* 1944, gives a suggestive treatment of the way the financial powers of the government may be utilized to provide for public planning by a writer who does not share Simons' economic theories.

Harold M. Groves, *Financing Government,* 4th ed., 1954, is the best standard work on public finance dealing both with the multitude of fiscal and monetary methods and also their public policy implications. This volume is comparative in that it treats both national and state problems and because it does not hesitate to draw on foreign experience.

Bureau of Census, *Compendium of State Government Finances* (Annual), Bureau of Census, *Compendium of City Government Finances* (Annual) includes fairly detailed statistical materials on large cities and only a sampling on other municipalities. *The Book of States* (Chicago: Council on State Governments, Biennial) has both useful articles and statistics. J. R. McKinley, *Local Revenue Problems and Trends,* 1949, deals with some of the important issues of local government finance in a systematic way. L. H. Kimmel, *Government Costs and Tax Levels,* 1948.

3. JAMES N. MURRAY, JR.

Foreign Policy

IT has become commonplace that the position of the United States in world affairs has undergone a revolutionary transformation. For almost 150 years the American people felt insulated politically as well as geographically from the major centers of international politics, and could turn to the task of shaping their common destiny in the New World free from the influence of important international commitments and responsibilities. True, we sometimes negotiated treaties and even fought an occasional war, but before the first World War neither the treaties nor the wars with foreign powers made much of an impact on the average citizen. And even as late as the 1920's it was our tradition of insulation that in part led to a policy of retreat from international commitments following that war. What the "return to normalcy" meant in the area of foreign policy was a return to the tradition of noninvolvement in affairs of Europe and Asia.

Today, of course, the situation is very different. Not only is the United States at the center of the whirlpool of international politics, where our very existence as a nation may well be at stake, but the life of almost every American is closely affected by our attempt to cope with the problems of foreign policy. The situation is strikingly illustrated by noting that only 35 years ago our total expenditures on matters relating to foreign affairs were about 2.65 billion dollars—a not inconsiderable sum. Yet in 1956 the corresponding figure was almost 20 times that amount.[1]

Nor can we find clear-cut, well-defined solutions to the problems we face. The United States has interests, commitments, and responsibilities that are today literally global. And any action we may take in one area of the world may have the most profound repercussions in other areas. For example, it may seem obvious both from the point of view of our historic tradition and our contemporary national interest that the United States should support the aspirations of the Algerian Arabs for independence from France. This would raise our prestige throughout the Middle East and would be consistent with our anti-colonial heritage. But France, for whom Algeria is both politically and economically important, is a prominent member of NATO. If we support the Algerian Arabs we do so at the risk of undermining our relations with France, and possibly jeopardizing the entire NATO structure for the defense of Western Europe. In attempting to grasp the tremendous complexity of the issues facing those responsible for formulating American foreign policy it is useful to remember the story of Alexander and the Gordian Knot. Analogously, the United States faces simultaneously a multitude of Gordian Knots; and perhaps more important, a successful attempt to untie any one of them may make others that much more difficult to unravel.

Clearly one of the crucial problems facing America as a nation is the formation of effective, coherent foreign policies not only because the stakes include the very existence of our society, but also because of the extraordinary complexity and fluidity of international relations today. Given the most efficient, well-organized system for forming policy, the problems would be staggering enough. But this question arises: Is our society organized in such a way as to promote the formation of intelligent foreign policy? Implicit in this question is the important consideration that the *process* by which policy is formed may have great consequences for the *substance* of policy. The suddenness with which the American people were thrust into the role of leader of the free world raises, then, not only misgivings about our experience in dealing with the substantive issues of international affairs, but at the same time questions as to the adequacy of our institutions to produce intelligent policy.

[1] Based on figures in James L. McCamy, *The Administration of American Foreign Affairs* (New York: Alfred A. Knopf, 1952), p. 5, and *Annual Report of the Secretary of the Treasury on the State of the Finances for the Fiscal Year Ended June 30, 1956* (Washington: U.S. Government Printing Office, 1957).

And there is yet more to the problem. For the goals and methods of policy formation cannot be stated in terms of efficiency alone, at least in a democratic society. We are committed to the idea that government in some way ought to reflect the demands of the governed. It is not enough, in other words, to achieve efficient, intelligent foreign policy if the price is the destruction of the institutions of democratic government.

In sum, our problems include both the substantive issues of foreign affairs and the capacity we have for dealing with those issues in terms of the organization of our government. Further, any attempt to create an efficient system of foreign policy formation must be attempted within the context of democratic values, lest in attempting to meet the challenges from outside we destroy the very things we are trying to preserve.

A BRIEF HISTORICAL SURVEY

Broadly speaking the history of the United States as a power in world affairs may be divided into two periods: pre- and post-Spanish American War. Prior to 1900 our two underlying foreign policies were (1) isolation of the New World from the affairs of the Old, as manifested in the Monroe Doctrine, and (2) expansion in the New World roughly as far as our relative power position could carry us. This meant, with respect to the second point, territorial acquisitions westward across the continent and southward as far as Mexico would permit. It did not mean northward for the primary reason that the nation in control of the territory to the north, Great Britain, was too powerful for us.

This two-fold basis of foreign policy—isolation from Europe, expansion in the New World—does not of course account for all our activities on the international scene until 1900, and there were, of course, occasional departures from these principles. But it does sum up our essential aims, and in these aims we were fortunate in facing a dying empire (Spain) in the West and South, a state anxious to liquidate its New World assets (France, with reference to the Louisiana Territory), and a state which, though it could have given us considerable trouble in pursuing either or both of these aims (Great Britain), viewed it as complementary to her interests to have the United States emerge as the dominant force in the New World.

The Spanish-American War marks a turning point in our diplomatic history because its conclusion saw American commitments now stretched far beyond our continental limits—for example, controlling the Philippines—and it saw an industrialized America capable of sustaining the national power necessary to defend those overseas commitments. At that time it might have yet been possible to turn back— to withdraw from the Philippines and remain aloof from the developing maelstrom in Europe. We chose not to. We remained in the Philippines, thus establishing ourselves as a Pacific power, and became inextricably intertwined in the fate of Europe with our entry into World War I. Viewed with hindsight the "return to normalcy" of the 1920's and early 1930's in the arena of international politics seems little more than an emotional reaction against the responsibilities that our ever increasing national power and our chosen overseas commitments ineluctably brought on.

World War I sapped the strength of the heretofore major powers of Western Europe and left the United States potentially more powerful than any state in the world. Any expansionist country, whether in Europe (where our ties with England had been increasingly strengthened since the middle of the nineteenth century), or in Asia (where we were committed to the defense of the Philippines), had to—and did—take the United States into account, whether Americans liked it or not. Without attempting to argue the immediate responsibilities for American entry into World War II, it seems obvious—again from the vantage point of historical hindsight—that given the relative decline in British and French power, given our economic and emotional ties with Europe, and given our commitments in the Pacific—such entry was inevitable, the only questions being those of time and place.

The post World War II era has been characterized on the international scene by the existence of two superpowers, the United States and the Soviet Union. The significance of this for Americans is that the Western European countries, particularly France and Britain, have declined in their relative power positions. This in turn means that as France or Britain withdraw from their overseas commitments the United States is faced with the hard choice of either filling the vacuum by guaranteeing the integrity of the area concerned or being faced with the possible consequence of Soviet domination of that area.

CURRENT PROBLEMS AND POLICIES

Faced with this situation the basic decision that the United States has had to make is whether to liquidate our commitments in Europe and

Asia and attempt to create an impregnable position in the New World, or to support non-Communist states in Asia, Europe, and Africa in an effort to contain Soviet expansion before it threatens the New World directly.

The grand alternative: containment or Gibraltar?

While there is some debate as to the precise meaning and implications of "containment" as a policy, most of its basic assumptions were spelled out in the Truman Doctrine which, specifically, was a request from the President to Congress in 1947 for funds to aid Greece and Turkey. The President in justifying his request asserted:

At the present moment in world history nearly every nation must choose between alternative ways of life. The choice is too often not a free one.

One way of life is based upon the will of the majority, and is distinguished by free institutions, representative government, free elections, guarantees of individual liberty, freedom of speech and religion, and freedom from political oppression.

The second way of life is based upon the will of a minority forcibly imposed upon the majority. It relies upon terror and oppression, a controlled press and radio, fixed elections, and the suppression of personal freedoms.

I believe that it must be the policy of the United States to support free peoples who are resisting attempted subjugation by armed minorities or by outside pressures.

I believe that our help should be primarily through economic and financial aid which is essential to economic stability and orderly political processes.

The world is not static, and the status quo is not sacred. But we cannot allow changes in the status quo in violation of the Charter of the United Nations by such methods as coercion, or by such subterfuges as political infiltration. In helping free and independent nations to maintain their freedom, the United States will be giving effect to the principles of the charter of the United Nations.

It is necessary only to glance at a map to realize that the survival and integrity of the Greek nation are of grave importance in a much wider situation. If Greece should fall under the control of an armed minority, the effect upon its neighbor, Turkey, would be immediate and serious. Confusion and disorder might well spread throughout the entire Middle East.

Moreover, the disappearance of Greece as an independent state would have a profound effect upon those countries in Europe whose peoples are struggling against great difficulties to maintain their freedoms and their independence while they repair the damages of war.

It would be an unspeakable tragedy if these countries, which have struggled so long against overwhelming odds, should lose that victory for which they sacrificed so much. Collapse of free institutions and loss of independence would be disastrous not only for them but for the world. Discouragement and possible failure would quickly be the lot of neighboring peoples striving to maintain their freedom and independence.[2]

Although the remarks of the President applied specifically only to Greece and Turkey there is implicit in them an argument for similar action in other parts of the world should the occasion necessitate it. Just what areas of the world we should support, and to what degree, are debatable, but in any case the notion of containment involves commitments by the United States to the support of non-Communist countries on both the Asiatic and European continents and, should the need arise, in Africa as well.

As opposed to this some Americans have argued that such a policy would commit the United States beyond its capacities. We should, they argue, confine our defense against Communist imperialism to the New World and the oceans separating us from Europe and Asia. This would mean supporting countries on the periphery of the European and Asiatic continents, but not those on the continents. A notable statement of what has come to be called the Gibraltar approach was made by former President Herbert Hoover in an address outlining his conception of what America's basic foreign policy should be:

> First. The foundation of our national policies must be to preserve for the world this Western Hemisphere Gibraltar of Western Civilization.
>
> Second. We can, without any measure of doubt, with our own air and naval forces, hold the Atlantic and Pacific Oceans with one frontier on Britain (if she wishes to cooperate); the other on Japan, Formosa and the Philippines. We can hold open the sea lanes for our supplies. I devoutly hope that a maximum of cooperation can be established between the British Commonwealth and ourselves.
>
> Third. To do this we should arm our air and naval forces to the teeth. . . .
>
> Fourth. We could, after initial outlays for more air and navy equipment, greatly reduce our expenditures, balance our budget, and free ourselves from the dangers of inflation and economic degeneration.[3]

One other element in this grand alternative deserves mention. In an age of potential nuclear warfare a crucial weapon of deterrence is the

[2] Quoted in R. J. Bartlett, *The Record of American Diplomacy,* 2nd ed. (New York: Alfred A. Knopf, 1950), p. 728.

[3] From "Our National Policies in This Crisis," broadcast over the Mutual Broadcasting System in December, 1950. Quoted in *Vital Speeches,* Vol. 17 (1950–51), p. 164.

known capacity to strike back. And where such warfare would be largely carried on through the aerial delivery of nuclear explosives it is obvious that the advantages lie—as between two states—with the state that surrounds the other with bases. In other words, as long as we can maintain a circle—or semicircle—of Strategic Air Command bases around the Soviet Union that country cannot hope to avoid calamitous effects in attacking the United States, for the simple reason that our ability to strike back is not confined to bases in this country. Were we to withdraw to continental isolation, this of course would no longer be the case.

But for whatever reasons, there can be little doubt that to date we have, under both Democratic and Republican administrations, pursued the general policy of containment. Having done this, however, does not relieve us from several other hard questions.

What kind of containment?

One such question is: just where should the line of containment be drawn? Is our national power together with that of our allies sufficient to contain the Communists along the present borders of the cold war? If not, where should we concentrate our efforts? If we decide we cannot possibly hope to defend every bit of territory not now in Communist hands, should we make clear just what we will defend and what we won't? If we do make this clear, we are in effect writing off those territories for which we make no commitment. If we do not, even assuming our policies are enough to avert direct Soviet imperialism, how do we know that the Russians won't guess wrong and precipitate a conflict by attacking a territory about which our position is unclear? Such might well have been the case in Korea, where prior to the invasion from the North, it was an open question whether or not the United States would in fact aid South Korea.

Even if we can decide where to draw the line of containment, there remains the question of how to draw that line. Specifically, even if we were capable of arming every non-Communist country in the world to the teeth, what is to prevent an internal Communist coup? Hence it can be argued that military aid must be buttressed by economic aid, lest in our concern with potential overt military aggression we forget that the same end might be achieved by internal coup, economic penetration, or even through successful campaigning in free elections. The latter point brings up the question of whether or not both military and economic aid will avail little without a proper information program that can spell out our objectives in various parts of the world in order to combat Communist charges of imperialism against us.

Implicit in all these questions is the very fundamental one of whether our national strength is or is not sufficient to sustain our international commitments. This, in many respects, is what underlies much of the criticism of containment by those who prefer the Gibraltar approach in our struggle with Communism. If there is a limit to what we can do, and if that limit is something short of what we would like to be able to do, then the very complicated question arises of just how much strength should be expended to support any particular aspect of containment. Concretely, if it is desired to prevent the communization of Indonesia, and if our capacities are not unlimited, to what extent should we expend wealth for arms, for economic aid, or for propaganda purposes? A related choice is whether it would be better to devote twice as much of our wealth in the attempt to support one country, or with the same amount spread it more thinly in the attempt to support another as well. None of these questions admits of an easy or precise answer; yet we are forced to provide answers to them in any decision we make to carry out the general policy of containment.

Finally, there is the question of the ultimate goal of containment. One criticism of the policy is that it seems essentially static in a world that is ever changing. Suppose, that is to say, that the Soviet Union and its allies can be contained in roughly their present geographic position—what then? Do we write off those areas now behind the iron or bamboo curtains; or is our ultimate policy one of rolling back the curtain and helping nations now under Communist control to determine their political destinies freely? If we do desire a roll-back of the iron curtain, how far? Again it is difficult to give a precise answer to any of these questions, but they nevertheless cannot be avoided.

The above questions by no means constitute an exhaustive list of the problems of a general policy of containment; but they do illustrate the variety and difficulty of arriving at effective foreign policies in this era of the cold war. To choose the most effective alternatives, to secure the support of the American people for these alternatives, and to do this without destroying democratic institutions and values—these are the challenges that face our society; challenges the answers to which may well involve our continued existence as a free society.

The revolution of rising expectations

The situation facing Americans would be worthy of our best efforts even if it were confined to the cold war. But there is a whole range of problems stemming from a situation that is intrinsically distinct from the cold war, though the latter aggravates some of these problems. This is what has aptly been called the revolution of rising expectations among the traditionally underprivileged people of the world. Since the end of World War II, some 655 million people in 20 states [4] have achieved their political independence. Colonialism is almost dead in Asia, dying rapidly in Africa. Nor are expectations confined to political emancipation. The newly independent countries face great economic problems in the attempt to raise the abysmally poor levels of living among their peoples. Our tradition as an independent, largely anti-colonial country, and our self-interest in seeing economically viable, democratically oriented states emerge in Asia and Africa force us to be concerned with these areas. Add the fact that most of the colonial powers are our Western European allies, distrusted in large measure in areas they have left, under constant pressure to retreat from areas they still hold, but anxious for strategic reasons to retain effective if not formal control over many of their remaining possessions—add this and the issues become as complex as they are crucial.

But despite the extreme complexity of all these problems it should not be forgotten that answers to them cannot be avoided, for failure to deal specifically with a particular problem of foreign policy is in itself a policy. Within the general context of the cold war and the revolution of rising expectations, then, what have been our major policies with regard to various regions of the world?

Europe

The central fact of post World War II Europe has been its division between East and West, reflecting essentially the military distribution of power at the end of the fighting. The development of the "cold war" was given formal recognition in the Truman Doctrine mentioned above, which, in effect, put the United States on record as ready to oppose any further Communist advances in Europe or, potentially, anywhere else in the world. The specific implications of our policies in Europe are perhaps best illustrated with respect to three basic prob-

[4] Vernon Van Dyke, *International Politics* (New York: Appleton-Century-Crofts, Inc., 1957), p. 407.

lems: economic disequilibrium, military weakness, and the physical split of Germany.

After World War II the economies of the major European western powers were in bad shape. Over a long period of time the economic dislocation caused by the war might have been remedied, but in the interim the Communist parties—particularly in France and Italy— might have made sufficient gains to capture control of the governments. Faced with this possibility, and the general desire not to see any western democracy sink into economic chaos, the United States responded with the boldly conceived Marshall Plan, which in essence was a proposal to furnish the necessary American capital to enable western European countries to get on their feet economically, provided they in turn worked cooperatively toward the same end.

As the various European economies became increasingly stabilized, and as the Korean fighting seemed to indicate the possibility of overt Soviet military action in Europe, American aid became increasingly military rather than economic, so that by 1953 by far the most amount of dollars were allotted for arms. The two most crucial questions rising out of the aid program have been (1) to what degree could the European states sustain a shift from economic to military aid, since our aid is dependent on their making sacrifices; and (2) to what extent could the United States, by reducing its trade restrictions, promote continued European economic recovery and stability through trade rather than aid? While there has been considerable discussion concerning the promotion of trade, not aid, actually little has been done to promote the increase of European exports to this country.

A second fundamental aspect of American policy with respect to Europe has been the development of the North Atlantic Treaty Organization, in essence a military alliance of some 13 states in which the participants have agreed that an attack on any one of them will be considered an attack on all. Perhaps more than anything else NATO symbolizes the revolutionary character of America's post World War II foreign policy, for it is graphic evidence that the United States is committed to maintaining the defense of free Europe. It is the first peacetime "entangling alliance" since the period of the Revolutionary War. It is important also as a tacit recognition by the United States that the peace and security provisions of the United Nations Charter had become inoperative due to the breakdown of East-West (that is, Soviet-American) relations. Regardless of how one strains to reconcile NATO with commitments under the Charter, the fact remains that the U.N. was designed to be *the* peace-keeping agency following World War II, and the creation of the North Atlantic alliance indicated that its members feel the basic assumption underlying effective U.N. operation as a peace-keeping agency—amicable relations among the Big Five—has not materialized.

While the treaty establishing NATO speaks of an Atlantic community and provides for increasing economic as well as military cooperation, to date practically all efforts have been directed toward the second of these considerations. What is unique about NATO in this respect is that a continuing international agency has been created with a standing international army in constant readiness. That is, where traditional alliances call for aiding an attacked state NATO provides for military cooperation *before* such an attack occurs, in order better to prevent that attack or to meet it should it occur. Thus, under one Supreme Commander, NATO army, naval, and air forces are stationed throughout Europe on constant guard against attack. What this means for Americans is that should an attack come, American personnel will be immediately involved, and there is little doubt we would be in the middle of the conflagration immediately. This has the effect of removing any discretion concerning entering a war in Europe—as was the case in 1914 and 1939—but it also has the effect of making it clear to any would-be aggressor that he cannot move against a NATO country without facing the opposition of the United States. The defenders of NATO often argue that had Hitler known this as clearly as Khrushchev does, World War II might well have been avoided.

The chief strains on NATO have been (1) the capacity of the various economies to sustain the military build-up necessary to make the NATO forces a real obstacle to possible aggression; (2) the fact that one of the two leading European members—France—is a colonial power faced with almost continuous armed revolt against its authority since the end of the second World War, first in Indo China, then in Algeria, in turn necessitating the withdrawal of troops originally earmarked for NATO to carry on the war against the rebels; and (3) the German question.

The last represents in microcosm most of the problems of Europe as a whole and the general line taken by America in meeting those problems. Essentially the question of Western Germany has been whether or not to re-militarize it so that it could contribute to NATO. The French, who have been invaded by Germany twice in this century already, naturally fear this policy. But even with France's eventual acquiescence in the rearmament of Germany—that is, Western Germany—the question arises as to how this affects the eventual unification of Germany. For the Soviet Union has made it crystal clear that it will never allow unification of Germany if the unified state becomes a part of NATO. One possible alternative is for the West to agree to a neutralized, unified Germany; so far, however, the United States has not accepted this idea. Essentially the issues come down to: (1) re-arming West Germany makes the crucial difference in our NATO manpower; but (2) it creates a gigantic obstacle to German re-unification, and makes France uneasy. As long as *military* considerations appear to be predominant, the case for German re-armament is indeed strong; but critics of our present policy argue that military considerations—at least those of German manpower—are *not* in fact predominant, that if the cold war in Europe will ever be settled it will be on the basis of negotiation with the Russians, which cannot be done as long as West Germany is remilitarized. In other words the critics of the policy ask: in view of atomic weapons, how important is a West German army to the preservation of world peace? Important enough to justify the continued partition of Germany?

China and Japan

The basic fact concerning contemporary China is of course the successful revolution staged by the Communists and their ultimate control over the mainland. During the period when the ultimate issue between Mao and Chiang was in doubt, American policy was to try to promote some kind of coalition-compromise between the Communists and Chiang; with the expulsion of the Nationalists from the mainland, however, American policy has consistently supported Chiang against the Communists, although the fervor of that support has varied. Whatever antipathy there was between the United States and the Communist government of China was of course greatly intensified once the Chinese had entered the Korean fighting. At present American policy includes continued aid to Chiang Kai Shek on Formosa, refusal to recognize the Communist government of China, refusal to vote for its admission to the United Nations, and an almost complete severance of private intercourse—commercial or even informational.

The basic dilemma facing American policy-makers in China and Formosa is that continued support of Chiang to the point of nonrecognition of the Communists flies in the face of (1) our allies' attitude on the matter (2) what at least many responsible observers see as the facts of life—Communist control of the Chinese mainland. The most salient argument in opposition to recognition is that it might lead to a vitiation of the will to resist Communism among the free areas of Southeast Asia. On the other hand, it is held, continued nonrecognition may well be playing right into the hands of the Soviets by pushing China into the embrace of the Bear.

One suggestion to meet this difficulty, offered by a number of close students of the Far East, is the doctrine of the "two Chinas"—while we would recognize the fact that Communists are in control of the mainland, we would continue to support the Nationalists, *on Formosa*.[5] This implicitly would mean admission of both the Red Government and Formosa to the United Nations. Whether this is feasible in terms of the avowed Communist goal of "integrating" Formosa to China, not to mention the violent opposition to any move toward recognition of Red China in this country, is a matter of conjecture.

The basic problem regarding Japan is simply enough stated, though not as easily susceptible of solution: (1) Japan must trade to live; (2) the United States does not want it to trade with Red China; (3) United States tariffs effectively cut off considerable Japanese-American trade; (4) either Japan trades with China, or we continue to make up the export-import gap with financial assistance. In addition to this basic economic-political question, there remains the degree to which Japan has genuinely accepted the democratic processes that were imposed upon her by the American occupation forces under General Douglas MacArthur. Allies such as Australia and New Zealand are somewhat leery of the revival of Japan as a major military power, just as France is similarly concerned over Germany. And, while the fact that our original policy of making China the major Far Eastern power had to be reversed in view of the rise of the Communists there may make the shifting to Japan explainable, it does not make the Australians, New Zealanders, or other free peoples of Southeast Asia particularly happy; for Japan has been the one far-eastern imperialist power in modern times.

So far we have met the economic dilemma largely through outright grants of dollars to make up the trade deficit, although we have permitted a little increase in trade with the Communist area. As for the question of Japanese democracy, we have apparently been more willing to support the extreme right than the moderate center in our

---

[5] See, for example, Edwin O. Reischauer, *Wanted: An Asian Policy* (New York. Alfred A. Knopf, 1955), pp. 242-49.

aversion to Communism. Whether this policy in the long run will prove effective in preventing both Communist inroads *and* undemocratic remilitarization remains to be seen.

Southern Asia and Africa

From Viet Nam to Morocco, from the Mediterranean to the Union of South Africa, hundreds of millions of people are in political, economic, and social turmoil—for it is in this tremendous area that the revolution of rising expectations proceeds apace. Actually this revolution has at least three distinct though entwined strands, the individual importance of which will vary depending on the historical situation in the specific area. There is first of all a revolt against imperial control—and with it a revolt against white western peoples, for in this area are the yellow, brown, and black-skinned peoples whose traditional overlords have been white westerners. There is also a revolution in the ownership of the means of production and distribution of goods and services; and in many if not most of the areas socialism rather than free enterprise appears to many people as the most promising solution to their economic problems. There is, finally, in many areas (particularly the Middle East) a revolt against the old indigenous ruling classes with the attendant struggle for support of the masses.

America's policies in the face of this three-fold revolution have been (1) economic aid for newly independent states, (2) support for legitimate nationalistic aspirations; (3) attempts to induce the independent states in the areas to join in anti-Soviet military coalitions—SEATO (Southeast Asia Treaty Organization) and METO (Middle East Treaty Organization). The primary problems of these policies concern (1) the type of aid given to these underdeveloped territories —whether or not a larger initial investment would pay off to a greater degree than comparatively small annual appropriations; (2) the dilemma brought on by the fact noted above that nationalistic aspirations are mainly at the expense of our important allies in Western Europe; and (3) the understandable neutralism of many newly independent countries, one of whose main objectives is to stay out of the cold war. It is probably fair to say that to date we have attempted to steer a middle course on all three policies: economic aid—but not a great deal of it; support of nationalism—but not to the point of engendering French, British, or Belgian enmity; promotion of military alliances—but not to the point of cutting off all aid for those nations not joining the alliances. The "hunt and peck" policies toward South

Asia and Africa, as compared to the rather bold and far reaching decisions made in Europe in the late 1940's and early 1950's, is doubtless a manifestation of our comparative inexperience in dealing with the peoples of the former area, and our still greater inexperience in dealing with a situation that does not admit of clear military answers.

It cannot be over-emphasized that it is one thing to play Monday-morning quarterback about the feasibility or desirability of American foreign policy and quite another to be responsible for making the actual decisions; and it also bears re-emphasis that these decisions cannot be avoided—failure to act is action itself in the area of foreign policy, and action that may have the most profound consequences.

THE EXECUTIVE AND FOREIGN POLICY

In making foreign policy, almost from the beginning of our nation's history, it has been the President rather than Congress who has been looked to for leadership. Of course Congress plays an important role. Indeed, as Professor Corwin has pointed out, the constitutional provisions concerning responsibility for foreign affairs are "an invitation to struggle for the privilege of directing American foreign policy." [6] Yet for a number of reasons, constitutional and otherwise, the executive branch generally and the President in particular have assumed primary responsibility for the formation as well as the execution of foreign policy.

Reasons for executive supremacy

The Constitution itself is characteristically brief in its delegation of authority in this area. In general, presidential powers in foreign affairs are confined to three matters: (1) the President is Commander-in-Chief of the Armed Forces; (2) he may receive and, with the consent of the Senate, appoint ambassadors; and (3) he may, with the consent of two-thirds of the Senate, make treaties with foreign powers. At first glance this constitutional delegation of authority may not seem sufficient to uphold presidential supremacy in the field. If the President can command the armed forces, only Congress can declare war. The Senate must consent to appointments and the ratification of treaties. And the reception of ambassadors is after all largely a formal act. It would seem, then, that the Constitution envisaged cooperation between the

[6] Edward S. Corwin, *The President, Office and Power*, 3rd ed. (New York: New York University Press, 1948), p. 208.

executive and Congress rather than executive supremacy in the foreign field.

Yet a moment's reflection will reveal that even in the constitutional provisions, implicitly at least, the *initiative* lies with the President. The Congress may refuse to declare war, the Senate may refuse to consent to an appointment or a treaty, but the responsibility for proposing clearly lies with the President. Further, while Congress itself can, and on occasion has attempted to, take the initiative in foreign affairs, its organization is such that, compared to the President, it operates at a tremendous disadvantage. Thus, while the Constitution in one sense divides authority in the area of foreign policy between the President and Congress, at the very least it implicitly places the responsibility for initiation in the hands of the executive. But in addition to the Constitutional provisions, Presidential supremacy has been buttressed by three other sets of factors relating to control over foreign affairs: traditional, representational, and informational.

Traditional factors

Traditional factors buttressing Presidential supremacy are those notions either accepted at the outset of our history or developed through custom that have served to center control over foreign affairs in the executive. Four such may be mentioned.

In the first place it is customary in almost all countries that the executive assume primary responsibility in this field. This idea dates back to the beginnings of the Western state system when dynastic diplomacy among the monarchal heads of states was the order of the day, and remained even after the various dynasties were replaced by republics. Thus when the framers of our Constitution assembled at Philadelphia they accepted the view that over and above any explicit provisions in the Constitution, the President, by the very fact of his position as chief executive, would pre-eminently represent the new nation in its intercourse with other states. This did not mean, of course, that the President was in sole control of foreign policy, but it did mean that in the words of John Marshall, "The President is the sole organ of the nation in its external relations, and its sole representative with foreign nations." [7]

Closely related to this idea of the President being the sole inter-

[7] Quoted in *ibid.*, p. 216. The author after citing numerous instances in which this doctrine was challenged, concludes on page 224: ". . . there is no more securely established principle of constitutional practice than the exclusive right of the President to be the nation's intermediary in its dealing with other nations."

mediary in our foreign relations is his exclusive power to recognize new states or governments, usually through the device of receiving their ambassadors. Again, potential Congressional hostility may in fact limit his discretion, but ultimately the President, and he alone, decides if and when to extend recognition.

Still another traditional factor leading to Presidential supremacy in the field of foreign policy is the gradual emasculation of the constitutional injunction that the President shall seek the "advice" as well as the consent of the Senate in the negotiation of treaties.

Again, this does not mean that the President can afford to ignore the Senate in his negotiation of treaties. Certainly the classic episode of Wilson and the League of Nations illustrates that point. But it does mean at best that he will seek the advice of Senatorial leaders, sometimes confined to his own party, and that so far as initiative is concerned what may have been the constitutional intent of coordinate authority has developed through custom into the normal practice of Presidential action. And even when the President feels constrained to seek the support of Congress for a statement of policy, many Congressmen will feel they should give him that support even if they have some misgivings about the policy; for to do otherwise might weaken the stature of the President internationally and thus undermine our foreign policy generally. This was apparently the case when a number of Democratic Congressmen voted to approve the Eisenhower Doctrine for the Middle East, even though they by no means favored all or any of its aspects.[8]

Finally, the treaty-making provisions of the Constitution themselves may be circumvented to a degree by the use of *executive agreements*. These may be defined as legally binding agreements between the heads of two or more states. There is some disagreement as to whether or not such an agreement is binding on the United States after the administration of the President who made it, but it has long been accepted that at least while the President involved remains in office, he may commit the United States to international obligations every bit as binding and important as those involved in treaties. The reasoning behind the practice of executive agreements is itself an aspect of the preeminence of the President in international affairs. Because of the need for secrecy and speed, very often the debate and delay associated with the treaty-making process cannot be safely brooked. It is customary during war, for example, for the President to make military agreements

[8] See *The New York Times,* January 3, 7, March 6, 1957.

with our allies, which by their very nature could not be openly debated. Yet, as the Yalta Conference demonstrated, such agreements may not be confined to military matters, but may include political commitments as well. While some people, particularly Congressmen, have deplored this extra-constitutional aspect of Presidential power, usually with reference to some specific executive agreement, so far attempts to limit it by constitutional amendment have failed.

Representational factors

If there is one genuinely national officer elected by the people in this country it is the President. Congress as a collective whole represents all the people, but only the President centers in one person the notion of national representation. From this it follows that only the President, or some one he allows to speak for him, may make foreign policy pronouncements for the nation as a whole. Congress may pass a resolution declaring our opposition to recognizing the government of Red China, but no single Congress*man* can authoritatively make such a policy pronouncement. The President can. As our nation must act as a unit in international affairs, so the nature of our government has placed responsibility for that action in one office—the Presidency. This point has been accepted to the degree that it is a federal offense for a private person to speak abroad claiming to express United States policy, but lacking Presidential authorization. Further, even Cabinet members have got themselves into difficulty by speaking out in foreign affairs without the full approval of the President.

Another aspect of this representational factor is this: since the President represents the people nationally, they tend to look to him for leadership in areas in which our nation acts as a single unit. Thus the President becomes the chief governmental molder of public opinion in the area of foreign affairs. When international crises face the United States, it is to the President that the people turn for initiative. It is significant that important policies in the domestic area are often named for the originators of the bills spelling out those policies: the Taft-Hartley Act, the Wagner Act, the Smith Act, and so on. Yet in the area of foreign policy it is the *Eisenhower* or *Truman* Doctrine, *Roosevelt's* interventionist policy, the *Monroe* Doctrine, and so on, even though the Congress ultimately might have just as much to say about the policy as the President.

In sum, because our nation must act as a single unit in international affairs, because the President is our one important policy-maker elected by all the voters, it is natural that the people will look to him for leadership and initiative in foreign affairs.

Informational factors

Finally, the executive's position of supremacy in foreign policy results from his exclusive access to all sources of information on which foreign policy is based. Any policy quite obviously will be affected tremendously by the policy-makers' view of the factual situation—their picture of reality. And while the normal channels of communication are open just as much to Congress as to the President, the latter has at least three sources not always available to anyone but himself. These are (1) the diplomatic reporting of our ambassadors; (2) military intelligence; and (3) the information gathered by the Central Intelligence Agency, a data-gathering body primarily concerned with obtaining accurate and largely secret information about other states. It has long been established that not only is the information gathered by these sources intended primarily for the President's ears, but also that Congress has no right to compel the President to reveal any information which he deems would jeopardize the national security. Further, the activities of the Central Intelligence Agency are so secret that Congress has so far refrained from attempting to supervise its activities through the device of legislative investigation. Under these circumstances even the most hard-working and sincere Congressman, concerned with foreign policy issues, might well feel constrained to go along with the President on the grounds that the latter may know more about the situation.

In sum, while the President is by no means in sole control of foreign policy, he, and under him that part of the executive branch concerned with foreign policy, normally takes the initiative in such matters and in any case assumes primary responsibility for the effective formation as well as the execution of foreign policy.

So far we have been using the words President and executive almost interchangeably. While there is of course an important distinction between the President himself and the executive branch under him, this distinction should not cloud the fact that *only* the President, under our system of government, is responsible for the acts of his administration. Yet the nature of his multitudinous tasks means that he must operate with and through his administration. If he is chief foreign policy formulator, he must nevertheless rely on the advice, abilities, and wisdom of his subordinates. The organization of the executive branch for developing foreign policy, then, takes on extreme importance—for the President is physically unable to make every decision on foreign policy, and even where he attempts to make all the important ones, his decisions will be no better than the information supplied to him or than the effectiveness with which they are carried out.

The Department of State

While it can be argued that every department, agency, bureau, or division within the executive branch is in some way connected with foreign policy, since any action taken in any field may well have international repercussions, historically and presently the Department of State has played the role of chief assistant to the President in both formulating and executing policy. Broadly speaking, the chief question in the internal organization of the department is whether to organize around *functions* performed—political, economic, cultural—or *areas* dealt with—Western Europe, the Soviet Union, Latin America. Essentially, the problem has been dealt with on the principle that one can have his cake and eat it too—while the core of the department is organized on a geographic-area basis, there are also important functional offices. While this may not seem logically very tidy, it does make sense to create a functional division whenever such function—say economic policy—becomes sufficiently important to require over-all rather than area-by-area policy.

By far the most important aspect of the department's role in foreign policy formation for our purposes, however, is the two-fold problem of the relations between the Secretary of State and the President, on the one hand, and between the Secretary and other Cabinet officers, particularly the Secretary of Defense, on the other. The latter aspect of this problem will be discussed presently. What is meant by the first is the degree to which the President is guided by the Secretary of State, ignores him, or permits him in fact to be the chief executive in matters of foreign policy. Chart lovers may draw lines of responsibility from the Secretary of State to the White House *ad infinitum,* but the fact remains that even though the President is constitutionally and politically responsible for foreign policy, the Secretary of State may have a great deal to say about its actual development. This appears to have been the case during the first six or seven years of Franklin Roosevelt's administration, when the President, concerned primarily with the domestic problems of the depression, left foreign affairs to a considerable degree in the hands of Secretary Hull. On the other hand, when the international crisis mounted toward the end of Roosevelt's second term, for all practical purposes the President became his own Secretary of State even though Hull ostensibly continued to run the department. There is no hard and fast rule about this relationship. The point is that at all times the Secretary of State is a man ordinarily of significant, potentially of decisive, influence on the development of policy. Even when the President reserves to himself the making of the important decisions on foreign policy, his picture of reality may well be what the Secretary of State supplies him, and a moment's reflection will make obvious that that picture will possibly be more influential in the determination of policy than the value predispositions of the President. Nor is there any institutional gimmick that will provide a foolproof method of assuring the "proper" relationship between the Secretary of State and the President—whatever that may be.

The position of the Secretary of State in this age of crisis is considerably different from that of most other Cabinet officers. If the Secretary of Agriculture, for example, takes the initiative in the formation of agricultural policy, Congress still ultimately determines what that policy will be to a much greater extent than for foreign policy. Thus while it might be argued that whomever the President wants as his Secretary of Agriculture (or any of the departments primarily concerned with domestic affairs) is the President's business, and his alone, the same is not true for the Secretary of State—who may well be, in a unique way, genuinely a policy-forming official.

ICA and USIA

Over and above the functional units within the State Department, two semi-autonomous agencies have been created since the end of World War II that reflect the increasing importance placed on two aspects of foreign policy and that deserve special mention.

Beginning with the Marshall Plan, the United States has spent many billions of dollars in both economic and military aid to countries all over the world. A new agency had to be created; the question was its relation to the Department of State. Many different arrangements were tried; as now constituted, the International Cooperation Administration has charge of virtually all overseas aid, and is semi-autonomous, although its head reports to the Secretary of State.

A similar development has occurred in the area of our overseas information program. To explain ourselves and our policies effectively to other peoples it was felt that a separate agency should be created.

This body, the United States Information Agency was until a short time ago autonomous in the sense that its director was not directly responsible to the Secretary of State. Recently, however, this status has been changed so that the agency now occupies a position similar to that of ICA.

The Defense Department

While all the other major departments are in one way or another concerned with foreign policy—Treasury with international monetary policy, Labor with the International Labor Organization, Commerce and Agriculture with economic policy, and so on—the Defense Department, other than State, is most crucially concerned with foreign affairs. Strictly speaking, the military arm of government is one of execution rather than formation of policy. But it is easy to see that as long as the United States is faced with a clear threat of involvement in a third world war the military implications of any proposed policy cannot be ignored. Further, the policy itself may result at least in part from military rather than political or economic considerations. Illustrative of both these points is our policy toward the Middle East and more particularly the Arab-Israeli dispute. Without attempting to disentangle the various threads of our policy in that area, it is obvious that our Air Force bases in Libya and Saudi Arabia are and will remain important considerations. Thus even though for other reasons it might be desirable to support Israel in any and all disputes with the Arabs, the protection of these bases by maintaining friendly relations with the Arabs doubtless will act as important brakes on any over-friendly actions by the United States toward Israel in a dispute with her Arab neighbors. These military considerations may not in themselves be controlling; but we omit them from foreign policy only at the risk of jeopardizing our national security.

That military considerations have become inextricably bound up with foreign policy is, then, obvious. A result is the not quite so obvious yet crucial problem of how to coordinate the military with the economic and political aspects of policy—or in institutional terms how to coordinate State and Defense—and perhaps more important, how to control these enormous agencies of policy formation to keep them responsible to the people whom they serve.

Largely in response to this challenge, Congress in 1947 created the National Security Council whose functions include the assessment and appraisal of the "objectives, commitments, and risks of the United

States in relation to its actual and potential military power in the interest of national security . . . and to advise the President with respect to the integration of domestic, foreign, and military policies relating to the national security so as to enable the military services and the other departments and agencies of the Government to cooperate more effectively in matters involving the national security." [9] The National Security Council represents a top level attempt to mesh all aspects of public policy involving the security of the United States. Since the emphasis is on security, detailed discussion of that body and its subsidiary agencies will be deferred to the chapter on military policy.

In addition to the Departments of State and Defense, the ICA, the USIA, and the NSC, brief mention should be made of three other agencies, all in the Executive Office of the President, whose functions relate in some manner to foreign policy.

The Office of Defense Mobilization is both the policy planning and coordinating agency of our national mobilization effort, including current defense activities and readiness for any future national emergency.[10] As such it has a great deal to say about the capabilities of the United States to pursue any given policy. Its director is a member of the National Security Council and occasionally sits in on Cabinet meetings at the invitation of the President.

The duties of the Bureau of the Budget include assisting the President in the preparation of the budget and the supervision and control of the administration of the budget. As such it plays an important role in any long-range policies involving expenditures and can act as a coordinating body for those agencies concerned with foreign policy.

The Council of Economic Advisers is probably less directly concerned with foreign policy than either of the other two, but its function of advising the President on long-range economic developments will impinge on foreign policy to the extent that the latter is, as it must be, partly dependent on our own internal economic health.

Coordination and control

Broadly speaking there are three general ways by which coordination of the various agencies concerned with foreign policy formation may be effected: (1) by the President himself; (2) by agencies in the executive office of the President; or (3) by inter-departmental or agency cooperation.

[9] *U.S. Government Organization Manual, 1957–58,* p. 63.
[10] *Ibid.,* p. 68.

All the agencies participating in the executive's formulation of foreign policy should also be considered as organs of coordination. For while it is theoretically possible to separate the functions of policy formation from coordination, in practice most agencies do both. Even the State Department, which has traditionally held that its job was to make foreign policy and the job of others to execute it, is faced with the problem of coordinating the activities of its own internal divisions as well as cooperating with other major agencies that take part in the foreign policy process. And the National Security Council is both the *formulator* of long-range security policy suggestions and the *coordinator* of agencies charged with carrying out that policy. But despite this welter of staff agencies and inter-departmental committees, ultimately the President, and he alone, is responsible for foreign policy.

This has important implications for both coordination and control. For coordination it means that while some integration of policy can take place below the level of the President, if two major departments— say State and Defense—cannot agree, it is the President himself who must make the ultimate decision. In this sense foreign policy-making within the executive branch can be viewed as the clash of competing interests both within and between departments. As long as the clash stays within a department, the Secretary concerned can resolve the issue; when it develops between departments, only the President can ultimately decide. Even the National Security Council cannot perform this function, for as President Truman has written:

> . . . the Council does not make decisions. The policy itself has to come down from the President, as all final decisions have to be made by him. A "vote" in the National Security Council is merely a procedural step. It never decides policy. That can be done only with the President's approval . . .[11]

In terms of control it means that the President is the one popularly elected official who can be held accountable for policy-making in the executive branch. It is true that the Vice-President is popularly elected, and under President Eisenhower has participated in top level policy decisions, but any control he exerts is derived from the authority of the President, who alone is responsible.

Both the process and the problems involved in the executive determination of foreign policy are perhaps best illustrated by a case study. While the issue itself was not of monumental importance, the

[11] Harry S. Truman, *Years of Trial and Hope* (New York: Doubleday and Co., 1955), p. 59.

process involved in reaching decision resembles that for more vital questions.

A case study: strategic trusts

In the years immediately preceding the end of the second World War, the United States sought, as part of its general planning for post-war international organization, to develop policies for the future status of colonial territories. Initially, the responsibility for formulating proposals on this subject was in the hands of the State Department. The original plans called for international supervision of all colonies, but largely as the result of unfavorable reactions on the part of the British and French, under the Secretary of State's direction the types of dependent territories to be placed under international supervision were confined to those that had been under League of Nations supervision (in what was called the Mandates System), those to be detached from enemy states at the end of the war, and those that might be voluntarily placed under the new system (to be called the Trusteeship System of the United Nations) by the mother countries.

To this point the policy developed as we might think it ordinarily would—within the State Department, modified by reactions of our allies. But the former mandates which were to be placed under the Trusteeship System included many of the islands, specifically in the Carolines, Marshalls, and Gilberts, that we had wrested from Japan only at heavy cost. And it could be argued that American retention of those islands was vital to our security in the Pacific, as the terrible days of early 1942 demonstrated. This is precisely what the military leaders argued when they saw the State Department proposals. Admiral King asserted, for example, that "American possession of the bases in the Pacific islands, which have been taken from Japan, was essential to the United States and world security after the war." [12] Earlier, Henry L. Stimson, then Secretary of War, had sent a memorandum to the Secretary of State in which he argued that the islands were "not colonies; they are outposts, and their acquisition is appropriate under the general doctrine of self-defense by the power which guarantees the safety of that area of the world." [13]

The State Department offered the counter-argument that exempting the former Japanese mandates from the new Trusteeship System would

[12] Quoted in *The New York Times*, April 19, 1945.
[13] Quoted in Henry L. Stimson and McGeorge Bundy, *On Active Service in Peace and War* (New York: Harper & Bros., 1948), p. 600.

lead "to reservations of other territory by other nations until the non-aggrandizement plan of the Atlantic Charter would become a mockery." [14] Implicit in this policy difference between the State Department and the military was a fundamentally different view of the world situation as it would exist after the war. The State Department's proposals reflected the general position that America's best interests lay in wholehearted support of the United Nations, and that any reservations to such a commitment meant subverting the chances of maintaining peace through that organization. The military leaders, on the other hand, took the view that we had to preserve our own security position, whether in the Pacific or elsewhere, irrespective of commitments in the direction of promoting international organization for peace.

It is idle to speculate at the moment on which side was "right." The point is rather that the case shows how two important agencies within the executive branch can fundamentally disagree on policy; how each in a sense acts as a pressure group—a public pressure group—for the policy to which it adheres. In such a situation either a compromise or Presidential decision was necessary. Actually, it involved both. At a meeting of the President, the Secretaries of State, War, and Navy, and advisers, it was decided to introduce the notion of strategic territories in the Trusteeship System, which territories would be formally placed under the system, but which the administering state could close to direct international supervision should the interests of security so require.

It should be noted that opposition to the State Department plan was not confined to the military leaders. Congressmen also voiced disapproval at proposals that would entail anything other than unhampered control of the islands by the United States. And this Congressional opposition doubtless played a part in the willingness of the State Department to compromise and the President's decision to approve it.

Certainly one can see from the case that the executive branch is not a monolithic institution composed of nicely integrated parts all working smoothly with the same means toward the same goal. In the largest sense, of course, all Americans want to pursue the national interest of the United States; but what that national interest is and how best to pursue it may be subject to honest disagreement among honest men. The struggle over foreign policy, that is to say, is a struggle within the

[14] Article by Arthur Krock in *The New York Times,* April 3, 1945.

executive as well as between the executive and, say, Congress, or between political parties.

It deserves re-emphasis that the President, though constitutionally and electorally responsible for executive foreign policy-making, cannot possibly oversee even all the important aspects of foreign policy, much less personally coordinate agencies within that branch. And this problem—the discrepancy between the legal and political responsibilities of the President and the physical impossibility of personally carrying out that responsibility—is one of the crucial problems of contemporary American government; crucial, that is, as long as Americans feel that effective policy is not enough, but that those who decide what in fact is effective policy be held accountable to the people.

The mention of Congressmen in the case study, however, raises the general question of Congress' role in foreign policy-making and the more particular question of the degree to which Congress can reinforce popular control of foreign policy, either through direct participation or by controlling the executive branch.

CONGRESS AND FOREIGN POLICY

Implicit in the constitutional provisions concerning foreign policy is the notion that Congress has a two-fold role to play: (1) in part as the initiator of policy; (2) in part as the single most important device for popular control over the executive agencies that carry out foreign policy. Because of constitutional provisions and the structure of Congress, however, that body plays its major role in control rather than initiation.

Until comparatively recently, even though the House was necessarily a participant in any foreign policy involving appropriations, the Senate had the main part in Congressional foreign policy-making. One striking bit of evidence of this was the difference in prestige of membership between the Senate's Foreign Relations Committee and the House Committee on Foreign Affairs. The former has always been a much sought after assignment, while the latter was viewed, in the words of one Congressman, as "a dump heap, where service was a chore rather than a privilege." [15] At least since the end of World War II, however, the House has come to play a crucial role in Congressional participation in foreign affairs. This is undoubtedly due in the first

[15] Quoted in Robert A. Dahl, *Congress and Foreign Policy* (New York: Harcourt, Brace and Co., Inc., 1950), p. 147.

instance to the increased importance of appropriations necessary to underwrite American foreign policy. For example, our fundamental program of military and economic aid to countries all over the world necessitates House as well as Senate acquiescence. Secondly, much of our foreign policy is dependent not on treaties but on legislation passed by both houses. Finally, the increased use of executive agreements which, more often than not, are based on Congressional authorization has enhanced the position of the House as participant in foreign policy-making.

More generally, if we review the foreign-policy milestones since the end of World War II—participation in the United Nations, the Truman Doctrine, the Marshall Plan, Point IV, The North Atlantic Treaty, military aid to our allies, the Eisenhower Doctrine—we see that in each instance the House had an almost equal part. So that despite the special Constitutional position of the Senate in the foreign policy field, the upper house is hardly more significant than the lower in making foreign policy.

Congress as participant

Broadly speaking both the House and the Senate are organized to participate in foreign policy-making in about the same way as for the consideration of other aspects of public policy. As already indicated, each house has a permanent committee on foreign relations. In addition, from time to time temporary investigatory committees have been created to look into some aspect of foreign policy. Thus the House appointed a temporary committee on foreign aid that toured Europe to gain information on the actual conditions in various countries to whom it was proposed Marshall Plan aid be extended. Further, the committees and sub-committees of the House and Senate concerned primarily with overseeing administration within the executive branch may well have an influence on foreign policy. One has only to recall recent investigations of the overseas information activities of the State Department to be reminded that these legislative committees, and sometimes their aides, can have an important impact on just about any phase of our over-all policy.

To aid the various committees in research and analysis on various foreign policy questions Congress in the Legislative Reorganization of 1946 authorized each committee to employ up to four experts. The primary purpose of these professional staffs is to remove some of the otherwise impossible burden on Congressmen of becoming fully informed on every relevant question concerning a proposed policy. The implications of such a professional staff for Congress will be discussed below.

Other important standing committees in both the House and Senate include the appropriations committee of each house, and, since military and foreign policies have become so closely interwoven, the military affairs committees of the two houses. Finally, mention should be made of the role of "bellwethers" in both the House and Senate. This term refers to Representatives and Senators who may or may not be members of the committees immediately concerned with foreign relations, but who have gained a reputation of expertness in foreign policy, usually with respect to a particular problem or area of the world. Thus Congressman Judd of Minnesota has been looked upon as an expert on the Far East, and the late Senator Vandenberg, after his striking change from isolationism to internationalism and his role in the formation of NATO, came to be acknowledged as an expert in foreign policy matters, especially with respect to the United States role in collective security arrangements against the Soviet Union.

While, as we have already noted, executive initiative is the rule in foreign-policy formation, this does not mean that Congress has not in the past attempted to exert initiative.

During the 1930's, for example, several so-called neutrality acts, passed and signed by the President only reluctantly, attempted to make sure that the United States would not be drawn into any future European conflict as had occurred in World War I. But such examples of Congressional initiative are more notable for their rarity than for anything else. Again, one has only to review the major foreign policy of the post-World War II period to be reminded that Congress' role is one of considering proposals, not of proposing itself. One important reservation should be made to this point, however. Congress' power to disapprove or modify executive proposals in one sense means it has the power, at least in certain instances, to formulate policy. This is especially true in those cases where a question of policy can be phrased essentially in Yes or No terms. For example, even though it was the executive that took the initiative in drafting the Covenant of the League of Nations as well as proposing American membership in that organization, it was the Senate that ultimately decided our policy on that issue.

One other point about the general role of Congress as participant in foreign policy-making should be noted. Congress collectively represents a microcosm of the American people, at least to the degree that it is a genuinely representative body. In this sense it mirrors the views of the people on all issues, foreign as well as domestic. But Congress, and especially leaders of Congress, not only reflect but help to *mold* public attitudes on various issues. Thus the executive, even when no one would doubt its authority to make decisions, may well hesitate to pursue a particular policy in the face of known and intensive opposition by Congressional leaders. This appears to be the case, for example, in the hesitancy of the executive concerning our policy toward the Communist government of China. Especially after the Formosa riots in the spring of 1957 there was evidence that many members of the executive including both the Secretary of State and the President had serious doubts about the advisability of continuing support for the Nationalist government on Formosa and refusing to consider recognition of Communist China. Yet in the face of known opposition of Congressional leaders, both Republican and Democratic, any administration might well feel the necessity of caution concerning a marked change in our China policy. Even though at first a majority of the American people might be opposed to such change, in the absence of marked Congressional opposition it might be "sold" to the people. But as long as Senators of such divergent beliefs and eminent positions as Knowland of California and Douglas of Illinois manifest antipathy toward such a change, the administration would find it difficult indeed to muster public support for any radical shift in policy. This, again, because individual Congressmen doubtless lead as well as reflect current public attitude. The degree to which Congress will be influential in foreign policy determination in this regard is, of course, dependent upon the Congressmen involved, the popularity of the President, and the specific issue. But that Congress in this informal way can and does materially affect executive decision, even in those matters constitutionally under executive control, is an important aspect of the foreign policy process.

Power of the purse

Except for the Senate's role in consenting to treaties (and the much less important power of approving ambassadors), by and large most Congressional participation in foreign policy, especially in the contemporary era, involves the funds requested by the executive to implement its policies of military and economic aid to foreign nations. The crucial committees involved here are the foreign relations and appropriations committees in each house. Because the Constitution itself distinguishes between legislation on the one hand and appropriations on the other, the appropriations process is a two-stage transaction: (1) authorization, providing the legal basis for executive expenditure of funds; (2) appropriation, providing the necessary funds to carry out the authorization. This explains why many times the executive in defending its budget before Congress will emphasize that the actual appropriations called for will not be nearly as much as the total figure in the budget (funds authorized in previous years but not expended, can be, with Congressional approval, used for the current program).

Essentially the foreign relations committees consider the authorization requests while the appropriations committees of each house pass on the actual appropriation of funds. Because the foreign relations committees are for all practical purposes exclusively concerned with foreign policy, while the appropriations committees must consider domestic needs for funds as well as those for foreign policy, there is sometimes disagreement over the total amount to be authorized and appropriated. Again, with a ceiling on the national debt and an economy-minded Congress, not only the appropriations committee, but also the Ways and Means Committee of the House may well play an important role; if money cannot be borrowed it must be forthcoming through taxes before it can be spent.

This over-all power of the purse gives Congress its most effective tool in the foreign policy formation process. Obviously executive initiative would come to naught if Congress chose not to furnish the necessary financial wherewithal. But the importance of this power of the purse can be overstated. After all, Congressmen no more want to see the United States suffer diplomatic, economic, or ultimate military defeat than does the executive. And, for information on which it will base its consideration of executive requests for funds, Congress must depend primarily on the executive branch itself. Consider for example, President Eisenhower's request to Congress to give him authority to spend some 200 million dollars in the Middle East. Given the most sincere, hard-working, and intelligent Congressman, on what basis must he make up his mind? On newspaper and other accounts of the Middle East situation and, more importantly, on what the executive itself reveals as to the nature of that situation on the basis of its own, partly secret, information. It would be difficult indeed for a Congressman to vote against such a request, especially when a President of tremendous prestige concerning matters of foreign policy is doing the asking.

Despite this reservation, the Congressional power of the purse remains an important aspect of the foreign policy process. And, together with other types of participation mentioned above, it means that Congress remains a vital part of that process. Still, Congressional participation, even when the purse is involved, and especially when it is not, remains intermittent at best. American foreign policy is a continuing, literally day-by-day process—it is the day-by-day relations with other states, both friends and enemies, that ultimately produce the "big situation" in which Congress is called upon to approve and support executive action at the very time when the pressure of events is such as to coerce Congress into accepting the President's proposals. Again to use the Eisenhower Doctrine as an example, by the time the President went to Congress for support and authorization to use funds in the area, Congress had little or no control over the situation. It may well be that many Congressmen would be highly critical of the position taken by the United States State Department in its dealing with France and the United Kingdom in the events leading up to the Suez invasion. But at no time was Congress really in a position to influence vitally the position taken by Secretary of State Dulles in those negotiations. These same Congressmen, however critical, still felt constrained to support the Eisenhower Doctrine given the situation in the Middle East at the time of the Presidential request. The point is that while Congress can and does play an important part in foreign policy, its role is essentially of an intermittent rather than a continuing nature. And this intermittency itself may lead to a situation when the choice left to Congress is more formal than real.

Can Congress limit the President?

That Congress itself has been aware of this situation has been demonstrated more than once in recent decades. The neutrality legislation of the 1930's mentioned above is a good example of Congress attempting to take the initiative in foreign relations. Yet even there, during the late 1930's, the United States under Roosevelt's leadership became increasingly interventionist, culminating in the repeal of those acts. More recently, in an attempt to limit the treaty-making power of the President and Senate, and to place limitations on the President's authority to make executive agreements, Senator Bricker of Ohio introduced a proposed Constitutional amendment providing that:

1. A treaty which conflicts with this Constitution shall not be of any force or effect.

2. A treaty shall become effective as internal law in the United States only through legislation which would be valid in the absence of a treaty.

3. Congress shall have power to regulate all executive and other agreements with any foreign power or international organization. All such agreements shall be subject to the limitations imposed on treaties by this article.

Particularly the third aspect of the amendment would attempt to give Congress a greater share in the shaping of American relations with other states. One of the decisive arguments against the amendment, however, was precisely on this point: that the executive ought to be left free to reach agreements with other states on his own initiative, on the grounds of needed flexibility of policy and of secrecy.

Other congressional weaknesses

From what has already been said, it may be summarized that constitutionally, representationally, organizationally, and informationally the executive is naturally in a much stronger position than Congress to be the effective formulator of foreign policy.

In addition to these comparative weaknesses of Congress, two others are important. The first concerns the nature of the legislative process itself. Implicit in that process is the notion of discussion, with a view toward pointing up rather than obscuring issues, compromising among various interests, and assuring sufficient deliberation so that all interests may be heard. Yet by its nature foreign policy is the more effective when based on unified support; compromise may well mean disaster, and many times speed in action precludes the delay associated with deliberation. It is these considerations that underlie the phrase "politics should stop at the water's edge." To have an effective foreign policy, it can be argued, we cannot afford to have the deliberation, delay, and compromise usually associated with the legislative process. Hence the tendency of even the most conscientious Congressmen to "go along" with the President rather than risk the dangers of delay and compromise.

But by far the most important weakness of Congress as a participant in foreign policy making, and one underlying many of the others mentioned, is simply the lack of time. When it is remembered that a Congressman, in addition to his responsibility to think and vote intelligently on matters of foreign affairs, must also concern himself with all other aspects of public policy, *plus* worry about his political fences back home, and perform all varieties of services for constituents, it is easy to see the physical impossibility for any Congressman, let alone every Congressman, to keep fully informed on every aspect of foreign affairs. Both houses of Congress have, of course, attempted to meet this situation in a number of ways. The committee system itself is designed in part to allow some degree of specialization so that Congressmen can become expert in certain areas; funds for the committees to hire experts to help provide informational and analytical ability as noted above, have been provided; and the committees have subdivided themselves to provide for greater specialization within the general area of foreign relations. But all these are ameliorative rather than remedial measures. Comparing the vast numbers of people in the State Department whose *sole* concern is with some area or function of foreign policy, not to mention the large numbers of persons in CIA, Congress is at a tremendous disadvantage when confronted by the executive.

One example of this problem illustrates the point nicely. The following is an exchange between the Staff Director of the Republican Senate Policy Committee and Senator Ferguson of Michigan:

MR. SMITH. Now, Senators, for your amusement as well as to bear out my point on the impossible work load put upon Members of Congress, I have gathered here a group of the books and reports, limited solely to an official character, you should be reading right now on the Marshall plan.

(Mr. Smith here presented a stack of material 18 inches high.)

You are going to take the most momentous step in the history of this country when you pass upon the Marshall plan. . . . That is what you ought to be studying. It contains the Krug report, the Harriman report, the State Department report, the reports of the Herter committee, the Foreign Relations Committee digest; it includes part of the hearings just completed of the Foreign Relations Committee. It does not include hearings yet to be held by the Appropriations Committees. This is one work load you have now on a single problem out of the many problems you have to decide.

SENATOR FERGUSON. How long would it take in your opinion . . . for a person to read it?

MR. SMITH. Well, Senator, I have been reading for the last 35 years, nearly all of my life, in the field of research; and if I could do an intelligent job on that in 2 months of solid reading, excluding myself from everything else . . . I would credit myself with great efficiency.

SENATOR FERGUSON. A normal person would probably take 4 to 5 months.[16]

16 Quoted in *ibid.*, pp. 129-30.

What has been discussed so far may be summed up as follows: (1) Despite the general proposition that the legislature is the primary agency for policy formation in the area of foreign relations, initiative lies largely in the hands of the executive, with Congress playing its most important role as the agency of control over the executive. (2) In this control function Congress is handicapped in a number of ways, so that control is intermittent, at best, and may introduce ignorance and shortsightedness into the foreign policy process. The question arises: What has been and could be done to provide a more effective role for Congress?

A more effective role for Congress?

One conceivable answer to this question is to recognize the necessity for centralized direction and control of foreign policy, to recognize that the President is best equipped to provide this direction and control and remove Congress as much as possible from the foreign-policy process—in short, to develop a kind of constitutional dictatorship in the field of foreign affairs. The case for this cannot be dismissed lightly. Given all the natural handicaps faced by Congress in its attempts to play a meaningful role in the development of foreign policy, and the converse advantages of the executive, and given the need, perhaps crucial, of effective, coherent, and consistent policy based on expert analysis of the exigencies of the world situation, it can be argued that the executive should not only be the supreme, but the *sole,* formulator and executor of contemporary American foreign policy. The stakes, it can be argued, are too high (ultimately the very existence of the country) to permit Congressional interference by men without adequate information, training, or time to participate intelligently in foreign policy making. This general line of argument is relevant to perhaps the most basic problem facing us today, for it is really an attack on democratic government generally. But in one sense the answer is too easy—for it ignores the fact that one of the things our foreign policy is designed to preserve is American values—values that include a commitment to democratic government. And if, in order to promote more effective foreign policy, we remove democratic controls on the foreign policy makers, are we not subverting those very institutions that our foreign policy is obtensibly trying to protect? It may well be that democratic government cannot cope successfully with the problems of a crisis age; but until such time as we are prepared to admit this, any discussion of foreign policy formation in the United

States must include the *promotion* not the *abolition* of democratic controls.

Congress and the expert

Congress itself has attempted to meet this problem in at least two general ways. First, it has tried to develop expertise concerning foreign relations through the devices of sub-committees of the major committees and the hiring of experts on the substantive questions faced by the committees. The essential problem concerning the development of Congressional expertise is that if one or two members of a sub-committee of the Senate Foreign Relations Committee become expert on a given problem or area, and the rest of the Senate relies on their judgment concerning executive proposals in this area or function, democratic controls are not advanced very much. The same thing applies to the committee experts. Yet it is the latter who offer the hope that real progress can be made in developing a more effective role for Congress.

As Professor Robert Dahl has pointed out, there are at least three different roles that the expert may play for the committee. The committee may in fact abdicate its responsibility for making decisions and merely follow the advice of the expert—a situation that may make for good decisions but one that does not solve the problem of control. Or the committee may confine the expert to a role of providing information that committee members do not have the time to absorb for themselves. This is obviously helpful, but it does not take full advantage of the expert's ability to suggest intelligent courses of action that the limitations of training and study may cause the Congressmen to overlook. Third, the expert may, in addition to providing information, suggest possible alternative courses of action indicating the implications of each, but leave the ultimate decision as to what course is chosen to the Congressmen. This arrangement combines greatest utilization of expertise with meaningful Congressional participation in decision making.

Bi-partisanship

Another way Congress has attempted to overcome some of the obstacles in the road to effective participation in foreign policy is through bi-partisanship. As this word is used popularly it involves two assumptions: (1) that party leaders in Congress should consult among themselves and with the executive in order to develop an executive-legislative consensus of foreign policy issues, and as an aspect of this (2) that opposition to foreign policy proposals should not be based on "political" considerations, that is, embarrassment to the administration, emotional appeals to constituents, or aggrandizement of personal political power. In terms of the second assumption, a better word would probably be non-partisanship. While bi-partisanship has had considerable appeal in recent American history, there are a number of things that limit its possibilities.

In the first place Congressional leaders do not have the time to engage in intra-Congressional consultations as well as Congressional-Presidential consultations on a systematic enough basis to develop consensus on all matters of foreign policy. Secondly, even if they did, the lack of party discipline characteristic of the American Congress would not assure Congressional agreement with that consensus. Thirdly, what may seem to be an irresponsible disagreement with administration proposals on the part of some Congressmen may actually be based on very serious considerations. Consider, for example, the possibility that the executive and legislative leaders agree that "trade not aid" should underlie American economic relations with Western Europe; that from this it follows that there should be a general reduction of tariff barriers on the flow of European goods to the United States; that Swiss watches are included in tariff reductions. If a Massachusetts Congressman violently objects to such reductions because they would have an adverse effect on the watchmakers in his district, is he playing "politics" with foreign policy? And if all other Congressmen similarly object to tariff reductions on commodities produced in their districts or states, are they too playing politics? The point is, simply, that foreign policy cannot be separated from domestic considerations, and to ask Congressmen to support bi-partisanship at the expense of the immediate economic interests of their constituents is to ask them to sacrifice concrete local demands for comparatively vague national advantages.

Finally, there is implicit in the notion of bi-partisanship—at least in the way the word is often used—the notion that disagreement should stop at the water's edge; that, at the extreme, severe criticism of an administration's policies weakens America's dealings with foreign powers. Yet democratic government means the right, not to say duty, of legislators to criticize as constructively as they can any public policy, foreign or domestic. To argue the dangers of criticism is to argue the dangers of democracy. Certainly it is hoped that the criticism will in fact be constructive; but to view criticism itself as by definition a hindrance to the pursuit of foreign policy goals, is to challenge one of the basic functions of the legislature.

In the sense that bi-partisanship means executive-legislative consultation, it is doubtless a real attempt to bring Congress more effectually into the foreign policy-making process. If the chief problem, as has been suggested in this chapter, is essentially the relation between the executive and legislative branches, then anything promoting closer collaboration among those two branches is probably useful. In this sense the problem of Congress' role in foreign policy is just an aspect of the problem of the relations of Congress and the President generally.

The many proposals for closer collaboration suggested by students of Congress and the Presidency are all relevant for the question of foreign policy. Professor Corwin's suggestion for a joint legislative-executive Cabinet, Senator Kefauver's proposal for a question period in Congress similar to that used by the English parliament in which executive leaders are called upon to account for their policies to the legislature, and Professor Dahl's contention that even the Central Intelligence Agency, however necessarily secret its activities must be, should not be immune from Congressional oversight, are all to the point.

In the absence of any marked institutional change, however, perhaps the most effective device for developing close executive-legislative collaboration is the informal consultation between the White House and Congressional leaders, combined with the use of experts as policy-advisers to Congress. Certainly no institutional changes will accomplish any more than a desire on the part of Congressmen and the executive to cooperate effectively in the development of foreign policy. This reliance on the desires of the people involved rather than institutional "gimmicks" may seem a weak recommendation for improvement in Congress' role—until it is remembered that it is not institutions, but people, who make foreign policy.

THE ROLE OF PUBLIC OPINION

When Senator Snodgrass stands up in Congress and declares "The public wants this foreign policy," to what public is he referring? He cannot mean everybody, for there is bound to be some difference of opinion among 60 million voting Americans. But he probably cannot mean even a majority because polls show that only 25 per cent of the people consistently show knowledge of foreign problems,[17] much less have an articulate opinion on them. When we speak of the "public" in public opinion on foreign affairs, then, we are usually speaking of a much smaller group than the total public—what have aptly been called the "attentive publics."

Who composes these attentive publics? Generally speaking, their membership may be divided into two broad categories: (1) *articulate leaders of opinion* (newspaper editors, commentators, columnists, educators, and the like) who, while they have a concern for the formation of effective, intelligent foreign policy, have no direct or immediate interest that will be affected thereby; (2) *organized interest groups,* whose concern will ordinarily be with the effects of a policy on their particular interests. The latter, while concerned with promoting America's international position, are more immediately involved in the domestic implications of any foreign policy and are likely to view the national interest in terms of their particular interest.

When the Senator used the words ". . . wants this policy," what did he mean? Did he mean that certain people interested in the policy banded together and attempted to influence Congress and the President in behalf of it? Or did he mean that a proposed policy, formed largely in the executive branch, is acceptable to that segment of the total public that knows and cares about it? Whether an attentive public is attempting to influence government, or whether the executive is essentially trying to "sell" policy proposals depends largely on the issue involved, but in any case it is rarely completely either one or the other.

The executive reaches down

In the attempt to "sell" policy proposals, the executive has a number of devices at its disposal. One technique is that of the strategically timed announcement. Many Democrats charged President Eisenhower with just such a maneuver when he appealed for support for the so-called Eisenhower Doctrine in the Middle East. They argued that during the Fall of 1956 the administration had indicated that the Middle East was relatively quiet and that the sudden announcement in early January 1956 of crisis conditions in that area was designed to coerce Congress into supporting the Doctrine without taking the

[17] Martin Kriesberg, "Dark Areas of Ignorance," in *Public Opinion and Foreign Policy,* ed. by Lester Markel, p. 51. Cited in Gabriel Almond, *The American People and Foreign Policy* (New York: Harcourt, Brace and Company, Inc., 1950), p. 82.

time necessary for a thorough investigation into the recent history of American policy in the Middle East.[18]

Another technique, used a good deal by President Franklin Roosevelt, is the trial balloon, launched either at a press conference or during fireside chats. This device is the practice of indicating that a proposed policy is under consideration and awaiting popular reaction to it. If such reaction, in the form of letters, editorials, and commentators' remarks, is favorable—or at least is not strikingly unfavorable—the policy may then be formally proposed.

Still a third technique is that of the weighted announcement. While informing the public of an important international event the executive may, by his choice of words, hope to build up support for his policy. Suppose, for example, that the Truman administration had not wanted to commit this country to the defense of South Korea in the face of the North Korean attack. An announcement mildly indicating that "a series of border incidents on both sides has led to the development of full scale hostilities which your government is watching with grave concern," might well have removed the connotation of aggression from the action of the North Koreans and thus have reduced the moral impetus to defend the South Koreans against aggression.

The process works both ways, for the executive does make some systematic attempts to collect and analyze at least some manifestations of articulate opinion. The State Department's Division of Public Studies, for example, reads editorials, columns, and feature stories in the press as well as the *Congressional Record,* analyzes findings of public opinion polls, and covers radio broadcasts and pressure group policy announcements. Based on these sources, a daily two or three page summary is circulated to officials in the department and every two weeks a 10 to 15 page summary is sent to our representatives abroad as well. Finally, a weekly digest of outstanding articles on foreign affairs is distributed to department officials. But in practice these devices for bringing public opinion directly into policy formation apparently do not count for very much. In the first place, the measurements of popular views do not always reveal *intensity* of opinion, which may be a decisive factor in the minds of the policy-makers. Secondly, members of the State Department, or other governmental officials, are probably more influenced by their individual reading and thinking about a problem than by scanning the office mimeographed reports on public opinion. Finally, in many cases policy cannot await

[18] *The New York Times,* January 6, 1957.

the initiative of a public outside the government or, specifically, the executive branch.[19]

The attentive publics push up

The question of the extent to which attentive publics participate actively in the formation of foreign policy is a deceptive one. This is true in part because of the tradition of executive supremacy in foreign affairs and in part because of the distinction between foreign and domestic policy.

One of the first things the student of American politics learns is that the how and why of policy formation cannot be completely explained solely by reference to the formal institutions of government. To get a clear picture of just why Congress passes one law rather than another, or of how the executive goes about "faithfully executing" the laws, it is necessary to look behind the scenes and identify those groups that are actively interested in any policy question, and to attempt to measure their relative influence on the ultimate policy decision. Put briefly: scratch the Taft-Hartley Act and you will find not 435 representatives and 96 senators sagely stroking their metaphorical beards, and deciding on a suitable labor policy, but whole congeries of individuals and groups both in and out of government attempting to influence the direction of policy on labor in a way they conceive to be favorable to their particular interests or ideas.

When the student turns to foreign policy, however, he may well look in vain for identifiable interest groups whose complex of activities will explain the emergence of a policy. By and large, every major area of concern of our government has its counterpart in one or more identifiable interest groups. When we think of labor questions we may expect that the AFL-CIO, the National Association of Manufacturers, and the United States Chamber of Commerce will, along with other groups whose interests may be somewhat less directly affected, take an active part in the attempt to steer public policy in the direction they want it to go. The same kind of thing is true for agricultural questions, civil liberties problems, transportation policy, and so on. When we turn to foreign policy, however, such easily spotted groups may seem notable by their absence.

The second reason that the role of attentive publics in the formation of foreign policy is obscured is a matter of historical tradition.

[19] See McCamy, *op. cit.,* pp. 329-32.

Throughout most of our history, matters of foreign policy were of secondary concern to the vast majority of Americans because of our geographic isolation from the vortex of international affairs. Throughout the nineteenth and even the early twentieth centuries, American interests and efforts were directed toward carving out and developing our own nation; what happened in Europe or Asia seemed of little consequence to us. It was thus not unnatural that governmental foreign policy-makers, particularly the executive, were left comparatively free to exercise their initiative. And while the exigencies of our present status as a major world power have made foreign policy issues of immediate concern to all Americans, the tradition of executive initiative in foreign affairs is still very much with us.

Yet, no matter how obscured their activities may be, attentive publics may have an important influence on foreign policy. In the first place, there are a number of highly articulate individuals and groups concerned with America's general international position that take stands on public issues. An incisive analysis by a man like Walter Lippmann may have considerable influence on any one of a number of important governmental officials, though how much or on whom is difficult to ascertain.

Groups such as the League of Women Voters and the Council on Foreign Relations spend a considerable amount of energy and funds on foreign policy. But the primary function of such groups is education, and there is little evidence that the groups as groups have had a great impact on the formation of any particular policy. They may, however, act as intermediaries in bringing together important governmental officials and thoughtful students of international affairs—an activity carried on by the Council on Foreign Relations.

Turning to those groups with specific domestic interests on which foreign policy will impinge we can discern a much more immediate impact on the formation of that policy. This impact may take the form of direct influence on the executive, or it may be revealed through congressional representation of the interest. As interests manifest themselves in Congress they may be immediate, in the sense of a congressional threat not to approve a presidential proposal, or long range; for example, when the President, having discretionary authority based on annual or biennial legislation, is threatened with a limitation on that authority. And the very fact that many people tend to assume that, while "special interests" participate in the formation of domestic policy, the "government" makes foreign policy unhindered by such interests, gives those groups that much greater leverage. This is further buttressed by the fact that foreign policy will ordinarily be defended in terms of America's international interests, almost never with reference to the domestic considerations involved.

By way of illustrating some of these points, two examples may be cited. During 1956 the United States first offered, then withdrew the offer, to aid the Egyptian government under Colonel Nasser in the construction of the Aswan dam on the Nile river. The withdrawal was defended in terms of the failure of the riparian states to make the necessary agreements concerning the dam, and Egypt's apparent inability to make her necessary financial contribution to the project. Another, and very important, factor in the decision, however, was the known opposition of Congress. This congressional opposition was based primarily on the fear that a "big investment in Egypt would offend Zionist sympathies and on the fear of Southern legislators that Egypt might raise more cotton than the U.S.[20] Here, both ethnic-religious and economically oriented interest groups were influential in determining policy.

Another example illustrates how the specific application of a general policy may produce a reaction sufficient to threaten the general policy itself. As part of the broad policy of promoting "trade not aid" with friendly nations, President Eisenhower, in December, 1956, rejected a Tariff Commission proposal to increase the import duties on groundfish fillets, which this country imports from Canada, Iceland, and Denmark. Representatives of both management and labor in the fishing industry immediately protested, and it is significant that such otherwise staunch supporters of "trade not aid" as Senators Saltonstall and Kennedy of Massachusetts indicated their disappointment with the President's decision.[21] Here, since the President is empowered to act on the basis of the Reciprocal Trade laws that underlie our "trade not aid" policy, the interest group concerned could not do very much about it. But similar presidential action in other fields has led to a growing opposition to further extension of the Reciprocal Trade laws. Should a sufficient number of interest groups become "disappointed" with presidential action in this regard, "trade not aid" might be negated, one case at a time, when extension of reciprocal trade again comes up for consideration in Congress in 1958.

Interest groups do, then, play a significant role in many aspects of

[20] *The New York Times,* July 20, 1956.
[21] *The New York Times,* December 11 and 12, 1956.

policy formation. In general, those organized around economic, religious, or ethnic interests appear to be the most active and influential. The degree to which they do impinge on foreign policy will be, other things being equal, roughly proportionate to the degree in which the proposed policy affects their concerns. Thus if we look at the development of the treaty setting up NATO we find that identifiable interest groups did not play a role comparable to that with regard to the Aswan dam decision—in large part because, while no one would dispute the importance of NATO, the proposed treaty did not have immediate effects on any interest groups as did the Aswan dam project. One other situation in which private interest groups would not exert direct influence on the decision-making process is a crisis situation, such as the invasion of South Korea, when speed and secrecy are both imperatives, and the stakes are too momentous to be reduced to interest group calculation.

We have said that insofar as public opinion impinges directly on foreign policy formation the public by no means consists of all Americans, nor on most specific issues, even of most Americans. It is, rather, a comparatively small number of people—the attentive publics. We have also said that the role of interest groups, as attentive publics, is an important one for many, though not all, aspects of foreign policy. This leads to two further questions: (1) Is there any sense in which the public—the "at-large public"—affects foreign policy? and (2) How does public opinion at large impinge on foreign policy indirectly through the electoral process?

Opinion and mood

The answer to the first question is necessarily speculative, but it seems fair to say that the at-large public sets the outside limits within which initiative may be exercised. Put another way, the at-large public has *moods* rather than specific opinions; moods that provide thresholds over which foreign policy-makers cannot step. Of course these moods are themselves subject to change and to a certain extent can be altered by the effective use of the devices the executive has to mold opinion. But in any given period, certain alternatives would appear to be closed to foreign policy-makers because the American people generally would be overwhelmingly opposed to them.

Perhaps even more important than setting the outside limits of policy formation, mood will affect the terms in which our policies are articulated. So long as our mood is one of bitter hostility toward the

Soviet Communists, any projected negotiated settlement with the Soviets in any part of the world runs the risk of being viewed as appeasement. Thus any concession our government makes must be disguised and any public position taken by an American official must be couched in "tough" language. This in turn tends to minimize or restrict the possibilities of negotiation with the Soviets.

Elections as measurements of opinion

Turning to the question of the public's influence on foreign policy through the devices of representative government, the classic formulation of the public's role is stated in terms of the two major political parties taking stands on foreign policy issues and the public—that is, the electorate—choosing between alternatives proposed by the parties. But the United States is noted for its absence of party discipline and responsibility. It is traditional in American politics that party positions on major issues as spelled out in the national platforms are vague rather than clear cut, and this is especially true of foreign policy issues.

On the other hand, meaningful alternative domestic policies are often presented to the voters in the individual congressional, senatorial, or presidential campaigns. Here, again, it is by way of exception that foreign as opposed to domestic issues are posed in terms of clear alternatives. In most congressional and senatorial races domestic questions are almost always of first concern (to the extent that policy issues enter at all). At the Presidential level, campaigns are marked by vagueness rather than specific proposals in the area of foreign affairs. In the campaign of 1952, for example, both candidates favored ending the Korean War if possible, and Eisenhower's declaration that he would go to Korea in person if elected indicated no real difference in his position on the war from that of Stevenson.

This whole question of campaigns and elections as devices by which public opinion can play a role in the shaping of foreign policy is illustrated by the election that perhaps more than any other is viewed as a solemn referendum on an issue of foreign policy—the Presidential election of 1920. Yet a close examination of that election shows that, however solemn it may have been, the election was something less than a referendum on the League. Given statements by candidate Harding and other leading Republicans during the campaign, it would have been perfectly logical for a voter to have believed that Harding's election would not constitute a rejection of the League. More important, it would have been perfectly possible for a voter to have viewed the election as a referendum on the League, to have been in favor of American entry, yet to have voted for Harding, because he felt other issues to be more crucial. In short, what we are saying here is that even at election time where the public is called upon to express direct preferences on issues, the results very rarely, perhaps never, give a clear indication of the public's view on any one issue. And in the interim between elections, of course, concrete manifestations of the public's desires are still less in evidence.

In sum, if we mean by the public the American people, generally it is more realistic to talk of moods rather than opinion—moods that at any given time set the outside limits for initiative in the making of foreign policy. Articulate opinion based on some knowledge of a foreign policy issue is ordinarily confined to a small part of the total public and here its role is often, though not always, confined to the comparatively passive role of accepting, rejecting, or perhaps causing the modification of proposals emanating from the government, particularly the executive branch. And, finally, our elections—the means by which the total public may directly impinge on foreign policy—are intermittent in time and inconclusive in results.

FOREIGN POLICY AND THE DEMOCRATIC PROCESS

This discussion of the major groups of participants in the foreign policy process brings to light four important points that often tend to be obscured in our concern with developing effective foreign policy, and that deserve special emphasis.

Domestic necessities and international responsibilities

No matter how much, for purposes of discussion, we differentiate foreign and domestic policies it should never be forgotten that the two in practice are very much related. Regardless of how beautifully thought out and constructed any foreign policy is, if it does not take into consideration the domestic needs and desires of the American people as manifested primarily through Congress, its adoption will be jeopardized. Nor is this a one-way street. Our international responsibilities may, and do, have important repercussions on domestic policy as well. We cannot spend 40 billion dollars a year to build up our own and our allies' military might without sacrificing a considerable amount of domestic goods and services. Any attempt to understand American foreign policy, then, must take into account the total picture of American public policy, with foreign policy viewed as an important, but still only one, aspect of that total picture.

Relation of substance and process

Another point that may well be obscured in our concern for effective foreign policy is that the *substance* of that policy is related in at least two significant ways to the *process* of arriving at it. First, it does make an important difference as to who in fact makes policy—whose picture of reality will serve as the basis for action. We have seen an example of this in the case study on strategic trust territories. On a broader screen, the degree to which we emphasize military build-up of the free world as opposed to aid for economic development and stability will be largely conditioned by the questions of whose analysis of the nature of the Soviet threat is used as the basis for policy development. Secondly, regardless of who in fact does make policy, the question arises as to whether or not they are in fact controlled by the American people, either directly or through their elected representatives. If we are not to throw out the baby with the bathwater, democratic controls over policy-making—foreign or domestic—must be retained.

Continuing control versus elective aristocracy

We have seen that these controls are by and large incomplete and intermittent. Necessity has led to considerable independence of the executive branch in the formation of foreign as compared to domestic policy. Does this mean that in fact about all we can do is elect a President every four years and turn over foreign policy decision-making to him, and the executive departments under him, in the hope that we have selected a wise man and able administrator? Perhaps so— and certainly a case can be made that the tendency in that direction is present, if indeed the end has not already been reached. But if so, there is no use in beclouding the fact that a vital aspect of democratic government has been vitiated. To the extent that in our quest for security we are willing to sacrifice democratic institutions, to that extent we destroy what we hope to preserve. Again, the exigencies of crisis may necessitate such a sacrifice—just as most of us accept the need for less democracy in wartime. Perhaps the real danger is one of drift. In wartime we are aware of the temporary crisis and aware that democratic controls are temporarily removed to a large degree. In the uneasy peace of the cold war, it is perhaps more understandable that we should tend to forget the more gradual accretion of decision-making authority into the hands of appointed rather than popularly elected officials. But such forgetfulness tends to make the decision in favor of what may be called an elective aristocracy as against continuing control, without our even being aware of it.

Institutional change versus responsible citizenship

But is this tendency irreversible? Must we of necessity turn our backs on the question of continuing control in order to achieve effective foreign policy? Or what might be done to promote more rather than less democracy without at the same time sacrificing intelligence and flexibility in our foreign relations? Several suggestions have been made on this point, some of which have already been discussed. In addition, one might mention the oft-repeated assertion that the development of disciplined, responsible political parties would make our elections more meaningful in terms of popular choices among alternative policies while at the same time promote greater Congressional effectiveness in controlling the executive. None of these proposals should be disparaged; but the possibility of developing responsible political parties itself indicates the real nature of the problem: that democratic government is after all a belief system as well as a structure of formal institutions. As students of political parties have pointed out, while institutional changes may affect the structure of parties, we will get responsible parties only when we want them. Similarly, no institutional change— reorganization of the executive branch, question periods in Congress, joint legislative-executive Cabinet meetings—will, however useful, in and of itself assure effective popular control of foreign policy. However trite it has become, the statement that in democracies people get the kind of government they want is still very much the case.

In the last analysis, then, democratic controls on foreign policy-making depend not so much on institutional change as on responsible citizenship. In a very real sense one of the great challenges of our age is whether in our concern with earning a living, going to parties, and achieving equal status with the Joneses, we are to turn over the responsibilities of decision-making to a kind of elective aristocracy; or whether American citizens can effectively cope with the problems of foreign policy themselves, can, that is to say, become sufficiently educated and interested to make thoughtful judgements on important issues and demand that their government be responsive and responsible to them. Responsive government calls for responsible citizens.

BIBLIOGRAPHICAL NOTE

An excellent general work, dealing with both the substance and the process of American foreign policy, is Richard C. Snyder and Edgar S. Furniss, Jr., *American Foreign Policy: Formulation, Principles, and Programs,* 1954.

A number of very good monographs on various aspects of foreign policy formation have been published, their titles indicating the subject matter with which they are concerned. Included among these are Gabriel A. Almond, *The American People and Foreign Policy,* 1950; Robert A. Dahl, *Congress and Foreign Policy,* 1950; James L. McCamy, *The Administration of American Foreign Affairs,* 1952; and H. Bradford Westerfield, *Foreign Policy and Party Politics: Pearl Harbor to Korea,* 1955.

Dexter Perkins, *The Evolution of American Foreign Policy,* 1948, provides a fine brief summary of the historical development of American foreign relations.

Useful collections of readings and documents may be found in L. Larry Leonard, *Elements of American Foreign Policy,* 1953, and Ruhl J. Bartlett, ed., *The Record of American Diplomacy,* 2nd ed., Alfred A. Knopf, 1950.

4. JAMES N. MURRAY, JR.

Military Policy

As noted in the preceding chapter, the problems of foreign policy can be adequately understood only in the context of the revolutionary transformation of the position of the United States in world affairs. Yet this change in the international role of the United States has had, if possible, even greater implications for military policy. It was something less than 50 years ago that a President directed the War Department to cease all war planning because, in addition to its inconsistency with America's position as a peace-loving nation, our security did not require it.[1] A similar directive today or for the foreseeable future, would be unthinkable.

BACKGROUND FACTORS

To appreciate the significance of this change, and the implications of it, it is necessary to recall the traditional position of the military in public affairs. Essentially, the role of the military was that of an agency of policy execution, whenever the civilian formulators of foreign policy, in trying to preserve our security, so directed. And since during the eighteenth and nineteenth centuries our geographic isolation from Europe and Asia meant our military isolation as well, we had no need

[1] Townsend Hoopes, "Civilian-Military Balance," *Yale Review,* Vol. 43 (Winter, 1954), p. 219.

of a large standing army and felt little necessity for a sizeable navy. Traditionally, the assumptions underlying America's relations with other states were that peaceful intercourse was the rule, armed conflict the temporary aberration. In this sense Clausewitz' famous statement that war is an extension of diplomacy by other means, was modified in the United States to include the notion that these "other means" were at most temporary, to be discarded immediately after having fulfilled their purpose. It has been as much a boast as a complaint to assert that America has never been prepared for a war. And our uninterrupted record of very rapid disarmament at the conclusion of wars further bears this out. Underlying this tradition of the abnormality of war was the fact that for over a century before World War II the physical security of the United States itself was never directly threatened.

Consider, then, the implications of the cold war for this tradition. The Soviet Union is not only a state whose interests conflict with those of the United States; it is as well a nation capable of inflicting untold damage, if not total destruction, on us. At present there is little doubt that the threat to American security posed by the Communists includes not just strategically located countries and territories overseas, but the United States proper as well. Further, the phrase "cold war" itself implies a struggle between two groups of states—an uninterrupted struggle which, although not at the moment a matter of armed conflict, is for the highest stakes. In addition to these considerations, technological developments have tremendously enhanced the importance of actual rather than potential military might. That is to say, the fact that the United States can out-produce any nation in the world does not mean it can, as it has in the past, wait until the outbreak of war to develop military striking power sufficient to win the war. Ballistic missiles with atomic warheads no longer permit any nation that luxury. While it is an overstatement, there is an element of truth in rephrasing Clausewitz' dictum to read for our own times: diplomacy is the extension of war by other means.

What the revolutionary transformation in America's role in world politics means, as much as anything else, then, is the revolutionary transformation of the military in the shaping of that role. Today it is fair to ask whether or not the traditional roles of the diplomat and military should be reversed—whether in view of the tremendous threat to our national security, strategic-military considerations ought not to govern our foreign policy.

Military-civil relations

The Gargantuan growth of military considerations in all aspects of public policy raises a further fundamental problem: the relations between the military and civilian participants in policy-making. It has long been recognized that one of the greatest threats to democratic government is the emergence of a strong military organization not easily susceptible to control by civilian officials. The framers of our Constitution were acutely aware of this, and it was not by accident that the President was made Commander-in-Chief of the Armed Forces, that Congress was empowered to raise and maintain an army and navy, that Congressional appropriations for the military were limited to a period not to exceed two years, and that army and navy officers were excluded from nonmilitary governmental positions. Indeed, one of the arguments used to support the adoption of the Constitution was that Congressional power to raise and maintain an army and navy provided safeguards against possible military dominance.[2] This attitude was further buttressed by the very fact that throughout most of our history we did not need a large military establishment. Until recently, civilian-military relationships did not cause grave concern because the problem simply did not arise to any significant degree.

Now, however, the problem is very much with us. With our tremendous military establishment, with the apparent necessity of viewing the world through the lenses of military strategy, and with the aura of prestige surrounding the military leaders as the result of victory in the second World War, we are faced with the danger not only of the predominance of military considerations in forming public policy, but with the dominance by military men as well. Any discussion of the problems concerning the development of adequate military policy must, then, include the basic question of control of the military by the civil. Nor is it enough to say, "If the military is getting too powerful, then let us remove them from the councils of policy-making." For military men participate in policy-making precisely because they are indispensable. The real problem concerns the development of a governmental system which can make use of the necessary military expertise in the formation of policy, and at the same time provide for authoritative, effective civilian control. We ignore the problem of control at the peril of our democratic institutions; we ignore military considerations at the risk of our security; we can afford to do neither.

[2] *The Federalist Papers*, No. 26.

A word about words

Before proceeding to a discussion of these problems, it will be useful to distinguish between three phrases with overlapping connotations: foreign policy, military policy, and security. Traditionally foreign policy has meant that collection of activities—largely political and economic—used to pursue our goals with respect to other states. Military policy has been concerned with the ways in which specific objectives should be pursued using military means—the objectives themselves ostensibly being defined by those in control of foreign policy. It is obvious that given our present position in the world the line between foreign and military policy will be vague at best. But in an age when the physical security of the nation is threatened with total war, attention must be paid to the mobilization of potentially all the domestic resources we have for the maintenance of our security. In this sense security policy may be viewed as a three-dimensional composite of foreign, military, and domestic policies.

To take a concrete example, consider the question of American policy toward Germany. Our foreign policy generally favors an economically viable, politically friendly, democratically organized state. The State Department is aware also that any efforts at German rearmament will be viewed with deep suspicion by other western European nations, France in particular. Our military policy, however, must consider Germany as a potential friend or enemy in the event of war, and may well include, as it does now, the rearmament of Western Germany as an ally against the Soviet Union. Our total policy toward Germany, then, will be some combination of what has been traditionally considered foreign policy on the one hand and military on the other.

But rearming Germany is only one aspect of a total program of foreign military aid to build up non-Communist states against possible aggression by the Soviet Union. To what degree will our internal economy be affected by an additional increment of sacrifice for foreign aid? Actually, two questions are involved here: (1) Can the economy physically sustain the effort? (2) Even if it can, will the increased diversion of national wealth to another country be acceptable to Congress, which represents varied economic interests? Thus, our total policy on Germany will be affected by foreign, military, and domestic considerations. This total policy we may call security policy. To generalize, we have security, rather than merely foreign or military, policies today because superimposed on our relations with any given area of the world is the cold war conflict with the Soviet Union—a "war" that can become both total and nuclear at any time. Potential total war calls for total planning both for its prevention and for its outbreak, and this in turn necessitates consideration of domestic capabilities, in addition to foreign and military policies. Finally, those domestic capabilities themselves include the degree to which American people are willing to make the necessary sacrifices to pursue any tactic, policy, or grand strategy.

Problems of military policy, then, must be discussed in terms of the more general question of security.

ORGANIZING FOR SECURITY

The attempt to develop security policy, as distinct from the more specialized foreign or military policy, is essentially a product of the post World War II era. As a consequence, the hallmark of American efforts in this direction has been change—trial and error, reorganization, shift of function. No better example of this can be found than the impact already made on America's defense organization by the launching of the two Soviet earth satellites. Already the President has appointed a Special Assistant for Science and Technology, and a Congressional investigation into the state of our preparedness has been undertaken. Concern for our military position was heightened by the initial failure of the Vanguard Project. Despite the success in launching Explorer I and subsequent satellites in 1958, it seems very likely that further changes in the organization for security, perhaps including the establishment of Congressional committees on science and technology, will be introduced in the 85th Congress.[3] In any event, a description of our present institutions concerned with military policy must be made with the important reservation that significant changes in those institutions may occur at any moment.

The basic legislation underlying our present arrangements is the National Security Act of 1947. In general, two considerations lay back of this law. The first, already alluded to, was the growing realization that it was impossible to separate rigidly the functions of the State Department and the military services. Even during the late war, when the military was theoretically running most of the show, it became obvious

[3] Senator Hubert Humphrey has advanced this proposal, among others. See *The New York Times,* November 16, 1957.

(1) that military-strategic decisions might have grave political implications—for example, bringing the Soviet Union into the war in the Far East or deciding not to invade Europe through the Balkans—and (2) that the problems of occupying defeated countries would call for close cooperation between the civil and military agencies of our government. In response to this, a joint State, War, Navy Coordinating Committee (SWNCC) was created, in the hope that our foreign and military policies could be effectively coordinated. When, after the end of the war, it became apparent that "peace" was giving way to the cold war, there was obvious utility in continuing this kind of joint policy-making agency.

The second reason for enacting the National Security Act was the increasing acknowledgement, though not without bitter controversy, that the traditional distinction of functions between the military services made less and less sense. At one time technological limitations on military power provided the basis for this distinction in fact as well as principle. Throughout most of our history the army was pretty much confined to the ground, the navy to the sea. Aircraft, upon their invention, were confined to tactical roles in connection with either of the other two. But with aircraft able to journey thousands of miles, with land-based rocket launchers capable of sending air-borne missiles hundreds of miles, with carrier-based aircraft able to penetrate far inland, and with any of these capable of delivering tremendous nuclear explosives, this military separation of powers needed re-assessment.

With these considerations in mind Congress did two things in the National Security Act: (1) provided for the unification of the armed forces—now including a separate air force as a concession to the fact that air power could be strategic as well as tactical—under a single Secretary of Defense; (2) created a National Security Council whose job it is to formulate and review basic policies of the United States relating to our national security. Thus the act dealt with developing more unified military policies in the more confined sense and with promoting comprehensive security policies in the broadest meaning of the term.

The National Security Council

As presently constituted, the NSC consists of the President, the Vice-President, the Secretaries of State and Defense, and the Director of the Office of Defense Mobilization. In addition to this formal membership, the President may invite other officials to participate without vote in its deliberations. Ordinarily the Director of the Central Intelligence Agency, the Chairman of the Joint Chiefs of Staff, the Secretary of the Treasury and the Director of the Bureau of the Budget attend the weekly meetings.

The *Central Intelligence Agency* was created by the National Security Act "to coordinate the intelligence activities of the several Government departments" and to advise the NSC "in matter concerning such intelligence activities . . . as relate to national security." [4] The CIA, then, is the apex of the intelligence agencies and is directly subordinate to the NSC. In addition to CIA there is another body concerned with information, the *National Security Agency,* whose work is classified, but whose main functions apparently are primarily those of analysis of information and preparation of reports for the NSC. Other important subordinate units of the NSC are: (1) the *Planning Board,* composed of representatives of the same departments as are represented on the Council, under the chairmanship of the Special Assistant to the President for National Security Affairs, whose main duty is to formulate security policies for considerations by the Council; (2) the *Staff,* under the executive secretary of the Council, whose job it is to keep the machinery of the Council running smoothly; and (3) an *Operations Coordinating Board,* composed of the Undersecretary of State, as chairman, the Deputy Secretary of Defense, the Director of CIA, the Director of the United States Information Agency, and a representative of the President. This board was created by executive order in 1953 to coordinate the implementation of Council policies and report to the Council on how its policies are being carried out. It may also initiate policies that are within the framework of previously established Council policies, as the opportunity and occasion warrant.

The creation of the board is a good illustration of the changing nature of our organization for security. It is one thing to have an agency develop security policies, quite another to see that those policies are carried out. Originally, the department that initiated a policy finally approved by the President was charged with overseeing its execution. But it became apparent that the Secretary concerned was busy enough running his own department without the added responsibility of coordinating the activities of his own with others as well. Hence the need for an intermediary agency between the Council as policy formulator and the various departments as policy implementers

---

[4] *United States Government Organization Manual,* 1957–58, p. 64.

to coordinate the various agencies responsible for carrying out that policy.

So much for the machinery. The question is: does it work? And if so, how?

NSC in action

Essentially the function of the NSC is two-fold: (1) to deal with the immediate problems of security as they confront the nation; (2) to develop long range policies, laying out at least tentative paths in the direction of the goals we should like to achieve. This second point is important. One of the chief difficulties the United States has faced in attempting to develop long range policies is that the departments were too concerned with their day-to-day business without taking on the additional responsibility of engaging in long-range planning. Yet without such planning our policies for the cold war and other security matters would have a tendency to be dictated by what other states do—we could not take the diplomatic offensive. One criticism of the policy of containment is that it is essentially negative in this respect, for it implies that we "hold the line" around the borders of the East and necessarily wait for some action from Peiping or Moscow before we do anything. Such a policy means turning over to the opposition all the initiative—letting him choose the time and place for action. Such considerations underlie the oft-expressed proposal that the United States seize the initiative, that we have positive not merely negative policies. But we cannot have a positive policy without having some idea of our long-range goals. Thus the need for some agency which, in addition to concerning itself with the major issues of the day, attempts to spell out more far-reaching goals and ways to achieve those goals.

To date, the NSC has been relatively successful as a body that can deal with the more immediate issues, but the fulfillment of the second function has left something to be desired, largely because, again, the NSC has had enough to do in meeting the more immediate problems. One suggestion for improving the situation is the addition to the Council of members without other governmental responsibilities. The objection to this is that planning by people who do not have the responsibility for executing those plans tends to introduce an element of unreality into the planning process. So far, then, the development of long-range foreign or security policy-planning remains one of the essentially unresolved problems of our government.

With respect to the more immediate problems, the ordinary process usually begins with a draft proposal in one of the departments, sometimes Defense, more often State. The Planning Board, in cooperation with the Staff, refines the proposal, taking into account the positions of the various agencies or departments affected. Ultimately a proposal emanating from the Board will be passed on to the Council for final consideration. The Council itself does not vote on a proposal; rather it reaches a consensus based on the discussion of all the factors involved. For example, in the Trieste incident, when we found out that the Russians were about to announce their support for the return of Trieste to Italy in the hope that this would influence the forthcoming Italian elections in favor of the Communist Party, a proposal initiated by the State Department, refined by the Council's subsidiary agencies, eventually reached the NSC, calling for an allied announcement supporting the return of Trieste to Italy *before* the Russians made their proposal. When the Council met, Secretary of State Marshall was still dubious about the proposal, even though it had originated in his department, since he felt that in effect we were stooping to the level of Soviet tactics. But other members brought up the strategic disaster that would be entailed should the Communists win the election in Italy, and with this in mind Secretary Marshall eventually acquiesced in the proposal.[5] No vote was taken—consensus was reached. But it is important to remember that consensus in the Council does not turn a proposal into policy; this can be done only by decision of the President. Only after President Truman wrote in the right hand corner, "O.K., HST," did we have a policy on the Trieste issue. It should be remembered further, that we could not easily act unilaterally in this case. Trieste was a matter of concern to Britain and France as well, and any policy had to be cleared with those countries before an *allied* policy could be announced. Had such approval not been forthcoming, the Council would have been called upon to discuss whether we should go ahead and make the announcement alone, or what modifications should be made to take account of British or French objections. In this case, however, the British and French approved, and the decision was eventually announced as a tri-partite statement.

The President is not kept waiting in the wings until the Council brings forth a proposal. Actually he has a daily briefing from the executive secretary of the Council on the upcoming major issues, and

[5] See Joseph and Stewart Alsop, "How Our Foreign Policy Is Made," *Saturday Evening Post*, Vol. 221 (April 30, 1949), p. 30 ff.

often knows as much (or more) about a proposal as the other members of the Council.[6] But this does not destroy the real function of that body: bringing together all elements involved in a situation and, through discussion, arriving at a joint recommendation to the President.

Setting up an agency, however superficially important it may appear, does not give that agency power, authority, or vitality. The role of the NSC is influenced by the degree to which its members can work together, and more importantly by the amount the President wishes to rely on it. He can ignore its recommendations; he can even prevent its consideration of a problem—as President Truman did in 1948 when he refused to let the Palestine question be put on the Council's agenda. Both Presidents Truman and, especially, Eisenhower, however, have increasingly relied on the Council, and it is hardly an overstatement to say that the NSC has become the chief formulator of our over-all security policy. In an age when security considerations predominate, this means that below the President the NSC is our most important governmental agency within the executive branch.

The Pentagon

The accompanying chart shows the general organization of the Defense Department. Two or three points call for special comment. Atomic energy, so important to our total military effort, is under the control of a separate civilian agency, the *Atomic Energy Commission*. Liaison between that Commission and the Defense Department is maintained through a Military Liaison Committee. Information on all matters relating to the military uses of atomic energy is provided by the Commission through the Committee to the Defense Department. Of course, basic questions such as whether or not to produce the hydrogen bomb remain the decisions of the President.

Liaison with the *Civil Defense Administration*, which develops and coordinates policy designed to protect us in case of attack, is maintained through a Civil Defense Coordinating Board, with representatives of the departments and agencies, including Defense, affected by any civil defense program.

[6] The operations of the NSC have been described by two former Special Assistants to the President for National Security Affairs, and one Executive Secretary of the Council. See Dillon Anderson, "The President and National Security," *Atlantic,* Vol. 197 (January, 1956), pp. 42-46; Robert Cutler, "The Development of the National Security Council," *Foreign Affairs,* Vol. 34 (April, 1956), pp. 440-58; and Sidney Souers, "Policy Formation for National Security," *American Political Science Review,* Vol. 43 (February-June, 1949), pp. 534-43.

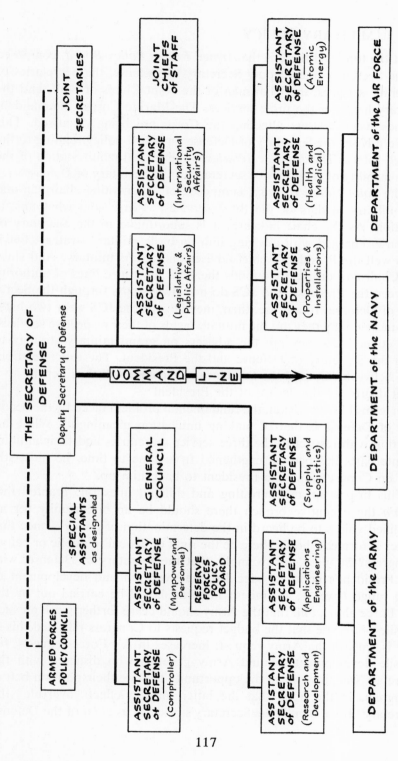

Fig. 4.1. General organization of the Department of Defense

117

At the top level there is the *Armed Forces Policy Board,* composed of the Secretary and Deputy Secretary of Defense, the Secretaries of the three services, the Chairman of the Joint Chiefs of Staff, and the military heads of the three services. The Marine Corps Commandant attends when matters affecting the Corps are being discussed. This Board advises the Secretary of Defense on broad policy relating to the armed forces. The *Joint Secretaries* is the formal manifestation of the responsibility of each service secretary to the Secretary of Defense.

The *Joint Chiefs of Staff,* composed of a nonvoting chairman and the military leaders of the three services, is in a somewhat unique position. As the chart indicates it is subordinate to the Secretary of Defense, charged with advising him on basic military strategy, but it is as well the President's chief adviser on matters military. And since the Chairman ordinarily attends the NSC meetings, lines of authority between the President and JCS do not always pass through the Secretary of Defense. In a sense, then, members of the JCS wear two hats: (1) individually they are the military heads of their respective services; (2) collectively they are the advisers on grand military strategy to both the Secretary of Defense and the President. The exact relationship between JCS and the Secretary of Defense will thus depend to a great degree on the desires of the President.

In terms of supervision, the fundamental problem faced by the Secretary of Defense is that of making unification meaningful. While his position with respect to the three service secretaries and their military counterparts has been strengthened from time to time, he must still rely on Congress and the President to back him up.

This brings up an interesting and difficult question: granted that *within* the executive branch there should be an opportunity for all qualified voices to be heard in the determination of policy—once that policy is formed, should there be the right of dissent in public or before Congress? Suppose, for example, that the Secretary of Defense, with the President's approval, decided that research and development of long range (over 1,500 miles) missiles should be carried out by the Air Force alone, and that the Army should cease further work on such missiles. Suppose that the budget requests to Congress reflected this— that is, cuts in the Army request, increases in Air Force requests, for missile development. Should Army generals who disagree with the Secretary's decision have the opportunity to state their position before Congress, in the hope that the latter may in effect "overrule" the Secretary? If so, then is the Secretary's position as *chief* of the Defense

Department meaningful? If not, is not Congress being deprived of expertness on the basis of which it may check the feasibility of the Defense Department's proposals?

As we shall see below, this type of problem is a very real one and has arisen more than once in the post World War II era. By and large, though not without some bitter infighting, military leaders have been allowed to speak their pieces in such situations. The line between insubordination and the exposure of differences for the public welfare, however, has not as yet been clearly defined, if indeed it ever could be.

Basic to this ambiguous position of the Secretary of Defense as head of his department is what might be called the functional inertia of the services. Even though unification implied coordination of military effort among the three services, this did not mean the end of bitter disputes concerning the proper role of each in any grand strategy. Primary reliance on air power, for example, might well make naval leaders feel not only that the Navy was being slighted, but that our national security was being jeopardized by insufficient recognition of other factors. Indicative of this was an episode that produced just such feelings and was known popularly in its time as the "Revolt of the Admirals."

The Revolt of the Admirals [7]

In the Spring and Summer of 1949 the problems involved in unification of the three services, and in the related, more basic, question of grand military strategy, were given public airing in a Congressional investigation of unification and strategy. What lay behind the investigation was the growing feeling on the part of many admirals that "unification" was becoming "domination," specifically by the Air Force over the Navy. One of the inducements to Navy acquiescence in unification had been the appointment of a known supporter of naval power, James Forrestal, as first Secretary of Defense. When Louis Johnson succeeded Forrestal, however, he gave indications of placing increasing reliance on strategic bombing as the king-pin of our defense efforts. Illustrative was his order to stop all work on a 65,000-ton super-aircraft carrier, which was interpreted as a full victory of the Air Force over the Navy.

Bitterness within the Navy reached a point where one of the Navy's most noted airmen, Captain Crommelin, made public a confidential

[7] The description of this episode is based on an unpublished manuscript by J. Dale Chastain of the State University of Iowa.

letter from Vice Admiral Bogan, commander of the First Task Fleet in the Pacific, to Secretary of the Navy Matthews. Bogan asserted that it would be "sheer balderdash to assume that there has been anything approaching unity. . . . Bickering is still the rule." And referring to the doctrine of strategic air power, with its consequent diminution of the role of the Navy in the total defense effort, he asserted "we are fearful that the country is being, if it has not already been, sold a false bill of goods." [8]

Shortly thereafter, Crommelin admitted he had "leaked" the letter to the press, hoping it would "blow the whole thing open and bring on another Congressional investigation. . . ." [9] The Captain was suspended and the House Armed Services Committee began public hearings into the dispute.

The Navy's position was not confined to the fact that it was getting a "raw deal" in unification. Rather the admirals argued that the basic assumptions underlying the "raw deal" were really at issue. They argued that reliance on strategic bombing as a major deterrent to war, and as a weapon for victory if war should come, was dangerous. With regard to its use as a deterrent, Admiral King asserted that its effectiveness "depends on the amount of fear it will instill in the would-be aggressor. This is a matter of speculation." [10] As a weapon for victory, the Navy had still greater doubts. Naval arguments in this connection were essentially that: (1) Strategic bombing of the Soviet's basic war-making plant could not prevent its initial success in overrunning Western Europe. (2) Should the latter occur, the Soviets would control vast reservoirs of war capabilities which we would be most reluctant to bomb, since it would involve atomic destruction of our traditional allies in Western Europe. (3) While air power, and within it, strategic bombing, are important, it is just as important to be able to strike effectively at the enemy's "armed forces and the transport system which moves him and his supplies. The targets must have a direct connection to the fighting which our troops and our allies are conducting. Bombing of cities and industrial areas will not have an immediate and direct effect in delaying or stopping the advance of enemy armies." [11]

[8] *The New York Times,* October 4, 1949.

[9] *Ibid.,* September 11, 1949.

[10] *Unification and Strategy,* Hearings, U.S. House Armed Services Committee, 81st Congress, 1st Sess. (Washington, D.C.: U.S. Government Printing Office, 1949), p. 253.

[11] *Ibid.,* p. 238. The remarks are those of Admiral Halsey.

What is important to note in this "revolt" is not only the fact that unification on paper is sometimes quite different from unification in fact, but also that underlying the organizational question of the Navy's role in unification was the doctrinal question of the validity of strategic air power as the basis of our military strategy. This in turn raises the question of whether, in an age of atomic warheads and guided or ballistic missiles, even a "unified" military organization makes sense so long as it is based on the traditional tri-partite functions of land, sea, and air forces.

One acute student of the military has suggested that it does not. He proposes the reorganization of our services along the lines of more realistic functions in the contemporary world.

> The Army, Navy and Air Force would continue as administrative and training units, much as the training commands *within* the various services function today. But for all other purposes two basic organizations would be created: the Strategic Force and the Tactical Force. The Strategic Force would be the units required for all-out war; it would include the Strategic Air Command; the Air Defense Command; those units of the Army required to protect overseas bases; and the units of the Navy which are to participate in the retaliatory attack. The Tactical Forces would be the Army, Air Force and Navy units required for limited war. The Strategic Forces would probably be under Air Force command, the Tactical Forces under an Army officer. The training and doctrine of each Force should be uniform and its officers should attend the same technical and service schools. The schools would continue to be administered by a parent service but the curriculum and student body should be determined by the Force commander.
>
> Such a division would reflect the realities of the strategic situation.[12]

Others, notably General James Doolittle, have suggested removing one of the hats worn by members of the Joint Chiefs of Staff by creating a military staff for the Secretary of Defense in charge of formulating over-all military planning. Members of this staff, unlike the Joint Chiefs, would not be the leaders of their respective services and, it is argued, would therefore be able to visualize the total military picture free from implicit obligations to their particular service branches.[13]

Whether this proposal will be given serious consideration or not, the fact remains that organizational problems are not confined to matters of hurt pride among the leaders of the traditional services, but include

[12] Henry A. Kissinger, "Strategy and Organization," *Foreign Affairs*, Vol. 35 (April, 1957), pp. 390-91.

[13] Testimony of General James A. Doolittle before the Senate Preparedness subcommittee. Summarized in *The New York Times*, November 27, 1957.

important questions as to the development of military doctrine sufficient to meet the challenges of our age.

While the Navy arguments did not materially change our emphasis on air power, it should be mentioned that the carrier program was eventually renewed.

PROBLEMS OF CONTROL

The description of the organization for security is but partial. Besides the agencies and departments mentioned, there are countless inter-agency committees and liaison offices, not to mention those extra-organizational devices for coordination: the telephone and the luncheon date. How is this maze of organizational activity controlled? How, that is to say, is security policy generally, and within that military policy specifically, made responsive to the "will of the people." Broadly, this problem of control has two aspects: (1) control over the executive by the Congress and the people and (2) control within the executive by the President and his civilian assistants over the military.

An over-view of the problem

Generally speaking what has already been said about the roles of the President, Congress and the people in foreign policy holds true for military policy as well. But if anything the problems are more acute.

In the case of the public, the lack of information—not to mention expertise—on military matters consequent on the necessary secrecy such matters involve, means that even the attentive publics have comparatively very little impact. While it is true that veterans' organizations such as the American Legion concern themselves with military policy it is usually in terms of supporting the position taken by military leaders in the government rather than on the basis of independent positions that may or may not be in harmony with the professional military.

In at least one instance, however, a combination of what we have called *mood* and vigorous assertion of a position by a number of interest groups apparently did have an important effect on a military proposal. This was the idea of universal military training, proposed by the executive but forcefully opposed by a number of organizations, especially church groups, which argued that it was inconsistent with our traditions and would open the door to further encroachments of the military on the civilian control of our society. Yet even here, public action was in fact reaction to policy emanating from the executive.

And it is difficult to think of many instances of a similar nature, or any instances where attentive publics have taken an active role in the development, as opposed to approval, of military policy.

Congress also faces great handicaps as an organ of control. Its military affairs committees are faced with the same problems of information and expertness as its foreign relations committees. Further, there is as yet no single committee that could be called the legislative counterpart of NSC. The organization of Congress is essentially based on the traditional distinction between military and foreign policy, and any sort of security policy developed in Congress will necessarily be a haphazard conglomeration of compromises among the appropriations, foreign relations, and military affairs committees, not to mention all the other committees whose domain will be affected by security matters.

As in foreign policy formation, probably the most effective device for congressional control of the military is the power of the purse. But here again the constitutional provisions are vitiated by the circumstances of contemporary military affairs. In the first place, a decision on military policy today often commits expenditures over a period considerably longer than two years. Once Congress has agreed to such a decision, in the form of the first appropriations, it can change its mind only at the cost of the great sacrifice of the already expended funds. And secondly, since we live in an age of fantastic technological change, research on, and development of, new weapons must proceed constantly, even though the cost is enormous. Our present research and development program, for example, includes work on some 40 missiles at a cost of around three billion dollars in fiscal 1958 alone.[14] Certainly the decision to allocate that amount for one aspect of defense is one of great importance. Yet Congress, for lack both of information and expertness, is for all practical purposes coerced into making the necessary appropriations, lest the "Russians beat us to the punch." Added to this is the fact that in five or ten years three-fourths of these weapons may be obsolete. Congressmen have expressed concern with this situation. As the chairman of the Joint Committee on Atomic Energy once declared, the choice seemed to be "financial ruination" or "atomic devastation." [15] But with our security apparently at stake, and in the absence of any real evidence other than that provided by

[14] Based on an article and accompanying chart in *The New York Times,* November 18, 1957.

[15] Quoted in Richard C. Snyder and Edgar S. Furniss, Jr., *American Foreign Policy: Formulation, Principles, and Programs* (New York: Rinehart and Co., 1954), p. 375.

the military, it is little wonder that Congressmen feel constrained to vote the requested funds.

Within the executive branch the problem of control of the military concerns the relationship of the civilian and military authorities. What this in turn means is the assurance on the one hand that military policy, as developed by the military, must undergo the constant scrutiny of civilian chiefs, and that on the other hand in any combined councils of decision-making, the civilian viewpoint must be sufficiently represented so that the military members do not run the show. One good example of an attempt to promote the latter goal was the reorganization of the NSC in 1949, at which time the three service secretaries—who had originally been members along with the Secretary of Defense—were removed and the Vice-President was added as a formal member. And an executive order of 1953 transferring such functions as integrating research and development, coordinating procurement and translating strategic plans into industrial requirements, from boards within the department to the Secretary of Defense, is an example of the former.

Could anything be done to strengthen the institutions of control? Some interesting suggestions in this connection were offered by the Research and Policy Committee of the Committee on Economic Development in December 1949. Among other things, it suggested the addition of three full-time civilian members to NSC without other governmental responsibilities, and the strengthening of the Secretary of Defense. The latter proposal has been attempted, the former not, undoubtedly in part because of the argument against participation in policy formation by persons not responsible for its execution." [16]

With respect to Congress' role, the Committee recommended the establishment of a Joint Congressional Committee on National Security, made up of members of all Congressional committees affected, to provide that organizational counterpart to NSC now lacking. As for public influence on security matters, it is suggested that one full-time member of NSC be responsible for a continuous flow of information concerning NSC activities to the people. Regardless of what institutional changes are introduced, civilian control in the development of military policy faces a number of obstacles resulting from the crisis we face, the developments of science, and the new status of the mili-

[16] "Civilian Control or Militarism," Statement by the Research and Policy Committee of the Committee on Economic Development. Reprinted in *U.S. News and World Report*, Vol. 27 (December 23, 1949), pp. 36-43. The argument against increasing NSC membership is found in Cutler, *op. cit.*

tary. The general nature of the problems will be indicated, followed by a case study illustrative of many of them.

The new technology

On August 5, 1945, the word "mushroom" to most people was a noun connotative of steaks and gravy. On August 16, it became an adjective, descriptive of a cloud, connotative of unparalleled, almost inconceivable, destruction. Since that time a considerable portion of our national resources, material and human, have been expended in the development of nuclear military weapons large and small. Nor has technological research and development been confined to the explosive power of nuclear weapons; of necessity a great deal of attention has been paid to the means of delivery of nuclear and conventional warheads, as well as the use of nuclear power to propel war craft.

The basic problem raised by this new technology is whether our policies, military and/or foreign, have in fact become the consequences of, rather than the controlling factor in, technology. More specifically, the new technology raises questions concerning military strategy, the strain on our internal economy, the foreign policies we pursue, and the logic of our military organization. Questions that are new, terrifying, and complex—but questions we cannot escape.

Secrecy

Closely connected with the problems of the new technology is the attendant question of the great secrecy needed in developing weapons. This has at least two important consequences. (1) It means that effective debate on policy alternatives even by Congress, much less by the public, is precluded—at least to the extent that policies themselves are determined by our military capabilities. (2) It means an extensive elaboration of governmental controls to preserve secrecy, with a consequent limitation on individual liberties. The second point is perhaps best discussed as an aspect of the contemporary dangers to civil liberties generally. As an illustration of the first point, the decision to produce the hydrogen bomb was made solely within the executive branch; there was no public or even congressional consideration of this basic policy decision. If the decision were, in effect, merely one concerning the best way to carry out an already agreed upon policy, this fact would not be of crucial importance. But if this decision had important consequences for security policy generally and foreign policy specifically, as it did, then the necessity for secrecy meant

another increment in the wall separating policy-formation from popularly elected representatives of the people.

The growth of the military

It is perhaps difficult for a person who has grown to maturity since
the end of World War II to imagine a time when important military
leaders were not intimately concerned with fundamental policy decisions. Yet, as an aspect of the traditional role of the military,
admirals and generals were until recently few in number and outside
the main stream of American social, economic, and especially political
life. As a consequence partly of our new position in the world, partly
of the prestige gained during World War II, and partly of the kind of
training involved in the development of a professional military officer,
the military today has become very much a part of the warp and woof
of our society.

The current esteem in which military leaders are held has its roots
in our traditions as well. Even in the days when the military played
no significant role in the development of major public policies, it was
accepted as a kind of political axiom that the army won wars in the
field while the diplomats lost them at the conference table. Despite
the fact that men not only control but are controlled by events, the
resort to war carries with it implications of failure by the civilian states-
man and of need to call out the military to "solve the problem." As
General MacArthur put it: "When all other political means fail, you
then go to force; and when you do that, the balance of control, . . . the
main interest involved, the minute you reach the killing stage, is the
control of the military. . . . You have got to trust [the military] . . . at
that stage of the game when politics fails, and the military takes
over." [17]

As long as a situation in which "the military takes over" is considered the abnormal case, the implications of prestige are not very
important. But when the military becomes a vital factor in the formation of the crucially important public policies, this prestige has profound repercussions. Our fundamental policy of containment, for
example, was influenced in large measure by the then Joint Chiefs of
Staff. When this policy becomes the subject of sharp criticism on the
part of opponents of the Truman administration, what action seems
more natural than to call on the Chairman of JCS—General Omar
Bradley—to explain (that is, defend) that policy? But there were

[17] Quoted in Hoopes, *op. cit.*, pp. 225-26.

military men of equivalent prestige who disagreed with containment and favored the Gibraltar approach to security policy. It is just as understandable that the political opponents of President Truman call upon these military leaders to support their positión. Thus the spectacle of Senator Taft, supported by men like Generals MacArthur and Wedemeyer debating with the Truman administration, supported by General Bradley. What this means is that the military is now no longer confined to the rule of supplying expert advice concerning possible alternative policies ultimately made by civilians; it means they themselves have become politicized. By the growth of the military, then, we mean not only that military considerations have come to occupy a pre-eminent position in the councils of policy-making. We mean also that the military leaders have come to take an active role in the political debate concerning fundamental policy decisions. At least two dangers are inherent in this situation.

The military mind

One danger lies in the infusion into the democratic decision-making process of thought patterns that are essentially foreign to such a process at best and at worst undemocratic themselves. While there is no precise definition of "the military mind," the phrase itself indicates certain predispositions, inculcated by rigid training, that are inappropriate for forming public policy. Professors Richard Snyder and Edgar Furniss list five attributes that seemed to represent a consensus on just what the military mind involves:

(1) rigidity in thought and problem analysis—the rejection of new ideas and reliance on tradition rather than on lessons learned from recent experience; (2) inadequate weighting of nonmilitary factors in military problems and inability to understand complex politico-military relationships; (3) an authoritarian approach to most social issues and situations accompanied by a disrespect and disregard for civilian authority; (4) insulation from nonmilitary knowledge or anything beyond what is narrowly defined as militarily relevant; (5) judgment of policy goals and techniques primarily in terms of military force and total victory from total war. Clearly these qualities would rarely be found completely dominant in any one military leader. Rather they typify collective attributes which are shared in at least a minimum degree by all military personnel.

As those authors put it:

The problem which arises from inappropriate habits of military thought is twofold: first, to minimize and counterbalance such habits in the training and organization of the military; and second, to minimize the impact of such habits on the policy-making process.[18]

The military, in attempting to meet the first problem, has developed a number of schools where officers are trained in the political-economic aspects of international problems. This in itself, however, is no guarantee that military considerations will be tempered by appreciation of other factors involved in any situation. It might just as well produce officers who, because they understand the point of view of their civilian counterparts, are just that much more effective in persuading them to their viewpoint. The second problem is usually approached by strengthening civilian representation on important bodies—for example, the removal of the three service secretaries from NSC—or by buttressing civilian control over military leaders, as was done by the executive order in 1953. The efficacy of such attempts brings up the second danger resulting from the growth of the military.

Who defines reality?

What is sometimes forgotten in discussions of the military mind is that, while not all military men reveal the attitudes encompassed in the term, those attitudes are not confined to people who wear army or navy uniforms. It can hardly be overemphasized that policy formation is as much influenced by the picture of the problem in the policy makers' minds as by anything else. Given certain assumptions about the world, conclusions as to how to meet problems may follow as night follows day. But the important thing is, are those assumptions correct? If, in other words, such public debate on policy issues as does take place occurs within the context of essentially military analysis on the world situation, alternative policies based on alternative assumptions are effectively precluded from consideration. The debate on containment versus Gibraltar mentioned above is a good example of this. In both cases the arguments rested on the views of military leaders as to what was the proper security policy for the United States. But if military considerations are all that underlie security policy, military policy and security policy are then equated, which we have seen is not necessarily the case, especially in time of peace. Containment versus Gibraltar is essentially an argument over the most effective way militarily to deal with the Soviet threat. What such an argument does is tend to ignore the fact that other, nonmilitary considerations, may be involved.

[18] Snyder and Furniss, *op. cit.*, p. 369.

To take a contemporary example: One difficult choice facing American policy-makers is that of our posture toward the situation in Algeria, where Arab nationalists have been in armed revolt against the French authorities. Starting with the assumption that basic to our whole security system is the cardinal factor of the Soviet military threat, the underlying rationale for supporting the French in Algeria follows logically enough. The argument in simplified form would run something like this: (1) the greatest danger we face in Europe is the danger of Soviet military aggression; (2) our best defense against the aggression is a military collective security arrangement—NATO; (3) any policy that jeopardizes NATO jeopardizes our whole security position in Europe; (4) France, already displeased to some extent with the rearmament of West Germany might consider withdrawal from NATO should the other Western powers, and particularly the United States, espouse the cause of Arab nationalism in Algeria; (5) however much we would like to do otherwise, the United States must support the French position. Once the assumption of (1) is accepted, (5) follows logically enough.

But is the greatest threat to our over all security the danger of overt Soviet military aggression? It is at least arguable that one could start with an entirely different first premise. For example, take the assumption that the most important complex of problems of our age is not that of the cold war, but the political, social, and economic revolutions among the traditionally underprivileged peoples of the world. Since World War II the great continents of Asia and Africa have been boiling with political and economic unrest. And in any competitive struggle between East and West, it is the "grey" area of the world—Southern Asia, from Viet Nam to Syria, and Africa—that will ultimately determine the course of history. It is precisely in this grey area that the revolution of rising expectations—political, social, and economic—is in full force. Thus this revolution of rising expectations will affect the cold war—according to this assumption—more than it will be affected by it. From this it follows that, while we cannot afford to let down our guard against the possibility of overt Soviet military aggression, the crucial problems are political (assuring that nationalism takes the form of liberal-western nationalism), economic (viable economies, to which the necessary repressions in the Soviet system do not appeal) and social (promotion of equality of status of the yellow, brown, and black-skinned peoples with that of the white). This means that wherever the revolution of rising expectations is a factor, the United

States *must* be on the side of the revolutionists, attempting to do what it can to direct the revolution along the lines of liberal democracy. Therefore, we must do everything in our power to promote the legitimate aspirations of the Algerian Arabs.

Notice that in neither case does one set of considerations monopolize the basis of policy. No proponent of the military analysis would discount the revolution of rising expectations; no opponent of such an analysis would say the Soviets do not represent a military threat. The question is one of emphasis. For while military and political considerations are inextricably bound up with one another, there is a difference between the military implications of a foreign policy, and the political implications of a military policy. The real point here is not that either of these alternative ways of picturing the world we live in is "right" and the other "wrong." Rather it is that as long as essentially military assumptions underlie our security policy, nonmilitary approaches may not even be discussed. Herein lies the greatest danger consequent on the growth of the military in authority and prestige: for if the civilian leaders of government, executive and congressional, accept the essentially military assumptions about the problems of security policy, civilian "control" is no longer control in any meaningful sense. And if the people generally accept it, the chances of ever effecting control are remote indeed. Again it is not a question of who is "right" or "wrong" in a particular situation. The real question is who is likely ultimately to make the better decisions: statesmen or soldiers?

There are at least two reasons for the tendency in our society to accept the military picture of reality. The first, mentioned in another connection, is the matter of prestige. No other group of experts, with the possible exception of the physical scientists, has anywhere near the prestige of the military. If, for example, a group of distinguished economists and political scientists should argue for increased economic aid, even at the expense of military build-up, and this should be opposed by military leaders on the grounds that such a shift in emphasis might jeopardize our "security," there is little doubt which group of experts would be listened to. The military has, in contemporary parlance, "paid off"; economists and political scientists have yet to demonstrate their utility to the same degree.

Secondly, there is a natural enough tendency for any public official, military or civilian, to "play it safe." Going back to our example of Algeria, the military analysis is strictly in terms of the here and now. There are Soviet divisions in Western Europe; the Soviets have nuclear weapons; military weakness anywhere along the line may prove fatal. On the other hand, the potential decisiveness of the "grey" areas of the world is just that: *potential*. We have no way of knowing what the next ten or even five years will bring in the form of political, economic, or social change in those areas. Support of Arab nationalism can be justified only in vague terms of what the world will be like in the future; support for France is an immediate military necessity. Can we afford to gamble military security for long-run political gain? But while such considerations may be understandable, they should not becloud the fact that the vague, long range, nonmilitary factors are those which may be crucial.

NATIONAL SECURITY: POLICIES AND ALTERNATIVES

When the Eisenhower administration took office in January, 1953, one of its first concerns was a re-examination of our total national security program as it had evolved under President Truman. The resulting proposals, dubbed almost immediately the "New Look," provide excellent illustrations of the kinds of problems involved in developing security policy, as well as a graphic example of the interconnection between foreign and military policies and domestic capabilities. For the New Look was announced by the Secretary of State, defended in terms of military strategy, and based largely on domestic economic considerations.

Much of the debate surrounding the New Look tended to obfuscate some of the main issues involved. This was true for at least three reasons: (1) to the extent that it implied criticism of the Truman administration's policies it brought forth arguments from those associated with that administration, not excluding the former president himself; this meant of course that the issue became involved in the general Republican versus Democratic political hassle; (2) since January, 1955, the Eisenhower administration has been faced with a Democratically controlled Congress, which means that the budgetary underpinnings of the New Look face congressional examination that, by natural party inclination, would be unsympathetic; and (3) the New Look became involved in the presidential campaign of 1956, and presidential campaigns are not notable for the calmness of debate and the measured consideration of proposals. But this obfuscation itself is important; for, to the extent that policy proposals are debated before Congress and the electorate, one must expect the lack of precise issues, logical arguments, and positions defended with no thought to party considerations. Partisan politics is democratic politics, and to expect major policy issues to be formulated in a "nonpolitical" atmosphere is either to demand the impossible or to remove the issues from democratic processes.

"More Bang for a Buck"

Table 4.1 provides ample evidence of the ever-increasing strain on our economy resulting from defense expenditures (figures rounded off to nearest billion):

TABLE 4.1

FISCAL YEAR

(Billions of Dollars)

	1949	1950	1951	1952	1953	1954	1955	1956	1957	1958
Total budget receipts	38	36	48	61	65	65	60	68	71	74
Total national security expenditures	13	13	22	44	50	47	41	41	41	43

Based on a chart in *The New York Times,* January 17, 1957.

It should be noticed that while the Korean fighting accounted for a tremendous increase in spending, armistice did not produce a rapid decrease in the defense budget. Rather, it was felt by the Truman administration that Korea should teach us a lesson: we cannot rely on our atomic superiority alone to prevent aggression. In the words of former Secretary of State Acheson:

> There [Korea] the attack had to be met—and was met—on the ground where it occurred. And this, in turn, required the raising, equipping, supplying and training of forces, our own and others, which could do this.
>
> So a sound military program . . . requires [in addition to a great atomic striking force] forces that can deal on the spot with lesser aggressions which, if unchecked would go far to undermine the integrity, and certainly the power, of the free world. . . .
>
> Now the military program we have been discussing cannot be acquired on the cheap. It is very expensive indeed.[19]

But do we need, or are we *able,* to stand that expense? Essentially, the New Look, recommended by the Joint Chiefs of Staff and approved by the National Security Council, was a military program designed to ensure national security at a bearable cost. Three things

[19] From "Instant Retaliation: the Debate Continued," *New York Times Magazine* (March 28, 1954), p. 13 ff. Reprinted, in part, in Herbert L. Marx, Jr. (ed.), *Defense and National Security* (The Reference Shelf, Vol. 26, No. 6), pp. 98-103.

were involved: (1) reshaping our military power around our air-atomic advantage; (2) gradually disengaging American forces from exposed positions; (3) arriving at a stabilized budget that our economy could be reasonably expected to bear over the long haul. As Secretary of Defense Wilson put it, "The increasing capabilities of new weapons and new techniques are sweeping into discard the practice of gauging military strength solely by count of men, and a census of ships, tanks, guns and planes." [20] By gearing our defense program to the technological revolution, the ever-mounting burden of armaments could be diminished. In terms of the relationship of military policy and our economy, then, what the New Look meant was that it was unnecessary, if not impossible, to attempt to create and maintain large conventional armies and navies of the World War II variety as well as a nuclear striking force. Rather, by the judicious use of the weapons our technological superiority was producing, we could develop both strategic and tactical striking forces at greatly reduced cost. Table 4.2 indicates the budgetary manifestations of this, as the New Look was proposed for fiscal 1955.

TABLE 4.2

FISCAL YEARS

(Approximate Billions of Dollars)

	1949	1950	1951	1952	1953	1954	1955	1956	1957	1958
Army	5.2	4.0	7.5	15.6	16.2	12.9	8.9	8.7	8.6	9.1
Navy	4.4	4.1	5.6	10.1	11.9	11.3	9.7	9.7	9.7	10.3
Air Force	1.8	3.6	6.4	12.7	15.1	15.6	16.4	16.5	16.9	17.5

Based on a chart in *The New York Times,* January 17, 1957.

The underlying question concerning the budget of the New Look is, is it enough? When Congressmen hold hearings on these budget proposals they do not confine themselves to listening to the civilian members of the administration, they also call in military leaders. And while it would border on insubordination for an admiral or general to disagree publicly with the budget proposals, Congressmen on several occasions have almost urged the military leaders to ask for more. In the 1956 hearings, for example, after the Air Force Chief of Staff, General Nathan Twining admitted that the budget "meets only our essential needs on a minimum basis," one Congressman asked if there

[20] From "Wilson Explains Program to Gain Maximum Defense Without Waste," *New York Herald Tribune* (October 12, 1954). Reprinted, in part, Marx, *op. cit.,* pp. 39-44.

was anything the matter. "Can it be corrected by dollars? If it can be, why have you not got them? If there is anything the matter with you this Congress will give you the dollars. You know it. You are literally and figuratively the white-haired boy here." General Twining replied, "We can always use more dollars," [21] and, in fact, the Congress eventually appropriated around $900 millions for the Air Force over and above the original budget request.

What this illustrates is a basic dilemma faced by Congress: how can it be sure that economies in defense are not risking national security? They have the word of the Joint Chiefs of Staff, but this word is given in the context of two important considerations. As Admiral Radford, former Chairman of JCS, has said, it is not the business of JCS to concern itself with fiscal policy. Secondly, it is fundamental to the Eisenhower program that defense effort should be on a "pay as you go basis." With this in mind it is not difficult to see how Congressmen, especially Democratic congressmen in the case of the New Look, may argue that fiscal policies, a desire to balance the budget, have determined military strategy rather than vice-versa. And how can any Congressman, in the absence of expertise and military information, be blamed for wanting to "play it safe." As the above episode illustrates, Congressional controls on the military through control of the budget may well have the opposite effect from that intended. It may mean that Congress will act as a friendly court of last resort for military men, whose initial budget estimates have been cut substantially by their civilian chiefs.

One other difficulty in attempting to arrive at maximum security at a price we can afford is that of rapid technological change. Once given air-atomic weapons as the nucleus around which our defense effort revolves, what happens when scientific research demonstrates the possibilities of intermediate and long-range missiles replacing aircraft? Inevitably, development of missiles must be pushed, but this can be very costly, especially when each service has its own missile program. In part the substantial increases in the budget proposals for all three services for fiscal 1958 results from the current emphasis on missile development, which costs in the billions of dollars. If the New Look offers the advantage of flexibility in military policy, the cost of that flexibility is necessarily high.

[21] *Department of Defense Appropriations for 1957*, Hearings, U.S. House Subcommittee on Appropriations, 84th Congress, 1st sess. (Washington, D.C.: U.S. Government Printing Office, 1956), pp. 764, 769.

Balanced forces versus air-atomic power

While critics of the New Look argued that it was a program designed to make big wars out of small ones because it necessarily relied on nuclear air attacks as the deterrent of aggression, administration leaders at all times took pains to point out that this was not necessarily the case. Rather, as Admiral Radford asserted, it is ". . . a matter of emphasis. We are putting emphasis on our advantages—our long suits —in other words, on modern air and naval power, on new weapons, on a highly mobile and offensively equipped strategic reserve." [22] But if that was true in principle, there were important people who argued that in practice too much reliance was being placed on "our long suits," which if they were effective would not be used. These important people were represented in the military by Army leaders, for both the Air Force and Navy were involved in air-atomic strategy. The Army argument was that with Russian development of air-atomic power roughly equivalent to our own, a state of "mutual deterrence" would be reached. Neither side could afford an all-out atomic assault on the other for fear of retaliation. In such a situation, the military threat was one of potential conflict between ground forces. This meant that a wise military policy would include emphasis on manpower, armed with tactical nuclear weapons as well as the conventional type.

Typical of such opinions were those expressed by former General Matthew Ridgway, upon his retirement, after having served as Army Chief of Staff on the JCS during the first two years of the Eisenhower administration. In a letter to the Secretary of Defense he wrote:

> . . . with [the] improvement of Soviet air defense capability, the United States nuclear-air superiority will have lost most of its present significance.
>
> . . . military power . . . must be real and apparent to all concerned, and it must be capable of being applied promptly, selectively and with the degree of violence appropriate to the occasion.
>
> It is my view that the commitments which the United States has pledged create a positive requirement for an immediately available mobile joint military force of hard hitting character in which the versatility of the whole is emphasized and the preponderance of any one part is de-emphasized.
>
> While a "mobile ready force" element is provided for in published policy statements, the actual development of a mobile ready force must

[22] From a statement made before the Senate Foreign Relations Committee on April 14, 1954. Reprinted in Marx, *op. cit.,* pp. 58-59.

[at present] compete with increasingly emphasized continental defense, and with, in my opinion, overemphasized nuclear-air requirements. . . .[23]

The question of emphasis on air-atomic power is not the only important military implication of the New Look. A little-discussed, but equally important, question concerns the implications of centering a military effort around atomic weapons of any variety. The problem here is whether it will ever be possible to fight a *local* atomic war. While it is possible in theory to make a distinction between tactical and strategic nuclear weapons, it can be argued that once such weapons have been used, the side that begins to lose in any conflict will naturally resort to larger and larger warheads; this will in turn be reciprocated by the initially winning side until the ultimate weapon, the thermonuclear bomb, will be called upon. The logic of this argument is historically buttressed by the concept of fighting until unconditional surrender by the opposition has been obtained, a concept thoroughly ingrained in twentieth century thinking by both of the world wars.

The New Look and foreign policy

There is probably no better contemporary illustration of the relationship of foreign and military policies than the questions raised about the New Look. As that program related to American foreign policy it was spelled out in a now famous address to the Council on Foreign Relations on January 12, 1954, by Secretary of State John Foster Dulles. After pointing out that attempting to meet local Communist aggression on its own terms, as in Korea, meant that we were accepting the enemy's superiority in manpower and not bringing our superior technology to bear, the Secretary went on to say:

> . . . Local defense will always be important. But there is no local defense which alone will contain the mighty landpower of the Communist world. Local defense must be reinforced by the further deterrent of massive retaliatory power. A potential aggressor must know that he cannot always prescribe battle conditions that suit him. . . .
>
> The way to deter aggression is for the free community to be willing and able to respond vigorously at places and with means of its own choosing.
>
> So long as our basic policy concepts were unclear, our military leaders could not be selective in building our miltary power. If an enemy could pick his time and place and method of warfare—and if our policy was to remain the traditional one of meeting aggression by direct and

[23] The letter is reprinted in Edgar S. Furniss, Jr. (ed.), *American Military Policy* (New York: Rinehart and Co., Inc., 1957), pp. 141-48.

local opposition—then we needed to be ready to fight in the Arctic and in the Tropics; and in Asia, the Near East, and in Europe, by sea, by land, and by air; with old weapons and with new weapons.

. . . This could not be continued for long without grave budgetary, economic, and social consequences.

. . . [The New Look means that henceforth we shall] depend primarily upon a great capacity to retaliate, instantly, by means and at places of our own choosing. That permits a selection of military means instead of a multiplication of means.[24]

The initial question raised by the speech was its real meaning. Was the United States pinning its defense against any and all forms of aggression on massive retaliation by our Strategic Air Command, or was massive retaliation, as the Secretary stated in a subsequent interview, a means of supplementing local defense? While there has been a good deal of speculation on this point, the continued emphasis on air-nuclear weapons, coupled with the explanatory remarks of the Secretary of State himself, seemed to mean that the chief instruments of deterrence would be the Strategic Aid Command and its naval counterpart.[25]

To the extent that "massive retaliation" does imply the possibility of strategic nuclear bombing as the chief deterrent to aggression, important questions are raised for foreign as well as military policy.

The first of these concerns credibility. If strategic bombing is going to deter an aggressor, he must be convinced that in fact strategic bombing will follow aggression. And if aggression has so far not resulted in the use of nuclear weapons, as it did not, for example, in Korea, will it in the future? Relevant to this question is the fact that the Soviet Union is increasing *its* capacity for massive retaliation, and if nuclear weapons were not used when the United States had a clear superiority will they be used at a time when Russia is capable of strategic bombing of the United States?

This notion of mutual thermo-nuclear capability has led a number

[24] The transcript of the entire speech may be found in *United States Department of State Bulletin*, Vol. 30 (January 25, 1954), pp. 107-10.

[25] In a press conference following his "massive retaliation" speech Secretary Dulles is reported to have said, "What I meant . . . was that if you have the capacity to strike an aggressor at the points which will hurt him, the deterrent power of that is sufficient so that you do not need to have local defense all around the twenty-thousand-mile perimeter of the orbit of the Soviet world because your deterrent power, to a large extent, reinforces your local power so that you do not have to depend upon having in place forces-in-being sufficient to stop an attack in its tracks anywhere where it could occur because you rely primarily upon deterring that attack, not necessarily upon being able to stop it." Text of the press conference on March 16, 1954, reprinted in part, Marx, *op. cit.*, pp. 64-71.

of people to argue that strategic bombing, while remaining a mutual deterrent to all-out nuclear war, will become less and less effective as a deterrent to local aggressions of the Korean variety. Suppose tomorrow, they say, the Soviets were to invade Pakistan. The basic question facing the United States would be: is the defense of Pakistan sufficient to retaliate massively—that is with nuclear warheads—against the Soviet Union, when we know the Soviet Union can retaliate massively against us? As one student of military policy has put it, the corollary to massive retaliation is simply that there is no alternative to peace.[26] This means that we would either have to choose some policy other than massive retaliation or let Pakistan fall to the Soviet Union.

In terms of foreign policy, then, massive retaliation—the doctrinal manifestation of the New Look—raises questions as to our capacity for flexibility in dealing with the Soviet Union. If our policy of containment means resistance to Soviet encroachments on the non-Communist world, but if our chief weapon of resistance is massive retaliation (which the Russians are able to reciprocate), any encroachment must result in success for the aggressor, or all-out nuclear war, or abandonment of massive retaliation, the weapon on which we are staking our policy. Critics of the policy have pointed to Korea, Indo-China, and lately Hungary as precisely the kind of situation that presents problems of foreign policy to which, in view of our reliance on massive retaliation, we cannot find suitable answers. Succinctly, the argument against massive retaliation as it affects foreign policy is that (1) foreign policy to be effective must be backed by military power; (2) reliance on thermo-nuclear power, in the face of Soviet possession of it, means that in any negotiations with the Soviet Union we deal either from weakness or must be prepared to risk total nuclear war; (3) total nuclear war will not be resorted to in any but the gravest emergencies; (4) as a result we have little or no basis of power for negotiating on issues of less than the gravest emergencies—for example, Korea, Indo-China, Hungary, or the Middle East.

Graduated deterrence

A number of students, concerned with the implications of the policy of massive retaliation, have addressed themselves to the problem of how to deal with these issues that do not warrant the use of the Strategic Air Command. If, in other words, mutual nuclear deterrence will

[26] See the article by Henry A. Kissinger, "Force and Diplomacy in the Nuclear Age," *Foreign Affairs*, Vol. 34 (April, 1956), pp. 349-66.

allow the Communists to nibble the West to death with local actions on the perimeter of our containment line, how can we deal with the nibbles?

One suggested line of thought in this connection is the development of the concept of graduated deterrence.[27] This involves the notion, essentially, of making the punishment fit the crime. It accepts two premises underlying the New Look: (1) capability for massive retaliation is fundamentally necessary, and (2) we should use our technological superiority to offset the manpower advantages of the Communists. With respect to massive retaliation, it seems obvious that it must be retained as the ultimate deterrent to an all-out nuclear attack; the point is that, of necessity, it is limited to that function. For local situations the doctrine of graduated deterrence requires that the West employ sufficient military power to deter or defeat any aggression, short of precipitating an all-out conflict. This means creating a distinction between *tactical* and *strategic* nuclear weapons, and applying, or threatening to apply, nuclear weapons only to the point of successfully meeting the local challenge.

Implicit in this doctrine is the concept of limited war. If all wars must be fought to "victory"—that is, unconditional surrender—then tactical nuclear conflict will ultimately result in all-out nuclear war as the enemy is pushed further and further into defeat. Admittedly, the notion that "in war there is no substitute for victory" would be difficult to remove from the American mind—as witness the tremendous dissatisfaction with the ultimate turn of events in Korea. But if local aggression is to be met on American terms, with weapons based on our technological advancement, if we are not to try to meet manpower solely with manpower, and if we are to prevent little wars from turning into big wars, the proponents of graduated deterrence would say that limited wars, fought for specific and limited purposes, must become part and parcel of American thinking.

Another difficulty with the doctrine of graduated deterrence concerns the feasibility of realistically distinguishing between tactical and strategic nuclear weapons. Suppose, for example, the Communists in

[27] For discussion of this concept see Rear Admiral Sir Anthony Buzzard, "Massive Retaliation and Graduated Deterrence," *World Politics,* Vol. 8 (January, 1956), pp. 228-37; Henry A. Kissinger, "Military Policy and the Defense of the Grey Areas," *Foreign Affairs,* Vol. 33 (April, 1955), pp. 416-28, as well as his article cited above; Paul Nitze, "Atoms, Strategy and Policy," *Foreign Affairs,* Vol. 34 (January, 1956), pp. 187-98; and William Kaufmann (ed.), *Military Policy and National Security* (Princeton, N. J.: Princeton University Press, 1956), pp. 12-38.

Viet Minh invade Viet Nam. Clearly the use of atomic cannons, where practicable, against the invading armies would be considered tactical; but what about air strikes with low kiloton atomic bombs against their bases of supply in northern Viet Minh; or, if they were supplied with Chinese materiel, what about similar air strikes on China? Would the latter be tactical or strategic? If we thought of them as tactical, would the Chinese? Might not they in turn bomb bases in Formosa, leading to further American bombing of China, possibly leading to Russian entry into the conflagration? The answer is simply that it is certainly possible; but, assuming that *both* East and West want at almost any cost to avoid all-out nuclear war, it seems just as logical to argue that both sides could develop rules for a "tactical atomic game" in future "brush-fires" as they did for convential weapons in Korea.

By no means all the relevant questions concerning the New Look have been raised in this discussion; for example, there are also the questions of its applicability to internal revolutions inspired by Communism, or how it affects America's relations with other members of the Western coalition. But the discussion does point to some fundamental aspects of national security policy. Regardless of whether massive retaliation alone, graduated deterrence, or some other alternative doctrine is developed in the future, it is clear that military and foreign policies are mutually interdependent. This means that the development of military doctrine that incorporates meaningfully the great and continuing technological advances of our time and the meshing of that doctrine with the goals of our foreign policy is one of the great, if not the greatest, challenges facing our country today. Finally, whether or not this challenge can be met depends ultimately on the capacity and the willingness of the nation as a whole to underwrite a rational national security policy.

THE ROLE OF THE MILITARY IN A DEMOCRATIC SOCIETY

Implicit in this challenge is the question of how best to integrate the military into our policy-making processes. This involves the recognition of some basic points that deserve re-emphasis.

The new role of the military

However regrettable it may be from the point of view of the traditional place of military men and military thinking in American society, it seems an inescapable corollary of the revolutionary transformation of America's position in the world that the military have played and will continue to play a central role in public affairs.

Certainly it is clear that our national security constitutes one of the crucial problems with which our government is faced. And it is just as clear that Americans can no longer afford to await the coming of an international holocaust before preparing for it, as we have been so prone to do in the past. What the atomic age means, if it means anything, is that the preservation of our security is an everyday, continuing task of *preventing* all out war, while at the same time deterring local aggression. Such a job calls for preparedness above all; preparedness in terms of military strategy and power. This in turn means that military men and military considerations must play an important part in the development of policy.

Military security and democratic values

To say that the military is important, however, is not to say it should be predominant. In the broadest sense the preservation of our national security does not mean only the military defense of the United States; it means also the preservation of values held by Americans, preeminent among which is liberty. In these terms, the risk implicit in the new role of the military is that in our excessive concern with physical security, we will permit the militarizing of our society to the point of undermining the liberties that lie at the basis of that society. This danger has been expressed in terms of the trend toward the garrison state, a state in which all other values are subordinate to the requirements of military security. As Professor Harold Lasswell has written:

> . . . To militarize is to governmentalize. It is also to centralize. To centralize is to enhance the effective control of the executive over decisions, and thereby to reduce the control exercised by courts and legislatures. To centralize is to enhance the role of the military in the allocation of national resources. Continuing fear of external attack sustains an atmosphere of distrust that finds expression in spy hunts directed against fellow officials and fellow citizens. Outspoken criticism of official measures launched for national defense is more and more resented as unpatriotic and subversive of the common good. The community at large, therefore, acquiesces in denials of freedom that go beyond the technical requirements of military security.[28]

[28] Harold Lasswell, "Does the Garrison State Threaten Civil Rights?" *The Annals,* Vol. 275 (May, 1951), p. 111.

Further, this trend toward the garrison state is induced every bit as much by the tendency to view the world through military lenses as it is by having military men in high places.

Recently this concern with the increasing militarization of our society has itself evoked criticism. If over-concern with security may result in the garrison state, it is argued, over-concern with the preservation of liberal democratic values jeopardizes our very survival. "Previously the primary question was: what pattern of civil-military relations is most compatible with American liberal democratic values? Now this has been supplanted by the more important issue: what pattern of civil-military relations will best maintain the security of the American nation." [29]

Striking the balance

Preoccupation with democratic controls may blind us to the very real need for considering strategic-military factors in our foreign policy. But to say this is not to say that such factors are the *only* relevant ones, or in many cases even the predominant ones—the preservation of our national security includes values as well as territory. If we can no longer afford to ignore military considerations, the answer now is not to ignore everything else. If there is a potential conflict between democratic values and military requirements, surely we can afford neither to destroy the values nor ignore the requirements. Rather it is incumbent upon us to develop the capacity for weaving the military fiber into the cloth of our total security policy, remembering always that the military is properly the servant and not the master of our society.

BIBLIOGRAPHICAL NOTE

The new role of the military in American public affairs is considered in Samuel P. Huntington, *The Soldier and the State: The Theory and Politics of Civil-Military Relations,* 1957, and Arthur A. Ekirch, Jr., *The Civilian and the Military,* 1956.

As the title indicates, Alfred Vagts, *Defense and Diplomacy: The Soldier and the Conduct of Foreign Relations,* 1956, devotes considerable attention to the role of the military in the development of foreign policy in the form of a historical analysis.

The chapter, "The Role of Military Institutions and Agencies in American Foreign Policy," in Richard C. Snyder and Edgar S. Furniss, Jr.,

[29] Samuel P. Huntington, *The Soldier and the State: The Theory and Politics of Civil-Military Relations* (Cambridge: The Belknap Press of Harvard University Press, 1957), p. 3.

American Foreign Policy: Formulation, Principles, and Programs, 1954, is an excellent short analysis of contemporary problems concerning the role of the military.

William W. Kaufmann, ed., *Military Policy and National Security,* 1956, and Edgar S. Furniss, Jr., *American Military Policy,* 1957, are selections of essays and readings, respectively, that deal with contemporary problems of military policy.

Walter Millis, *Arms and Men: Study in American Military History,* 1956, after relating American military history, discusses the impact of atomic weapons on war.

Herbert L. Marx, Jr., ed., "Defense and National Security," *The Reference Shelf, Vol. 26, No. 6,* 1955, is a selection of readings embracing our contemporary defense policies in terms of the New Look, our relations with our allies, and the new weapons.

The threat posed to individual freedom by the new role of the military, and what can be done about that threat, is the subject of Harold D. Lasswell, *National Security and Individual Freedom,* 1950.

5. ROBERT H. SALISBURY

Transportation

PEOPLE who talk about transportation often talk of "the transportation industry," "the transportation problem," and propose "the transportation policy" for the future. This attitude, in which all persons and groups engaged in transportation are thought of as performing the same economic function and therefore as a single monolithic group, has typified much of the debate on policy in the field. But even a cursory examination of the industry reveals that there is not one transportation industry but several. Railroaders, truckers, airlines, and bus companies by no means have identical interests. On the contrary, they behave according to different economic imperatives, they compete with varying degrees of vigor both across industry lines (for example, trucks versus railroads) and within given industries (for example, TWA versus Eastern Airlines), and they seek very different policy goals through government. The conflicts are numerous and shifting and involve not only various interests within transportation but also other segments of the society.

Thus in order to understand transportation *policies* we must look at transportation *politics*—the conflicts of interests that give rise to policy demands. And to understand the interests involved in transportation politics, we must understand the economic forces that shape the interests at stake. If the emphasis in this discussion is on economic matters, it is because these are the factors of which transportation politics is made.

TRANSPORTATION ECONOMICS AND POLITICS

The size of the transportation industries in comparison with the rest of the economy is deceptive. Only the railroads loom large in the American economy in terms of assets or employees. But size does not determine the political significance of economic activity so much as the relationships between particular economic and social groups. In this respect the significance of the transportation industries can hardly be overstated. Perhaps no other single economic function is more central to the entire economic life of a people so mobile and technically interdependent as Americans. The size and character of the political and social community is much dependent upon the degree to which means of transportation and communication break down physical isolation and promote mobility of people and goods. The location and development of centers of trade and industry are closely related to the available transport facilities. Rivers and harbors, mountain passes and, in modern times, rail lines and highways have had incalculable consequences for every aspect of the social system.

Further, as an economic system reaches the stages of industrialization of the United States—marked by extreme mobility of persons and goods and incredibly complex interdependence of millions of people and billions of dollars worth of products—the system of transportation is of first importance to all members of the society. Thus public concern with transportation is bound to increase as the society grows more complex, and the result of increasing concern is seen in the growth of governmental policy.

"Consumers" of transportation

Since transportation costs are also an important factor in the costs (and thus the profits) of virtually all businesses, the size of these costs will be a matter of direct and deeply felt concern to many people. If a user of steel should find the price of steel too high, he may sometimes be able to substitute aluminum or wood. But the user of transportation services is usually unable to find alternatives. Either he ships his products to market or he does not sell them. In the past there was typically only one seller of transportation service available. The railroad was so far superior to the horse that a shipper had no real choice.

And if there was only one railroad available, then the shipper was at its mercy in a very real sense. For many decades in the United States there was a strong tendency toward railroad monopoly of transportation, particularly in areas outside the larger cities. Although the situation has been substantially changed by the rise of motor and air transportation, the earlier tendency toward monopoly has been a major factor explaining why shippers sought early to use *political* power to control transportation costs while relying more upon *economic* power to secure lower costs on raw materials and labor.

Farmers have been particularly vulnerable to railroad power. Specialized commercial farming, in which each farmer grows one or a few crops to be sold for cash in the market, depends upon transportation facilities for its commercial success in a way that few other industries do. Many agricultural crops are perishable if they cannot be taken to market quickly. Transportation is a principal item of cost to a farmer who may provide his own labor but who cannot carry his own cattle to market. The transportation industries loomed as industrial giants against the solitary farmer, and the latter often felt at the mercy of the railroad so far as economic bargaining power was concerned. The prices received by farmers tended to fluctuate widely according to weather and other factors beyond the farmer's control, but rail rates did not fluctuate in similar fashion. Thus, if a bumper crop caused a decline in the price of wheat while rail rates remained steady, the farmer might suffer a severe loss—a loss due, in part, to the railroads.

But inequality in the economy might be redressed in the political arena. There, greater numbers and general rural over-representation could give farmers the opportunity to control transportation costs that they could not control through economic bargaining. The result was that the early farmer organizations, such as the Granger movement, had as a central goal the control of transportation rates. The establishment of regulatory commissions at state and national levels came about largely as the result of efforts by the agricultural protest groups. The attempt to solve farm problems by regulating rates gave way in later years to the more fundamental goal of gaining governmental support for farm prices. The rise of competition in transportation also has made rate regulation less important to farmers and indeed to most shippers. It is important to recognize, however, that the earlier conflicts over transportation—roughly, those prior to the first World

War—were between the railroads and their allies on the one hand, and the shipper groups, particularly farm groups, on the other. Since that time, however, and more relevant for our concerns, the conflicts have been largely among various groups *within* the transportation industries.

In explaining the extensive political action concerning transportation, one other general factor should be mentioned. If transportation is basic to the economy in peacetime, it is doubly so in war. Since military affairs are preeminently a governmental responsibility, in time of military stress governmental action is almost inevitably directed toward the transportation industries. The first World War, particularly, brought significant government action in transportation in the form of government seizure and operation of the railroad system which had broken down in the attempt to meet wartime demands.

The interest groups

Transportation politics involves the interests of a wide range of groups which, either because of direct concern or because of alliances with transport groups, devote much effort toward influencing public-transport policy. These groups cannot all be dealt with at length, but it is well to understand the nature and functions of the more significant ones.

Carrier Organizations. The organized mechanisms through which the various industries speak are trade associations. The railroads have formed the most comprehensive of these: the Association of American Railroads, which includes railroad firms doing 97 per cent of the business in North America (including Canada and Mexico). The present AAR was established in 1934 through a merger of several other more specialized organizations. It provides many services to the industry through research into common problems, through technical assistance of many kinds, by enhancing cooperation among various companies in handling such joint problems as the use of freight cars, and by mobilizing the resources of the industry to meet emergencies. The AAR also appears to provide the machinery through which disputes between rail companies can be resolved and competition moderated. Control of the AAR tends to be oligarchic, with effective power wielded by eastern roads.[1]

[1] See John Schott, *The Transportation Monopoly* (Washington, D.C.; Public Affairs Press, 1944).

On the directly political front, the AAR *is* the railroad industry. The Association is regularly among the leaders in reported expenditures for lobbying, and it carries on broad gauge propaganda campaigns on behalf of the railroad point of view. The AAR is the chief spokesman for the railroad interests on matters of public policy. It has also provided the machinery for negotiating alliances with other business interests, notably through the Shipper Advisory Boards formed to enable railroads and shippers to work out their mutual problems. Through such regular contacts the railroads have improved their channels of communication with their "natural enemies" and have thus strengthened their political position vis-a-vis their main antagonists, the rival carriers.

The motor carriers have also established an association linking the major firms in their industry, the American Trucking Associations.[2] This federation of state associations was formed in 1933 to do for the motor carriers the same sort of task that the AAR does for the railroads. A wide variety of types of motor carriers are eligible to join the ATA, but a much smaller proportion of those eligible has actually done so than in the case of the AAR. Motor transport is engaged in by firms ranging from very small—one truck and an owner-driver— to very large, and by many types of carriers: for example, common and contract, taxicabs and interstate trucks. Many smaller carriers, however, do not feel the need to carry on a broad campaign on the political front. Their chief competition comes not so much from railroads as from the large truckers who dominate the ATA; in turn, the large truckers have found one of their most persistent problems the control of rate-slashing by small truckers. As a result the ATA represents only a segment of the motor carrier industry,—the larger interstate truckers—although on questions of national policy it is clearly the most active segment.

Air carriers have established an even more exclusive organization, the Air Transport Association. Only scheduled airlines are eligible to belong, and the nonscheduled lines are excluded. Since one of the most vigorous disputes with respect to air carrier policy has been whether the "non-skeds" were to be allowed to operate, the position of the Air Transport Association has been one of far more involve-

---

[2] See *Hearings* before the Senate Special Committee to Investigate Political Activities, Lobbying, and Campaign Contributions, 84th Congress, 2nd Session, Vol. II, pp. 731-34.

ment in intra-industry disputes than is the case with other carrier organizations.[3]

The American Waterways Operators is the organization joining the water carriers plying the lake, river, and intercoastal water routes of the United States. Water transportation accounts for about one-sixth of the total ton-miles of shipping in the United States, but the political significance of water carriers is quite different from that of the other forms of transportation. Although water transportation is low in cost, it is slow and limited in the markets that it can serve. Much of the cargo transported by water is handled by private carriers, such as subsidiaries of steel or aluminum firms carrying raw materials to processing plants. Despite substantial federal aid to improve river and harbor facilities and local government help on port facilities, the business of water carriage has not been very profitable. The carriers themselves are not very strong, either economically or politically. The major political force supporting the interests of the water carriers has been the various local groups seeking federal money for rivers and harbors construction.

"Satellite" groups. Many other organizations are active in one phase or another of transportation policy. Any major policy battle will find impressive lists of organizations established along regional or state lines or on the basis of some specialized function supporting—or appearing to support—one or another of the major carrier groups. The labor organizations of each industry are also significant. Railroad brotherhoods may make wage demands on management and Teamsters may go on strike against trucking firms, but on questions of national transportation policy the labor group of each industry is generally found on the same side as management. Organizations such as the American Automobile Association and the Transportation Association of America frequently take positions on controversial transportation questions, and the latter, at least, is often referred to as a railroad "front" group.[4]

Shippers and suppliers. Industries in which transportation is a big part of total cost of products are often active in transportation politics. Indeed, as we have noted, it was these groups that provided much of the early impetus for regulation of railroads. These industries are typically those whose products are high in bulk and low in value, such as

[3] See Robert Bendiner. "The Rise and Fall of the Nonskeds," *The Reporter,* Vol. 16 (May 30, 1957), pp. 29-34.
[4] See Senate *Report* Number 26, pt. 2, 77th Congress, 1st Session (1941).

most farm products, coal, cement, and the like. Shipper interests have
also been organized along sectional lines. For example, Southern shippers tried to mobilize their political resources in an attempt to eliminate what they regarded as discrimination in rate structures.

Industries that supply products to the transportation industries also
have a considerable interest in the economic success of their customers.
Steel companies have an interest in the economic well-being of railroads as major users of steel. Coal producers also had a large stake
in the railroad industry, although the switch to diesel engines has
altered that relationship and brought oil companies into greater prominence. Airplane manufacturers are clearly interested in the airline industry, as is the automotive industry in the motor carriers. The relationships of these suppliers to transportation firms or with transportation politics are not always clear, since, for example, steel companies
both supply railroad equipment and ship steel on railroads, and in
addition are linked with some railroads through common financial
ties. Nevertheless, such groups are an important part of the total picture of transportation politics, and mentioning these connections at
least serves to emphasize the fact that these issues involve broad and
diverse interests embracing much of the economy of the nation.

Financial control groups. Of very considerable importance in the
group struggles over transport policy, especially when the railroads are
involved, are what may be called financial control groups.[5] These
groups include (1) persons in positions to make vital decisions, who
(2) are associated primarily with financial institutions such as banks
or investment houses rather than with transportation firms as such. In
the railroad industry the need for large capital investment has always
been great, and when the foreign capital that had provided much of
the early railroad investment was replaced by American capital around
the end of the nineteenth century, J. P. Morgan, Andrew Mellon, E. H.
Harriman and other financiers entered the scene to reorganize and consolidate many of the railroad systems and to take over many of the
key centers of decision in the industry. Trucking firms and airlines
have not needed as much capital and consequently have remained
largely outside the orbit of finance capital.

The importance of the finance groups cannot be estimated with any
confidence, since little real documentation is available for recent years.
Certainly the potential power of these interests is great, and it is fairly

[5] See Merle Fainsod and Lincoln Gordon, *Government and the American Economy*
(New York: W. W. Norton & Company, Inc., 1941), pp. 240 ff.

clear that in the past financiers played a major role in shaping railroad policy.[6] The fact that the same groups are also allied with much of the rest of basic American industry gives a powerful potential to the railroads in their conflicts with other carriers. It would appear, however, that the financial control groups are not completely united in behalf of the railroads. Such conflicting interests as lower rates for the transportation of steel may prevent the railroads from mobilizing the finance groups to vigorous support of the railroad position.

THE ISSUES

The political issues in the transportation field have varied, of course, over different periods of time and according to changing political and economic circumstances. Each type of carrier, as it developed, faced certain problems unique to it and found a particular environment with which to deal. But there have also been basic similarities in the issues that have faced each carrier, and as the field of transportation has become an arena of competition among several competing types of carriers, these similarities have become more relevant to an understanding of the field than the historical differences. We shall examine three broad categories of issues that have particular significances: (1) right of way and roadbed provision, (2) rates and service, and (3) combination, and cooperation.

Right of way and roadbeds

The roadbeds upon which operates each of the major carriers were provided with the aid of some form of governmental subsidy. In the earliest days of the republic, highways were built with the help of the federal government as part of the plans to develop the interior of the nation. Canal boats operated on ways built with substantial assistance from state and local governments, and some canals were dug entirely by public funds. In the early days of railroad development, state and local governments often tried to outbid each other in financial inducements to persuade the railroads to extend their lines through particular communities. Land grants, tax exemptions, and subscriptions to securities were commonly used to attract the new transport companies, particularly in the midwestern states. And between 1850 and 1871, assistance amounting to nearly 500 million dollars was extended to

[6] See Shott, *op. cit.*

railroads in the form of federal land grants.[7] Probably only about 10 per cent of the total mileage built in the United States received land grant aid, and most of this was located west of the Mississippi, where the immediate prospects for profitable railroads were not good, due to the lack of settlers. Nevertheless, it is fair to say that the building of the railroad system in the United States received substantial help from government in the early stages of development. Without such help it is questionable if enough capital could have been attracted to construct the western roads at such an early date, and this in turn would have meant much slower settling of the west. At the same time, the building of the railroad system was accompanied by a considerable amount of stock watering and other questionable financial dealings. This, combined with too rapid expansion, produced financial difficulty which forced many of the roads to the wall when the anticipated demand for railroad services never did develop.

The assistance received from governmental authority in providing the roadbed in no way distinguishes the railroads from competing carriers. All highways in contemporary use were built exclusively by government, whereas many of the railroads built their own lines unaided. The vast majority of waterway facilities have been improved through governmental action and many routes would not be in operation without such aid. And while the air was freely available, the airways have been set out by governmental authority, and the charts, weather reports, beam signals, and many airport facilities—the airlines' equivalent to railroad trackage, roadbed, and terminal—also come from public agencies. The carriers themselves, and the shippers hoping to benefit, have actively sought this public assistance and rarely has there been sufficient opposition from the taxpayers to prevent such subsidies.

None of the transportation industries could have developed as rapidly as they have without substantial assistance from public funds. The costs of providing a system of highways for motor carriers would ob-

[7] Federal Coordinator of Transportation, *Public Aids to Transportation* (Washington, D.C.: U.S. Government Printing Office, 1940), Vol. II, pp. 3-103; Board of Investigation and Research, *Public Aids to Domestic Transportation*, 79th Congress, 1st Session, House Document 159 (1944), pp. 105-88. Robert S. Henry argues that the value of the federal land grants was substantially less, perhaps 130 million dollars. Also the federal government received considerable financial return since land-grant railroads were required until 1940 to carry mail for 80 per cent of the rates applying to other roads and until 1946 government military and naval personnel moved at much less than normal rates. "The Railroad Land Grant Legend in American History Texts," *Mississippi Valley Historical Review*, Vol. 32 (Sept., 1945), pp. 171-95.

viously have been prohibitive for any private interests. Only recently have the airlines been able to operate profitably, and even so, without paying for their own airway system; certainly they could not have met by themselves the huge expenditures that flight safety requires. As noted earlier, the railroads did provide much of their own roadbed unaided, partly because the virtual monopoly of commercial transportation that they enjoyed seemed to assure a profitable future, and partly because the fact that the nation was expanding rapidly at the same time made any enterprise as vital to that expansion as transportation look very attractive to investment capital.

With the development of competition among different forms of transportation, the competing interests have sought to increase the proportion of the costs of keeping up or expanding the roadbeds that *other* carriers must pay. Thus the railroads have tried to get truckers to pay a greater share of the costs of building highways and have sought a deduction in the tax burden on their own right of way and roadbed. The truckers, of course, have taken an opposite stand. We shall see more of this conflict when we consider the highway program. Suffice it to say at this point that this is an important issue because the costs of roadbed provision and maintenance are, or could be, important to the profits of the carriers.

Rates

Although public assistance to carriers for their roadbeds has been usually the first issue to arise, after the carrier is in full operation the central issue has soon become the rates charged. Particularly with respect to the railroads, the problems of rate regulation have monopolized attention since the latter part of the 19th century. A number of aspects of the general issue of rate regulation must be understood in order to talk sensibly about the problems. Three major issues— maximum rate control, valuation and rates, and discrimination among different shippers in rates—will be considered here.

By spreading the network of their service throughout most of the United States, the railroads achieved substantially a position of monopoly in transportation. Most shippers had no real choice about which company would transport their products. Some areas, of course, were served by more than one railroad, and shippers in those areas could bargain between competing roads. In other areas, like much of the sparsely settled West, there was not sufficient traffic to permit the railroads to abuse their monopoly position, since this would merely keep away further settlement. But in many parts of the country the railroads did enjoy monopoly conditions and as a result could set their rates as high as the shippers could pay without going bankrupt. The shipper paid the rates or went out of business. Any railroad achieving this position was a very profitable operation, which explains part of the attraction the empty expanses of the west held for railroad promoters.

Since shippers, particularly farmers, had no way to combat railroad rates in the market place, they turned to the political arena. The passage of state and later national legislation providing for regulatory commissions empowered to fix maximum rates was the result of this effort. When the commissions were first established, it was widely anticipated that they would be able to curb the monopoly power of the railroads and reduce rates to levels bearing reasonable relation to the costs of the service. However, the complex forces at work were more involved than they had appeared to be, and many unforeseen problems developed.

The Interstate Commerce Act of 1887 provided, among other things, that the Interstate Commerce Commission could review rail rates and, if the Commission found the rates to be too high, it could order them to be changed. Only "just and reasonable" rates were to be permitted. The Supreme Court held early, however, that the ICC had no power to specify the rates to be charged,[8] and so a railroad could change a rate found to be unjust by a fraction of a cent and make it legitimate. The support of the railroads by the courts effectively emasculated the ICC's authority, and it was not until the passage of the Hepburn Act of 1906 that the Commission was given specific power to set maximum rates. The Mann-Elkins Act of 1910 extended the Commission's authority over rates by empowering the ICC to suspend proposed rate increases while examining their reasonableness and to consider the rate schedules as a whole rather than confining attention to specific rates. As a result of these changes, the authority of the ICC to control the maximum rates charged was fully established.

This authority was not sufficient to control the profits that railroads might earn, however. The definition of what rates were "just and reasonable" depended not just upon what the shippers thought was fair, but what brought the railroads a "reasonable" return on their invest-

[8] *Cincinnati, New Orleans and Texas Railway Co. v. Interstate Commerce Commission,* 162 U.S. 184 (1896).

ment. The Supreme Court held in *Smyth v. Ames* [9] that "just and reasonable" rates were those that assured the railroads of a "fair return on a fair valuation" of the railroads' investment. This formula was designed to protect the railroads against Commission action so zealous as to reduce rates below what was necessary to keep the railroads in business. The railroads were able, for a number of years, to argue that the rates set by the ICC were not fair, and it was difficult to demonstrate that they were. [10]

"Fair return" was generally agreed to mean a return of between 5 and 8 per cent on the investment. The really difficult problem was how to determine the "fair value" of the investment. The early days of railroad promotion had seen a considerable amount of financial manipulation that severely inflated the paper value of the railroad investment without actually adding any productive facilities. Were these paper assets to be included as part of the base upon which the percentage return the railroad was entitled to earn would be figured? Even if this problem were solved, how was the value of the railroad plant to be calculated? If the *original cost* of building the railroad, minus depreciation, was used as the basis for ratemaking, this would reward the wasteful construction that often characterized railroad building. If the *cost of reproduction* of the facilities were used, this would give the railroads the benefit of increases in the general price level that had occurred since the railroad was built. Or if a compromise—the *prudent investment* of a reasonable man—were used, who was to determine what was prudent and what was not? The issues raised by the "fair return on a fair valuation" formula were immensely difficult and so long as the courts insisted that control of railroad rates must also guarantee the railroads a fair return, the railroads were given an important weapon to stave off the rigors of control. By taking ICC rate decisions to the courts and protesting that the rates were unfair, the railroads were able to protect some of the fruits of their monopoly position in transportation. When this monopoly position gave way before motor and air competition, the question of maximum rate control lost much of its original significance, since monopolistic rates might merely force shippers to use the other means of transport.

[9] 169 U.S. 466 (1898).

[10] For a convenient summary of the development of these doctrines see D. Philip Locklin, *Economics of Transportation,* 4th ed. (Homewood, Ill.: Richard D. Irwin, Inc., 1954), Chap. 17.

Rate discrimination. Rate discrimination was another type of con-troversy that grew during this period of 1870 to 1917. This issue was one of discrimination by carriers in the rates charged competing ship-pers for the same service.[11] Rate discrimination took two different forms; discrimination against specific shippers producing the same product, and discrimination between different localities. In the early days of agitation for rate regulation, one of the main charges against the railroads was that lower rates were being extended to a few fav-ored shippers as part of a concerted effort to eliminate competition and build the trusts. A particularly flagrant example of this practice was the granting by the Marietta and Cincinnati of a rate of ten cents a barrel to Standard Oil for a particular haul of crude oil, charging smaller oil companies thirty-five cents a barrel for the same haul, and giving Standard the additional quarter.[12] Rebates of rates and special rates were sometimes induced by competition between railroads for a large shipper's business, but more often they appeared to be part of the move-ment toward monopoly that marked so much of American business in the late 19th century.

The Interstate Commerce Act of 1887 contained prohibitions against rebates to favored shippers and generally outlawed discrimina-tion among persons. These prohibitions were strengthened by later legislation, and this aspect of discrimination in rates was substantially eliminated, so far as it was possible for governmental action to do so. It remains true, however, that since rival shippers do not ordinarily ship in exactly the same quantities or over equal distances, charges of favoritism through different rates not accurately based upon cost dif-ferences continue to be made.

It has proved far more difficult to eliminate discrimination in rates between *places.* One fairly common type of such discrimination in the pre-regulation days of railroad transportation was the situation in which the railroad charged the same product more for a short haul than a long one. Usually this type of discrimination resulted from the fact that competition over the longer haul forced the railroad to reduce its rate, while for the shorter haul the railroad enjoyed a monopoly. Obviously this sort of discrimination worked serious disadvantages upon the city or manufacturer located on the short haul. Higher trans-

[11] For more extended discussion of these problems see Locklin, *op. cit.,* pp. 479 ff.; Marvin L. Fair and Ernest W. Williams, *Economics of Transportation* (New York: Harper & Bros., 1950), Part III.

[12] Cited in Fair and Williams, *op. cit.,* p. 463.

portation rates meant a weaker competitive position *vis-a-vis* the man-ufacturer in a city served by more than one railroad. The 1887 Act prohibited charging more for a shorter haul than for a longer haul, when the former was contained within the latter, over the same line in the same direction. Railroads could receive specific exemption from the prohibition, and the prohibition applied only when the two hauls were under "substantially similar circumstances." However, the Su-preme Court held that competition between railroads over the longer haul made the circumstances dissimilar,[13] and it was not until the Mann-Elkins Act of 1910 that the "similar circumstances" clause was dropped and the blanket prohibition enforced. Railroads can still apply for and obtain specific exemptions for specific rates when the ICC finds that lower rates for a longer haul are necessary to meet (but not to undercut) competition from other carriers.

Another aspect of rate discrimination which had profound conse-quences for the economic development of the nation was the discrim-ination between different *regions* of the country. The railroads of the United States were built in three fairly distinct groups, each serving a different type of economy, each separately controlled, and each cut off from the others by river barriers.[14] The eastern roads served an area that already was emphasizing manufacturing, and the rate struc-ture of this region was designed to encourage the shipment of manu-factured goods to other parts of the country. In the south, the rail rates were fixed to encourage the flow of agricultural products north-ward, and the southern roads recouped by charging high rates on the shipment of manufactured products. The railroads west of the Missis-sippi followed the same pattern as the southern roads. The result was that, although the cost of transporting manufactured goods by rail was actually lower in the south than in the northeast, the rates were higher in the south, and rates were higher in the west than in the south. The rate structures developed by the three groups of railroads were designed to maximize their profits, and when rates were brought under the control of the ICC it was very difficult to discard the main outlines of transportation rates for the whole nation.

In the years around 1900, effective control of many southern and western railroads was brought into the same hands that controlled the eastern roads—those in centers of financial power—thus assuring

[13] *Interstate Commerce Commission v. Alabama Midland Ry. Co.,* 168 U.S. 144 (1897).

[14] On the development of basic rate structures, see Fair and Williams, *op. cit.,* Chap. 22.

united opposition among the railroads to any proposals for scrapping the sectional classification. The effects of this system were mainly to make it difficult for manufacturing, particularly of basic industry products, to develop in either the south or west where transportation costs for manufactured goods were so high. Not until the TVA was established and sought to promote industrialization in the south were there politically effective protests against the discriminatory rates.[15]

The Transportation Act of 1940 specified that no unreasonable preference be given in the rate structure to any region or territory and, after revising the rate structures to make them more equitable as between sections, the ICC finally put a uniform classification into effect for all territory east of the Rocky Mountains. Transportation costs are not the only factor, of course, affecting the economic development of an area, and other factors also have worked in the past to keep manufacturing concentrated east of the Mississippi and north of the Ohio. Nevertheless, more equitable transportation rates appear to be one of the factors contributing to the expanded industrialization of the south and west during recent years.

The discussion of discrimination in transportation rates has focused on the railroads. Discrimination in rates charged by the newer types of carriers has been a much less significant policy problem. Rates of water carriers, motor carriers, and airlines all tend to be set with reference to railroad rates. If particular rail rates are low, other carriers will charge low rates in order to compete. Water carriers follow essentially the same classifications of freight that railroads use, while truckers have fewer classes and airlines still fewer. Many of the firms engaging in water and highway transportation are contract carriers or are owned by the shippers themselves, which means that they are exempted from ICC rate control and can charge whatever rates they deem advisable.

Among the common carriers in air and motor transport, the temptation to discriminate in rates in order to attract more business is not as great as it is for railroads.[16] Railroads must bear heavy fixed costs of investment in plant and rolling stock, roadbed, administrative overhead, and so on, which do not vary much even though the railroad is doing little business. The costs of doing additional business are a smaller proportion of the railroad's total costs than they would be for a trucking firm or an airline. The major proportion of the costs of the

---

[15] The Southern Governors' Conference also became active on this issue. See H. C. Nixon, "The Southern Governors' Conference as a Pressure Group," *Journal of Politics,* Vol. 6 (1944), pp. 338-45.

[16] See Locklin, *op. cit.,* pp. 138-41 and 685-86.

latter are out-of-pocket costs—those extra costs incurred for each additional piece of business done—which in the case of truckers would include wages, gasoline, tires, and so forth. Since the railroad must pay such heavy fixed costs regardless of whether or not it operates, it is to its advantage to try to get additional business even at rates that do not cover its total costs—that is, fixed plus out-of-pocket costs—so long as the rates cover out-of-pocket costs and contribute something to fixed costs. The railroad tends to set lower rates, therefore, to secure traffic in competitive markets. Their cost structure is not so likely to induce truckers to set discriminatory rates, and they will do so usually only following the lead of the railroads. The fact that the railroads and truckers differ in the nature of the costs of doing business has other consequences that will be noted later on. We are concerned here only to note that this is one factor causing discriminatory rates.

Rate-making machinery. The ICC has the authority to suspend any rates set by carriers under its control, pending investigation, and then to fix the maximum and minimum, or the precise rate that the carrier may charge. In practice the ICC acts mainly in response to complaints brought to it by shippers or on requests from the carriers for across-the-board percentage rate increases on all commodities. The carriers establish their own specific rates, cooperating with other firms in their industry through private rate bureaus. When a carrier desires a new rate, the rate bureau must approve it. Then the carrier posts his intention to change the rate and unless protests from shippers are forthcoming within 30 days, the rate goes into effect. If shippers object to the proposal, the ICC will review the case, and on across-the-board increases will study them of its own volition.

But many of the rate changes and adjustments which carriers put into effect receive no direct attention from governmental authority and are reviewed only by the rate bureaus of the carriers themselves. These private rate bureaus have effective authority very similar to that of the ICC, and the operations of these agencies raise some interesting problems for public policy which we shall examine later in this discussion.

Service

The problems of the adequacy of transport service cannot entirely be separated from those of rates discussed above, since service at rates that are too high is not adequate service from the point of view of the shipper. But the provision of service that is satisfactory in quantity and quality to both the shippers and the carriers, has engendered considerable conflict among several interested groups, and, in turn, this conflict has resulted in governmental action. The problems of service have two main aspects—the *addition* of service at the behest of would-be shippers or of new transport firms anxious to tap a promising market, and the *abandonment* of service in unprofitable markets by carriers seeking to cut their losses at the expense of the few remaining customers in the area to be abandoned.

In the early days of railroad building, many communities, as well as states and finally the federal government, offered substantial assistance in order to persuade the railroads to come through a particular locality or area and provide their invaluable service. Many of the communities in the midwest and west expected that massive growth and commercial success would follow the railroad, and many railroads were built in hopes that turned out to be only dreams. The railroad system expanded beyond the needs of the economy, and despite the reorganization and concentration of control that took place in the early twentieth century, many railroads found themselves in awkward financial condition and were unable to continue operating many of their lines at a profit. However, by this time many communities had come to depend upon these lines. To abandon the service, some feared, would virtually turn these communities into ghost towns. Clearly, all the available political resources of the communities where abandonment was threatened would be mobilized to resist. The general result was that the Transportation Act of 1920, of which more will be said later, provided that no rail lines could be built or abandoned without permission of the ICC. Thus the problem was frankly made political rather than simply a question of business judgment of the profit and loss situation.

As automobiles and trucks have increased, however, the railroads have steadily sought, and eventually received, permission to abandon unprofitable service, particularly passenger lines.[17] Since 1920 more than 40,000 miles of railroad line have been abandoned while only about 10,000 miles of new line have been built, a shrinkage of the railroad network in the United States of about 12 per cent. The abandonment of rail service is often necessary to the financial health of the railroads, but the social health of communities may depend upon retaining railroad service. The problems are difficult to solve, but they

[17] See Charles R. Cherington, *The Regulation of Railway Abandonments* (Cambridge, Mass.: Harvard University Press, 1948).

are unavoidable in a dynamic society where people and industry are continually shifting locations.

The older carriers serving older markets may have sought retrenchment of service, but the newer forms of transportation and the newer markets have tried to obtain expanded service. Common motor carriers and airlines must receive certificates of convenience and necessity from the ICC and CAB respectively before being allowed to add new routes and before new firms can compete over established routes. The rationale of regulation here is based upon the memory of railroad overexpansion and the resulting financial troubles, plus the fact that the airlines have, until very recently, required government subsidy to make them profitable. To these considerations must be added the concern of existing carriers to resist the expansion of service; for example, railroads seeking to limit truck service, or one airline trying to maintain a monopoly over a particular route against the threatened competition of another airline. The communities to be served are on the side of the new carriers, and in this situation the long term victory generally has gone to those who desire increased transportation service.

Competition, cooperation, and combination

One of the most difficult subjects to discuss accurately and dispassionately in the whole field of public policy is the degree of competition existing among the firms of an industry. Even when all the necessary data are available, which they seldom are, reasonable men continue to disagree about what the data mean. These problems are not less difficult to handle in the field of transportation than elsewhere. But an attempt to grasp the extent of competition or cooperation within the several transportation industries is fundamental to an understanding of public policy in the field and of the political activities of many of the groups interested in transportation questions.

The traditional reliance on competition among several firms to assure reasonable prices and service has never been held in transportation quite so firmly as in many other industries. Since the latter part of the nineteenth century, transportation (meaning until recently railroads) has been regarded as a public utility for which competition could not function as an adequate regulator. Government regulation had to be substituted to hold prices and service at levels acceptable to the public. This image of transportation was never entirely accurate, since even in the days of railroad domination of transportation, several railroad companies competed for traffic in many of the markets of the country, particularly the major cities, such as Chicago, New York, and Philadelphia. It was primarily the rural areas and agricultural shippers who faced one-railroad monopoly.

In the late nineteenth and early twentieth centuries, public policy toward transportation was directed largely toward the restoration of competition in transportation, through preventing the pooling of revenues, by breaking up railroad combinations under the Sherman Act, and so on.[18] Despite this emphasis on governmental action, consolidation of many independent railroad firms into fewer, larger firms went on during this period, usually under the auspices of financial control groups. Following the near disastrous failure of the railroads to provide adequate service during World War I, public policy underwent a shift as the desire of the railroads themselves to decrease competition and a widespread public desire to shore up a financially weak railroad system coincided. The Transportation Act of 1920 aimed to reduce the overexpanded industry through consolidation and merger while guaranteeing to the industry as a whole a stable financial return. The ICC was to develop a comprehensive plan for the integration of several hundred roads into a relatively small number of systems that would be able to operate more efficiently and economically. Many firms in the railroad industry continue to support consolidation schemes that would reduce inter-railroad competition and strengthen the railroads for competition with motor carriers.

Since World War I, however, the rise of new forms of transportation has cut deeply into the near-monopoly once held by the railroads. The private automobile and to a lesser degree buses and airlines have almost destroyed passenger business for railroads, and competing carriers have taken an increasing share of the freight traffic as well (see Table 5.1). This "new competition" in transportation has changed drastically the problem of regulation of transportation. The railroads argue that government control is no longer needed to assure low prices and adequate service since competition with other carriers can provide that assurance. Shipper groups and rival carriers continue to claim, however, that public control of the railroads is necessary to prevent a resurgence of railroad monopoly. In any event, the "new competition" has brought new arguments to the debate over transport policy.

[18] An early but thorough treatment of this general problem can be found in W. Z. Ripley, *Railroads: Rates and Regulations* (New York: Longmans, 1912).

TABLE 5.1

PERCENTAGE OF DOMESTIC INTERCITY TRAFFIC CARRIED BY
MAJOR TYPES OF TRANSPORTATION

	1916	1939	1949	1955
Railroads				
Passenger-miles	98.00	8.7	9.3	4.5
Freight ton-miles	77.2	62.2	60.6	49.4
Motor carriers				
Passenger (including				
private automobiles)	—	90.5	88.5	92.0
Freight	—	8.0	10.6	17.7
Inland waterways				
Passenger	2.0	.5	.4	.26
Freight	18.4	17.8	15.8	16.9
Petroleum pipelines				
Freight	4.4	12.0	13.0	15.9
Airways				
Passenger	—	.25	1.8	3.4
Freight	—	.002	.025	.04

Data for 1916 from Marvin Fair and Ernest Williams, *Economics of Transportation* (New York: Harper & Bros., 1950), p. 132. Data for other years from *Annual Reports* of Interstate Commerce Commission of 1941, p. 9; 1951, p. 20; and 1956, p. 43.

The problem of consolidation has also taken on a new meaning. While at the turn of the century consolidation of railroads under the guidance of financial control groups was often a means by which monopoly was strengthened and "wasteful" competition among railroad firms reduced, by 1920 railroad consolidation was actually fostered by public policy as a means to strengthen a financially weak railroad system. ICC-promoted consolidation did not get very far, but it is important to note that the combination of firms into larger and stronger ones—whether rail, air, or truck—is no longer regarded with the same fear of monopoly. In many cases, combination and consolidation are looked on as means toward more effective competition among financially stronger companies.

The "new competition" has not, however, eliminated either the demands for continued public regulation or for efforts within each of the transportation industries to reduce competitive pressures. As noted earlier, one of the functions performed by each of the trade associations in the transportation field is the moderation of competition within the industry. The trucking association tries to prevent "cutthroat" rate-cutting among rival truckers while at the same time it promotes the trucking interests against the railroads. The AAR and the Air Transport Association have done the same thing in their industries. This is not to suggest that competition between railroad firms, between rival airlines, or among several trucking companies is entirely absent. It is not. But in each of these industries the tendency toward combination of lines under common ownership and the activities of the trade association have moderated this kind of competition. Certainly the most significant competition so far as transportation politics is concerned is that between the industries, and especially railroads versus trucks.

Governmental limits on competition. Governmental authority has been used by the carriers to reduce the competitive pressure within each transportation industry. The rationale in each case is that by preventing extreme competition the firms of the industry are made financially stronger and are thus able to operate more efficiently over the long run. Two major techniques by which governmental authority is invoked to moderate intra-industry competition are *control of entry* and *minimum rate control.*[19]

Control of entry is a useful device for reducing competition only if the industry is sufficiently attractive that entry by new firms is sought. For many years the railroad industry has not been attractive enough, and although new firms would have to obtain permission from the ICC in order to start offering rail service, almost none has done so for several decades. Interstate trucking, on the other hand, has presented financially promising opportunities, and thousands of applications for permission to enter the industry have been filed with the ICC. A basic part of the original legislation providing for federal control over interstate trucking—a provision that helped secure support from the larger existing trucking firms for the whole Motor Carrier Act of 1935 —guaranteed the right of continued operation to all existing firms, but provided that new firms thereafter would have to obtain certificates from the ICC that the service they proposed to offer was "in the public interest." Existing trucking firms thus secured a measure of protection against an ever-growing number of companies engaged in motor transport, and competition was correspondingly moderated.

Airlines likewise must secure permission from the Civil Aeronautics Board before inaugurating service or expanding routes.[20] The basic regulatory legislation affecting airlines was passed in 1938 and provided "grandfather rights" to protect existing firms in their right to con-

[19] See Fair and Williams, *op. cit.*, Chap. 32, especially pp. 644-56.
[20] See Lucille Keyes, *Federal Control of Entry into Air Transportation* (Cambridge, Mass.: Harvard University Press, 1951).

tinue to operate. Since until quite recently the regular airlines did not operate at a profit, the control of entry was concerned not so much with regulating competition among airlines as with protecting the meager earnings of the existing companies.[21] In recent years, however, most of the major trunk airlines have made substantial profits, and repeated demands by new firms to be allowed entry to the industry have arisen. The CAB, supported by the existing airlines, has resisted these pleas and by refusing entry to new firms has moderated the competitive pressures that the airlines have to endure.

Governmental action to prevent carriers from setting excessively low rates has quite a different purpose than the control of maximum rates. *Maximum rate control* is designed to limit the profits of the carrier who is in a relatively monopolistic position; this sort of control is asked for by shippers. *Minimum rate control* is designed to prevent "cut-throat competition" among the carriers and is desired by the carriers themselves. Particularly among the railroads but also among small truckers, there is often the temptation in the face of competition to reduce rates below the actual cost of providing the service, to attract more business. If the carrier can stand the temporary loss, the hope is that the competitors will be forced out of business and that the losses will be regained later by raising the rates again. If the carrier can thereby put to work idle equipment, he may not lose very much money even though his rates are not equal to his total costs. However, unless the lower rates bring a larger volume of business to the whole transportation industry, frequently all that happens is that some of the firms go bankrupt. Except for air passenger traffic, the volume of transportation traffic does not change much with rate changes, and, as a result, price-cutting competition, which is particularly common in time of depression, tends to throw the whole industry into chaos. Even shippers do not necessarily welcome these rate wars, since the rates will not stay low, and the violent fluctuations in rates and service are difficult to deal with in planning business operations. The result of these considerations is that the ICC and the CAB are empowered to establish minimum rates for the carriers under their control.

The ICC requires that rates be at least equal to the added cost to the carrier of providing service and that the rates be no lower than necessary to meet competition. Thus a railroad has difficulty setting rates below those of a competing water carrier in order to win back busi-

[21] See Civil Aeronautics Board, *Role of Competition in Commercial Air Transportation* (Washington, D.C.: U.S. Government Printing Office, 1952).

ness, unless the ICC agrees that lower rates are "necessary" to meet service advantages of water carriers. As we shall see later, this restriction on the ability of railroads to lower rates in efforts to win back business is a matter of current controversy. Our concern with it at this point is to consider its effects on competition. Clearly this kind of control substantially reduces the extent of rate competition that will exist between railroads and truckers, for example, since the rates will tend to be about the same. Minimum rate control also minimizes the extent of competition within the railroad or the trucking industries. Competition within the railroad or trucking industry has also been controlled, in many instances, through the trade associations, but through minimum rate control, the force of governmental authority is added.

In summary, we may say that competition *between* the several transportation industries is reasonably vigorous and is pursued both in the market place and in the political arena where each industry seeks to secure advantages in law. The importance of this inter-industry competition in holding prices at reasonable levels should not be overlooked, and it may well be that some of the legal rules adopted in a day of transportation monopoly that restrain rail-truck rate competition are anachronistic today. It must be remembered, however, that *within* each transportation industry, competition has been moderated substantially. Both the private associations in which transportation firms are joined together and various portions of public policy have been found to be useful means to "soften" competition.

ARENAS OF CONFLICT

We have examined the interest groups most active in transportation issues and have explored the major issues of public policy in this field. Let us turn now to the agencies in which the public policy decisions are made. It is not surprising that, since transportation is so central to the rest of the economy, disputes over transportation policy may involve many agencies at all levels of government. Only the most important of these can be dealt with here. These agencies may be viewed as arenas within which the contending groups struggle to gain the support of governmental authority as a means of advancing their interests. Thus railroads hope to get support from the Interstate Commerce Commission for a rate increase, scheduled airlines find the Civil Aeronautics Board "on their side" against the nonscheduled lines, and so on. It is from this point of view that the major agencies shall be described.

The Interstate Commerce Commission

The Interstate Commerce Commission was established in 1887 as a basic part of the first great national attempt to regulate railroads.[22] Regulatory commissions had existed in some of the states, but railroad lines commonly extended beyond the boundaries of a single state, and state commissions lacked both constitutional authority and political power for adequate control. The ICC was to attack the problem on a national scale. The Commission was to be "independent" and expert. Its independence was to consist of freedom from direct pressure or influence of political party interests, and this independence was to be achieved by appointing members for fixed, overlapping terms, longer than those of the President, and by requiring that the Commission be bipartisan in composition. It was expected that long terms and the absence of political pressure would permit the Commission to develop the experience and expertise necessary to deal with the complex field of railroad regulation. It had been felt that one of the chief difficulties confronting the courts when they were called upon to restrain predatory railroad practices was their lack of really intimate acquaintance with the problems. A full-time group dealing with the problems could remedy inequities more swiftly and effectively than was possible in the courts.[23]

"Independence" was not a guarantee of effectiveness of the Commission, however, nor was the Commission removed from the political scene. The courts could and did review its decisions with the early effect of sharply reducing ICC authority to control railroad practices. The agrarian protest groups that had provided the political impetus to establish the Commission lacked sufficient strength to give it continuing power. Indeed its very "independence" meant that the ICC was cut off from important political support, since no President or party could make much use of the Commission in building a majority. As a result the ICC achieved comprehensive control of rates, service, and financial structure of railroads only gradually.[24]

By the second decade of the twentieth century the Commission had

[22] On the history of the ICC, see I. L. Sharfman, *The Interstate Commerce Commission*, 5 Vols. (New York: Twentieth Century Fund, 1931–1935); R. E. Cushman, *The Independent Regulatory Commission* (New York: Oxford University Press, 1941).

[23] On the theoretical virtues of independent commissions, see Marver H. Bernstein, *Regulating Business by Independent Commission* (Princeton, N. J.: Princeton University Press, 1955).

[24] See the brief discussion of statutes expanding ICC authority during this period, *ibid.*, pp. 20-25.

broad legislative grants of authority, the specific exercise of which was generally sustained by the courts. By this time, however, the political power and the economic interests of the railroads themselves had changed considerably. Railroad expansion had ended by 1916, and by that time more and more railroads found that their hopes of earlier years were not fulfilled. Although some fairly strong systems had been put together, many roads were in grave financial difficulty. For this reason, government control did not have the unpleasant taste that it might otherwise have had for the railroads. These changes in attitudes were speeded by the virtual collapse of the United States railroad system in the face of the demands of World War I. Seizure and operation by the national government was unavoidable in 1918, and when Congress revised basic public policy toward the railroads in 1920, it confirmed the view that the array of interests had changed drastically since 1887. The Transportation Act of 1920 was designed to revive the railroads as a strong and healthy system, though still regulated against any predatory actions. Under the new policy, the railroads were conceived of as a *system* rather than as many firms with few formal connections. The new conception conformed more closely to the realities of railroad cooperation and control and in addition provided the basis for one extension of ICC authority. The Commission was directed to draw up a plan under which the railroads would be consolidated into fewer and stronger companies; enough to provide some competition for each other, but few enough to avoid waste and duplication. After several years the Commission completed a plan calling for nineteen systems in various parts of the country. The Commission could not force combination in accord with its plan, however, and the railroads that did seek to combine did so along different lines. Until 1933, railroad holding companies were outside ICC jurisdiction, and combination through the holding company device could not be prevented. In 1940 the consolidation plan, having achieved little real reorganization, was dropped from the legislative mandate of the ICC.

The Act of 1920 transformed the relationship between the ICC and the railroads in still another way. The principal reason for establishing the Commission had been to provide for the regulation of railroad rates so as to prevent those rates from being discriminatory and too high. Prior to World War I the main business of the ICC was to hear and act upon complaints from shippers. If the complaint was found to be justified, the ICC was empowered under the Hepburn Act of 1906 to prescribe the maximum rate that could be charged. But the change in the philosophy of regulation which was embodied in the 1920 Act made protection of shippers only a part of the story. The railroads themselves had to be protected against too severe competition and against unwise management. Consequently, the 1920 Act authorized the ICC to set minimum as well as maximum rates. Rates were to be such that the railroad industry as a whole would earn a satisfactory return (5½ per cent of their investment), and provisions were made to allow the weaker roads to "recapture" part of the earnings of the stronger roads when the latter exceeded the "fair return." The recapture clause actually produced little but litigation, but the positive authority that the 1920 Act gave to the ICC to regulate in exact detail the whole rate structure of the railroad industry was indeed significant. The ICC would still protect shippers, of course, but it would also provide a floor under railroad earnings to protect railroads against themselves and against the competing transport industries. The ICC was to become a confidant and friend of the railroads rather than an implacable adversary.

During the 1920's the rapid expansion of motor transportation made it clearly impracticable to assure railroad earnings simply by setting high rates. High rates would merely shift traffic to truckers without necessarily producing increased revenue for railroads. And when rising motor competition was followed by the railroads' severe financial distress during the Depression, it became clear that a more complex approach to the problems of transportation regulation would have to be developed. The Emergency Transportation Act of 1933 marked the beginning of a new era in transportation policy. The ICC was no longer to attempt to guarantee the railroads a fixed percentage return on their investment nor even to base rates on the value of investment. Instead the Commission was to "give due consideration, among other factors, to the effect of rates on the movement of traffic; to the need, in the public interest, of adequate and efficient railway transportation service at the lowest cost consistent with the furnishing of such service; and to the need of revenues sufficient to enable the carriers, under honest, economical, and efficient management, to provide such service." Thus the ICC was to view the problems of the railroads as part of a broader transportation industry, and the criteria the Commission was to apply were made a great deal more flexible than before.

Another side of the railroads' difficulties was dealt with in 1935 when commercial motor carriers were brought under ICC control. Many states had enacted regulatory statutes aimed at trucks, but these had not provided adequate protection for the two major groups concerned: the railroads and the larger truckers. The railroads, of course, resented the general lack of rate, safety, and service controls that contributed to the competitive advantage motor carriers often enjoyed over railroads. They sought to bring the motor carriers under ICC supervision to equalize some of these conditions. Larger truckers were not averse to federal regulations, even though it might entail some loss of advantage *vis-a-vis* the railroads, for the large truckers were troubled by competition, often of a "fly-by-night" sort, from small one-truck carriers. The latter were quite numerous during depression days, since money for a down payment on a truck and a tankful of gas set a man up in business. Such businesses usually did not survive long, but with a great many of them continually appearing, the confidence of shippers in the trucking industry was faltering. The large truckers were willing to trade ICC control of themselves for protection against too easy entry into the trucking business by small truckers.[25] The Motor Carrier Act of 1935 provided that "certificates of public convenience and necessity" must be obtained to engage in business as common motor carriers, protecting the continued right to operate of all existing carriers through a "grandfather clause."

The authority of the ICC had long (since 1906) been extended to cover oil pipelines, express companies, sleeping-car companies, and refrigeration and storage services, and in 1940 all common carriers operating on domestic waters were brought under Commission jurisdiction. In 1942, freight forwarders—middlemen who collect and consolidate small shipments of goods, ship them in carloads, and unload and deliver them—were added, as were rate-making bureaus of the several industries in 1948. Thus all the major carrier groups except the airlines were made subject to ICC control.

In 1940 the basic statement of transportation policy was revised to take fuller account of the new competition in the transportation industries. The ICC was directed to:

> . . . provide for fair and impartial regulation of all modes of transportation subject to the provisions of the Act, so administered as to recognize and preserve the inherent advantages of each; to promote safe, adequate, economical, and efficient service and foster sound economic conditions in transportation and among the several carriers; to encourage the establishment of reasonable charges for transportation services, without unjust discrimination, undue preferences or advantages, or unfair or destructive competitive practices . . . to the end of developing, co-or-

25 See Locklin, *op. cit.,* pp. 707-8; Fair and Williams, *op. cit.,* pp. 509-11.

dinating, and preserving a national transportation system by water, highway, and rail, as well as other means, adequate to meet the needs of the commerce of the United States. . . .

The Transportation Act of 1940, in effect, placed the several transportation industries under ICC control and specified that that control was to be exercised in such manner as to produce "sound policy," with the criteria for determining "soundness" largely left undefined. In turn, this meant that the contending groups in the transportation industries would all conduct continuous campaigns within the framework of ICC authority to secure the maximum advantage.

In one sense, of course, the Commission has broad discretion and authority to shape the whole transportation system of the United States, airlines excepted. Not only are questions of rates, service, and competition among carriers within the authority of the ICC, but the less dramatic, yet important functions of prescribing safety devices, investigating accidents, controlling the issue of securities, and supervising accounting methods give the Commission extensive authority over the management of the carriers. Given the sweeping powers of the ICC, much is at stake for the carriers. Consequently, they devote much of their resources to the struggle for advantage, far more than any group not directly and primarily engaged in transportation. The ICC has thus been transformed from a symbol of anti-railroad sentiment and an agency to protect shippers against railroad monopoly to an arena within which rival carriers contend for competitive advantage.

Who wins?

If the Interstate Commerce Commission is viewed as an arena where rival carrier groups compete, the question becomes "Which carriers benefit most from ICC decisions?" Such a question is often difficult to answer with assurance because the decisions deal with very complex matters, and the effects of these actions on the interest groups is not always clear. In the case of the ICC, for example, the Commission must operate in an environment circumscribed by Congressional actions, economic circumstances, and a political climate that greatly narrow the choices that the Commission itself can make. Further, none of the carrier groups realizes its goals to its own satisfaction from ICC action, so that in most cases all the carrier groups may insist that the Commission favors the other fellow. Each case is unique in some respects and the Commission will seem to veer now this way, now that way, depending on the specific circumstances. Finally, the policy declaration contained in the Transportation Act of 1940 stated that decisions of the ICC were to insure that each type of carrier preserved its inherent advantages, and that no carrier was to be given any preferred position. Still, when railroads and truckers are in conflict over the whole range of policy decisions, any decision the ICC makes affecting the interests of either group is bound to benefit one group and hurt the other. Thus if one can identify tendencies, even though they are not clear-cut and simple, some answer to the question "Who wins?" may be given.

One extensive review of the decisions of the ICC concludes that the Commission has tended to align itself with the interests of the railroads as against motor and water carriers.[26] The mass of data upon which this judgment is based cannot be reviewed here, and it must be remembered that the railroads have not necessarily been made "happy" by ICC support, only "less unhappy." Specifically, ICC support of the railroads has entailed: support for extension of ICC authority to include motor and water carriers so that minimum rates might be established for those carriers and competition against railroads reduced; permitting, almost without exception, increases in railroad rates while requiring more rigorous standards to be met before granting increases to other carriers; opposition to Justice Department attempts to prosecute railroads for violations of the antitrust laws; granting railroad requests to reduce rates selectively, notably through exemption from the long-and-short haul requirements, with the effect of diverting profitable traffic from other carriers. Some of these policies may have been of questionable long-run value to the railroads—increases in rail rates, for example, which diverted more traffic to motor carriers— and extension of ICC authority over motor carriers was supported not only by railroads but also by the larger motor carriers themselves. Nevertheless, the analysis cited concludes that in general the ICC has granted substantially what the railroads thought they wanted in their struggle against the new carriers.

In return for ICC support, the railroads have vigorously defended the Commission against any proposed reorganization which might have the effect of transferring authority to some other agency, such as placing the more clearly administrative duties of the Commission in the Commerce Department, or abolishing the "independent" agency alto-

[26] See Samuel P. Huntington, "The Marasmus of the ICC," *Yale Law Journal,* Vol. 61 (April, 1952), pp. 467-510; Charles S. Morgan, "A Critique of 'The Marasmus of the ICC,'" *Yale Law Journal,* Vol. 62 (Jan., 1953), pp. 171-226.

gether and vesting all transportation matters in an agency directly under the control of the President.[27]

It should not be concluded that the members of the ICC have followed base motives in supporting the demands of the railroads. Just what constitutes the most desirable transportation policy is a matter of substantial disagreement, and the paths of action followed by the Commission can be defended as representative of the public interest. Moreover, the Commission was required to extend a protective umbrella over the railroad industry following the first World War. The failures of service in World War I, the alarming number of bankruptcies during the Depression, and the continuing facts of a relatively declining industry might well persuade the ICC to continue to assist the railroads to build up their competitive position.

It may also be argued that no agency of government can follow any line of policy without organized political support.[28] The farmer and shipper protest groups that invigorated the ICC in its early years turned to other policy goals for the most part following World War I and left the well-organized railroad interests occupying the field. Transportation policy in Congress and the ICC reflected this change. As motor carriers came into prominence they had fewer problems of staying alive with their smaller investments, and they were less cohesive and less well organized politically. Moreover, the most influential trucking lines were content to suffer regulation as protection against other truckers and also to benefit from the traffic lost to the railroads by steadily increasing railroad rates. Water carriers were not politically strong enough to resist railroad influence or to provide a counterweight with the Commission. In this situation, which extended from the end of World War I to the end of World War II, the ICC could hardly do otherwise than to work closely with the railroads, and the evidence suggests that it did.

Inflation and transportation politics

A basic fact about the railroad industry is that at least since World War I earnings have been lower than a financially healthy industry should enjoy. The efforts of the ICC to reorganize the industry met

[27] See David Truman, *The Governmental Process* (New York: Alfred A. Knopf, 1951), p. 421.

[28] See, for example, the early and classic statement of this position with reference to the regulatory commissions, E. Pendleton Herring, *Public Administration and the Public Interest* (New York: McGraw-Hill Book Co., Inc., 1936); Truman, *op. cit.* pp. 416 ff.

with little success, and the Depression of the Thirties drove many roads into bankruptcy. Not until World War II did railroad earnings begin to recover. But even the heavy traffic and relatively good income of the war period were not an unmixed blessing, for enormous strain was placed on already obsolete equipment. At the end of the war, railroads were faced with hardening competition, which could be met only with new and modern equipment, since a major drawing card of motor and air carriers was speed and comfort of service. Wartime earnings might have given the railroads an outside chance to renovate their plants and hold more of their traffic, if it had not been that the war was followed by seven years of substantially uninterrupted inflation. Rising costs were not so serious for motor carriers, since they did not have such a huge investment in obsolete and worn-out equipment.

The result of this situation was that railroads had to seek large rate increases in order to make any headway in modernization. Between 1946 and 1952, rates were increased an average of 78.9 per cent. This was not the way to win back business from the trucks, and during the same period the motor carrier share of traffic rose from 7.28 per cent to 16.21 per cent of the volume and considerably more of the value.

After 1952, prices rose more slowly, and the railroads began to catch up with their task of renovation. They continued to seek rate increases from time to time, and these were usually granted. Some railroads seemed quite content to give up passenger traffic altogether except for "expense account" luxury riders. But the respite from rising costs permitted railroads to make a strong effort to win back freight traffic from the trucks.[29] This effort has taken many forms. The introduction of "piggy-back" service to combine truck and rail facilities is one of the most novel developments. Railroads have also increased their political activity on many fronts, not only to improve their own relations with governmental authority, but also to disadvantage truckers through such measures as heavier highway use taxes. An important part of the railroads attempt to compete more successfully has been their effort to get permission to set rates more flexibly, and in particular to reduce specific rates in order to undercut competing carriers. More flexible rate-making, in turn, means a change in the scope of ICC authority, and this has been a central issue in recent transportation politics.

[29] See John P. Fishwick, "The ICC's Regulation of Rail-Motor Competition: A Study in Administrative Lag," *Virginia Law Review,* Vol. 41 (June, 1955), pp. 559-81.

The President's Advisory Committee

In 1954 President Eisenhower appointed a committee consisting of the Secretary of Commerce, the Secretary of Defense, and the Director of the Office of Defense Mobilization to examine federal policy toward transportation industries in the light of the competition now existing between various types of carriers. The Committee issued its report in 1955 and proposed several revisions of public policy aimed at enabling each type of carrier to realize its inherent advantages primarily through competition rather than through regulation. We shall consider some of the most significant of these proposals.

Whereas now the ICC can establish the precise rates charged by carriers, the Advisory Committee recommended that Commission authority be limited to fixing minimum and maximum rates. This would give the carriers greater flexibility in competing ratewise for traffic. Minimum rates would be determined, under the Committee proposal, by out-of-pocket costs of carrying the specific traffic. Since the railroads have relatively heavy fixed and low out-of-pocket costs this proposal would give them an advantage. The truckers would be adversely affected since out-of-pocket costs compose the bulk of their total costs. Maximum rates could not be set lower than the fully distributed costs of the service including all fixed costs such as depreciation and overhead. The range between maximum and minimum rates within which the carriers could maneuver without ICC control would be greater for railroads than for truckers.

The Advisory Committee recommended that the ICC's authority to suspend proposed rates for examination be narrowed by shortening the period of suspension from seven to three months. The Committee added that the burden of proof be upon the party protesting the new rate whenever that party was a rival carrier, rather than always requiring the carrier proposing the change to justify it.

The requirement of prior ICC approval for exemption from the long-and-short haul clause would be dropped under the Committee's plan if the competitive situation justified the higher rate for the shorter haul. Shippers of large volumes of commodities could be granted lower rates based on cost savings, which would be of help primarily to the railroads since they can handle larger shipments than motor carriers. The Committee would define somewhat more narrowly the contract and private carrier and the freight forwarder so as to bring these firms under greater ICC control.

These proposals have been widely discussed as "railroad proposals,"[30] and the AAR and the ATA have purchased considerable national advertising to defend and attack them. Judging from the support given them and from their probable effects, this is an accurate charge. Whatever the conscious motivations of the Committee, or of the Eisenhower Administration, the recommendations seem in every case to give advantages to the railroads and thus injure their competitors.

Nevertheless, it also is true that *any* proposal designed to give greater initiative and flexibility to the carriers so as to allow the new competition in transportation to achieve the benefits expected of it must be a "railroad proposal." Flexibility in rate-making is a goal sought primarily by railroads while truckers can rely more upon their advantages in service to compete against other carriers. It must also be recognized, however, that the fear with which rival carriers regard the railroads has a basis in fact. Despite their relative moribund condition over the past four decades, the railroads retain potentially far greater economic power than do their rivals. They represent many times the financial investment, their associations with other basic industries are closer, and their leadership is nearer the corporate core of the American economy. In a knockdown fight the truckers are convinced that the railroads have the financial power, despite their low earnings, to overcome the relatively small motor carriers. The result the latter particularly fear is not the elimination of motor and water transport but railroad ownership and control of all these transport media. Whether the truckers are correct or not is certainly a matter of argument, but there is sufficient logic in their position to excite potent political opposition of the truckers and their allies to the Advisory Committee's Report.

When viewed from the standpoint of transportation politics, inflation and depression both appear to work to the greater disadvantage of railroads than of motor carriers, again emphasizing the importance of the heavy fixed costs of railroads. The problems of reequipping the railroads, particularly the high-cost eastern roads, during times of rising prices were seen in 1957 when the president of the Pennsylvania proposed to a Congressional committee that the federal government establish an agency with an initial capital of 500,000,000 dollars to buy railroad cars and lease them to the carriers. Such a proposal, departing as it does so drastically from the "free enterprise" ideology

[30] See, for example, the statement by Wayne Morse, *Congressional Record,* 84th Congress, 2nd Session, pp. 9694 ff.

emphasized by the railroads in their discussion of the Advisory Committee Report, suggests that even in a period of moderate increases in the general price level the railroads face a difficult task.

Congress, President, and Court

Although many of the basic decisions concerning transportation interests are made by specialized agencies like the ICC, the major institutions of the national government are, of course, intimately involved in this policy struggle. Congress writes the basic legislation setting forth the policies the ICC is to follow, and, as we have seen, important transportation legislation has been produced every few years of this century. Legislative questions of indirect effect on transportation interests, such as many tax issues, frequently induce the affected groups to mobilize any influence they have on Capitol Hill. Annual Congressional decisions determining how much money the ICC is to be allowed to spend to enforce its rules and to investigate rate cases may also be of great consequence. In the early days of the Commission the lack of funds was a major factor forcing the Commission to retreat into a relatively passive approach toward rail regulation. Appropriation control as well as general legislative authority are important weapons, potential or actual, that make Congress an important arena for conflicts among transport interests.

The President, and indeed much of the executive branch, is frequently involved in transportation politics. Of course, members of the ICC must be appointed by the President with the consent of the Senate, and this could give the Chief Executive considerable opportunity to shape Commission policy. Appointments run for seven years, however, and the chance that a single President could remake a Commission is not good. At any rate, Presidents have not appeared to try to direct transportation policy in this manner. More important examples of executive influence can be seen in the recommendations of several presidential commissions that have studied both the administration and policies in the field. We have already discussed the controversial recommendations of President Eisenhower's Advisory Committee. Several other proposals have been made, however, to transfer some or all of the functions of the ICC to an executive department directly under presidential authority. Such transfer would vitally affect the ability of particular groups in the transportation field to secure their interests, and railroads, for example, have generally opposed shifting authority away from the ICC to an executive department.

The courts have played an important role from time to time, as noted above, in shaping transportation policy as they followed particular formulas for determining the fair value of railroad investment, or as they interpreted in narrow and restrictive ways the authority of the ICC. In recent years the courts have not had an important part in resolving conflicts in this field, but the judiciary remains a potential battleground for the interests at stake.

State and local government

Many agencies of state and local governments make decisions of interest to transportation groups. Federal regulatory authority is based on the constitutional power to regulate interstate commerce. Today this is a broad enough grant to embrace almost all rail and air traffic and much motor transport too. For example, since 1914 the courts have sustained federal control of rates for entirely intrastate traffic when such control was necessary to effective control of interstate transportation.[31] Nevertheless, states continue to make decisions, usually through some type of commission, regulating rates on intrastate traffic such as interurban passenger lines. Abandonments by intrastate railroads of lines no longer profitable must usually be approved by these state commissions. Motor carriers are subject to more extensive regulation respecting licensing, height, weight, and length, and service. Many of these questions are the subject of bitter struggle between rival transportation groups as railroads and truckers bid for support from the state legislatures.[32] Indeed, restrictive state legislation seems to present one of the primary weapons by which railroads can reduce the competitive advantages of the trucks. State regulations of this kind are not unlimited, however, since the Supreme Court has from time to time struck them down for placing an "undue burden" on the free flow of interstate commerce.

All transportation interests must also be closely concerned with state and local taxation. Property taxes are particularly important to railroads since the huge investment in rolling stock, the trackage and right of way, and any terminal facilities are subject to taxes that in

---

[31] *The Shreveport Case,* 234 U.S. 342 (1914).

[32] The struggle in Pennsylvania over truck weight restrictions was so intense that trucking and railroad associations *plus their respective public relations firms* became embroiled in a colorful lawsuit. See "The Railroad-Trucker Brawl," *Fortune,* Vol. 47 (June, 1953), pp. 137 ff.; Robert Bendiner, "The Engineering of Consent," *The Reporter,* Vol. 13 (Aug. 11, 1955), pp. 14-24.

turn place a burden on railroad income. Both the rate of taxation and the level of assessment are therefore of great concern. Gasoline and other state and local highway use taxes represent an important cost of doing business to the truckers and thus draw much attention. In some states in the past, the stakes for transportation interests were so great that particular rail firms dominated virtually the entire political life of the state. Interest group conflicts have grown more complex and no firm today occupies the position that the Louisville and Nashville or the Southern Pacific once did in Tennessee and California respectively. Nevertheless, the decisions of state and local governments continue to attract the political attentions of transportation groups.

The rate bureaus

The tasks given by law to the Interstate Commerce Commission and other transportation agencies are exceedingly broad and complex. Although the ICC is the largest of the regulatory commissions in point of personnel and appropriations, it is far short of the size necessary to supervise every detail of the industries. The Commission operates around the edges, so to speak, hearing complaints brought by shippers and unhappy carriers, spot-checking financial accounts and compliance with safety requirements, and setting general rate structures. In practice, the individual rates for specific shipments of specific commodities are set by the carriers themselves, subject only to ICC veto in case of protest. The mechanisms through which this *private* rate-making process takes place are the *rate bureaus* that serve the carriers of each industry.[33] Carriers make rate proposals to the bureau, and the bureau in turn makes to the carriers recommendations that the latter normally accept as binding. Shippers also often seek rate adjustments through the rate bureaus. If some of the parties are sufficiently aggrieved by the rate bureau decisions, the authority of the ICC can be invoked to suspend and investigate the rate, and the Commission may modify it later. The *de facto* authority of the rate bureaus remains extensive, however. Through these mechanisms competition between rival carriers within the railroad industry or within the trucking industry is substantially modified, since the attempt by one to secure traffic from another by changing the rate can often be blocked in the rate bureau. The rate bureau has been an important technique

[33] See Board of Investigation and Research, *Report on Rate-Making and Rate-Publishing Procedures of Railroad, Motor, and Water Carriers,* House Document 363, 78th Congress, 1st Session (1944).

by which some firms in an industry have been able to dominate others in the quest for traffic.[34]

The activities of the rate bureaus constitute cooperative price-fixing and would almost certainly be in clear violation of the antitrust statutes were it not for the specific exemption granted by the Reed-Bulwinkle Act, passed over President Truman's veto in 1948. It was argued that the practice of fixing rates through rate bureaus was an indispensable means of preserving order and stability in transportation. Shippers of products over long distances will usually need the services of several transport firms to complete the haul. To assure equitable treatment of the shipment throughout the haul and equitable division of the revenue among the several carriers involved, cooperation among the carriers is needed. Opponents of the bill contended that the rate bureaus were control mechanisms which, among other things, have contributed to the dominance of eastern railroads over southern and western roads. It would seem that some kind of control machinery to supervise the carriers in more detailed fashion than can the ICC is probably inevitable, especially in the railroad industry, in order to protect the huge investments against rate wars. It is also true, however, that such machinery will not benefit all the firms of a transportation industry equally. Rate bureaus contribute to the solidarity of each transport industry, thereby helping to assure that the major conflicts in transportation will take place between different transport industries rather than between firms of the same industry.

AVIATION POLICY AND POLITICS

The commercial aviation industry, although a transportation industry and competitive with motor carriers and railroads, carries on its major political activities on a different front. It is regulated by separate administrative agencies, both at the state and federal levels of government, and while aviation interests do engage in such general transportation controversies as highway construction, by and large the air carriers resolve their conflicts separately from those of competing carriers. The Civil Aeronautics Board and the Civil Aeronautics Administration are the principal governmental agencies dealing with aviation problems. These agencies were established in 1938 when the basic policies of control were enacted. Prior to that time safety regulations

[34] See Schott, *op. cit.*

and air mail rates were prescribed by various agencies, but little over-all control of the industry was exercised.

The CAA

The Civil Aeronautics Administration is located within the Department of Commerce. It plans and administers the system of airways in the United States, controls flight patterns, provides navigational assistance, examines and tests pilots and planes, administers the federal portion of the airport construction program, and investigates accidents. In this last function, the Civil Aeronautics Board also participates, especially when there is the possibility that the CAA itself was at fault. The CAA is essentially administrative, and most of the policy decisions respecting aviation are made either in Congress or the CAB. Nevertheless, the responsibilities of the CAA do involve it in some significant controversies. The amount of money to be appropriated for CAA operation has been a matter of some dispute in recent years as concern has grown over the adequacy of the airway system and control in these days of rapidly expanding air travel. Critics of the Eisenhower administration, for example, have charged that "budget-minded" tendencies, particularly strong in the Commerce Department, have undermined the CAA.[35] Thus strong supporters of civil aviation interests have proposed that the CAA be taken out of the Commerce Department and given independent status like the ICC. The CAA also has been the site of a struggle between operators of private planes and commercial and military interests over the issue of radio-controlled flying. Many private operators prefer to fly on a "see-and-be-seen" basis and avoid investing in radio equipment. Commercial and military interests argue for greater safety through radio-beam control and at the same time have sought to secure a greater portion of the airwaves for use of beam signal transmission. The private pilots' association has viewed the Commerce Department with alarm, particularly with respect to its treatment of the CAA.

The CAB and competition

The major arena for airline disputes, however, is the Civil Aeronautics Board. The CAB is primarily concerned with economic regulation: controlling entry, fixing routes and approving expansion or abandonment of service, regulating rates, and determining air mail payments and subsidies. The industry now regulated by the CAB developed

[35] See *St. Louis Post-Dispatch,* March 10, 1956, and May 5, 1957.

along lines quite different from other transportation industries. In the early years of aviation, the paramount concern of governmental policy was to develop aviation technology in time of peace which would be adequate in time of war. In the period following World War I, commercial aviation showed little likelihood of achieving commercial success without substantial assistance, so the air carriers were granted subsidy payments in the form of overpayments for carrying airmail. As commercial aviation developed and business expanded, various local communities sought service, and when airmail subsidies were expanded in 1934, the industry became somewhat more attractive.

After several shifts in the governmental control machinery, Congress established the CAB in 1938 as a semi-independent, regulatory agency. The CAB has been confronted with the task of encouraging what is still an infant and somewhat risky industry. This encouragement has taken the form of subsidies for airmail contracts, and limitation of the entry of new firms into the field. All firms operating at the time the 1938 legislation was passed were allowed under "grandfather rights" to continue operation. These firms are called "trunk" lines. New firms seeking to enter the field of commercial aviation must secure certificates of convenience and necessity from the CAB. No new certificates for trunk-line operation have ever been issued.

This does not mean that competition has been entirely absent within the airline industry. The 12 domestic trunk airlines (reduced through mergers from 16 in 1938) compete with each other over many routes and often quite vigorously. When a new route promises to provide adequate traffic, several lines may seek CAB permission to serve it. The CAB is faced with two difficult and intensely political problems as air traffic expands. In the first place, air traffic is almost all passenger traffic, and it is heavily concentrated in a small number of routes. In 1949, nearly 50 per cent of the traffic was concentrated in less than 1 per cent of the pairs of cities served. The airlines naturally seek to serve these profitable routes. Since no route has enough traffic to make it profitable for all lines to serve it, the CAB limits the number of firms that can gain entry. Those lines denied access to choice routes and communities may thus come into severe conflict with CAB policy. One former member of the Board has charged that Board decisions have favored the larger trunk lines.[36] Any policy of limiting expansion

[36] See the statement of former CAB Chairman Ross Rizley, *St. Louis Post-Dispatch,* November 18, 1955.

of service would assist those firms already serving the major routes. The CAB for its part has had the obligation to protect the financial position of certificated trunk lines, and it has followed a conservative path in resisting proposals to enlarge service or reduce rates until it was clear that the traffic justified the change.[37]

The other side of the coin shows traffic concentrated in a few routes involving in turn the plight of the communities with relatively sparse traffic. These communities demand air service, and the CAB has responded by granting certificates on a three-year basis to a number of "feeder" lines to operate on spur-type routes feeding into the main trunk lines. These lines have had greater financial troubles than the trunk lines in the postwar period and continue to need substantial subsidies to remain in operation. The feeder lines join the trunk line companies, however, in opposition to the nonscheduled airlines.

The nonskeds are firms or groups of firms flying a limited number of flights over a given route and not adhering to fixed schedules of flight. The nonskeds have generally offered lower rates and less luxurious accommodations than the regular airlines, and they have been a major factor in persuading the scheduled lines to adopt air-coach service. After World War II the nonskeds, which until that time had been exempted from CAB control, grew rapidly. The CAB decided to require them to register and to apply individually for specific exemption from certification and rate requirements.

Since 1955, nonskeds have been permitted to fly up to ten scheduled flights per month. Some nonskeds have worked closely together and provided what amounted to full scheduled service. The scheduled lines have vigorously opposed the nonskeds on grounds of inferior safety and also have argued that the nonskeds took the cream of the passenger traffic without serving less heavily traveled routes. The nonskeds reply that they have forced many innovations in the industry, such as air-coach service, which demonstrates that the competition of new firms in the airline industry is healthy for everyone. The CAB has taken the position that any large scale nonscheduled flight service would endanger the stability and earnings of the certificated carriers, and in line with this policy the Board has revoked the permit of Trans-American Airlines which was the largest of the nonsked group.[38]

---

[37] See Keyes, *op. cit.*

[38] See Robert Bendiner, "The Rise and Fall of the Nonskeds," *The Reporter,* Vol. 16 (May 30, 1957), pp. 29-34.

Airline earnings and subsidies

Whether the earnings of the airline industry are really marginal and need continued CAB protection has been questioned. Localities that want more air service and taxpayers who want less subsidy payments are both strongly represented in Congress, and both groups have had reason to be unhappy with the trunk airlines from time to time. There were moves in 1956 to reduce the appropriations for subsidies, and demands for a general investigation of airline earnings. Although the results of the full CAB inquiry into this problem are not yet available, preliminary data shows that from 1950 through 1955 the 13 domestic trunk lines averaged more than 10 per cent return on their investment after taxes in each year. Some lines earned as high as 35 per cent return in one year. These earnings reduce the force of the argument against nonsked entrance into the industry. The trunk lines insist that averaged over all the years of operation their returns are not excessive, but the trends of the last several years show a major upswing in airline profits.

The result of the economic success of the trunk lines is that only one or two lines, it is estimated, will receive any subsidy for fiscal 1956 or 1957 and that all trunk lines will be in the black in fiscal 1958. The feeder lines, however, continue to rely heavily on airmail subsidies as do most of the lines engaged in international service. Even the trunk lines may not enjoy their newly achieved economic health for long, however. The transition to jet airliners is requiring a large investment, which increases even more as the price level rises. Terminal and other costs are rising too, and crowded airways make it difficult for airlines to increase their traffic. Thus in 1957 the major airlines were requesting a general rate increase which, however, may have the effect of slowing down their growth. Such conditions would make it unlikely that the nonskeds will be able to obtain permanent certification for some time.

The problems of providing airport facilities adequate to fast-growing needs, especially of large metropolitan centers, have been the basis for governmental action in the postwar period and promise to be of increasing significance in the years to come. Since airport facilities do not normally pay their way, and since most municipalities are already hard-pressed for funds, federal aid has been extended to local governments for airport construction. Since 1946 substantial grants-in-aid have been voted for this purpose by Congress. These funds, and those spent on developing the airway system, have not been sufficient to relieve all the dangerously overcrowded airports, or to provide an airway system regarded as adequate in a jet age. The latter project alone has been estimated to cost several hundred million dollars, and the needs of air transportation must, of course, compete with many other interests for public money. President Eisenhower recommended that an Airways Modernization Board be established to develop traffic control systems to deal with congestion and safety hazards, and in the summer of 1957 Congress authorized the agency. It is clear that problems of air transportation will be in the forefront of governmental activity for many years to come.

THE AMERICAN HIGHWAY SYSTEM

Although airplanes may be the most exciting aspect of modern transportation revolution, the most significant development from the point of view of commercial transportation and nonmilitary governmental programs is the phenomenal rise of motor vehicle transport.

TABLE 5.2

SURFACED ROAD MILAGE AND MOTOR VEHICLE REGISTRATIONS
IN THE UNITED STATES

	Surfaced road mileage	Motor vehicle registrations
1900	128,500	8,000
1920	369,122	9,239,161
1930	694,000	26,531,999
1940	1,367,000	32,035,424
1950	1,678,619	48,567,000
1954	1,905,871	62,020,000 (1955)

Data from U.S. Dept. of Commerce, Bureau of the Census, *Historical Statistics of the United States, 1789–1945* (Washington, D.C.: U.S. Government Printing Office, 1949), pp. 220-23; and *Statistical Abstract of the United States: 1956,* 77th ed. (Washington, D.C.: U.S. G.P.O., 1956), pp. 545, 551.

The growth of the automotive industry and of the industries related to automobiles and trucks has wrought far-reaching changes throughout the economy and in the political and social system as well. The manifold effects of this development can not all be considered here, but one area does deserve our concern—highways. The direct clash of many of the transportation interests over proposed highway programs in recent years affords an opportunity to examine these forces in case-study fashion as they relate to an issue of the broadest social significance. The highway programs are important in their own right too, for they are of enormous size financially, involve all levels of government, and call into play values and interests ranging from reservation Indians (states containing reservations want the federal government to provide the whole cost of highways through the reservations) to national defense.

Development of American highways

When the first automobiles appeared in the United States in the 1890's, the opportunities to drive them were severely limited. Although bicyclists had been trying to secure better roads, most of the roads outside the major cities were dirt tracks and even urban streets were often little more than mud. Long-distance transportation was almost inconceivable on these primitive roads; if motor vehicles were to have any future, highways had to be constructed for them. By 1900 many interest groups had begun to promote the cause of better highways.[39] The American Automobile Association, the American Road Builders Associations, promoters of "named highway" projects like the Lincoln highway, and others built political support to "get the traffic out of the mud." Although from time to time ever since 1806 the federal government had provided funds for road construction, the principal responsibility had remained with the county or township. The roads were normally built either by citizens who thus worked off their road taxes or by convicts. State officials had begun to establish state highway programs with state administrative control by 1916 when the first major federal highway legislation was passed. The Federal-Aid Act of 1916 authorized the expenditure of 75 million dollars in those states possessing responsible highway departments. World War I temporarily checked the program but also dramatized the possibilities of motor transport.

The Federal Highway Act of 1921 set the basic pattern followed by federal programs until 1956. The Act provided that grants were to be distributed to states one-third on the basis of population, one-third on the basis of area, and one-third on the basis of rural postal routes in the state. Each state was required to match the federal grant with its own funds and to submit to certain federally-prescribed standards of operation. The Act also provided that a system of interstate and intercounty roads should be designated up to 7 per cent of the total road mileage which would serve as the focus for federal aid. In 1925

[39] See F. L. Paxson, "The Highway Movement, 1916–1935," *American Historical Review*, Vol. 51 (1946), pp. 236-53.

this focal system of arterial highways was narrowed to a total of 70,000 miles.

In 1944 a separate system was authorized to be referred to as the National System of Interstate Highways and not to exceed 40,000 miles (increased in 1956 to 41,000 miles). The routes of this latter system were to connect the principal metropolitan areas of the country and were to receive a larger portion of their costs from the federal government. Also in 1944 federal aid was extended to urban extensions of routes receiving federal support in the rural areas. There are today four classifications of highways receiving federal aid; Interstate System, primary roads, secondary roads, and urban extensions. In addition, of course, states construct roads for which they receive no federal aid, as do counties and townships in some states. Cities are on their own so far as most of their street construction is concerned.

Highway finance. Throughout the first third of the twentieth century highway construction was expanded rapidly, and counties became utterly unable to finance the programs. Even at the state level, money from the property tax, the principal source of state and local income at that time, soon became scarce in the face of large capital expenditures for highways. At the national level the income tax was providing an ever greater share of the federal revenue and came predominantly from the eastern part of the country. Revenue for highway construction, however, was granted in larger proportion to the western states. Thus at both state and federal levels demands for new techniques to finance highways were heard, and the result was the gasoline tax, in most cases to be earmarked for highway construction purposes only. Through this tax the users of highways would provide the revenue to meet the costs of construction and maintenance, and the gasoline taxes imposed by federal and state governments have continued to be the principal source of revenue for highway purposes to this day.

Use of the gasoline tax and of other taxes imposed specifically on users of highways has not solved all the problems of highway finance, however. Most of the controversies that have developed in relation to highway problems in recent years have revolved around questions of finance. No one has successfully challenged the ever-increasing demand for highway construction and modernization as the traffic has grown, but how these highways were to be paid for has remained an area of disagreement. Truckers urgently want more and better highways but hope to avoid taxes that would bear especially upon them. Private motoring groups like the AAA also want an expanded highway program but hope to shift more of the financial burden onto the commercial vehicles which, because of their greater weight, account for a larger proportion of the wear and tear on the roads and necessitate heavier construction. Railroads and other competing groups seek to equalize what they consider to be an unfair advantage possessed by motor vehicles in not paying the full costs of their roads, and therefore ask higher taxes on trucks and buses. Farmers want to avoid paying taxes on gasoline used on the farm, and taxi drivers likewise oppose being taxed for the purpose of building highways they seldom see. Although some groups have argued that highway programs are so vital to national defense that part of their costs should be attributed to defense programs and paid for out of general revenue, this view has not so far been persuasive and financing highways from taxes on highway users has remained the basic principle. The only exception on a large scale occurred during the great Depression when highway projects were often built as relief measures to provide employment.

While finance is central, many groups are interested in other aspects of the highway programs. Many farmers are disturbed, for example, by the shift in the emphasis of federal programs to construction of intercity routes and away from secondary and "farm-to-market" roads. The American Farm Bureau Federation has opposed *any* expansion of federal highway programs, however financed, and has preferred to have states build the roads, hoping that at the state level farm groups would have more influence on which roads would receive the most emphasis. Another conflict in highway disputes has been between construction firms and labor groups over whether the prevailing wages of the area would have to be paid on highway projects, as is the case on most other federally financed projects. In the past, firms have sometimes imported workers to a high wage area so as to cut their costs, and labor groups tried successfully in 1956 to make sure that did not happen in the highway program. Proposals to increase taxes on the sale of trucks and buses and to tax rubber tires and retread rubber stimulated the affected groups to action. Problems of administrative organization—for example, whether to have state or federal officials determine the prevailing wage rates in each state—were matters of concern not only to the economic groups with stakes in the issue, but also to the affected bureaucracies. All of these groups actively tried to shape the course of legislation respecting highways with varying degrees of success, and their activities provided a broad panorama of politics at work.

The 1956 highway legislation

During World War II, highway construction in the United States came to a virtual standstill while, at the same time, there was substantial wear and tear on highways, especially from military vehicles. When the war ended the automobile population expanded rapidly, and the new cars moved at speeds that often made the old roads inadequate altogether. The financial problems of railroads of which we have spoken before helped stimulate the shift to trucks as means of commercial transportation. The net result was a substantial demand for repair and modernization of old roads and construction of new high-speed arterial highways to handle the new traffic. Congress responded to these demands by authorizing 2.4 billion dollars in total federal aid between 1948 and 1954. The biennial authorizations increased each two years of this period from 450 million dollars to 875 million dollars with an ever greater proportion being devoted to the interstate, metropolis-to-metropolis network. Despite these efforts the needs grew more rapidly than the appropriations, and from various sources proposals were made for long-range and massive efforts to overtake and get ahead of the highway demands.

Many states sought to meet the new demands by building toll roads. Following the prewar example of Pennsylvania, states issued bonds to be paid by the tolls received for use of the high speed, limited access superhighways over major long-distance routes. Through bond financing, these roads could be built in addition to those financed through gasoline taxes. Motorists, especially long distance truckers, received substantial savings in time and gasoline consumption. Some states found, however, that traffic on the new roads did not always provide toll revenue adequate to pay for the bonds, and problems of connecting toll routes for interstate travel were not always solved. In 1957 the Kansas turnpike still ended in an Oklahoma farmer's field.

In 1954, both Congress and the President began to study the possibilities of a long-term multi-billion dollar highway program to be financed primarily by the federal government to meet the needs of arterial highways. In early 1955, President Eisenhower released the report of his Advisory Committee which called for a program by all levels of government to cost 101 billion dollars over ten years. Of this total, 27 billion dollars was to be spent on the National System of Interstate Highways, 25 billion dollars to come from the federal government and be financed through bonds issued outside the regular debt structure of the federal government. These bonds would be retired from general revenue of future years. The Committee estimated that, with traffic continuing to increase and tax revenues from highway users also increasing, revenue would be adequate to pay off the bonds without raising taxes. The bond approach, however, would cost some 12 billion dollars in interest charges during the life of the bonds. Many groups vigorously opposed the bond issue proposal, among them the American Automobile Association and the Association of American Railroads, while the American Trucking Association supported the proposal. Many Congressional leaders argued that highways should be financed by increased user taxes and began to push in that direction.

One element of conflict in the situation involved competition between the political party groups in Congress as each tried to secure whatever advantages there might be in the highway programs. Senate Democrats sponsored a bill which finally passed the Senate providing for a five-year, 12¼ billion dollar program and which preserved more of the traditional emphasis on primary and secondary roads than the Administration plan did. In the House, alternatives to the bond issue approach to financing were developed, and higher taxes were proposed bearing particularly heavily on the things used by trucks, such as diesel fuel and truck tires, rather than on things used by automobiles. The AAA and AAR supported these proposals while the truckers and rubber manufacturers (and the American Farm Bureau Federation which opposed any extension of the federal program) opposed the tax increases. The "pay-as-you-go" tax proposals were defeated in the House, as was the Administration proposal to issue bonds. The bill passed by the Senate, containing no provisions for raising additional money, did not pass the House, so no final action was taken during 1955.

In 1956 the President again urged action on the highway program, and it was said that the Administration would now accept the "pay-as-you-go" principle insisted upon by most Democrats. The proposed tax increases were scaled down somewhat as they affected trucks and buses, and the American Trucking Associations supported the new bill. The AAA and the AAR continued to try to place a greater share of the costs of the program on the truckers, but the disagreements had been moderated sufficiently so that while many groups remained only partially satisfied, the bill finally passed without significant opposition.

The Federal-Aid Highway Act of 1956 authorized the largest road-building program in American history: 31.5 billion dollars are to be spent over a 13-year period of which nearly 27 billion dollars are to come from the federal treasury. Primary and secondary roads and urban extensions of these roads are to receive increased assistance matched in each case by the states affected. Roads through national parks, public lands, and Indian Reservations, for which the federal government traditionally has taken responsibility, will be given increased sums. The bulk of the funds, however—nearly 25 billion dollars—is to be devoted to the Interstate System. The federal government is to pay approximately 90 per cent of the costs of this part of the program, and states will be given credit for toll roads that fit into the system. The money for the Interstate System is to be apportioned among the states more in accordance with population than the other programs have been, which means that urban industrial areas will receive greater benefits and farm groups fewer benefits than they have from past highway programs.

To provide revenue for the program, gasoline taxes were increased from 2 to 3 cents a gallon; taxes on tires from 5 to 8 cents a pound; a 3 per cent per pound tax was placed on camelback rubber used in retreading tires; the manufacturers' tax on the sale of trucks, trailers, and buses was increased from 8 to 10 per cent; and a tax of $1.50 per 1,000 pounds was imposed on trucks and buses weighing more than 26,000 pounds. The Secretary of the Treasury contended that these tax increases would not provide enough revenue to cover the costs of the program, but his objections were not given effective support.

Many points basic to an understanding of politics are illustrated by the controversies over the highway program. No matter how strong the support for a program may be *in general,* there will surely develop conflicts of interest when *specific* problems arise. Tax provisions, formulas for the allocation of funds, wage questions, the administrative structure, and many other issues are not to be solved by invoking general concepts like "public interest" or "general welfare." Rather, some groups will succeed and others fail, while through the give-and-take of negotiation and compromise some kind of decision is reached. The highway program that finally was accepted did not wholly please the truckers. They would have preferred not to pay any increased taxes. The railroads would have put greater tax burdens on their competition in motor transportation. The farm groups would have preferred greater emphasis on farm-to-market roads. The Democrats would have preferred a more distinctively Democratic bill upon which they could have campaigned in the 1956 election; the Republicans would have preferred the reverse. Yet the Senate voted 89-1 and the House voted 388-19 to pass the bill.

CONCLUSION

By way of summarizing the discussion of transportation politics and policies, it may be useful to point out the patterns of policy development in the field and to note what appear to be the main factors operating to shape this area of political activity. Each mode of transportation has passed through one or more stages of what may be described as a three-stage cycle; (1) subsidy and promotion, (2) regulation, and (3) private inter-carrier competition. In their infant days the railroads, the motor carriers, airlines, and water carriers all received substantial assistance from government as potential shippers and travelers sought expanded means of transportation and utilized public authority and public money to get it. Then, as the market for each type of carrier reached some degree of stability, customers and/or rival carriers found they were not satisfied with rates and service and once again sought to improve their position through governmental authority, this time through regulation. The development of new forms of transportation competing with the old has set the stage for the third phase of the cycle. Each new carrier has represented a threat to the older groups and has been resisted both in the economy and through the governmental processes. The increasingly complex conflicts of interest among competing carriers and shippers have begun to produce in the present era a shift away from policies of public control to policies permitting greater adjustment of inter-carrier conflict to take place outside governmental area, each carrier utilizing its advantages through economic bargaining. The phases of this cycle are not exclusive. Transportation groups still receive governmental assistance, as do many other groups in the society. Regulation—of rates, service, accounting, safety, and so on —still is very important in the operation of every phase of transportation.

A complicating factor has been introduced by the growth of organization, both governmental and private. In the regulatory phase, governmental agencies were established to administer the laws. As the cycle moved on, these agencies have tended to become bastions of defense for the regulated carriers against the new carriers. The railroads have associated themselves with the ICC and the scheduled airlines with the CAB. Each group of carriers has developed its own organization which speaks for part but not all of the industry. Thus the AAR does not represent equally the interest of all railroads, and the Air Transport Association speaks only for scheduled air carriers.

The changes that have taken place in transportation policy have not been responses to recommendations of "sound public policy." They do not follow from definitions of the "public interest." They may be compatible with some versions of either of these concepts, but the concepts have not produced the changes. Rather transportation policy has evolved mainly in response to changes in the technology of transportation, in the economic relationships both within and outside of transportation, and to the activities on the political front stimulated by the first two factors. The invention of the internal combustion engine had fundamental consequences for railroad interests. The inflation following World War II had great effect on the nature of rail-motor competition. The shift in emphasis by farm groups away from monopoly regulation toward price-support programs changed the political position of the railroads by diverting a major part of their opposition. One must also note the effects of a war that permitted the railroads to increase earnings but wear out equipment while suspending highway construction and motor carrier expansion for want of materials. It is to such basic factors one must look to understand transportation politics and policy. How these factors will operate in the future remains unknown; one can predict only that the policies adopted by Congress, the decisions of regulatory commissions, and the goals sought by the carriers themselves will largely turn on them.

BIBLIOGRAPHICAL NOTE

Full-scale treatments of transportation development and current problems may be found in Philip D. Locklin, *Economics of Transportation,* 4th ed., 1954; Russell E. Westmeyer, *Economics of Transportation,* 1952; Marvin Fair and Ernest Williams, *Economics of Transportation,* 1950; and Charles L. Dearing and Wilfred Owen, *National Transportation Policy,* 1949. Each of these volumes deals with the economic aspects of transportation and includes discussion of the historical development of public policy in this field.

Few systematic studies of the organized interest groups active in transportation politics are available, but John G. Schott, *The Transportation Monopoly,* 1950; Arne C. Wiprud, *Justice in Transportation,* 1945; and Senate *Report* No. 26, pt. 2, 77th Congress, 1st Session (1941) contain valuable information concerning railroad groups.

Most general studies of transportation concentrate attention on the railroad industry. Students desiring more data about other transport industries may consult Charles A. Taff, *Commercial Motor Transportation,* 1952; and Richard Hellman, "The Air Transport Industry," in Walter Adams, ed., *The Structure of American Industry,* rev. ed., 1954.

The Interstate Commerce Commission is the subject of I. L. Scharfman's authoritative *The Interstate Commerce Commission* in four volumes, 1931–1935. A more recent analysis that emphasizes the ICC's relationship with the carriers it controls is Samuel Huntington, "The Marasmus of the ICC," *Yale Law Journal,* Vol. 61 (1952), pp. 467-509. See also the discussion of Huntington's findings in *Yale Law Journal,* Vol. 62 (1953), pp. 171-226, 561-74 and Vol. 63 (1953), pp. 44-63.

A brief but valuable history of the early years of highway development in the United States may be found in F. L. Paxson, "The Highway Movement, 1916–1935," *American Historical Review,* Vol. 51 (1946), pp. 236-53. The 1956 highway legislation may be conveniently traced in "13-Year Highway Program," *Congressional Quarterly Almanac,* 84th Congress, 2nd Session (1956), 1957, pp. 398-408.

6. ROBERT H. SALISBURY

Agriculture and Natural Resources

TO understand the political climate within which American agricultural policy has been made, we must understand first the *ideology* surrounding farming in this country.[1] At least since the days of Thomas
Jefferson, when small farmers were beginning to look on manufacturers and merchants as economic and political enemies, farming has
been vested by writers, newspapers, political orators, and farmers
themselves with special qualities—qualities that made it right and
desirable for government to protect farmers against those who would
take advantage of them. Three broad themes run through this type of
argument.

First, agriculture is regarded as logically prior to any other economic
activity. All of us must eat before we do anything else. Farming is thus
indispensable to the welfare of all, and if farmers are not given a "fair
share" of material rewards then governmental action should correct
the situation and place agriculture—the "first industry"—on a par
with other occupational groups. Then too, farming is harder work and
often less rewarding in a material way than work in most other fields.
No eight-hour day, no minimum wage, no plush offices are available
to the farmer. He rises before dawn, works fiercely all day, is isolated

---

[1] An excellent explanation of agrarian ideology in the United States can be found in
Richard Hofstadterm, *The Age of Reform* (New York: Alfred A. Knopf, Inc., 1955),
Part I.

195

from his fellows, enjoys fewer of the comforts of urban life, faces myriad perils from nature, and gets relatively small cash rewards for his efforts. Moreover, his income is uncertain. Not only do the fluctuations in market prices and farming costs plague him, but a hail storm at a critical time may destroy a year's crop and with it a year's income. Third, there is a strong strain in the talking and writing about American agriculture to the effect that farmers are better, more virtuous people than city dwellers. The city is the center of high crime rates and generally sinful activities—or, at the least, is filled with smoke and traffic. In the country, on the other hand, the air is pure, the grass is green, and man is part of nature's life-giving processes. For this reason too, then, farmers and farming deserve a preferred place at the hands of governmental authority.

The situation with natural resources is somewhat different. For most of our history the problem of resources was largely ignored; we had more resources than we needed, and in any event there was nothing that government need do, except see that the resources were handed out in a more or less equitable fashion. During this century, however, especially as a result of President Theodore Roosevelt's keen interest in the West, conservation of natural resources has become a major public responsibility at all levels of government. The relation between agriculture and resources, moreover, is a very close one. Farmland is surely our single most important resource, and the government seeks to protect its fertility even when the farmer himself may not see the need for careful protection of the soil. Our farm policy is based in part on such resource-protecting techniques as the soil bank, under which farmers contract to divert general cropland to soil, water, forestry, and wildlife conservation practices. For purposes of clarity this chapter will take up first agriculture and then natural resources, but both of these must be viewed as part of an inseparable whole.

FARM POLICY: ECONOMIC AND POLITICAL BACKGROUND

Farming is not only a way of life, it is a business. And admirable as the *way of life* may be, the *business* of farming has presented serious problems for decades. In the days when the pioneers settled the frontier and until after the Civil War, many farmers engaged in what was basically subsistence agriculture. They raised the food and fibers necessary to feed, clothe, and house their families, selling or bartering only enough to secure commodities, such as salt or calico cloth, that they could not supply themselves. Particularly in the Midwest of this period, where few people lived in cities, very little commercial agriculture took place.

The agricultural revolution

The coming of mechanization to farming, however, changed this pattern drastically. With a reaper and later with a combine one man could harvest a wheat crop that formerly had required many men. Gang plows, improved seed, and other technological improvements made it possible for a farmer to raise enough crops not only to feed himself and his family but to sell in substantial quantities as well. To buy the new machinery the farmer needed cash, and by selling in the market a farmer could get cash. Farming on a cash basis meant that farmers would specialize, raising those crops that gave them the greatest returns in their climate and soil, rather than trying to raise all the needs of the family. By specializing and using machinery the productivity of the farmer increased, and with the cash received from selling his increased output a farmer could begin to buy not only machinery and the necessities he formerly had raised himself but also some of the comforts previously enjoyed by his city cousins. Thus today electric freezers, automobiles, and television sets are bought by farmers from the proceeds of commercial cash agriculture—radically different from subsistence agriculture.

Cash farming brought many advantages to farmers, but it also posed many problems—problems that have provided the basis for most issues of modern agricultural politics. First and foremost, cash farming made farmers dependent on markets: markets in which their products were sold and where the object was to secure the highest possible price, and markets where farmers bought at the lowest possible price the machinery and other products they now needed. In order for cash farming to be profitable, farmers had to secure more for the things they sold than they paid out for the things they bought, and in the latter 19th century when cash farming really took hold this did not always happen. For one thing, the markets in which farmers sold their products were distant. To reach them, transportation, usually by rail, was necessary, and thus farmers became dependent on railroads. Moreover, some markets were "rigged" by grain speculators or meat packers who on occasion conspired to hold down prices paid to the unorganized farmers. Even in an honest market no individual farmer's product would be required to provide the needed supply of a commodity. The small number of flour mills or meat packers who bought from the farmers could often quite easily and legitimately play off one solitary small farmer against another. Nor could the farmer afford to wait until the price went up next year. His crop might spoil if it was not quickly sold or stored. The packer or miller, on the other hand, could wait. The tendency was strong, therefore, for farmers to operate at a disadvantage in selling their products. Often a great host of farmers selling identical bushels of wheat or bales of cotton faced a few, often highly organized, buyers.

At the same time, in the markets where farmers bought the things they needed, the manufacturers of farm machinery comprised one of the early trusts, and many other industries supplying farmers with indispensable commodities were few in number and highly organized. Again the solitary farmer was at a disadvantage. No manufacturer needed the custom of any specific farmer, yet no specific farmer could do without the manufacturer's product. Thus in selling and buying alike the farmer had less bargaining power than those with whom he had to deal.

A further problem was presented by the very fact of the farmer's increasing productivity. As machinery and technique improved, farmers could produce more and more. But an increasing output of a product will not bring the producer more income unless the demand for the product also increases. An expanding population in the United States meant more mouths to feed, of course, but farm productivity increased more rapidly than the population. Up to a point, as people earn more income they buy more food, so that as *per capita* income rose so did consumption of farm products. But as income rises a smaller and smaller proportion of income goes for food, and indeed, after a certain level is reached, the higher the income the less of such commodities as bread and potatoes are consumed altogether. More and more money is spent instead on services, appliances, and luxuries. The result of this tendency has been that as the economy has expanded the farm sector has occupied a less important place and has secured a smaller proportion of the national income.

In the face of the higher incomes available from industrial work a steady stream of farmers has left agriculture and moved to the city, and in recent years the farm population has suffered not only a relative loss of numbers but is actually smaller than formerly. However, the movement off the farm has not reduced agricultural productivity, and the remaining farmers have been confronted over and over with

TABLE 6.1

THE DECLINE OF AMERICAN AGRICULTURE

Percentage of total national income going to farmers		Percentage of U.S. population living on farms	
1869–1879	20.5	1910	34.9
1899–1908	16.7	1920	30.1
1919–1928	12.2	1930	24.9
1933	8.9	1940	23.2
1940	7.4	1950	16.6
1950	6.9	1954	13.5
1954	5.3		

From *Historical Statistics of the United States* and *Statistical Abstract of the United States: 1956.*

the specter of falling prices and incomes. Besides the reasons for falling prices already noted, the planning of farm production is very difficult. A farmer plants a crop or breeds his livestock long in advance of the actual sale and must guess at the probable future price. If he guesses wrong and the price is below his expectation, he must salvage what he can by selling a larger volume of goods. The tendency is for each farmer to produce as much as possible. But if all farmers produce to the maximum the supply will be so great that the bottom will fall out of the market price. Education and information on the nature and probable future state of the market can alleviate somewhat this tendency to overproduce, and the U.S. Department of Agriculture and state agriculture colleges carry out work of this kind. But even so, without some sort of disciplined control, whether private or governmental, American farmers today tend to produce more than can be sold at prices that are satisfactory to them. The main exception to this rule has occurred during the three war periods of the 20th century. During each period, foreign production declined and American demand increased, with the result that farm prices improved substantially.

The facts of farming as a business are thus in sharp contrast to the values often expressed by those who extoll farming as a way of life. As a group in society farmers are declining in numbers both relative to the rest of the population and absolutely. The economic strength of the farm sector of the economy likewise has been steadily reduced; virtually every other major industry has grown more rapidly than agriculture. The very productivity achieved through use of machinery and scientific techniques of farming often compound the problems of securing adequate income. This situation did not develop all at once, of course. It has, however, been the dominant tendency since the permanent full scale shift to cash farming during and after the Civil War.

The political representation of farmers

The economic and numerical decline of agriculture in American society has occurred in the context of the American political system, which gives to rural people political strength greater than their numbers alone would justify. In the United States Senate each *state* is equally represented, which means that a predominantly rural state with a small population like North Dakota will have the same voting strength as a heavily populated, mainly urban state like New York. In the House of Representatives seats are allotted to each state primarily on the basis of population. But House districts are drawn by state legislatures, and state legislatures in almost every state over-represent rural interests. Thus in the House, too, farmers have a louder voice than mere numbers or economic strength would give them. Trying to recoup in the governmental area the ground lost in the economy, farmers since the Civil War have made primarily political responses to economic adversity.

Basic to successful political action is organization, and, as we shall see later, there have developed in agriculture several fairly strong organizations representing various groups of farmers. At this point we should note, however, that disorganization has been a chronic problem in agriculture, too. Whereas business did become progressively better organized in the latter 19th and early 20th centuries, the farmers tended to remain relatively solitary and isolated. Indeed, therein lay part of their economic troubles. Since World War I farmers have developed stronger organizations, especially for purposes of advancing political objectives. Direct organization for economic goals, however, without intervening political and governmental action—for example, production control, price maintenance, and so forth—has not yet been very successful. Farmer cooperatives are perhaps the strongest kind of organized farm group operating primarily in the economic sphere with only incidental political concerns.

Early governmental programs for agriculture

The early attempts to organize discontented farmers for purposes of recovering their power were quite differently focused than those of the more contemporary era. The Granger movement of the late 1860's and early '70's, the Farmer's Alliance, and the Populist Party were three important organizations drawing most of their strength from agricultural interests. The Populists, of course, organized as a party rather than a specifically agricultural interest group, but the main themes of all three organizations and of others of this period of the latter 19th century were similar. The political program was twofold: (1) break up the trusts and combines of the business world through antitrust proceedings, and (2) regulate the rates charged by public-utility type enterprises. The image of the business firms with which farmers had to deal was one of conspiracy and monopoly, and the public policy goal was to control these monopolies through governmental authority. The image of business conspiracy was mingled with the image of agrarian independent and individualist virtue. These appeals continue to be heard in the rhetoric of agricultural debate. The policy objectives of farm organization, however, have changed substantially. Antitrust action still receives support from farm groups, and the most consistent opponents of railroad rate increases have been the several agricultural organizations. But the main theme of farmer demands since World War I has been for direct governmental support of farm prices and income.[2]

Although it took several decades to become fully operative, the idea early gained currency that the answer to the problem of declining farm prices was to increase those prices rather than try to decrease the prices of other commodities through antitrust and regulation. The first major step in this direction was the establishment of agricultural education and service agencies designed to teach farmers how to improve their methods, get bigger yields, and earn larger profits. Three major types of activity were undertaken in this direction and all three continue to provide important services today. In 1862 the federal government established the Department of Agriculture "to acquire and diffuse useful information on agricultural subjects." [3] The Department (USDA) for many years after its establishment confined itself to distributing free seeds and other similarly marginal functions. But beginning about 1900 the research and service functions of the Department were expanded until today over 70,000 employees supervise the expenditure of sums in the neighborhood of two billion dollars.

[2] The most comprehensive history of farm policies in the United States is Murray Benedict, *Farm Policies in the United States, 1790–1950* (New York: Twentieth Century Fund, 1953).

[3] John M. Gaus and Leon O. Wolcott have written the most comprehensive description of the development of USDA in *Public Administration and the United States Department of Agriculture* (Chicago: Public Administration Service, 1940).

In 1862 also a second approach to raising farm standards of living was taken with the passage of the Morrill Act, which provided grants of public lands to endow colleges "for the benefit of agriculture and the mechanic arts." These colleges, in most instances, became far more than simply centers of agricultural research and training, but the latter have remained central functions. The agricultural colleges have continued as an important element in the structure of agricultural politics, and as such will be further treated below. Suffice to say, for the moment, that they represent the attempt to educate farmers to higher income.

The service and education efforts were supplemented shortly after 1900 by the development of the extension program.[4] Extension was in one sense simply bringing education and research directly to farmers through face-to-face demonstration and training. This field education came to have more profound significance, however, with the organization and expansion of the Extension program, which was financed after 1914 partly by federal funds, partly by state governments, and partly by private groups of farmers and businessmen. Extension became a focal point for organizing the more prosperous farmers who tended to be more receptive to demonstrations of new techniques. To some degree the emphasis on education, research, and extension programs as means of increasing rural prosperity meant less support for direct programs of price support and production control. The latter type of program has achieved strongest backing from those farmers not so clearly benefitted by or closely linked to the educational approach.

Direct support for farmers

All the major farm organizations have sought more direct governmental assistance, however. The "golden years" for farm prices, 1909-1914, were followed by the heavy demands and high prices of World War I, but, following the war, demand collapsed and so did prices. Throughout the 1920's, farm prices remained relatively low despite the prosperity of other sectors of the economy. During this period also the American Farm Bureau Federation rose to prominence and power in farm politics and along with the older Grange began to seek various programs that would shore up domestic prices. A number of proposals were made, through the "Farm Bloc" in the Senate, and two versions of the McNary-Haugen bill were passed by Congress, only to be vetoed by President Coolidge.

[4] See Gladys Baker, *The County Agent* (Chicago: University of Chicago Press, 1939).

The McNary-Haugen bills and several other proposals of the period were based on a generally accepted control device, the tariff. The idea was to "make the tariff work" to achieve "equality for agriculture." Farm products were to be purchased by the federal government in quantities sufficient to raise the domestic United States price to acceptable levels. The stocks so purchased would be sold at the presumably lower world price and the losses recouped by some means of equalization fee subtracted from the supported United States price.

McNary-Haugenism never was put to the test of operation, but the establishment of the Federal Farm Board in 1929 attempted a similar program without the foreign trade features. The Federal Farm Board was endowed with a revolving fund of 500 million dollars, which was to be used in support of cooperative marketing associations. The associations were to stabilize farm prices by buying when prices were low and selling when prices were high. The Board stepped in to buy large quantities of cotton and wheat as well as several other commodities. By 1931 the combination of general depression and a bumper crop resulted in huge surpluses, and the Board ceased operation after losing nearly 400 million dollars.

The lessons of the Federal Farm Board failure were clear by the time the Roosevelt administration took office in 1933. Price support programs could not succeed in raising price levels for farm products unless one of two other situations obtained; either demand increased or production declined. General depression and a relatively inelastic demand for farm products meant that in many cases production would have to be reduced in order to achieve price increases. Since farmers normally tended to increase production in the face of falling prices, and especially did so when the Farm Board would purchase the increase at artificially high levels, the inescapable conclusion was that governmental policy would have to include provisions to curtail production. The first Agricultural Adjustment Act in 1933, therefore, provided that the Secretary of Agriculture could contract to make payments to farmers in return for reducing acreage or for raising less livestock. Money for the payments was to come from a tax levied upon processors of basic farm commodities such as cotton ginners, meat packers, and flour millers. Cotton, tobacco, and potato production control was soon made mandatory for all growers if controls were accepted by two-thirds of the growers in referendum vote.

In 1936 this legislative program was declared unconstitutional by the Supreme Court on the grounds that the tax on processors benefitted special interests rather than the general welfare and that the control of agricultural production was a state concern beyond the legitimate authority of Congress.[5] Congress quickly restored federal assistance to farmers by offering payments in return for taking land out of production of soil-depleting crops and for following other conservation practices. The object was to provide additional farm income under the guise of conservation, and crops adjudged to be soil-depleting were those in excess supply.

In 1938 Congress passed new basic farm legislation restoring the policy of supporting agricultural prices and of providing for production controls when necessary. The processor tax was eliminated and the post-1937 Supreme Court—now a "liberalized court"—sustained the legislation as a legitimate regulation of interstate commerce.[6] The 1938 law established three basic concepts of agriculture policy which continue in present-day legislation; *parity, acreage allotments,* and *marketing quotas.* Each of these will be discussed primarily as it is currently in operation.

Parity

Parity is a relationship—a relationship between the prices farmers pay for the things they buy and the prices farmers receive for the things they sell. The relationship or ratio varies from one period to another as farmers find themselves in better or worse position in relation to other segments of the economy. One way to look at the parity concept is to see it as a relationship in terms of prices between farmers and other producers. It has already been noted that farmers are in a position of economic decline relative to other sectors of the economy. By trying to secure parity prices the farmers seek to recoup through government what they have lost in the economy.

Parity is not, of course, just any relationship between prices received and prices paid. It is rather an ideal relationship based on some period in the past. Until 1948 the base period—the ideal relationship—was 1909–1914 when farmers had enjoyed their greatest peacetime prosperity in this century. Thus a program guaranteeing full, or 100 per cent parity would mean that farmers would be assured prices for their products sufficient to give them buying power equivalent to the buying power of 1909–1914. If the prices of things farmers buy have doubled, then farm products should also bring twice the return.

[5] *U.S. v. Butler,* 297 U.S. 1 (1936).
[6] *Mulford v. Smith,* 307 U.S. 38 (1939); *Wickard v. Filburn,* 317 U.S. 111 (1942).

Beginning in 1948 a "modernized" parity formula was introduced. It did not become the mandatory formula, however, until 1957, since Congress permitted farmers to use either the "old" or "new" formula, whichever provided the higher parity price for each commodity. "Modernized" parity is figured by calculating the average price received by farmers for each commodity over the previous 10 years, making certain adjustments to take account of changes in demand for various agricultural products, and then relating this figure to prices farmers pay for some 350 items. "Modernized" parity results in lower parity prices for many commodities, especially wheat and feed grains, while giving higher returns on livestock when that commodity is supported. In 1956 the "old" parity formula was dropped and except for some commodities going through a period of gradual adjustment, the "modernized" formula is now in operation.

Full parity would provide full equality of purchasing power per bushel of corn or per bale of cotton with that of the base period. Actual legislative protection has not normally provided 100 per cent of parity. The 1938 legislation authorized price supports at from 52 to 75 per cent of parity; supports being pegged higher when supplies fell and lower when production increased. During the war period farm prices rose well above 100 per cent of parity, and the OPA was forbidden to put ceilings on farm prices until they reached 110 per cent of parity. When price controls were removed in 1946, farm prices rose still further to 115 per cent in 1947. From 1942 to 1955 Congress required prices to be supported no lower than 90 per cent. During the war years farm prices were considerably higher than that, but price supports were used to encourage farmers to plant crops that were especially needed for the war effort. The Acts of 1948 and 1949 provided that price supports should range between 60 per cent (1948) or 75 per cent (1949) and 90 per cent of parity, depending on whether supplies were large or small. However, the application of this flexible principle was postponed several times and did not go into operation until 1955 and then only after a considerable struggle.

Not all farm commodities are supported at the same level. There are three categories of commodities: basics, designated nonbasics, and others. Basic commodities include wheat, corn, cotton, tobacco, rice, and peanuts. These crops must be supported between 75 and 90 per cent of parity. Certain other designated commodities like feed grains—oats, barley, rye, and sorghums—are supported at somewhat lower levels. Livestock and other products may be supported at any level from 0 to 90 per cent of parity. The price at which each commodity will be supported is determined separately by the Secretary of Agriculture on the basis of the anticipated production and expected demand. Generally, the greater the expected supply in relation to demand, the lower the support price.

The mechanism by which prices are supported centers around the Commodity Credit Corporation. When the Secretary of Agriculture announces the support level for a crop, usually prior to planting time, this means that the Commodity Credit Corporation stands ready to grant what are called nonrecourse loans at the announced level. If the support level for corn is $1.60 per bushel, then, if the market price at the time of harvest is below $1.60, farmers may place their crop in storage and get a loan from the CCC of $1.60 per bushel. If, at any time, during the next year the market price exceeds $1.60, the farmer may redeem his loan and sell his crop. If, however, market prices remain below support prices, at the end of the year the CCC takes full possession, and the farmer keeps the loan money. In this latter case surpluses are accumulated.

Acreage allotments and marketing quotas

Without some means of controlling production the price support program could not operate except by incurring astronomical cost and collecting mountainous surpluses. We have seen that the 1933 AAA offered farmers payments designed to raise their income in return for taking land out of production, and that under the conservation label the 1936 legislation did likewise. Since 1938 there have been three principal ways by which the problem of production control has been approached: flexible price supports, acreage allotments, and marketing quotas. When price support levels are permitted by law to vary, the Secretary of Agriculture tries to lower supports whenever it appears that there will be an oversupply of a commodity. It is hoped that the lower support price will encourage farmers to plant other crops instead. However, many farmers may be unable to grow other crops and may instead increase production so as to receive equivalent income at the lower per bushel price. Consequently, in the short run, while high support levels usually will encourage increased production of a commodity (and were used for this purpose during the war periods), low support levels may not result in decreased production.

In the light of this situation Congress has authorized the Secretary of Agriculture to establish *acreage allotments* for commodities that promise to be in oversupply. These allotments are allocated to states, counties, and, finally, to individual farms of the growing area, and although acreage allotments are voluntary a farmer may not produce on more than his allotted acres and still be eligible for the full support price. A farmer may, however, use fertilizer and other means to increase his yield on his allotment, and a cotton farmer, for example, may devote his extra acreage to corn production, thus diminishing the effect of corn acreage controls. Moreover, Congress has provided limits below which basic crop acreage may not be reduced. Thus acreage allotments are often not effective means of bringing production down to a level at which market demand will return full parity prices.

Considerably more rigorous control of production is achieved through the use of marketing quotas. When supplies of a commodity exceed by more than a stated percentage the "normal" supply, the Secretary of Agriculture is required to present a choice to the growers of the commodity. Either they must accept by a two-thirds majority limits on the amount they may market (in bushels or pounds, not acres), or price supports will fall to 50 per cent of parity (0 per cent for tobacco). If marketing quotas are accepted in referendum vote, any farmer who sells or consumes himself more than his quota must pay a heavy tax on the excess. The rigor of marketing quotas notwithstanding, almost every time they have been proposed the farmers concerned have accepted them in referendums. Marketing quotas were imposed several times prior to World War II and again, especially for wheat, in the attempt to reduce the surpluses of the 1950's.

Conservation and the soil bank. We have already noted that after the first AAA was declared unconstitutional in 1936 Congress adopted as a temporary means of assisting farm income the Soil Conservation and Domestic Allotment Act, which made payments to farmers who followed soil-conserving practices, especially that of taking commercial cropland out of production. Since that time one of the available techniques by which farm production could be controlled has been through practices designed to conserve and strengthen the soil. The payments made to farmers who follow these practices (payments which currently cover only a portion of what it costs the farmer) are inducements to farm more efficiently and productively. In this sense conservation payments in the long run may increase production and perhaps decrease farm prices. But in the short run conservation often means putting cropland into grass or planting timber, and in turn production may decline. Except for the 1936–1938 period conservation payments have not been the major means of controlling farm production or income but the general technique is potentially an important one. The fact that the benefits of conservation have somewhat wider political appeal than price supports and production control suggests that conservation payments may occupy an important place in farm programs of the future.

Actually, under a slightly different name they already have come into substantial prominence. The *Soil Bank* program passed by Congress in the late spring of 1956 has received considerable attention as a device to reduce farm production without reducing income, all in the name of conservation. The origins of the soil bank are somewhat confused as leaders of both political parties have sought to secure whatever advantage might accrue to the sponsors of the program. Some Democrats advocated a plan similar to the one finally adopted when farm income dropped precipitately in 1955. At that time Republican Secretary of Agriculture, Ezra Benson, rejected the proposal, but in January, 1956, President Eisenhower asked Congress to pass a soil bank program. After a strenuous legislative struggle the soil bank was approved but was linked with provisions restoring price supports to 90 per cent of parity. The President vetoed this bill and again asked for the soil bank alone, which Congress then passed.

Under the Soil Bank program farmers may contract with the Secretary of Agriculture to place a portion of their *allotted* acres either in what is called the *acreage reserve* or in the *conservation reserve*. A farmer placing land in the acreage reserve may not plant or graze the acres. In return the farmer receives payments equal to a portion, usually about 50 per cent, of his average income from the acreage. Farmers participating in conservation reserve must use conservation practices on the acreage removed from cultivation and in return receive payments to meet part of the cost of the conservation practices as well as payments equal to a portion of the average return. The acreage reserve program has been authorized until 1959 and the conservation reserve until 1972. Money for the program, however, has been appropriated on a year-to-year basis. 260 million dollars were paid out during 1956 under the soil bank program, most of it in the corn belt, where corn growers had to join the program to qualify for crop supports.

Prior to the 1956 election there was a good deal of speculation concerning what effects these payments might have on the voting in rural areas. In 1957 many farmers seemed reluctant to put acres into the bank and payments were lower than the Administration had anticipated. Just how much effect "conservation" programs of this sort will have on production and income remains uncertain. Although rather large sums of money are to be allocated to this program, its effects seem so far to be relatively modest. The difference between the expected and the actual benefits may be the basis of change in the original wide support for the soil bank given by leaders of both parties and a broad assortment of interest groups, and of the increasing volume of criticism of the soil bank during 1957.

The administration of agricultural conservation

The soil bank is primarily administered by the Secretary of Agriculture, but the older conservation program involves two rather distinctive administrative groups, the Soil Conservation Service and the Agricultural Stabilization and Conservation farmer committees.[7] The former agency provides technical advice and assistance to farmers to aid them in planning more efficient use of their land and water. SCS works through soil conservation districts and has at times been regarded by such groups as the American Farm Bureau Federation as a potential basis for building a powerful interest group. The Federation has tended to oppose SCS programs and sought to place SCS in subordination to the Extension service with which AFBF enjoys very close relations.

The ASC committees are composed of farmers in each rural county elected by the farmers of the county. The committees supervise the local operation of several basic programs, including acreage allotments, marketing quotas, and conservation payments. For many years Republicans charged that these committees, formerly part of the Production and Marketing Administration, were means of dispensing Democratic party favors. When the Eisenhower administration came into office, a federally appointed official was placed in charge of each county committee office,[8] but, except for the patronage advantage, the transfer of power in Washington does not seem to have changed drastically the operation of the committees.

THE POLITICS OF AGRICULTURE

We have noted that the administrative structure of the conservation programs has been a subject of conflict among different groups. What is true of conservation is true of all of agriculture. The agricultural

[7] See Charles M. Hardin, *The Politics of Agriculture* (Glencoe, Ill.: The Free Press, 1952); Grant McConnell, *The Decline of Agrarian Democracy* (Berkeley and Los Angeles: University of California Press, 1953).

[8] See Wesley McCune, *Who's Behind Our Farm Policy?* (New York: Frederick A Prager, 1956), pp. 323-25.

community is not a single homogeneous group, united in its interests or agreeing in its demands. All of the preceding discussion of programs and policies must be understood in the light of the conflicting interests and competing activities of many groups of farmers and their nonfarming allies.

The commodity bases

The key basis of division among farmers is the fact that different farmers grow different crops. The interests of a wheat farmer may be quite different from those of a corn-hog farmer, those of cotton growers different from dairy farmers. These differences have endless ramifications; here we can distinguish three main groups of commodity interests: wheat, cotton, and corn-hog farmers.

Two main types of wheat are grown in the United States: spring wheat is raised mainly in the upper Great Plains States, winter wheat grows mainly in the lower Great Plains. Other regions, such as the Pacific Northwest, also produce wheat, and many farmers elsewhere grow some wheat. Politically, though, the "wheat states" are mainly the Plains States, especially Kansas and the Dakotas. The geography of wheat-growing is important, for the Plains States are located in a marginal rainfall belt.[9] That is, the adequacy of rainfall is always uncertain, and drought is an ever-present possibility. This, in turn, means that while some years may produce bumper crops, others may produce little at all. Moreover, technological development has had enormous impact on wheat farmers. The broad flat fields of wheat are ideally suited to mechanical harvesting, resulting in greater productivity of wheat farmers, who by increasing the supply of wheat create a downward pressure on price unless increased demand for wheat makes up the difference. But demand for wheat, especially American wheat, has not increased with production. When income levels rise generally, as they have in recent years in the United States, people eat less bread and cereal and more meat, vegetables, fruit, and dairy products. Prosperity for the economy as a whole does not, therefore, mean prosperity for wheat farmers. Finally, the United States has long exported wheat, but in the years since the Korean War its export market has declined drastically. All these factors taken together make wheat farming a more risky type of farming than many other kinds, and wheat farmers tend to seek more

[9] The factors which contribute to the political behavior of many wheat farmers are discussed in Carl F. Kraenzel, *The Great Plains in Transition* (Norman: University of Oklahoma Press, 1955).

governmental protection against those risks than do some other types of farmers.

By contrast, corn growers feed much of their crop to hogs and most of what is not consumed on the farm is sold for livestock feed. The corn-hog area is concentrated east of the wheat belt in Iowa, Illinois, and Indiana. Here the weather is much more reliable. Prosperity has increased the demand for meat as it has for the milk and eggs that many farmers in this same area produce commercially. Technology has had some effect in corn-growing, especially through the use of hybrid seeds, but the impact of machinery on the corn-hog production has not been as great as it has on wheat growers. Corn-hog farmers are not necessarily pleased with market conditions and have sought some degree of governmental protection, but generally they have been more restrained than wheat growers.

The position of cotton growers in recent years has usually been somewhere between corn-hog and wheat farmers. Mechanization has increased cotton yields, and vast cotton-growing undertakings in Egypt and other former colonial areas have taken away much of our onetime export market. But except when disease strikes, cotton production is fairly steady. Cotton farmers have sought more governmental assistance than corn growers but somewhat less than wheat.

Although these three crops, plus dairying, engage far more farm families than any others, many other crops are involved in agricultural policy and politics. An Oklahoma Senator, for example, may be primarily concerned with feed grains, such as sorghums, and with beef prices. A Kentucky Representative's chief problem is tobacco, while Arkansas raises large quantities of rice. Many products are the objects of specific programs of price supports and quota restrictions. A number of other products of more specialized type, such as avocadoes, are not much affected by these programs. In trying to generalize about agricultural politics these many variations must be kept in mind, and while corn, cotton, and wheat are the three major forces, most issues have a multitude of other interests involved.

Farm organizations

Farmers who specialize in corn, cotton, or wheat have tended in recent years to fall into two main camps; each vitally concerned with the direction of public policies, and each joining with a variety of other sympathetic groups.

The first camp is that of the wheat farmers, who have led the demands for greater governmental protection of farm prices, 90 per cent price supports (or, preferably, the Brannan Plan to be discussed below), federal crop insurance, expanded federal credit for farmers, adherence to the "old" parity base explained earlier, and so on. These programs have become increasingly identified as Democratic party programs, and although traditionally the Great Plains wheat belt has been strongly Republican the 1956 elections saw a number of Democratic victories in that area. Increasingly associated with this group are the Southern cotton belt farmers and their representatives, the feed-grain and range cattle interests of the Southwest, and those corn-hog farmers injured by drought. Many younger farmers who invested heavily in machinery in the post-war years and were hit hard by falling prices of 1952–1956 have also joined this alliance.

The chief organized spokesman for this point of view is the Farmers' Educational and Cooperative Union, usually referred to as the National Farmers' Union.[10] The "heartland" of the NFU is the Great Plains wheat belt, but in recent years the organization has moved into some parts of the Midwest and South. The NFU lays heavy emphasis on the "family farm" theme as it attacks corporate farming and "big business enemies" of agriculture. It was the only farm organization to support the original Brannan Plan and has consistently advocated maximum government help to the farmers. The NFU has come to work more and more closely with the Democratic leadership in Congress and has achieved a rather close alliance with the major elements of organized labor on legislative issues. The NFU has been the vigorous opponent of the Eisenhower Administration generally and of Secretary of Agriculture Ezra T. Benson in particular.

The second main camp, consisting of the bulk of the corn-hog farmers, many cotton growers, part of the dairy farmers, and scattered, but generally more prosperous, farmers in other areas, is represented mainly by the American Farm Bureau Federation.[11] Of the three major farm organizations the Farm Bureau is the youngest, as it was organized only in 1919. AFBF grew in close association with the Extension Service. Particularly after federal grants-in-aid were extended for Extension work in 1914, the county agents organized committees of the leading farmers of the county to arouse enthusiasm and provide some of the

[10] There is no recently published study that treats the NFU in any detail. McCune, *op. cit.*, and McConnell, *op. cit.*, both give the organization some attention.

[11] The "official" history of the American Farm Bureau Federation is O. M. Kile, *The Farm Bureau Through Three Decades* (Baltimore: Waverly Press, 1948). McConnell's study, *op. cit.*, is also primarily concerned with the Farm Bureau.

funds for Extension work. When these county bureaus were organized into state and national organizations the result was a powerful spokesman for the more prosperous and politically more active farmers. The AFBF has always had very close—at times almost semi-official—relations with the U.S. Department of Agriculture and with most of the land grant colleges. The main link has been Extension, and while the use of county agents as recruiting agents for the Bureau has declined under pressure from other farm groups, the policy views of these three organizations remain in harmony. The Farm Bureau played an enormously influential role throughout the 1920's and 1930's, and took much credit for writing the New Deal farm legislation. The Bureau fought the Soil Conservation Service and Farm Security Administration (see below), as potential rivals for power in farm politics. Not, however, until the Farmer's Union emerged in the post-war period as a cohesive organization, ready to work through the major parties for a full legislative program, was the AFBF presented with a real threat to its general position as principal spokesman for farmers on matters of public policy.

The Farm Bureau has been primarily a sectional alliance of Midwest corn-hog and Southern cotton interests. In the last decade the corn-hog interests have clearly been dominant, and the Bureau has much less political strength in the South than formerly. It has moved more and more firmly to a position of opposing broad-gauge government assistance to agriculture; at most it advocates flexible price supports and seeks restrictions of many other programs, not including extension or land grant college work. The Bureau has tried to decentralize the administration of many farm programs in order to give more authority to state governments, with which the Bureau's relations are more dependable than they are with a sometimes Democratic national administration. The AFBF has been closely aligned, increasingly in recent years, with Republican leaders and has warmly supported Secretary Benson. The Bureau has always worked more closely with business leaders, especially the Chamber of Commerce, than other farm groups, as local businessmen have always been active in support of county agent work. As the Bureau has moved toward advocating that more emphasis be placed on a free market in agriculture, its business ties have been strengthened. For the last several years the Bureau and the Farmers' Union have been almost diametrically opposed on issues of farm policy as each organization leads a broad alliance of interests.

A third general organization of farmers is perhaps of more historical interest than of contemporary political importance. This is the National

Grange. In the latter nineteenth century the Grange was a powerful force in advancing the political interests of farmers, but in recent decades its membership has found more attraction in the social side of Grange activities. Politically the Grange generally followed the position of the Farm Bureau, but in the past few years such influence as it can muster has been exercised in a "middle" position, somewhere between the Bureau and the NFU. The principal commodity base of the Grange is dairy products, and it is strongest in Northeastern United States, although its large membership is found from coast to coast.

Many more specialized organizations are active in farm politics on particular issues.[12] Such groups as the National Council of Farmer Cooperatives, the National Livestock Producers' Association, and many others, representing interests not only of farmers but also of processors and other businesses related to agriculture, may be very effective on specific issues of farm policy. Farm policy is an immensely complex combination of many different and often incompatible interests, and the activities of a wide variety of groups will normally be involved in its development.

CONTEMPORARY CONFLICTS

The close association of Democrats with the alliance headed by the Farmer's Union, and the ties between the American Farm Bureau Federation and the Republicans, represent a significant change from previous patterns of farm politics. The original "Farm Bloc" of the early 1920's which tried unsuccessfully to secure general price support legislation was essentially a bipartisan group of midwestern (especially Great Plains) Republicans and Southern Democrats. This coalition embraced the major commodity groups in agriculture and led by the AFBF it continued to dominate most farm policy-making throughout the period of the New Deal. Following World War II, however, the dominant corn-hog wing of AFBF began to move away from the Southern cotton and tobacco groups. The latter sought a continuation of maximum governmental supports including 90 per cent of parity that had been achieved during the War, and this meant closer relationships with the wheat farmers.

[12] McCune, *op. cit.*, and in his earlier study, *The Farm Bloc* (Garden City, N. Y.: Doubleday, Doran and Company, 1943), examines a wide variety of the organizations interested in farm policy.

Farmers and party conflict today

President Truman's victory in 1948 and the vigorous efforts of his Secretary of Agriculture, Charles Brannan, to expand protection of farm income through the Brannan Plan in 1949, were significant turning points. Southern Democrats joined with AFBF and Republicans to oppose the Brannan Plan while the NFU and labor groups supported it. But the demands of Southern commodities for stronger protection, which Brannan's proposal represented, persuaded Southern Democrats to change their position once the Truman Administration, which most of them had opposed vigorously, was out of office. Since 1952 the basic compatibility of wheat and cotton and feed grain interests, and the opposition to these interests of the Republican Administration, have made for a closer alliance. Wheat farmers, main strength of the NFU, had traditionally been Republican, however, and to weld a firm alliance of Southern Democrats and NFU wheat growers to oppose the Republican-AFBF administration, this voting tradition had to be broken. The NFU leadership had for some time been thoroughly Democratic, and in 1954 and especially in 1956 NFU members began to vote Democratic; they played a part in electing Congressmen from South Dakota and Kansas, in nearly defeating Senator Case of South Dakota, in electing a Democratic Governor of Kansas, and in registering substantial voting gains throughout the NFU area. The AFBF, by contrast, has continued vigorously to defend Secretary Benson and increasingly to associate with solidly Republican interests.

The implications of this new partisanship in agriculture are many. For one thing, no longer can farmers, in any sense, be regarded as a homogeneous group, strongly represented in Congress and in the Department of Agriculture regardless of which party holds power. When Democrats control Congress the Farmer's Union alliance is able to achieve considerable success, especially to the extent that it can hold the support of the Southerners. The Farm Bureau, by contrast, has nothing like the influence it had from the 1920's to 1949. The AFBF works most effectively when the Republicans control the Congress. The same is true of the Executive Branch, where under the Eisenhower Administration the AFBF has been well represented and the NFU almost completely shut out. A change in party control presumably would reverse these relationships. The AFBF remains more influential at the state level and has argued that many federal programs be decentralized and turned over to state administration.

Recent struggles over basic farm legislation have showed these political forces at work. In 1955 the House passed a 90 per cent price support bill, 206 to 201; 87 per cent of the Democrats voted for the bill and only 9 per cent of the Republicans. Most of latter were from NFU territory. Democrats from the five largest urban centers in the country supported 90 per cent supports 33 to 3. Both the Republican and Democratic percentages represented changes over previous position as Republicans decreased and Democrats increased their support of 90 per cent supports. In 1956 the Senate passed a similar bill, including the soil bank requested by Mr. Eisenhower, and with a similar alignment of interests supporting and opposing. President Eisenhower was urged to sign the bill by the Farmer's Union, the Grange, and several labor groups. The Republican leadership, the Farm Bureau, and many business groups urged a veto. The bill was vetoed, and a separate soil bank bill then was enacted.

The Brannan Plan

The Brannan Plan for revising agricultural policy has been, and may again be, a focal point for conflict over farm policy. Briefly, Brannan's proposal of 1949 recommended the substitution of farm *income* supports for farm *price* supports. Under the usual price support program the farmer is guaranteed that what he sells in the market will bring at least the support price. Brannan proposed to support farm income while at the same time allowing market prices freely to find their own level. This would be achieved by *production payments,* direct subsidies paid to the farmer for his crop in the amount necessary to bring his income up to the parity standard. Brannan's plan was to use a formula that would increase the farm *income* needed to achieve parity and also to guarantee 100 per cent of this higher parity. While farm income was increasing, market prices would decrease since the latter would no longer be supported. Thus consumers could buy more food, and there could be no surpluses in government storage. Brannan's proposal was warmly endorsed by the NFU and many labor unions but vehemently opposed by the AFBF and most business groups. The latter argued that Brannan's proposal would either be fantastically costly to the taxpayer (since farmers would greatly increase their outputs to get maximum production payments), or it would involve strict production controls that the AFBF contended would amount to "regimentation" and "socialism." Brannan had specified that production payments be limited to a maximum of 26,000 dollars and larger farmers were not pleased by this cutoff.

Production payments as a device to lower consumer prices and increase demand, to eliminate surpluses held in expensive storage by the government, and to enable a more direct approach to the problem of public assistance to a disadvantaged economic group has not come close to enactment, except in the case of wool for which the Republican administration provided a kind of "Brannan Plan in sheep's clothing." The approach presents several problems. It makes obvious the subsidies to farmers and weakens the traditional argument that price support programs merely equalize the farmer's bargaining power in the market. The proposal would increase the income level of most farmers, especially of those whose commodities are suffering relative decline in demand, like wheat. The 26,000 dollar cutoff would mean that the large scale farming enterprise in wheat, cotton, rice, or beef cattle would receive support on only a portion of its production. If such a program were to go into effect, it seems likely that strict production controls would be imposed. This is an issue about which farmers seem not to have made up their own minds. The Farm Bureau leadership vigorously opposes the whole idea of controlled agricultural production, but many farmers, especially those of the NFU, seem willing enough to accept controls if the result is effective support.

Relief programs, rural and urban

The controversies over the Brannan Plan point up two other related issues in agricultural politics: rural relief and rehabilitation, and programs to increase the consumption of farm commodities. At the beginning of this chapter it was observed that the shift to cash crop farming had broad consequences for agriculture. Later the change in farm group strategy from seeking to break up or regulate business concentration to seeking support for farm prices was noted. These two developments brought a significant division in the interests of those listed in the census as farmers. In order to benefit from price support programs a farmer has to produce cash crops *for the market*. Approximately one-third of the farms in the United States had total sales worth less than 600 dollars in 1950. Some of these were part-time residential farms whose owners work in nearby cities. But many are subsistence farms whose occupants raise little more than required to feed the family and who have little or no other income. These are the "rural slums," and the major farm programs have little to do with them. They market little and thus receive little benefit from price support programs. Subsistence farmers have not been politically effective, and programs to assist them have received little support from commercial farming interests. Not until 1933 was a continuous program established to provide low-interest loans and expert advice to make subsistence and tenant farmers more secure. In 1937 these programs were placed under the Farm Security Administration, but this agency was caught up in conflict between the Farm Bureau which attacked and the Farmer's Union which supported it. In 1946 the FSA was superseded by the present Farmer's Home Administration. The FHA continues to extend loans to farmers who cannot obtain credit elsewhere, but has devoted more attention to assisting commercial farmers and much less to rural relief and rehabilitation than did its predecessor agency.

It was said earlier that when income increases the proportion spent on food declines, and that this gives one clue to the plight of the farmer in the present expanding economy. This means that many people are not likely to eat more than they already do although they may eat one type of food rather than another. It does not mean, however, that there are no possibilities of expanding food consumption and thus improving farm prices. There still are many people in the United States whose income is too low to enable them to buy the food they want. For these people, many of whom are urban slum dwellers, various food stamp plans have been proposed whereby surplus food products could be purchased by these people at prices they could afford to pay. Such programs are supported by the NFU alliance, since they would assist farmers and urban labor interests alike. To date, however, the food stamp proposals have not been adopted. The school lunch program is another example of a program designed to increase food consumption.

A third area for increasing consumption is the international. Ever since the 1920's, there have been advocates of a two-price plan whereby domestic farm prices would be supported and export surpluses sold at whatever price the world market would bring. Such programs have not been adopted, but the surplus farm commodities are used as part of the foreign aid program and many farm interests would like to see this expanded. The State Department opposes many of these proposals, as it fears that to use American surpluses in this way will deprive other nations whom we want to help of markets for their agricultural products. The latter set of interests, however, is not so well organized for purposes of political action in the United States, and a considerable degree of tension between domestic and international policy has resulted.

NATURAL RESOURCES

The United States is blessed with a wide variety of valuable resources that underlie the economic strength of the nation. But despite substantial abundance, few of these resources are available in unlimited quantities.[13] Some vital materials like natural rubber are not found in this country. Others such as tin and tungsten must be imported to provide an adequate supply. And many resources including oil, water, and soil may be dangerously depleted in the future. In short, despite a great natural endowment, the United States faces problems of scarcity; problems that may not be as severe as those of some other countries but still give rise to political action and governmental response.[14]

Background factors

The definition of resources is not fixed. Peat has been an important resource in Ireland as fuel. It is not important in the United States where a higher economic level and other available fuels that heat more effectively make peat worthless. Coal was once the pre-eminent source of power. The development of large amounts of power from oil, gas, and falling water has reduced the significance of coal, and atomic energy may change this pattern even more drastically. The technology of the industrial system and the state of economic development in the United States affects our conception of what constitutes a valuable resource.

Government policy affecting resources in the United States has been further conditioned by two other "givens." For one thing, much of the land—and the minerals, soil, forests, and water that go with it—was owned originally by the federal government. Some of this public domain was acquired by purchase, some by treaty, some by exploration. But since it was not private property, the government could not avoid responsibility for it, and public conservation of resources was a much easier policy to sell. To some degree, public development of navigable waters was not blocked by free enterprise

---

[13] The most recent comprehensive survey of American resources can be found in the report of the President's Materials Policy Commission, *Resources for Freedom*, 5 vols. (Washington, D.C.: U.S. Government Printing Office, 1952).

[14] The most recent general discussion of the political conflicts over natural resources is Barrow Lyons, *Tomorrow's Birthright* (New York: Funk and Wagnalls Company, 1955).

ideology. Property rights in waterways did sometimes exist, but control of these waterways, especially in aid of navigation, was always clearly the legitimate responsibility of the federal government under the Constitution.

A final condition making governmental action regarding resources inevitable has been the economic character of much resource development. If a firm wishes to plan in terms of 100 years and has sufficient capital to do so, sustained yield forestry may seem attractive, but probably not otherwise. Private development of atomic power has lagged in the United States because of the huge risks involved, and the original atomic bomb, of course, would not have been developed by private enterprise. In short, the costs and/or risks of some types of resource development are very large. Moreover, from projects like parks, flood control, and navigation assistance the benefits are diffused among perhaps millions of people. It becomes impossible to operate these projects privately, since neither the customers nor the size of the purchase are known.

Ideology of resource politics

That governmental authority should be invoked to deal with conflicts over the use of resources was inevitable, but the scale of operation and to some extent the direction could be disputed. The public domain might be handed over to homesteaders or reserved for parks and forests. Multiple purpose dams might be built often or seldom, power might be sold at the dam or from transmission lines. The states or the federal government might control offshore oil. These and many more conflicts over policy may make enormous financial differences to groups concerned. In the process of seeking to secure their goals, the principal groups have developed sets of ideas and arguments to support their positions. Three general ideas have been especially prominent in this field: exploitation of resources by or for the benefit of private producers, conservation of resources by public authority, and exploitation of resources by public authority.

Historically, the first of these three positions was by far the most significant. The public domain was to be sold cheaply and sometimes given to private parties to encourage the growth and settlement of the nation. For the most part, private exploitation was uncontrolled. Charters were issued by public authority, and the courts were sometimes called upon to interpret the limits of private property rights. But there was little doubt in the minds of most people that American resources were unlimited and little suggestion that these gifts of a bountiful nature would have to be husbanded.

In the latter nineteenth and early twentieth centuries several factors combined to produce a different set of ideas about natural resources.[15] As the population expanded land values rose, and, especially in the latter half of the nineteenth century when farm prices declined, it became very attractive to settle low-priced Homestead land, farm it as extensively as possible for the required five years, and then sell it at the increased value. This process resulted in bringing millions of acres into the most depleting kind of cultivation. The disappearance of great forests of the Great Lakes area was an inescapable fact by this time, and a number of people began to show concern over the fact that at this rate of cutting there would soon be no trees at all. Moreover, there developed during this same period a considerable body of scientific data about natural resources, especially forests, and the scientists were prominent in promoting new concepts of resource use. These concepts stressed orderly, efficient utilization of resources to secure the maximum yield at a rate that would maintain the supply into the indefinite future. This was the beginning of the conservation movement.

The scientists and their supporters began an extensive campaign of public education for governmental action to enforce conservation. Despite their zeal, however, it may be doubted whether conservation would have been written into public policy without other developments of the period. The technology of industry produced electric power, petroleum, and chemical giants whose dependence on long-term supplies of natural resources placed these matters in a different light than had been held by the small-scale Homesteader. Scientific management concepts in industry made planning and efficiency politically more acceptable. Finally, the general shift in political and social ideology away from laissez-faire to one accepting some regulation of business allowed the conservationists to become part of the Progressive Era.

The first great surge of conservationist policy by the federal government occurred during the administration of Theodore Roosevelt. The factors which led to conservation thinking all came into conjunction in the first decade of the twentieth century. In time, although

[15] A brief but good discussion of the development of the conservation movement, stressing the group interest basis is found in Norman Wengert, *Natural Resources and the Political Struggle* (Garden City, N. Y.: Doubleday and Company, 1955), Chap. 2.

conflicts developed within the original groups, the conservation movement gained new adherents from two other types of interests. With the general increase in prosperity and leisure time, recreation attracted more and more interest, and many wished to preserve areas for hunting, fishing, and other outdoor recreation. National parks, forests, and fish and game preserves thus became important political goals to these people. Then too what might be called an antiquarian aesthetic interest, a concern to preserve some of the natural beauties of the country unmarred by urban "civilization," animated more and more people, particularly writers. Very recently, for example, it has been argued that the Dinosaur National Monument should be preserved against flooding from the proposed Echo Park dam because of the wild stark beauty of this inaccessible spot.

Conservationists have sometimes been allied with and sometimes opposed to a third approach to resource use, that of public exploitation. This view is a part of the broader demand for governmental development and protection of human and natural resources. Sometimes the goal grows out of the inability of private enterprise to raise the capital necessary to undertake the project or from the fact that the benefits of the project are so diffused as to make profits impossible to secure. Both of these conditions, for example, make it very unlikely that private enterprise will construct large *multi-purpose* dams. In many cases, however, the demands for public exploitation reflect a basic change in attitude toward resources. The feeling is that these resources belong to all the people of the country, not just a few, and that private exploitation, especially of the "strike it rich" or "cut and get out" type, is immoral and improper. There is not necessarily any thought of not using these resources, but only of using them to benefit as many people as possible. The assumption is that public dam construction, federal control of tidelands oil, or governmental development of atomic power will benefit more people than will private utilization of the resources involved.

All three of these general attitudes toward resources are prominent in the conflicts of today over natural resource policy.

Land resources

The federal government at one time has owned nearly one and a half billion acres of land in continental United States, over three-fourths of the total land area. Over 400 million acres still are in the public domain, most of them in the Western States. The story of the transfer of so much land from public to private ownership embraces much of American history.[16] For the first years after the Constitution was adopted the sale of public land was designed to bring revenue to the government. As the West gained greater political power, the emphasis was changed to using the public domain to encourage settlement, and successive Acts of Congress, culminating in the Homestead Act of 1862, made it easier and cheaper to secure private ownership of land. The Homestead Act provided that anyone over 21 who was or intended to become a citizen could acquire up to 160 acres of surveyed public land by living on the land for five years and making certain improvements. Grants of land were made to the states as early as 1787 to support common schools, and later to support universities and other institutions of the states. Land grants were made also to the railroads in the West and South.

The land policy throughout most of the nineteenth and early twentieth centuries was to encourage settlement of as much land as quickly as possible. In this process there was a good deal of fraud. The rapid increase of land values in some areas placed a premium on speculation. There was no suggestion that some land would be unsuitable to settlement or to cultivation. Consequently, much grassland was plowed only to blow away before the winds. Tacit encouragement was given to the illegal practice of entering the public domain and cutting the trees without pretending to settle. Cutting the forests permitted cultivation which in turn often resulted in dust storms and erosion, since the forest cover no longer held the soil in place.

A change in direction regarding land policy came as a consequence of several factors. By the latter nineteenth century most of the choice land was gone. What was left was arid and distant from markets. The universal dream of owning a farm had lost some of its attraction as commercial agriculture had suffered a prolonged slump. The erosion and waste of unrestricted settlement and cultivation had become a subject of more and more concern to the growing group of conservationists. In recent times, although Homesteading is still possible, the principal actions of the federal government in this century have been to withdraw, reserve, and sometimes even purchase land to conserve and regulate the use of land resources.

---

[16] An excellent study of the political struggles over the public domain is E. Louise Peffer, *The Closing of the Public Domain* (Stanford: Stanford University Press, 1951). Marion Clawson, *Uncle Sam's Acres* (New York: Dodd, Mead and Company, 1951), is a readable and useful account of policies and conflicts over the public domain.

Reservation of public land

The earliest actions setting aside public land for public use established Indian Reservations. Usually these reservations consisted of land unwanted by anyone else. It is illustrative of the nature of resources, however, that as new mineral depcsits were discovered and new uses were found for old materials pressure developed to take back the reserved lands for private exploitation. Today Indian Reservations contain much less than half the peak of 166 million acres reached in 1875.

National parks have survived in strikingly better fashion. There are few to speak politically in behalf of Indians, but as recreation and tourism have become major industries in many parts of the United States, the National Parks have had vocal defenders. Beginning with Yellowstone Park in 1872, some 180 parks, monuments, and historic sites have been reserved from public land, or in some instances purchased from private owners. The National Park Service administers these lands. Political conflict is not absent from this activity. Recreation and conservation groups often seek to expand the park system or at least to increase the appropriations for its maintenance. Others may seek to exploit mineral, timber, or grazing potentialities in the parks.

More controversial still has been the development of *national forests*.[17] Throughout much of the nineteenth century lumbering was a major industry in the United States and timber one of the most vital resources. The great forests of the Great Lakes area were thoroughly cut over in this period, and the forests of the West were attacked with vigor. Taking their cue and their training from state-owned forests in Germany, scientific foresters began to campaign for public action to conserve the fast-dwindling tree supply. For some 20 years this campaign of scientists achieved little, but in 1891 a law was passed, almost unnoticed, which permitted the President to reserve portions of the public domain as forest preserves. Successive Presidents withdrew land from the public domain and slowly funds and administrative machinery were secured to manage the forests. Gifford Pinchot, Chief Forester under Theodore Roosevelt, was perhaps the outstanding leader in this movement.[18]

[17] On forest policy the most recent extensive discussion is Luther H. Gulick, *American Forest Policy* (New York: Duell, Sloan, and Pearce, 1951).

[18] Pinchot's autobiography, *Breaking New Ground* (New York: Harcourt, Brace and Company, Inc., 1947), contains much valuable information from the point of view of an active participant in the movement for scientific forestry and resource conservation.

Western states were the only ones really affected by this policy since only in the West was there much public land remaining. In 1907 western interests finally secured legislation prohibiting further reservation in the western States. In 1911, however, the Weeks Act authorized the purchase of land for forest conservation, and, mainly in the 1930's, nearly 20 million acres were added to the national forests in this fashion. Most of the land purchased has been either in the South or in the Lake States of Minnesota, Michigan, and Wisconsin.

Most of the national forests are managed by the Forest Service of the Department of Agriculture. The forests are run on a sustained-yield basis, with private firms securing the right to cut timber by competitive bidding. Land included within national forests may also be leased in order to extract mineral resources. The Forest Service has been involved in some heated controversies concerning the administration of conservation programs. Rivalry has persisted between the Forest Service and the agencies now located in the Bureau of Land Management in Interior. Each agency administers much public land, and from time to time each has sought to unify public land management under its guidance. The agencies often diverge on policies respecting functions such as grazing control which they both perform, and each group tends to regard itself as the leading exponent of conservation and prudent resource use.

Another area of resource controversy has developed over *grazing* on public land. For many years the public domain was grazed essentially without control. Much of the land was unsuited to homesteading, but neither was private ownership for grazing purposes very attractive. Thus despite several legislative efforts to tempt stockmen into claiming some of this land, much of it remained under private use and public ownership. Disputes between cattle and sheep raisers and between stockmen and occasional "nesters" or homesteaders have provided much of the material for the Western stories and movies of today, and they well illustrate the absence of federal control over this vast expanse of grassland. Not until the Taylor Grazing Act of 1934 was the range land brought under continuous federal management. Under this Act stock raisers must secure licenses from and pay fees to the agency in the Interior Department responsible for the range. Originally this was the Grazing Service, but now this function is performed by the Bureau of Land Management. Grazing districts were established, each with an advisory board of licensed stockmen. It appears that these boards have virtually dominated the use of the range. Limited appropriations and continuing opposition from Western interests wishing to exploit the grazing lands, usually for mineral deposits, and from rival conservationists working through the Forest Service, have seriously limited the effectiveness of grazing administration.

Land and water—irrigation and reclamation

As the arable land in the public domain was occupied, pressure mounted to make some of the remaining land arable by irrigation.[19] Some irrigation projects had been privately constructed since the Indian days, but not until 1902 did the federal government embark on a program to reclaim arid lands. The Newlands Act of that year provided that irrigation projects could be constructed, the costs without interest to be repaid over ten years by the homesteaders claiming the irrigated land or by the owners of private land benefitting. Homestead claims of irrigated public land were limited to 160 acres and private owners were likewise limited to the amount of water necessary to irrigate 160 acres. Most of the land suitable for irrigation actually turned out to be private land. The terms of repayment of construction costs have been extended to 40 years, thus allowing the land to become fully productive before payments are required. The 160 acre limitation has survived, although many groups seeking to irrigate larger areas under single ownership or hoping to speculate in land values have sought to abolish it.[20] By 1956 more than 7 million acres in 17 states had been reclaimed; 135 storage dams and 105 diversion dams had been constructed.

Until the Hoover Dam was authorized in 1928, the irrigation projects were aimed at a single purpose, reclaiming arid land through irrigation. Yet a dam built to store water for irrigation can also be useful for flood control and power production and possibly also for helping navigation. The Bureau of Reclamation of the Interior Department finally began to try to fulfill these several purposes with each project, and the costs of the project were allocated among the purposes served. The prospect of developing hydro-electric power through governmental action greatly enlarged the political scope of the Bureau's program. The demands for power in the West were potentially great, but so were the stakes of the private utilities and their allies in opposing public power. Moreover, this expanded multi-purpose operation of the Bureau of Reclamation ran head-on into a rival bureaucracy, the

[19] On the development of irrigation policy see Roy E. Huffman, *Irrigation Development and Public Water Policy* (New York: The Ronald Press Company, 1953).
[20] See Lyons, *op. cit.*, Chap. 10.

Army Corps of Engineers. The Army Engineers had navigation and flood control as their main peacetime job. They operated with strong alliances throughout the country, whereas the Bureau of Reclamation was confined to arid regions.

Thus one cannot today speak of irrigation programs apart from the broader conflicts of interests in water resources. Bureaucratic rivalry, public versus private power interests, and rivers and harbors "pork barrel" legislation are all involved.

POWER AND ENERGY RESOURCES

Clearly the most important political issues surrounding the use of water resources in the United States concern the production and sale of hydroelectric power. Hydroelectric plants provide just under one-fourth of all electric utility power in the country. Many of these are privately owned, but government-owned utilities have increased until, federal and municipal together, public power accounts for about one-fifth of the nation's capacity. Whether or not the production of hydro-electric power by the federal government should be continued has become one of the central political conflicts of the day.

We have already noted that federal irrigation projects eventually were broadened into multi-purpose projects producing power as well. In other parts of the country federal funds had been spent since the beginning of the Republic to improve navigable streams, to develop harbor facilities, and later, to control floods. Most of this work has been directed by the Army Corps of Engineers.[21] The Corps has planned projects, usually in close association with the local interests involved, secured appropriations from a friendly Congress, and executed the plans for a wide variety of rivers and harbors improvements. Their warm relationship with the National Rivers and Harbors Congress, to which many influential Congressmen belong, and the Associated General Contractors who actually build the projects, has helped make the Corps a very powerful agency in the federal government. The Engineers did not until quite recently build projects producing hydro power. Their prime concern was, and still is, navigation and flood control. However, a dam built to store flood waters can be used also to produce power, and since 1936 many of the Corps' projects have been multi-purpose with power being one objective.

[21] The Corps of Engineers is the subject of Arthur Maass' excellent study, *Muddy Waters* (Cambridge, Mass.: Harvard University Press, 1951).

Thus, historically, federal development of water power has been largely incidental to other purposes, chiefly irrigation, navigation, and flood control. Until 1933 federal action in this field consisted mainly in the establishment of the Federal Power Commission in 1920. Any agency, public or private, wishing to build a dam on a stream subject to federal jurisdiction must first secure a license from the FPC. The dam or other installation must, in the Commission's judgment, contribute to the best comprehensive development of the waterway. The FPC regulates the accounting and some financial practices of licensees and has full regulatory authority over electric utilities engaged in interstate commerce. The Commission must approve rate schedules on power produced by the Interior Department, or under the supervision of the Army Engineers. A private license must also be approved by Interior or the Corps of Engineers when it affects waters under their jurisdiction. Despite rather extensive authority, however, the FPC has not played a major role in power development. On rare occasions, such as the Hell's Canyon case, the granting of the license can be important. But the crucial decisions are normally made by the Interior Department, the Army Engineers, the Administration, and Congress.

The TVA

One such crucial decision was made in 1933. This was the establishment of the Tennessee Valley Authority.[22] A few Congressmen, notably Senator George Norris of Nebraska, had campaigned for more than a decade for a comprehensive, multi-purpose, valley-wide program to develop all of the potentialities of the Tennessee Valley. The logic of valley-wide development was compelling. Rather than have many separate and only vaguely coordinated projects, the idea was to integrate into a single system the flood-control, navigation, and power projects and to plan consciously the rehabilitation of the whole valley region.

Logic, of course, was not all that was involved. TVA was intended to produce electric power and to buy out existing private utilities. It was to raise the economic level of the whole region and in so doing to work enormous changes. Many interests would benefit from these changes, but many others would lose—notably, the utilities. More important was the fact that TVA became a symbol of broad-gauge governmental action to promote welfare. Those opposing TVA regard

[22] There is much literature concerning TVA. Two volumes by former members of the TVA board are David Lilienthal, *The TVA: Democracy on the March,* 2nd ed. (New York: Harper & Bros., 1953), and Gordon Clapp, *The TVA* (Chicago: University of Chicago Press, 1955).

this as an interference with private enterprise upsetting to existing relationships and interests and in the long run producing less welfare. The supporters of TVA, and of other public power projects, argue that its larger resources enable government to undertake projects, like valley development, that private enterprise could not and would not afford. Each side produces statistics and rationalizations to support its position; symbols like "creeping socialism," "monopoly," and "public interest" are invoked; but neither group convinces its opponents. TVA has survived, but no other valley authorities have been established.[23]

The Tennessee Valley Authority is a semi-autonomous corporation, governed by a three-man board of directors appointed by the President. TVA operates under Congressional authorization, of course, and must get approval from Congress for new construction. Regular operating expenses, however, are from TVA's own revenue, and the Authority is much less subject to control and supervision than are most government agencies. TVA has engaged in a broad program. Floods have been substantially curbed and an even river flow is maintained all year, permitting navigation for over 600 miles. The income level in the valley area was raised from 40 per cent of the national average in 1933 to 60 per cent of that average in 1950. Huge amounts of power have been supplied to the Atomic Energy Commission projects at Paducah, Kentucky, and Oak Ridge, Tennessee. Much private industry has been attracted to the valley by the low cost power. TVA has priced its power in a manner calculated to stimulate its widest possible use. As a consequence, from one of the lowest per capita consumption rates in the nation, the region has changed to one of the highest, and, in turn, all kinds of economic activity have expanded on this base of low cost power.

The low cost of public power, in TVA and elsewhere, is an issue about which reasonable men do not agree. It is clear that the *price* of TVA power is less than half the nation's average. It is not so clear whether this price accurately reflects the cost to the government of producing the power, or whether, on the other hand, it amounts to a subsidy to the Tennessee region. A number of arguments are made

[23] The policies developed concerning other river valleys can be studied in Charles McKinley, *Uncle Sam in the Pacific Northwest* (Berkeley: University of California Press, 1952); Marian E. Ridgeway, *The Missouri Basin's Pick-Sloan Plan* (Urbana: University of Illinois Press, 1955); "The Kings River Project in the Basin of the Great Central Valley," in Maass, *op. cit.;* and William E. Leuchtenburg, *Flood Control Politics: The Connecticut River Valley Problem* (Cambridge, Mass.: Harvard University Press, 1953).

pro and con, but two seem to be central: taxes and cost allocation. Private utilities, of course, pay taxes to federal, state, and local authorities on both their physical assets and their income. These taxes are costs that the utilities must cover in their rates. TVA pays no taxes, though it does make payments to state and local governments in lieu of taxes. These payments admittedly are lower than the utility tax burden, however. The utilities claim that if taxes were subtracted TVA income would have failed to cover its costs. TVA supporters deny this, and the nature of TVA costs makes it difficult to reach an objective conclusion. The costs of constructing facilities used only to produce power may accurately be calculated and compared with income. But many TVA facilities are multi-purpose. What proportion of the joint costs should be allocated to power as against flood control and navigation? Almost any decision on this question is arguable, and the contending interests do not accept each other's conclusions.

The TVA has overwhelming support from the people in the valley. In a sense, however, it has succeeded too well. In stimulating the demand for power through low rates, TVA has been confronted with an unending need to expand its facilities, both by adding new capacity and by building steam plants to provide adequate power when water flow is slack. For such expansion TVA needs the approval of Congress, and those who oppose TVA have managed in recent years to block approval of many proposals. One result of this situation has been pressure from TVA advocates to pass legislation authorizing the Authority to borrow money on the open market without prior Congressional approval.

Another, more dramatic, example of the same political conflict was the Dixon-Yates contract controversy of 1954–1955.[24] The Atomic Energy Commission's demand for TVA power was becoming so great that the supply for other users, notably the City of Memphis, Tennessee, was threatened. TVA proposed to build additional facilities, but the Eisenhower Administration chose instead to have the Atomic Energy Commission contract with a utility group headed by Dixon and Yates to supply power to Memphis. Involving very little risk to the private utility, the contract was hailed as an advance for private enterprise. Public power and TVA supporters fought the contract vigorously, both in Congress and during the 1954 elections, and "Dixon-Yates" became a major slogan in the party battle. The Eisen-

[24] A discussion of the Dixon-Yates affair, critical of the proposed contract, may be found in Lyons, op. cit., pp. 247-57.

hower policy withstood these attacks, however, until 1955. First, it was discovered that a man had helped the government draw up the contract while also employed by the investment firm that would handle the Dixon-Yates securities. This "conflict of interest" added considerable fuel to the fire. Then the City of Memphis decided to build its own power plant, thereby making the Dixon-Yates facilities unnecessary, and the contract was cancelled. The defenders of TVA continue to maintain that the Republicans are opposed to the Authority and are determined to stop its future growth. TVA and public power policy generally have thus become a significantly partisan issue.

Petroleum

From the modest beginning of petroleum production in Titusville, Pennsylvania, in 1859, oil has grown to become one of the most significant resources in the United States, and indeed in the world. The early use of petroleum to light kerosene lamps was significant in the latter nineteenth century, but the gasoline and diesel engines of the twentieth century have made petroleum crucial to the transportation and defense systems of every nation. The result has been a mighty economic complex of interests throughout the world with substantial political power. At the same time, oil as an irreplaceable natural resource raises severe problems of conservation.

In the United States more than 20 states produce petroleum, but Texas, California, Louisiana, Oklahoma, and Kansas account for over three-fourths of the production. Oil is normally found in pools that may vary substantially in size, the larger extending over a considerable area. If a well is drilled and taps a pool, the normal property rights entitle the owner to pump as much oil as he can. But a pool usually lies under many properties and one well may pull the oil out from under another owner's land. To avoid this, other wells will be drilled, as many as possible, by each owner in order to pump the maximum amount of oil from his property before others siphon it away. Thus, in the absence of controls, discovery of a large field will be followed by a rush to drill and pump. This sort of exploitation is both wasteful and uneconomic. When so many wells are drilled much of the natural pressure in the pool is lost and consequently much of the oil cannot be recovered. Much of the oil may run off at the surface too in the scramble to drill and pump. Furthermore, a large unregulated field will produce huge quantities of oil that will hit the market hard and drive down the price.

Consequently, when some of the big strikes were made in Oklahoma and Texas, oil companies demanded some regulatory mechanism to save themselves from their own destructive competition. Oklahoma enacted legislation in 1915 authorizing the state Corporation Commission to estimate "reasonable market demands" and to limit production to that amount. The Commission was to prorate production among well owners. During and following World War I, however, demand for petroleum increased substantially and the Oklahoma plan was not put into effect. But in 1931 the huge East Texas field was brought into production, and the price of oil collapsed. The governors of Texas, Oklahoma, and Kansas acted swiftly to control production. An interstate compact was formed, originally without waiting for Congress to consent, to assure that all three states would limit production. Each state proceeded to prorate production along the lines of the Oklahoma system. The Texas Railroad Commission lacked authority to do this, but for a time its orders were enforced by martial law, and eventually the required legal authority was secured. The states called their regulation "conservation measures" but specified that both economic and physical waste were to be prevented.[25]

Twenty states joined the Interstate compact, but state action alone did not sufficiently guarantee effective production control. If one state refused to cooperate, there were no sanctions available to force its adherence to the program. Hence it was necessary for federal authority to back up the control machinery. Today the Bureau of Mines in the Interior Department makes monthly forecasts of consumer demand for petroleum products, divides these into estimates for each state, and sends these forecasts to the producing states. The states legally need not follow these estimates, but they all do. Each state prorates its quota among its wells, and the federal government forbids shipments in interstate commerce that are in violation of state quotas.

Regulation of production is not the only major governmental action affecting oil. Since oil is such a vital resource and is irreplaceable, exploration must be encouraged to discover new pools. Just how much encouragement is necessary is a matter of dispute, but the political power of oil interests is great and one result is the "depletion allowance." Twenty-seven and one-half per cent of the gross sales of oil and gas producers (but not to exceed 50 per cent of net revenue) is exempt

[25] Regulation of oil production in Texas is well-described by York Y. Willbern, "Administrative Control of Petroleum Production in Texas," in Emmette S. Redford, ed., *Public Administration and Policy Formation* (Austin: University of Texas Press, 1956), pp. 3-53.

from federal income tax. Other mineral producers also receive depletion allowances, though none as high as 27½ per cent. The depletion allowance unquestionably expands greatly the net return from oil and gas production.[26] The new "Texas oilionaire" has been made possible, in part, by this allowance which permits him to keep more of his income. Oil producing interests have used this capital to move into other industrial areas; for example, securing control of the New York Central Railroad, and into active politics; for example, H. L. Hunt and his *Facts Forum*.

The enormous stakes involved in the exploitation of petroleum made a major political issue of the control of the offshore oil deposits. Large oil reserves are located under the continental shelf off the coasts of California, Texas, and Louisiana. The question at issue was whether these reserves were under the authority of federal government or whether the states controlled them. The Supreme Court ruled that they were under federal jurisdiction.[27] The affected states, which would benefit hugely from royalties, and the oil companies, which expected more liberal terms governing exploitation from the states than from Washington, campaigned vigorously to reverse the Court's decision. Congress passed one quitclaim bill relinquishing the land in question to the states, but it was vetoed by President Truman. During the 1952 presidential campaign the "tidelands" was a major issue. General Eisenhower favored turning the land back to the states, while Governor Stevenson rejected the requests of Texas Democrats and supported continued federal ownership. Even after the Republican victory some of the Democrats tried to retain federal control and to devote the royalties toward aiding education. However, after extended debate, Congress passed a quitclaim bill which President Eisenhower signed into law in May, 1953.[28]

The international significance of United States petroleum policy was illustrated in 1956 and 1957 when the closing of the Suez Canal temporarily placed Europe on short oil rations. Many of the firms engaged in oil production in the Middle East are substantially American-owned and produce oil in the United States too. They might have been able to increase their U. S. production in order to supply Europe, but

[26] The effects of the depletion allowance on oil company income are discussed in Walter Adams and Horace M. Gray, *Monopoly in America* (New York: The Macmillan Company, 1956), pp. 75-85.

[27] *U.S. v. California,* 332 U.S. 19 (1947); *U.S. v. Texas,* 339 U.S. 707 (1950).

[28] For a brief resumé of these events, see the useful volume by Clair Wilcox, *Public Policies Toward Business* (Homewood, Ill.: Richard D. Irwin, Inc., 1955), pp. 348-50.

the Texas Railroad Commission refused to allow the increase for several months. It appeared that the smaller producers in the United States preferred to reduce existing domestic supplies before allowing increased production for export—export that they would not share in anyway.[29] The Texas Commission represented the smaller producer interest in this situation. These same smaller independents—as opposed to the "majors" who produce and refine petroleum both in the United States and in other parts of the world—have been pressing for quota restrictions on imports of foreign crude oil into the United States. Imported crude oil is usually cheaper, and more abundant reserves exist abroad, but importation creates a serious conflict of interest between the majors and the independents. President Eisenhower has requested the majors to reduce voluntarily their imports by 10 per cent. Whether this will have the desired effect remains to be seen.

Natural gas

Among natural resources none has come into more striking prominence recently than natural gas. The use of natural gas for heating, power, and in manufacturing has been multiplied more than a dozen times in the past 20 years and spread geographically from the Southwest, the major producing area, to most of the nation. Gas is usually associated in nature with oil and often provides the pressure forcing the oil out of the ground. For years natural gas was burned off as waste, but the development of seamless steel pipe made it possible to transport gas by pipeline over long distances and thus made it commercially significant as fuel.

The natural gas industry is divided into three phases; production, transportation, and distribution. There are several thousand producers, located mostly in the Southwest. About 20 of the producers, however, are corporate giants who also control pipelines that carry the gas to market. Some of the distributors also control pipelines, but most companies engaged in this phase of the business are local gas companies. Local gas companies are public utilities with a monopoly of the business in a given area. As such their rates and service are regulated by state commissions.

Under the Natural Gas Act of 1938, interstate transmission of natural gas and its sale for resale have been subject to rate and service regulation by the Federal Power Commission. However, neither state

[29] See Douglass Cater, "The General and the Umbrella," *The Reporter,* Vol. 16 (March 21, 1957), pp. 11-15.

nor federal regulation began until after the gas had been produced and entered interstate commerce. For the integrated producer-pipeline owner this meant that by charging himself high rates for the gas he produced he could escape much of the impact of regulation of the transportation rates. Some members of the FPC, notably Leland Olds, held that effective regulation of interstate transportation required also regulation of production. In 1949, when Olds was nominated by President Truman for another term on the FPC, the oil and gas interests successfully prevented his confirmation by the Senate.[30] A bill specifically exempting the production price of gas from FPC control was passed by Congress in 1950 and vetoed by the President. The FPC, however, then decided that it lacked the authority under the 1938 legislation to control the production price. The Supreme Court reversed the Commission in 1954 and directed it to set "just and reasonable" prices for gas entering the pipelines.

President Eisenhower had announced that he favored legislation to withdraw this authority from the FPC, and when in 1955 and 1956 the Harris-Fulbright bill, designed for this purpose, was considered by Congress it had Administration support. The argument of the proponents of the bill was mainly that the rapidly increasing demand for gas made it necessary to encourage maximum expansion of production. Many gas utility companies opposed the bill, however, on the grounds that it would raise the prices they paid for their gas. A large number of northern and eastern cities, labor groups, and other consumers of gas joined in this opposition. The bill nevertheless passed the Congress, but not before one Senator announced that a lawyer lobbying for passage had given $2,500 to the Senator's campaign manager. President Eisenhower thereupon vetoed the bill, approving its purpose but condemning the "arrogant tactics" of its supporters. In 1957 it was reported that utility opposition to the bill had been moderated following conferences with the oil and gas interests. At the same time, however, the Eisenhower Administration seemed less favorably inclined than it had been, and the issue remained in doubt. Natural gas conflicts, like so many other resource issues, drew sectional lines of division between representatives of producing areas, especially the Southwest, and representatives of consumer areas. Some Democrats tried to make a party issue out of what they termed "another giveaway," but, in contrast to Hell's Canyon, some Democratic leaders in Congress supported the bill

[30] See Robert J. Harris, "The Senatorial Rejection of Leland Olds: A Case Study," *American Political Science Review,* Vol. 45 (1951), pp. 674-92.

while a number of Republicans opposed it. It appeared further that voters were substantially indifferent.

Atomic energy

The amazing technological developments of the twentieth century have transformed much of the economic, social, and political life of the world, and the changes already experienced may be merely a prelude to the future. Surely one of the most fundamental changes has been in the field of energy resources where atomic and thermonuclear energy have drastically altered the nature of international relations. The impact of atomic energy may be almost as great on the economic development of the United States, when the power needed to run machines and heat buildings can be drawn economically from atomic reactors. Atomic energy is potentially unlimited in quantity, and as the power needs of the nation continue to increase and other sources of energy are depleted, the public policies affecting atomic development will be of vital significance.

Unlike any other resources in the United States, atomic energy was purposely developed as substantially a total federal monopoly. The enormous capital outlay of two billion dollars was required to perfect the atomic bombs of World War II, and it seems clear that no other source than government and no other purpose than world war could have combined to produce successful controlled atomic reaction so quickly. But there was a war, and Hiroshima and Nagasaki were bombed, and atomic energy had arrived. The military importance of atomic energy was so great, however, that civilian uses could be explored only under the strictest control. Since the American position in the world following World War II depended for several years on its atomic weapons monopoly, the strictest sort of secrecy was thought necessary concerning these matters. Some argued that this meant that control of atomic development should continue to be vested in the military as it had been during the War. This proposal was rejected in favor of civilian control, to be exercised by an Atomic Energy Commission of five members appointed for five years by the President, with the consent of the Senate.

The AEC was established by the McMahon Act of 1946. Its authority over atomic development was great. Private enterprise in mining uranium ore was permitted, but private ownership of fissionable materials made from the ore, of facilities for production, and of patents covering the production processes was forbidden. The AEC could lend or lease fissionables and by-products for research or medical use and license industrial use. The AEC could continue the earlier practice of entering into private contracts for research and production, or it could construct its own facilities. All AEC work was classified to protect security, and AEC contracts were let without competitive bids. The AEC was subject to general oversight by a joint Congressional Committee.[31]

This was an unprecedented act, but it dealt with a subject of unprecedented importance. The discretion granted the AEC was great, and the departure from standard images of American economic organization was also extreme. Many criticisms were leveled at the AEC, culminating in substantial revisions of the law in 1954. The secrecy and security provisions were attacked as inadequate, and when it appeared that atomic secrets had been given to the Soviet Union, the program was pulled into the whole loyalty-security conflict. The decision of the AEC to sever the relationship with physicist J. Robert Oppenheimer on security grounds was followed by a considerable debate over the desirability of some of the security restrictions. Many argued that fewer restrictions would enable freer communication among scientists which would lead, in turn, to more rapid advances.

Another area of controversy developed as rapid strides in technology made it apparent that economically feasible, peace-time atomic power was just over the horizon. This brought forth the whole range of public and private power interests. The issues between these groups centered around three main themes: (1) the contract system, (2) patents control, and (3) public power. The contract system in actual operation had worked to give a great head start in know-how and experience to a few, already large, firms. The AEC was concerned to secure production as quickly as possible and so turned to firms like General Electric and Union Carbide and Carbon to operate its plants. Yet it was clear that when the atomic field was opened to somewhat more free private exploitation, these firms would have a substantial advantage. There was little that could be done to change the contract system directly and give contracts to small companies. However, compensatory advantages regarding patents and public ownership could be required by law. Revision of the 1946 legislation to permit greater private development was requested by the President in 1954, and, during Congressional consideration of this revision, the possible com-

[31] See Morgan Thomas, *Atomic Energy and Congress* (Ann Arbor: University of Michigan Press, 1956).

pensatory advantages designed to ease entry into the field and prevent monopoly were debated at length.[32]

The 1946 legislation had made all patentable processes the property of the government. It was argued that private enterprise would not be tempted to enter the field of atomic power unless such inventions and discoveries as might be developed were protected from competitors. To achieve this protection many business groups sought normal patent protection of atomic technology. Opponents argued that patent protection, running for at least 17 years, would freeze out firms seeking to enter the industry later on and would thereby contribute to monopoly in the field. Democrats in Congress were united almost solidly in efforts to limit patent rights, while Republicans were equally united in their desire to extend patent protection. A compromise was finally worked out whereby patents on nonmilitary processes are permitted, but licenses must be freely granted for five years at royalties determined by the AEC.

The other main issue respecting atomic power was whether the AEC or other government agencies should be authorized to produce commercial power. Again the monopoly theme was raised as well as the argument that private enterprise lacked the capital and the incentive to develop atomic power soon enough to maintain American superiority in this field. Republicans sought to limit or prevent entirely public development of power and to confine AEC work to experimental and military uses. Again a compromise was achieved. Both private and public agencies could be licensed by the AEC to produce atomic power. The AEC itself was forbidden to engage in commercial power production but was authorized to sell any power produced incidental to the Commission's other work.

Thus since 1954 private corporations may, under AEC license and control, produce power from atomic reactors. The fuel for the reactors is purchased from the AEC, which buys back the ash left over after the power has been produced. But despite this opportunity few licenses have so far been issued. There are more reactors reported in operation in the United States than in any other country in the world, but none of these as yet is actually producing commercial power. It is expected that a few such reactors will be functioning by 1960. In the meantime, Britain has already begun to produce commercial atomic

[32] For a discussion of this issue and the effects of the 1954 legislation upon it, see Adams and Gray, *op. cit.*, pp. 142-64.

power, and the Soviet Union is reported to have a "crash" program under way.

In 1956 Senate Democrats again attempted to authorize the AEC to build experimental demonstration reactors. It was argued that this would assure continuing technological advances in the civilian power field, and that the example would stimulate private industry. Such a program would also enlarge the available public power and would be particularly appropriate in areas like the Northeast where little public hydro power is available. Mostly on the public power issues the Republicans opposed this proposal, and, after it passed the Senate on virtually a straight party vote, it died in the House. The debate over atomic power policy did not end, however.

The relative slowness of private industry to enter the field of atomic power is partly due to the fact that power is not nearly so scarce in the United States as in most parts of the world. Thus there is not so much pressure from consumers to persuade utilities to enter the field, and the uncertain economic feasibility of atomic power makes it a very risky venture. Representatives of the power industry have claimed that two other factors are holding them back—insurance, and the Public Utility Holding Company Act. The possible disaster resulting from a "runaway reactor" is enormous and far exceeds in potential damage the coverage offered by private insurance groups. Bills to provide federal insurance, with maximum liability of 500 million dollars, were introduced in Congress in 1956 but failed to pass in the midst of the party and public-private power conflicts. The same fate befell a bill to exempt utilities that combine to produce atomic energy from the Public Utility Holding Company Act (which forbids such combination). The bill's supporters argued that the great economic risk and capital outlay involved in atomic power projects made it difficult for a single utility to undertake them. Democrats and public power groups countered by interpreting the proposal as a rebirth of the utility empires that had engaged in unsavory financial operations during the 20's. Thus the development of atomic energy for commercial power was bound up in a whole range of controversies, some old and some new, between major political and economic groups.

BIBLIOGRAPHICAL NOTE

A variety of problems relating both to agriculture and natural resources policy are discussed in Clair Wilcox, *Public Policies Toward Business,* 1955, and Barrow Lyons, *Tomorrow's Birthright,* 1955.

There is much literature concerning the complex field of agricultural politics and policy. Leading works which deal primarily with the historical development are Richard Hofstadter, *The Age of Reform,* 1955, and Murray R. Benedict, *Farm Policies of the United States, 1790–1950,* 1953. Stressing the economic side of agricultural problems are Harold G. Halcrow, *Agricultural Policy of the United States,* 1953; Rainer Schickele, *Agricultural Policy,* 1954; and Theodore W. Schultz, *The Economic Organization of Agriculture,* 1953. The political side of agricultural policy is treated in Charles M. Hardin, *The Politics of Agriculture,* 1952; Grant McConnell, *The Decline of Agrarian Democracy,* 1953; and Wesley McCune, *Who's Behind Our Farm Policy?* 1956.

The two most useful general studies of land resources are Marion Clawson, *Uncle Sam's Acres,* 1951, and E. Louise Peffer, *The Closing of the Public Domain,* 1951. Irrigation policy is examined by Roy E. Huffman, *Irrigation Development and Public Water Policy,* 1953. The Army Engineers are given careful scrutiny in Arthur Maass, *Muddy Waters,* 1951.

There are many titles dealing with the TVA. One of the most recent is *TVA: The First Twenty Years,* 1956.

Two recent studies of atomic energy are Morgan Thomas, *Atomic Energy and Congress,* 1956, and Gerald Wendt, *The Prospects of Nuclear Power and Technology,* 1957.

Most of the subjects discussed in this chapter are in a fairly constant state of debate and often of rapid change. To keep abreast of current developments the *Congressional Quarterly Weekly Report* and *Congressional Quarterly Almanac* are extremely useful.

7. RICHARD W. TAYLOR

Government and Business

GOVERNMENT regulation of business activities involves perhaps the most controversial and complex issues of domestic politics. Not only do students of government offer a variety of judgements on the relation between business and government, but businessmen themselves give divided counsel on whether, when, and how the government should intervene in the economy. The advice offered, moreover, usually turns on ideological assumptions that are more likely to confuse than to enlighten. The air of charge and counter-charge of contesting groups is always murky. To comprehend the process of governmental participation in economic affairs will require (1) first, an examination of the system of property ownership that has developed in the United States; (2) a comparison of the existing property system with the ideology of noninterference by government in property relations; and (3) a summary of the methods of maintaining competition, the controversy over monopoly, the issue of public ownership, and the techniques of regulating private utilities.

PEOPLE, POLITICS, AND PROPERTY

Wealth when protected by law is called property and when used in business is called assets. When government intervenes in economic affairs it usually alters property rights and affects the assets of individ-

241

ual enterprises. For example, a price control statute limits the right of a seller to fix prices on his wares, while a luxury tax is often designed not only to secure revenue but to influence economic development and/or to redistribute income. Viewed in this way, the law of property must be regarded as the foundation of economic activity and a principal means of public regulation of business activities. Conceptions of property may also be regarded as changing under the impact of the technological and organizational revolutions that produced the modern capitalist economy in the United States. One of the central questions is whether or not the ideology of free enterprise that is usually advanced in justification of this system has kept up with these revolutionary times.

The legal foundations of capitalism

A fascinating chapter in the legal history of property in the United States is its common law origin. John R. Commons has demonstrated that in early common law property was identified with a "thing" or "skill" possessed by some person.[1] According to this early conception, land and buildings erected thereon provide good examples of the "thingness" of property; while the right to the fruits of one's labor from the field or shop provide examples of the occasionally inconsistent "skill" or labor theory of property. In the common law, the "thing" conception of property was generally considered a most important right, a right prior to the creation of society and superior to the worker's "skill property." Commons calls this kind of property *corporeal*.

An example of how the courts applied this *corporeal* theory of property is provided by the history of Granger legislation and the attempts of agricultural America to protect itself against what farmers thought to be exorbitant rates by railways and grain elevators. To prevent such abuses the Illinois legislature enacted legislation prescribing maximum charges for the storage of grain. This legislation was regarded by the owners of grain elevators as an interference with their natural right to do as they pleased with their property. Some members of the court sympathized strongly with this group of owners, but the majority of the court felt that this regulation by the State of Illinois was justified. The majority in the case of *Munn v. Illinois* [2] used the *corporeal* theory

[1] The following is from Commons, *Legal Foundations of Capitalism* (New York: The Macmillan Co., 1924), pp. 225-82.

[2] 94 U.S. 183 (1877).

of property when they reasoned that while the fixing of prices might interfere with the profit-making capacity of grain elevators it did not deprive the owners of any property. The grain elevators were not taken from the owners, merely some of the conditions limiting the owners' power to use the property were legislatively redefined. However, even the majority did not follow this theory completely because they did not wish to sanction all similar price regulation statutes. To justify this particular limitation on this property the majority had recourse to the words of an English common law justice, Lord Chief Justice Hale, who two and a half centuries previously had explained that when private property was "affected with a public interest, it ceases to be *juris privati* only." Although the majority provided this qualification, they maintained primarily the *corporeal* view of property. This view of property is occasionally expressed today when we describe a man owning much real estate as "a man of property."

Soon the *corporeal* concept of property, however, was found to be inadequate as a legal device to deal with the complex problems of modern business and technology. Modern business involves largely the exchange of pieces of paper such as contracts, promissory notes, stocks and bonds, and bank checks and paper money, and these pieces of paper under the *corporeal* view (if consistently applied) are worthless *per se*. Under the pressure of business, a new view of property as a bundle of rights has developed, according to which these pieces of paper become claims against others and evidence value; that is, they describe relationships between people. It is these *relations* that are significant since governmental institutions interpret them and require performance of the duties stated therein. This is the domain of *incorporeal* property, a bundle of rights that courts will enforce against the persons who have made commitments through some form of contract. As these bundles of rights were defined by lawmakers, the older common law concept of property as a physical thing was changed in business law to make prices the crucial feature of the business relationship.

Business found it necessary, moreover, to secure additional protections for *incorporeal* property by expanding the significance of this concept. Businessmen have been anxious to protect their market by trade marks and tariffs, their inventions by patents, their going concern value in goodwill, and their profits through price-fixing devices. These efforts have been directed toward the creation of what Commons calls *intangible* property. He says:

. . . it was not until the new idea of "intangible" property arose out of the customs and actual terminology of business magnates of the last quarter of the Nineteenth Century that it was possible . . . to make the new distinctions which clearly separate from each other not only ownership of debts, but also the ownership of expected opportunities to make a profit by withholding supply until price is persuasively or coercively agreed upon. This ownership of expected opportunities is "intangible" property.[3]

Of one aspect of *intangible* property—good will—he says, that it "can be seen and felt—not in commodities, but in the transactions of business; and felt, not in consumption and production, but in the confidence of patrons, investors and employees." [4] Manifestly, *intangible* property refers to no definite thing, nor does it refer to a contract or promise made by two parties. It is *intangible* in the sense that it refers to anticipated profits on the basis of present market conditions that are protected by law or it refers to expectations for profit stemming from changed market conditions resulting from changes in the law. Hence when a private utility extracts a promise from the government that it will always receive a profit in return for submitting to public regulation, the private utility has extracted from the government *intangible* property in terms of a *promised* income on investment no matter what may happen. Furthermore, when some group proposes to change this guaranty in such a way as to reduce the future profit expectations of the company, the private utility is likely to struggle to maintain its *intangible* property rights. It will argue that it would be deprived of its property (meaning anticipated profit) without due process of law.

The *intangible* property concept provides a useful tool for examining the aspirations of various groups as they seek help from the government to protect their present markets or to secure new ones. A monopolistic business will defend itself against a government antitrust suit in such a way as best to protect its market; a would-be competitor may well endeavor to support a government antitrust suit by supplying information, or it may go to Congress to get legislation that might break up the market control by the monopoly. The Lanaham Trade Mark Act (1946), passed by Congress at the behest of business interests wanting to protect their markets, vested an almost absolute property right in peculiar marks that distinguish particular lines. The

---

[3] Commons, *Institutional Economics* (New York: The Macmillan Co., 1934), p. 5. Quoted with the permission of Mrs. Anne Commons Polisar.

[4] *Legal Foundations of Capitalism, op. cit.,* p. 273.

object was not to promote competition, but to protect future profit expectations by controlling markets. Such market protections that individualize the products of different corporations facilitate also their advertising programs. Coca Cola can be sure that no other manufacturer of thirst quenchers can legally duplicate either their name or their container; they have legal control over both because they own them as property.

Property receives its meaning in the context of the conflict of economic interests. Most changes in the significance of this concept have come about under the pressure of business interests. When business activity was hindered by the *corporeal* conception of property, courts and legislatures were persuaded by businessmen to add *incorporeal* property. Finally, under the demand for protection of markets and profits the concept of *intangible* property was also added. This last concept helps to explain the strivings of various interests as they seek government aid to protect their assets or to deprive others of their *intangible* assets. The property system becomes a means of understanding the relations between government and business.

When we speak of "property rights" we are using merely a shorthand expression describing the rights of persons to ownership and control over things and expectations. This may be illustrated from the field of patents; when an invention is patented, the patent is the right of the owner to exclusive control over the invention for the prescribed 17 years. In practical terms the exclusive control means the right to exclude others *or* to charge a price for the invention; it may also mean that the owner may decide whether or not his patent is to be used by any one. It is not the invention that has the right but the man, and this man may not even be the person who made the invention. Nonpropertied persons often seek governmental aid in modifying or destroying existing property rights. Zoning laws limit the right of owners of real property to use their property except in accordance with ordinance. The Prohibition movement at one time successfully outlawed the use of liquor-making property for that purpose.

Property, in short, is a bundle of rights defined and protected by government as well as subject to change through governmental processes. It is the means whereby economic possessions are legally identified. In our country the states have primary responsibility for defining corporeal and incorporeal property. As state lines provide no useful boundaries for the large national markets, intangible property has become largely determined by national laws and regulations.

The organization of property

The changes in legal rules that resulted in the disassociation of the thing owned from the right to own correspond to some fairly fundamental changes in the manner of business organization and the marketing process. The technological revolution has had its counterpart in an organizational revolution. First the steam engine and then electric and internal-combustion motors have helped transform our economy from an agricultural to an industrial one, and from one of many local markets to one huge national market. The large-scale factories required by modern technology have involved to a considerable degree the replacement of the individual businessman by the corporate device. The corporate form of organization is a legal construction that makes possible the collection of a large amount of capital from a large number of different persons through the device of stock ownership. The corporation itself is only partially controlled by the owners, the job of running the corporation being largely delegated to management. This divided and multiple ownership through stock ownership is encouraged through the device of limited liability as well as limited responsibility. The separation of ownership from management has simplified and unified the administration of corporate assets and has made possible the perpetuity of the legal personality independent of the life of stock or bond holders.

Along with this commercial revolution the forms of ownership of the earlier period have continued to survive. The data summarized in Table 7.1 suggests that there is still a considerable economic role

TABLE 7.1

PARTNERSHIPS, CORPORATIONS, AND SOLE PROPRIETORSHIPS

Forms of Business Organization	Number of businesses			Total receipts ($1,000,000)		
	1947	1953	Per cent increase	1947	1953	Per cent increase
Partnerships	888,862	958,591	8	60,687	80,702	33
Corporations	551,807	697,975	26	366,821	556,977	52
Sole proprietorships	6,624,300	7,714,512	16	101,124	143,792	42
TOTAL	8,064,969	9,371,078	16	528,632	781,471	48

Source: *Statistical Abstract of the United States,* 1957, p. 483. Data on corporations for 1947 are accurate on basis of income tax returns filed with the Internal Revenue Service. Other data depend on sampling of returns filed by partnerships and business schedules attached to individual tax returns.

for the private entrepreneur. There are still young men who invest in land to build a farm; the retail business continues to embrace a large number of small establishments. The partnership continues to be a popular form of organization for retailing and for a number of professions, especially law and investment brokerage. However, statistics suggest also that these forms of ownership are of rapidly declining economic importance. M. A. Adelman estimates that 135 corporations own 45 per cent of the industrial assets of the United States.[5] This is approximately one-fourth of the entire manufacturing volume of the world. And even this figure underemphasizes the concentration of control that accompanies this ownership. The economic power reflected by these statistics of business concentration controls other businesses. For example, in the automobile industry the relationship between the marketers of automobiles and the producers is determined by contracts controlled by the producers. Approximately three billion dollars are invested in garages and facilities owned by these agents, and although called "independent businessmen" they can hardly be considered as such. As Berle says, "their policies, operations, and, in large measure, their prices are determined by the motor company whose cars they sell." [6] Other devices for concentrating power in the economy include interlocking directorates (directors of one company holding similar responsibilities in other, occasionally competing, companies), control of patents and licenses, as well as aggressive and predatory activities. Some of these we shall have occasion to discuss later, but a most important reason for this large-scale concentration of control is the activity of government itself.

The device of incorporation has not been exploited as a means of governmental regulation. The responsibility for incorporation has remained dispersed in each of the 48 states, although there is no constitutional barrier against the national government taking on this job. This responsibility for incorporation has rested lightly on the states, their activities being more permissive than regulatory and frequently motivated by the desire for tax revenues. For example, one state advertised for potential incorporators as follows:

> Incorporate in Arizona: Complete in one day. Any capitalization, least cost, greatest advantages. Transact business anywhere. Laws, bylaws, and forms free. Stoddard Incorporating Co., Phoenix, Arizona.[7]

In the corporation, the states have provided a device to facilitate the large accumulations of assets necessary to carry on modern business

---

[5] M. A. Adelman, "The Measurement of Industrial Concentration," *Review of Economics and Statistics,* Vol. 32 (November, 1951), pp. 289 ff.

[6] Adolph A. Berle, *The Twentieth Century Capitalist Revolution* (New York: Harcourt, Brace and Co., Inc., 1954), pp. 27-28.

[7] W. Z. Ripley, *Main Street and Wall Street* (Boston: Little-Brown, 1927), p. 29.

while the potential capacity of this device for regulation has been largely ignored. New Jersey laws in 1888, permitting corporations to own and vote shares of stock of other and occasionally competing companies, provided a legal formula that encouraged additional concentration of industry under the holding company device. Especially in the utility field this device was exploited to create holding companies of the second ("grandfather holding companies"), third ("great-grandfather"), and even higher degrees, a method of organization that permitted a few people with relatively small investment to control large economic empires. Under the pressure of business interests, the national as well as state governments have often framed other policies that have encouraged the development of large concentrations of business.

These two facets of modern industrial organization—the corporation and its large size—have resulted in other changes in the conception of property. Under the older forms of ownership two attributes of property were combined—the creative and productive aspect, and the consumption and enjoyment aspect—and this combination reflected the genuine possibilities of a handicraft barter civilization where the producer put his skill to the work of creation, the product of his efforts becoming his to use and enjoy. Under the newer forms of ownership, the corporate device has separated ownership from control. A person can still invest money, but he grants the corporate management all power to use that capital to create, produce, and develop. The investor retains virtually no control over the product, although he may retain a right to share in the earnings, and in return he has an investment that has the advantage of being quite liquid—it can be sold for money—without interfering with the ongoing productive process. What is true for capital investment is also true for labor. Labor is impersonalized; the employee of large factories rarely knows which of the products he has helped to create, and he has no control over what he is to help to produce, not to speak of the product once made. The worker receives instead liquid wages which he can use to purchase many of his family's requirements in a vast market.

From this brief survey of changes in property and industry, one may conclude that government has constantly been involved with the fortunes of commerce. Not only does the law of property lie at the base of the economic system, but public revenues, the maintenance of internal order, and foreign policy are affected by conditions of economic growth and development. It is not surprising, therefore, that government protects property, and that these protections (as well as the notions of what property is) change as economic conditions change. The legal alterations of property are largely the product of political conflict, because the direction of change as well as its instruments become political issues. To be sure, many important business decisions—automation, for example—are made with little reference to the public decision-making process.

The language of political-economic contest

The fundamental American ideology—the verbal frame of reference for most citizens—is that private ownership and control of property is the rule, and government regulation or ownership of property is the exception. Even though the government creates property rights and protects them, the fundamental assumption is that governmental regulation of property use or abuse requires justification. This ideological opposition to public interference is expressed in the Constitution, our literature, the editorials of newspapers, the statements of organized business, and even in the constitutions of a good number of trade unions. In accordance with this assumption, the American economy is generally called a free enterprise economy, meaning freedom from governmental control along with governmental action against invasion of and/or destruction of property. If one tries to put specific content into this ideology, he would find, as American political history evidences, that a host of different and conflicting points of view can happily co-exist within this frame of reference.

The National Association of Manufacturers (N.A.M.), an organization of about 16,000 manufacturing firms and corporations, has provided a fairly representative exposition of this ideology. In 1946, one of its committees published a report, which states that the individual enterprise system ". . . is interwoven inseparable into the whole fabric of American life," and that observance "of the principles of [this system] . . . has brought more benefits to the people than were ever obtained under any other economic system in history." [8] Among the principles that the N.A.M. regards as fundamental are (1) the competitive character of the economy, (2) the freedom to enter and leave various occupations, (3) the freedom and sanctity of contract, (4) "the right to accumulate property, as an incentive to the full use of

[8] *The American Individual Enterprise System: Its Nature, Evolution, and Future* (New York: The McGraw-Hill Book Co., Inc., 1946), Vol. I, p. 5. A provocative logical and economic criticism of this document appears in Richard Schlatter, *Private Property* (New Brunswick: Rutgers University Press, 1951).

productive activity," [9] and (5) the freedom to invest money in profitable enterprises. These economic principles are supported, according to the N.A.M., by "a distinctive philosophy,"—one that "regards the individual as of supreme importance, fundamentally responsible for his own welfare and entitled to the benefits he earns." [10] In this system, the government's responsibility is restricted to the protection of private property, the enforcement of contracts, and the maintenance of "certain conditions essential to the operation of an individual enterprise economy." [11]

Other representatives of business interests, such as the more influential and less conservative United States Chamber of Commerce, express fundamentally the same economic ideology. One reason for expressing this ideology in abstractions is that these general organizations represent to some extent competing and opposing practical business interests. The generalities cover up these conflicts of interest in order to protect the organization's size and unity, which partly depend in turn on lessened external and internal competition. Where industry is organized along special interest lines—for example, the American Association of Railways or the National Tax Equality Association—the organization is more likely to concentrate on the practical interests of its members than to engage in economic abstractions.

Even more significant, groups such as organized labor or the Public Affairs Institute, which are likely to oppose the political positions of the N.A.M. and the Chamber of Commerce and the special positions of the A.A.R. and the N.T.E.A., often base the philosophical part of their case on the same abstract generalities found in the N.A.M. statement. An example involves the Taft-Hartley Labor Management Relations Act of 1947, partly drafted by the N.A.M.[12] One provision of this legislation, the non-communist affidavit required of all union officials for unions seeking the protection of the Act, was designed according to its proponents to provide the government with protection against subversive infiltration of trade unions and industry. Organized labor generally opposed this provision as unnecessary and as unwarranted interference by government in union affairs. At the same time the N.A.M. thought the act a legitimate interference to protect the public and property interests. As in this instance, most people in the

[9] *Ibid.*
[10] *Ibid.*
[11] *Ibid.*
[12] Chapter **8.**

United States share this common realm of discourse while disagreeing sharply over particulars.

Another conflict among advocates of the free enterprise system involves the *pro* and *anti* protective tariff groups. The N.A.M. and the Chamber both support generally high tariffs to protect U.S. industry from "unfair" foreign competition. Various special interests, using these same arguments, lobby vigorously in the national capital to maintain and increase the rates on various imports, such as Japanese toys, British wool, and Swiss watches. Opposing groups contend that protection is an interference with free trade and a violation of the free enterprise system. Not only do importers hold this position, but also consumer organizations, the U.S. Department of State (especially under Cordell Hull), and most professors of economics. Fundamentally, these arguments are not debates about economic abstractions but conflicts about what kind of property should be recognized and protected by the government and what should not, as we have seen.

Occasionally the language of political conflict or ideological justification clearly signals the interest that is being expressed, but more often it obscures the expression of interest. Since groups try to secure as broad support as possible to achieve a specific goal, it is tactically effective to secure such support by appealing to those abstractions that unite rather than to the specifics that divide. One of the best examples of this tendency, as we shall note below, involves one of the basic concepts of our economic system, namely competition. Usually this word signals a "sacred cow"; our job will be to define it carefully and usefully.

Competition and monopoly

If we believe in a competitive economy, what types of facts are supposed to be designated by "competition" and what kinds of theoretical economic controls are to be accomplished by a competitive market? Economists have distinguished three characteristic types of markets, the *competitive*, the *oligopolistic*, and the *monopolistic* market. The *competitive* market is one embracing many buyers and sellers—where buyers are economically free to buy from a multitude of sellers after evaluating the relative quality of the goods and services as well as prices. Similarly, vendors are free to sell to those vendees who are willing to pay the highest prices. Theoretically, quality as well as price is subject to negotiation and bargaining, but market price will be determined by the relation between supply and demand.

At the opposite pole from a competitive market we find the

monopolistic market in which either one buyer or one seller controls the complete market. The Aluminum Company of America exercised such a control of the aluminum market in the United States until after World War II; this company was in an economic position to sell aluminum at any price it wished or to withhold sales if it chose. For this reason, Alcoa was subject to periodic suits brought by the government. Periodically, the U.S. Government has also instituted proceedings under the Sherman Act against the partial monopoly of the Atlantic and Pacific Tea Company because its extensive retail market gave it economic power to control the price of goods sold to it and to its competitors. Court decisions supported the Government's contention that the A&P was in effect a monopoly because as a buyer it controlled prices of a number of items on the market in spite of the fact that it was not the sole buyer.[13] The Aluminum and the A&P examples illustrate the two sides of the market on which *monopoly* may operate.

In fact the word "monopoly" has an even broader connotation; it was originally introduced into the English language by the utopian Thomas More in 1516 to describe the destruction of competition brought on by the English Enclosure legislation. Its early legal use, and occasionally its encyclopedia use today, was to describe the patents granted by the Crown giving exclusive right to manufacture and/or to sell specified products. This British use explains why the struggle against monopoly in that country has been generally a struggle against one prerogative of the Crown. On the other hand, in the United States "monopoly" has often been the product of economic combination by private individuals, and, consequently, the struggle in this country against monopoly has generally taken the form of opposition to large-scale concentrations of privately controlled wealth. It is partially for this reason that not until the last part of the 19th century did courts begin to expand the common law to make illegal those restraints on the market caused by private economic actions as well as by public grants. Today, "monopoly" is generally used to designate a wide variety of devices for eliminating competition.

[13] See, for example, *U.S. v. A & P,* 173 F. 2d 79 (1949). In this case, to which reference will be made later in the text, the Circuit Judge Sherman Minton explained that "The buying power of A&P was so to use its power as to get a lower price on its merchandise than that obtained by its competitors. This policy, as implemented by 'direct buying,' was referred to by top officers of A&P as a two-price level, the lower for A&P and the higher for its competitors. It used its large buying power to coerce suppliers to sell to it at a lower price than to its competitors on the threat that it would place such suppliers on its private blacklist if they did not conform, or that A&P would go into the manufacturing business in competition with the recalcitrant suppliers."

Rarely do single firms obtain a complete monopoly. Much more likely is the reduction of competition by some kind of combination or cooperation among competing firms. These "restraints" on trade were illegal under the common law. Although single firms rarely monopolize a market, in many areas a few concerns dominate the market, a condition that economists refer to as *oligopoly*. Oligopoly arises when these few concerns are so powerful that they are not subject to the influences of the market but rather influence the market *themselves*. Examples of oligopoly include the cigarette industry, flour milling, the aluminum industry today, and the steel industry. Oligopolistic control may be facilitated through intercorporation agreements, or the controls may be quite informal, existing independent of trade association action or explicit agreements.

Recent experience has shown that a competitive market is hard to maintain, for either buyers or sellers generally have a direct interest in controlling it so that they will not have to depend on the whims of competition to insure a supply or sale at a satisfactory price. When such controls are imposed, monopoly is said to exist. Whether control of the market is secured through economic or political action, it impedes to some degree the freedom of either vendors or vendees or both, as the case may be, to bargain freely with respect to price and quality of the monopolized product.

There are a variety of methods whereby reductions of competition may be achieved. Loose combinations—that is, the collaboration by separate firms in one industry—may result from formal agreement or merely from tacit understandings. Close combinations—complete integration under one management—may be accomplished through a voluntary merger, or through some type of predatory activity that results in the union of two or more previously competing corporations. Combinations may be either *horizontal* or *vertical*. A horizontal combination is the joining together of separate businesses engaged in the production or sale of the same or similar economic goods. A vertical combination is the integration of various stages in the productive process from raw materials to marketing of finished products. Each of these different types of combination involves a lessening of competition on the market with respect to entry, price, or quality or some combination of these.

An additional method by which competition is controlled and often monopoly created is by public grant. A franchise to a street railway, a certificate of public convenience and necessity to a private electric company, or a professional license to practice medicine all usually have the effect of reducing competition or eliminating it, no matter what the stated purpose of the grant is. Indeed, a multitude of trolley or electric power companies serving the same district is uneconomic because of the high investment cost and the lack of public convenience. The purpose of medical licensing is to prevent the untrained or quacks from competing with the medical profession. According to some authorities, government is itself the chief creator of monopoly.

The existence of technological forces that tend toward large scale enterprise and the fact of state and national encouragement of a number of monopolistic conditions raise the question of what should be done in those markets where competition does not serve as a regulator. There are, broadly speaking, three possible alternatives, each with its important advocates. One alternative is that technological forces should be allowed to control the market since large scale enterprise is efficient; according to this view, there should be no restraint by government except in those situations where the economic power is used in a way opposed to public policy.

A second alternative favors "bust the trusts," meaning that the government should use its legal weapons simply to break up monopolies except where a specific monopoly is clearly in the public interest. The third alternative is a compromise position between the other two: government should foster competition where this will encourage production and distribution, but it should take steps to control directly either through *ownership* or by *positive regulation* those industries that can only be carried on monopolistically; in other industries, where competition is restricted by economic forces to a few large corporations, the government should also protect the public by such regulations as are necessary. In this latter case, public authorities should intervene only where private economic power is used to frustrate public policy. These three positions, each of which has many advocates, reflect competing claims that can be resolved only in the political and the economic market places.

Another controversy surrounds the question of how competitive the United States economy really is. Many economists argue that the competition is declining. They use the facts of economic concentration, the concentration of investment in large banking and insurance institutions, and the increasing role of government in the economy to buttress their case. While some welcome these facts, others complain. Those who welcome the decline of competition argue that the increase in technological efficiency and economic security produced by these facts more than justifies the decrease in competition and the values that such competition theoretically might achieve. Those deploring the assumed decline of competition argue along two lines. One group holds that the decline of competition has been brought on by governmental interference, such as the granting and protection of monopolistic rights as in patents or in franchises to private utilities. The second group complains that the decline of economic competition has been the result of predatory large-scale business activities which the government has not attacked vigorously enough.

Many businessmen and economists argue, on the other hand, that competition is increasing. They use different sets of facts to justify their position. Some of these authorities point out that only large-scale enterprise has the capacity to deal with other large businesses. In the event that a business cannot purchase the raw materials or finished products at prices they consider reasonable, they put their hired scientists to work in the laboratories to discover substitutes. In any event, according to this view, there are few things for which no reasonable substitutes are available. When prices, services, or quality are unsatisfactory, there is always some other business eager and able to invade the market by providing an alternative product or method.

The question of whether competition is increasing or declining is indeed controversial. This is a political fact with which we must deal just as we deal with the political fact that most citizens believe in the virtue of competition. Students of business organization and economics may well be permitted to continue to study this question and, perhaps, come to some scientific conclusion. However, this study is an academic process; and until there is general agreement on these economic facts, we must continue to concern ourselves with the political facts relating to competition.[14]

[14] Regarding such controversies one of the most sophisticated students of scientific method writes, "The wisdom of absolutes, verities, facts, will be regarded as present before us in society, but not as potentially the master of knowledge or of life. Yes, even 'facts' must lose their sophisticated claim to dominance. My naiveté will regard everything as fact, even a wrong theory: and will admit no claim to independent actuality for any fact whatever as opposed to any non-fact whatever. But how indeed can a sociologist do other, when the world and life and mind are all his jumbled field?" Arthur F. Bentley, "New Ways and Old to Talk about Men," *The Sociological Review*, Vol. 21 (1929), p. 38, as quoted in *Life, Language, Law* (Yellow Springs, Ohio: Antioch Press, 1957), p. 23.

PROTECTION OF COMPETITION

A wide variety of means are at the disposal of public authorities either to further or to hinder competition. Among these means the following have been used to control private economic activity: *codes*—agreements among competitors, partially governmentally sponsored, as to what is appropriate business practice in a particular line of commerce; *publicity*—pressure through public exposure of particular commercial or industrial abuses to encourage reform; *licenses* and *franchises*—means for control of entry into a business or occupation that would be otherwise illegal; *inspection*—examination by public officials of the quality, price, and weight of commodities or services, used to control the safety of working conditions or public conveyances and the sanitation of food and to provide protection against fire; and *administrative rule-making* and *adjudication*—a more flexible device for governmental control. For purposes of governmental regulation at the national level, administrative rule-making and adjudication have become the most important means of regulation, replacing, to a large extent, two earlier methods of regulation, special legislation and judicial control. How these various devices are being used to support the governmental policy to encourage competition will now be examined.

Competition and monopoly in 19th-century America

The problem of monopoly became a serious issue during the late 19th century when radical changes in the economy took place, largely as a consequence of technological innovations in transportation and steel. These changes laid the foundation for the large business unit and the transformation of the market. The small firm gave way to the large firm with its greater technological efficiency, while the local market gave way to the national market. This process was facilitated by various financial manipulations involved in industrial combinations and by aggressive behavior such as price wars, espionage, preferential rebates, and even violence. Insofar as these activities were designed to prevent competition, to increase the size of business, and to establish economic empires, the problem of monopoly was evident. The growth of bigger business units posed a threat to many smaller vested interests and resulted in agitation from injured groups and reformist elements for government regulation and a policy of "bust the trusts." Neither the common law nor state legislation was able to prevent these "abuses," and the injured groups turned their attention to Congress and the national political parties. Under the threat of possible third party competition, reluctant Democrats and Republicans in Congress finally passed the Sherman Act of 1890, which was to become the cornerstone of governmental efforts to protect the competitive system.

The Sherman Act

An appeasement measure to combat the Populist Revolt, the Sherman Act did not result from either careful Congressional committee investigation or from extended Congressional deliberation. It was a simple, rather general piece of legislation, containing but eight brief sections. Section I made illegal "every contract, combination in the form of trust or otherwise, or conspiracy in restraint of trade or commerce among the several States, or with foreign nations." Section II was more inclusive in that it declared that "every person who shall monopolize or attempt to monopolize or combine or conspire with any other person or persons to monopolize or attempt to monopolize any part of the trade or commerce among the several States or with foreign nations shall be deemed guilty of a misdemeanor." The first section was directed only against the practices of two or more parties in their efforts to restrain commerce, while the second section is much broader in that it is not limited to two or more concerns nor is it limited by method of contract, conspiracy, or combination. The second section declared any monopoly illegal regardless of whether trade was restrained or not and whether or not it was the product of conjoint activities. However, the act provided no definition of the terms "monopoly," "restraint of trade," or "to monopolize."

The object of the Sherman Act was to maintain competition in interstate and foreign commerce. By neglecting to define what was meant by certain key words, however, the statute was left quite vague. In the event of a conflict between the common law (where not every monopoly or restraint of trade is illegal and where judges are guided by the principle of "reason") and the Sherman Act, which declares every monopoly and restraint of trade illegal, a broad avenue for judicial discretion was left open. Nor is the Constitution explicit on what is, and is not, interstate and foreign commerce. In the face of congressional reluctance to support the Justice Department with funds to carry through antitrust litigation, and in the face of similar executive lethargy, judicial discretion in favor of "monopoly" interests in the community has often been left unchallenged, while judicial opinions unfavorable to some large industrial combinations have often been reversed by acts of Congress. The vagueness of the Sherman Act itself makes possible conflicting interpretations of such phrases as "restraint of trade" and "monopolize or attempt to monopolize." These conflicting interpretations have been used by a variety of interests to persuade succeeding Supreme Courts that particular monopolistic activities were either monopolistic or not. Depending always on the type of controversy and on a judicial sense of fitness, and occasionally on the particular political-economic situation, the Courts have interpreted, reinterpreted, muted, and occasionally strengthened efforts to preserve competition.

Lack of clarity of purpose only partially accounts for the shifting antitrust policy. The sanctions that have been used to enforce antitrust policy have been both inappropriate and weak in relation to the economic purposes of the Act and to the power of the interests that have practiced monopoly. These sanctions are criminal and civil. Penalties for criminal violation of the Sherman Act are limited to a maximum of a 50,000 dollar fine (before 1955 legislation it was 5,000 dollars) and a year's imprisonment. Penal sentences have been only sparingly used, and then almost always against labor unionists and racketeers, not businessmen. Fines have been imposed in a large number of cases and have varied from 200 dollars to 638,000 dollars. To achieve the purpose of protecting competition, these criminal sanctions seem quite unrealistic. If the Act is supposed to promote an economic situation of competition, its concern is not primarily with such questions as criminal intent and reform of misdemeanants.

Furthermore, monopolistic results may be easily achieved without any collusion or criminal intent to monopolize. Businessmen are often very much like players at cards or baseball; they too wish to score all the tricks or runs. If this hazardous analogy may be carried a bit further, a comparison from the card game of Bridge may show how the competitive game may be rigged without intent. We need only hypothesize that all four players are using the same strategy, for example Culbertson's; in this case the results of the game are merely determined by the lay of the cards and by no intent to predetermine the result. Manifestly, each side is attempting monopoly by securing all the tricks; however, both sides agree (without even thinking about it) to divide the market by making rules of fair play and by using common strategy. There is, consequently, team effort to monopolize the results; there is collusion to divide up the market; and the results are almost entirely determined by the way the cards are dealt.

Similarly, we may describe the industry where the managers of the apparently competing corporations have received a similar training, can secure bank loans at the same rate of interest, read the same trade papers, and study figures presented to them by cost accountants who follow the common practices of their trade. In place of the deal of cards we substitute the variety of resources and markets, and we should not be surprised if the market was divided up not through the competitive situation but through the realistic appraisal of apparently competing businessmen as to which market they might most profitably serve. Another possibility in which criminal intent is inappropriate is the situation in which a business merely through efficiency might become large and achieve a monopoly status because it serves the public better than former competitors. Finally, the financial penalties are inappropriately small to act as deterrents to multimillion dollar monopolies; to be sure, few businessmen look forward to having the criminal tag placed on them, but this tag, as we have noted, is rarely levied against them.

Other remedies provided by the Sherman Act have proved of varying degrees of usefulness. One rarely used section authorizes courts to entertain suits by private persons who have been injured by monopolistic activity. If the suits are successful, courts are required to assess triple damages on the offending party. One reason for the infrequent use of this section is that private parties generally do not have the resources to provide the investigative groundwork for securing proof. Another reason is that in government cases the defendants are frequently permitted to plead *nolo contendere,* a plea that prevents the government from presenting its case. This means that injured parties do not have this potential government assistance.

The strongest civil remedy that the government may use is the court injunction, which may take the form of dissolution, divestiture, and divorcement proceedings. The injunction is designed to prevent named parties from continuing alleged illegal acts. However, dissolution, divestiture, and divorcement proceedings are drastic and rarely applied, for this type of action requires the complete destruction of the illegal combination, and this would injure the property interests of stockholders and other investors who are certainly not culpable. A much favored device of much more moderate character is the *consent decree* whereby the government and offending persons or corporations come to an agreement regarding the particular activities that the guilty party will cease.

Neither the simple prohibitions of the Sherman Act nor its inappropriate sanctions, however, provide the main cue to the economic significance of this legislation. To find this significance, one must inquire into the economic practices of various lines of business and the ensuing economic and political pressures on competitors, consumers, campaigners, elected officials, and administrators of the law. As Dean Acheson has explained:

> Now it is characteristic of those who have had the good fortune to escape the study and practice of law that to them the law is—or seems to be—both simple and clear. It would not occur to them, for instance, that the plain and simple words of the Sherman Anti-Trust law do not apply to professional baseball because it is a sport and not a business, but do apply to professional football and boxing because they are both sports and businesses. A Lawyer knows only too well what Longfellow meant when he wrote, "And things are not what they seem." [15]

The anomolous situation wherein contracts of baseball players are given a property status while contracts for boxers and footballers are not can be explained in terms of a special situation arising out of the history of these sports in their relation to the law. Other paradoxical decisions can also be successfully explained in terms of special circumstances.

Sherman Act cases

To illustrate the way in which economic circumstances and conflicts of interest give varying contents to the words of the law, a brief survey of the treatment of a variety of different situations is in order. Since a full survey of the different types of cases is impossible, what follows is merely illustrative. Three questions will be taken up.

First, what is the "interstate commerce" covered by the Sherman Act? One of the earliest cases arising under the Act was against a New Jersey holding company, the American Sugar Refining Company. The object of this action was to prevent this holding company from monopolizing interstate commerce in sugar. The government's case was directed by Attorney General Olney who had spent much of his time in his official position trying to persuade Congress to repeal the Sherman Act on the grounds that it would prevent the natural development of the economy. The Attorney General's feelings were reflected in the majority opinion of the Supreme Court which reasoned that the American Sugar Refining Company, in spite of the fact that it controlled 98

[15] Dean Acheson, "Foreign Policy and Presidential Moralism," *The Reporter* (May 2, 1957), p. 13. Printed with the permission of the publisher.

per cent of the refined sugar capacity in the United States, was not subject to the Sherman Act. This was because manufacturing was not commerce, but *prior to commerce*. Professor Edward Corwin has asserted that the "effect of this holding was to put the Antitrust Act to sleep for a decade, during which period most of the great industrial trusts of today got their start." [16] Since according to the opinion of the court *manufacturing* was not *commerce,* sugar refining was only subject to state regulation; and because the states were incapable of controlling giant interstate operations such as the sugar monopoly, this decision was the signal for the first great period of corporate mergers (1897–1903).

The Supreme Court has considerably broadened its conception of commerce since the sugar trust case. In 1899 following the change of one judge on the High Bench the ruling was modified to include *manufacturing* as part of *commerce*.[17] The broad sweep of national power with respect to commerce was more recently indicated in another sugar case,[18] in which the Supreme Court held that the Sherman Act applied to a loose combination of beet sugar refiners who had agreed among themselves on the buying price for sugar beets grown in their state, California. The sugar combination argued that the purchase of sugar beets by California firms in California was purely a local matter and beyond the reach of the Sherman Act. The Court held, nevertheless, that "the artificial and mechanical separation of 'production' and 'manufacturing' from 'commerce,' without regard to their economic continuity, the effects of the former two upon the latter, and the varying methods by which the several processes are organized, related and carried on in different industries or indeed within a single industry, no longer suffices to put either production or manufacturing and refining processes beyond the reach of Congress' authority."

Insofar as the commerce clause of the Constitution is concerned, the tendency of court decisions in recent years has probably been to broaden the scope of the Sherman Act beyond the intentions of its legislative authors. In the *Mandevelle* case the Court provided this test for the exercise of national power, "a showing of actual or threatened effect upon interstate commerce" which would be "substantial."

[16] Cf. Edward S. Corwin, *The Constitution and What It Means Today* (Princeton: Princeton University Press, 1947), p. 37. The sugar trust case is *U.S. v. E. C. Knight,* 156 U.S. 1 (1895).

[17] *Addyston Pipe and Steel Co. v. U.S.,* 175 U.S. 211 (1899).

[18] *Mandevelle Island Farms v. American Crystal Sugar Company,* 334 U.S. 219 (1948).

However, earlier courts held to a more restrictive interpretation. For example, it was not until 1944 that interstate contracts for insurance were held subject to regulation by the national government. Until that time combinations of insurance underwriters could operate free of control from the Sherman Act. However, only one year after the Supreme Court had declared that a combination of fire and casualty companies were a conspiracy to monopolize the insurance business, Congress passed the McCarran Act, which—by ensuring the continued legality of state legislation—partially reversed the effect of the High Court decision. This act provided that by 1948, state laws must conform to the requirements of the Sherman Act. This type of resolution is permissible under the present inclusive view of the significance of the term "interstate commerce," as expounded in *U.S. v. South-Eastern Underwriters Association.* Justice Black's opinion states:

> Our basic responsibility in interpreting the Commerce Clause is to make certain that the power to govern intercourse among the states remains where the Constitution placed it. That power, as held by this Court from the beginning, is vested in the Congress, available to be exercised for the national welfare as Congress shall deem necessary. No commercial enterprise of any kind which conducts its activities across state lines has been held to be wholly beyond the regulatory power of Congress under the Commerce Clause. We cannot make an exception to the business of insurance.[19]

Second, what contracts or combinations does the Sherman Act prohibit? Although the tendency of the court has been to expand the meaning of interstate commerce, the court has generally followed a narrow interpretation of the terms "monopoly," "to monopolize," and "restraint of trade." One of the first cases in which the question of whether or not the Act prohibits all monopolistic activities is *U.S. v. Trans-Missouri Freight Association.*[20] In this case the Government sought to enjoin a loosely knit association of railroad companies that fixed rates so that there would be no competition in rates. The opinion of the Supreme Court, written by Justice Peckham, stated that the "language of the act includes every contract, combination in the form of trust or otherwise, or conspiracy, in restraint of trade or commerce among the several States . . ." The majority of the Court felt that the Sherman Act prohibited *all* monopolistic activities in interstate com-

---

[19] 322 U.S. 533 (1944). For further discussion of the S.E.U.A. decision and explanation of the McCarran Act (Public Law 15), see William H. Rodda, *Inland Marine and Transportation Insurance,* 2nd ed. (Englewood Cliffs, N.J.: Prentice-Hall, Inc., 1958), pp. 502-5.

[20] 166 U.S. 290 (1897).

merce. From this position the Supreme Court has retreated. Indeed, Justice White, for the minority, argued in this case that the Sherman Act outlawed only "unreasonable" restraints of trade, and Justice White's view became the settled opinion of the court in the *Standard Oil Company* case in 1911.[21]

Although the court in this case declared the Standard Oil monopoly illegal, the prevailing opinion (written by Justice White) incorporated the distinction between "reasonable" and "unreasonable" restraints of trade. Thereafter followed a period of considerable uncertainty on the part of businessmen as to what actions violated the Sherman Act and what did not. Consequently, many businessmen asked Congress to clarify this matter. The consumers and small enterprises that were anxious to have a strict construction of the Act urged Congress to pass legislation to catalogue the various economic practices that would restrain trade. Mindful of these pressures, political parties promised strengthening of the law on these and other grounds, and this activity provides the background for the Clayton and Federal Trade Commission acts.

Besides introducing some general confusion into the interpretation of the Sherman Act, the "rule of reason" assisted the development of a remarkable double standard under which the courts became more lenient toward close combinations than toward loose combinations. Part of the reason for this leniency toward close combinations derives from their unitary character. While it is fairly easy to dissolve a trade association like the Trans-Missouri Freight Association or the South-Eastern Underwriters because they include separate corporations with separate managements who are cooperating together in a manner that can be easily prohibited, the remedy for close combinations is not as simple because separate ownerships and managements are not involved and the property interests of generally innocent investors are involved. Hence the courts have been reluctant to order dissolutions of close-knit combinations.

Third, does bigness itself constitute restraint? In general, large size has shared the same advantages under the "rule of reason" as have close combinations. The arguments of courts at least until after World War II generally followed the doctrine that mere size was no sign of monopoly. Thus a series of opinions following *U.S. v. United States Steel Corporation* [22] held that the law should not handicap the eco-

---

[21] *Standard Oil Co. v. U.S.*, 211 U.S. 1 (1911).
[22] 251 U.S. 417 (1920).

nomic efficiency that the courts have assumed to be a concomitant to large size. This view was most cautiously expressed by Justice Cardozo who explained that

> Mere size, according to the holding of this court, is not an offense against the Sherman Act unless magnified to the point at which it amounts to monopoly . . . but size carries with it an opportunity for abuse that is not to be ignored when the opportunity is proved to have been utilized in the past . . .[23]

This tolerant position toward large businesses was maintained until 1945, when Judge Hand ruled that the size of the Aluminum Company of America was such as to amount to a restraint on the entry of potential competition.[24] At present the Supreme Court's position is to condemn size unless dissolution would mean a substantial loss in technological efficiency.[25] Hence, large size no longer has the same advantages as close combinations under the "rule of reason" and judges are more likely today to regard economic size as an aspect of economic power which may itself prove restraining on potential and actual competition.

Businesses under indictment frequently defend themselves by pointing out that size is merely a relative matter. One small grocer in a small town with no competitors for many miles may have an effective monopoly, while a large industrial combination such as Du Pont or the United States Steel Corporation may be subjected to considerable market control either because of competing large scale enterprises or because of the countervailing power of raw material suppliers and purchasers. One should point out that this argument does not favor the competitive model with which this section was introduced. It is essentially an argument that oligopoly in this specific business will achieve better results. Opponents to large-scale enterprise do not view this argument favorably, and the courts have increasingly held that the Sherman Act barred this type of monopolistic activity.

Summary of Sherman Act cases

The account of the Sherman Act and its enforcement suggests conflict between a variety of different groups to give it different meanings, as owners and corporate managers feel their property in things or expectations is affected. As a consequence, the Act itself has had special and different meanings in the field of transportation, professional ath-

[23] *United States v. Swift & Co.*, 286 U.S. 106 (1932).
[24] *U.S. v. Aluminum Co. of America*, 148 F. 2d 416 (1945).
[25] Examine, for example, *U.S. v. Columbia Steel Co.*, 334 U.S. 495 (1948).

letics, insurance, and the production and marketing of sugar. Although the act declares all monopolies to be illegal, under the "rule of reason" integrated close combinations have generally been carefully protected, large size has only recently become suspect, and only loose combinations have been easily broken up. What types of activities the government may reach with the Sherman Act under the "interstate and foreign commerce" clause of the Constitution has also been controversial. We have noted how Congress quickly nullified a Supreme Court decision of 1944 finally recognizing that insurance was an interstate business by passing legislation that returned the regulation of this type of commerce to the states. This is but one example of how Congress has complicated the antimonopoly policy by granting exceptions to special industries.

The Clayton Act

Part of the surge of public opinion behind the election of Woodrow Wilson to the Presidency in 1912 stemmed from a popular reaction against executive and judicial enforcement of the antimonopoly policy. Businessmen were not altogether sure what the "rule of reason" applied to and they naturally wanted the greater security that comes from knowing what is legal and what is not. Small enterprisers were opposed to large competitors who had the economic power to force them out of business. Labor unions were very much handicapped by virtue of the very rigid enforcement of the Act against them, even though its author, Senator Sherman, had specifically explained that this Act was not to apply to trade union activity. These pressures resulted in a number of different types of legislative proposals that were to some extent finally included within the Clayton and Federal Trade Commission acts.

The legislative history of the Clayton Act shows that one of the directions of this pressure was toward an explicit enumeration of monopolistic practices that Congress should outlaw. The purpose of this specific listing of illegal acts was to take discretion away from the courts under the "rule of reason." However, Congress found the task of enumeration overwhelming, although the Clayton Act is primarily a remnant of this effort. In sections 6 and 20 of the Act, Congress directly exempted legitimate trade union activity from the Sherman Act, while in sections 2, 3, 7, and 8 various specific activities that interfered with competition were proscribed. Three specific evils are prohibited: (1) price discrimination, (2) exclusive agreements, and

(3) interlocking directorates or the purchase of stock in competing concerns. These prohibitions are limited to circumstances where these activities substantially interfere with competition in interstate commerce. Furthermore, the Clayton Act made corporate officers personally liable for violations, and it facilitated the bringing of suits by injured parties under both this Act and the Sherman Act. Responsibility for enforcement was lodged jointly in the Department of Justice and the Federal Trade Commission.

While other aspects will be treated below, here we may examine the specific provisions of the Clayton Act with regard to close combinations. This Act seemed to establish a more rigorous standard for holding companies than the existing interpretations of the Sherman Act. Section 7 provided "That no corporation engaged in commerce shall acquire, directly or indirectly, that whole or any part of the stock or other share of capital of another corporation engaged in commerce, where the effect of such acquisition may be to substantially lessen competition. . . ." This provision was generally regarded as meaningless and ineffective because the Supreme Court ruled that

> The statute does not forbid the acquirement of property, or the merger of corporations pursuant to state laws, nor does it provide any machinery for compelling a divestiture of assets acquired by purchase or otherwise or the distribution of physical property brought into a single ownership by merger.[26]

Since there was an easy way for a holding company to avoid the operation of Section 7, this provision did not prevent a practice that Congress presumably tried to forbid.

The Federal Trade Commission (F.T.C.), representing the spokesmen for small business and the consumer, repeatedly sought amendment of the law, efforts that were finally crowned with success in the adoption of the Anti-Merger Act of 1950. Curiously, public pressure may also have breathed life into the original wording of the Clayton Act on this question, for the Supreme Court recently reversed a dismissal of a government suit against du Pont de Nemours & Co. involving certain activities that come under the jurisdiction of the earlier wording of Section 7.

The *Du Pont* case involves a company that owns 23 per cent of the General Motors stock. Du Pont has been charged with using this position to ensure that General Motors buys a considerable proportion

[26] *Arrow-Hart & Hegeman Electric Co. v. Federal Trade Commission*, 291 U.S. 587 (1934).

of the Du Pont production of automotive finishes and fabrics. This is a vertical combination through stock acquisition, a type of combination that the government has never attacked before under Section 7. Furthermore, the acts of acquisition took place between 1917 and 1919, and they were finally brought to trial in 1954. This case appears to suggest a significant change, for the Supreme Court has given a much more forceful interpretation to the original Clayton Act than it had previously; seemingly, it has revitalized the old Section 7, and a less permissive view of combinations may be in the making. However, whether the decision of *U.S. v. Du Pont* will provide a new manner of interpretation will depend fundamentally on the strength of the property interests that are affected. The fact that not until 34 years after the Clayton Act became law was this type of case first litigated suggests the power of the opposition to this type of government action.

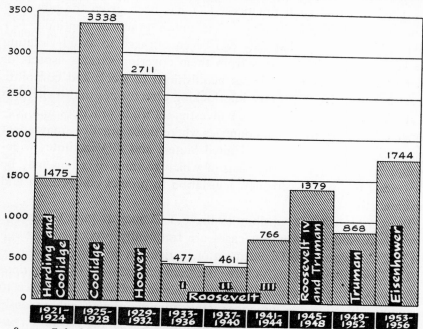

Sources: Federal Trade Commission, REPORT OF CORPORATE MERGERS AND REQUISITIONS (*House Doc. 169, 84th Cong. 1st Sess., 1955*); *and information supplied by Simon N. Whitney, Director, Bureau of Economics, Federal Trade Commission.*

Fig. 7.1. Number of corporate mergers by presidential administrations, 1921–1956

The Federal Trade Commission Act

To assist in the enforcement of the Clayton Act, the Federal Trade Commission Act was also passed in 1914, creating an administrative commission of five members with rule-making, administrative, and judicial functions. The F.T.C. was empowered to define and forbid unfair and dishonest methods of competition in interstate commerce. It was supposed also to enforce the Robinson-Patman Act of 1936, which amended the Clayton Act to illegalize transactions through which chain stores and other large purchasers received discounts, rebates, and other concessions that did not always correctly reflect all legitimate costs when these practices diminish competition or injure competitors.

In carrying out its many duties, the F.T.C. (1) enforces laws against unfair competitive practices of businesses, unless this responsibility has been vested in some other agency by special legislation; (2) works out lists of unfair practices (examine the appendix of any *Annual Report* of the F.T.C.) by holding conferences in which industries are encouraged to avoid such practices; (3) has been given the power to issue "cease and desist" orders when unfair practices continue; (4) advises businesses so that they can be encouraged to avoid violating the law, and requires reports from them covering various aspects of their operations; (5) scrutinizes acquisitions of stock and corporate structures in order to prevent interlocking directorates and ownership of stock in competing firms; (6) investigates trade practices and economic conditions in foreign countries where these practices may affect the foreign commerce of the United States; and (7) institutes widespread investigations on the basis of which recommendations may be forwarded to Congress for new legislation to protect competition and business ethics.

To carry out its responsibilities the F.T.C. may require testimony. For this reason Clayton Act cases are frequently processed through the F.T.C. because the Department of Justice has no similar power.

The Commission employs three different procedures: (1) the *stipulation* procedure by which defendants admit violations and agree to abandon objectionable practices (the admission may subsequently be used to support a cease-and-desist order); (2) the *industry conference* to secure industry-wide compliance with codes of fair competition; (3) legal enforcement action based on formal complaints that may result in a cease-and-desist order enforceable by the national courts. The types of practices with which the F.T.C. deals fairly effectively can be illustrated from the record of stipulations achieved in 1955:

Among the deceptions were claims that: A throat lozenge containing an antibiotic cure prevents or shortens the duration of the common cold; an analgesic tablet is of aid in arresting the progress of arthritis, rheumatism, sciatica, or neuritis; a vaporizing device or chemical compound used in it reduces the incidence of infection or the spread of communicable disease. . . . In other stipulations, a manufacturer of home-freezers and two distributors of freezers in combination with food purchase plans agreed to discontinue claims that savings in food costs will pay for the freezer. . . .

Nine importers or distributors of hooked rugs stipulated that they would not use the word "wool" to describe any rug which is not composed wholly of "wool" as defined in the stipulations. Two manufacturers of hair and scalp preparations agreed to stop representing that their products grow hair or prevent baldness.[27]

Complaints have been made against the F.T.C. that it has been mainly concerned with misleading advertising, and has not been concerned enough with the more important problems of maintaining competition. Furthermore, the F.T.C., it is argued, has been handicapped by the propensity of Presidents to reward party faithfuls by appointing them Commissioners, or, alternatively, that Commissioners have been appointed who are not very anxious to enforce the anti-trust acts. Another complaint has been made that the procedures of the Commission have been used by large business concerns to harass new entries in competition. For example, complaints by battery makers and distributors resulted in an extensive and expensive investigation of battery additives; and complaints by the organized medical profession have hindered experimentation with new methods to cure serious diseases. Despite these many complaints, support for the F.T.C. has increased both in Congress and in the courts, which increasingly place confidence in the factual findings and in the drafts of cease-and-desist orders. Perhaps it is because the F.T.C. does not act against the most important forces hindering competition that it has become increasingly effective in these side issues.

Exceptions to the policy of fostering competition

Along with the handicaps placed by Congress on the enforcement of the antitrust laws through inadequate appropriations, a series of exceptions have been made to the general anti-monopoly policy. Legislation to protect creative activity through the patent and copyright has always constituted an exception. These exceptions have been defended on the grounds that inventiveness and creativity should be

[27] *Annual Report of the F.T.C.*, 1955, pp. 68-69.

encouraged by the government. Patents have often been protected even when they are owned by others than the inventor and when they have been used as means for creating an economic monopoly. Further exceptions exist under national and state agricultural policies, transportation, electric power, communication, gas, banking, meat packing, and insurance, some of these exceptions being described elsewhere in this volume.

Among the politically most controversial efforts against price competition has been the movement to shackle the chain stores in order to preserve small independent businesses. This movement waxed most powerfully during the depression and has been considerably moderated in recent more prosperous times. It has been characterized by a relatively disorganized attempt to tax the chains out of existence through state legislation, and by efforts at price fixing through "fair trade" and "unfair-practices" acts at the state level and the Robinson-Patman Act and the Miller-Tydings Act at the national level.

A number of different groups have been differently involved in these efforts by independent druggists and grocers to protect themselves against the more efficient services offered by the chains. Producers have frequently welcomed these efforts in order to improve their bargaining position with the chains. Many wholesalers, and competitors, have been similarly interested in moderating the power of the chains. Agriculture has been divided through astute politicking on the part of the chains, which have tried to prove to farmers that the chains' efficient marketing system could be more advantageous to them.

The first attack on the chains came largely through state legislative initiative by the passage of laws designed to cripple chains by *taxation*. During the depression this type of legislation had additional support from those desirous of finding new sources for state revenues; some of the additional taxes could even be justified on the grounds that the chains have a tax advantage over independent grocers because of their relatively higher turnover of stock. However, many of the 27 state laws taxing chains were declared unconstitutional by state courts. Even though the U.S. Supreme Court upheld this type of legislation with respect to national constitutionality, the effort to tax the chains out of existence did not succeed.

Subsequent efforts were directed toward *resale price maintenance* legislation. This type of legislation followed two forms. The "fair trade" laws, adopted in 45 states, were designed to prevent price slashing of trademarked goods through private agreements between producers, wholesalers, and retailers. The "unfair-practices" legislation, adopted in 31 states, generally imposed a prohibition on the sale of all commodities on either wholesale or retail markets at "below cost of production." These types of legislation are designed to restrain price competition within the states where legislation is effective.

Under considerable pressure from these same influences, Congress adopted the Robinson-Patman Act of 1936 and the Miller-Tydings Act of 1937. The latter act suggests the strategy of anti-chain store forces in that it amends the Sherman and Federal Trade Commission Acts to exempt resale price agreements in interstate commerce where products are shipped into "fair trade" states. The objective of this act was to expand the reach of this type of anti-chain legislation to products involved in interstate commerce.

The relative futility of this type of legislative approach is best illustrated by the legislative history of the Robinson-Patman Act. This act was the result of a conflict in interpretation of Section 2 of the Clayton Act, which prohibited price discrimination against small firms where such discrimination substantially interfered with competition, except when price differentials were based on "differences in grade, quality, or quantity," when they made "only due allowances" for differences in selling or transportation costs, or when they were made "in good faith to meet competition." The independents claimed that this section as interpreted permitted precisely the type of unreasonable quantity discounts that made possible the destructive predacity by the chains. The chains retorted that their activities were more efficient and consequently more economical. Statutory loopholes and judicial interpretation in effect prevented the use of this section to protect the independents.

The chief organized force pushing for the Robinson-Patman Act was the U. S. Wholesale Grocers' Association; the original bill, indeed, was written by the general counsel of this organization. The USWGA secured the support of the retailers, and partial support from manufacturers and agricultural producers, with the chains in opposition. The proponents secured the support of Representative Patman who had launched an extensive investigation of the whole issue, and Senator Robinson. Under the pull and push of a variety of pressures as well as general Congressional confusion this bill was wedded to another proposal, the Borah-VanNuys bill which moderated the act in such a way that the chains were not substantially interfered with and agricultural and industrial producers were protected. As a consequence, the final law prohibited only excessive and unreasonable use of chains' mass buying power to discriminate against the independents. The chains have continued to grow and the independents have lost more of their market. On the other hand, wholesalers and producers have greater protections against the buying power of the chains.

The history of efforts to shackle the chains suggests a basic confusion in the idea of competition. Does competition mean a large number of sellers and buyers on the market actively seeking a share of the market? Or does competition mean the right of more efficient businessmen to drive the less efficient out of the market? Should established small independent businesses be given a continuing property right in the market in the face of more effective marketing techniques? Does the large size of the chains carry with it not only the power to abuse but actual abuse of their economic power against horizontal competition and vertical suppliers? The Federal Trade Commission, which had made an extensive investigation of this problem in the early 1930's, concluded that the commission should be given the power to proceed by the case-by-case method to expand the notion of unfair competition, but these recommendations were lost amid the pressure by retailers and wholesalers for their own pet bills.

Summary

To maintain competition in the market there must be freedom of entry, no collusive agreements or close combinations regulating prices and quality, no interlocking financial controls or predatory marketing practices conducive to monopoly. Main responsibility for protecting competition has been lodged in the national government because neither the common law nor state legislation was regarded as adequate by the antitrust forces to deal with the giant interstate enterprises. Accordingly, the Sherman Act was passed to require competition, the Clayton Act, to specify methods of competition that were "unfair," and the F.T.C. Act to help fill in the loopholes of the Sherman and Clayton acts by giving a quasi-legislative-quasi-judicial agency rule-making and enforcing powers.

The national policies have called forth criticisms by interests that have been interfered with by the law. One of their arguments is that agreements between businesses regarding trade policies often prevents cutthroat and ruinous competition. A second argument is that mere size is not necessarily monopolistic, and this position has frequently been given court support. A third argument extols the great efficiency of large corporations, while a related argument explains that each monopolistic activity can be counterbalanced at the market by the power of some prime user of the monopolized product, or some supplier, or by the development of some substitutable commodity. You may yourself judge the relative effectiveness of a monopolistic telephone system over the allegedly competitive railroad system as a means of communication; and some would-be home owners suspect that an integration of the building industry might produce economically and quickly mass-produced or custom-made homes. These three arguments should be recognized as potential criticism of the competitive system itself.

The government itself encourages certain types of monopolies in patents, copyrights, trademarks, and private utilities. Advocates of competition do not usually argue against all kinds of monopolies or anti-competitive practices. Frequently, retailers propose legislation such as state fair trade laws that have the effect of restricting competition from large "would-be-monopolistic" chains. Further, arguments by many private utilities that their business conditions are unfavorable to the development of competition usually imply the need of a grant of authority to create a monopoly.

Certainly few would-be monopolists proclaim their opposition to the competitive framework or even the antitrust acts, except in detail. In any event they do not speak loudly against the present pro-competition policy because an abolition of the present confused anti-monopoly policy would probably bring on another variety of regulations, which they cannot be sure will be favorable to their property interests. These opposing interests can work in the present legal haze dominated by the ideology of free enterprise and the free market even though they may oppose this ideology in their practice. The reason that the present anti-monopoly and pro-competition policy is continued is that the more powerful economic interests including those real or would-be monopolists are better protected under present laws than they would be under any political acceptable alternative. Perhaps the protection of competition today, then, is as utopian as it was in the time when Thomas More introduced the word into the English language. The conflicts that hide behind the doctrine of competition are conflicts about business opportunity, in short about intangible property rights.

PRIVATE AND PUBLIC UTILITIES

Although competition is the norm, in some areas public policy has been designed not to promote competition but to prevent it. In some of these fields governments have created monopolies and imposed special types of regulation to insure adequate service and rates. The conditions under which pressure for this type of regulation has been most effective include (1) conditions where duplication of service is uneconomic or physically impossible, for example street railway systems, gas works, electric light and power plants, sewage, and water; (2) conditions requiring heavy investment, with capital turnover occurring only over a long period, and giving rise to decreasing costs with increased use of facilities (as, for example, in the railway transportation field); and (3) conditions where a publicly necessary service requires the use of public rights of way, and where experience has proved that it is "undesirable to have parallel lines, poles, rails or mains on highways, streets or alleys." [28]

These three factors give rise to "natural" monopolistic conditions resulting in the creation of public utilities or private utilities subject to detailed public regulation. The law usually does not specify that monopolies be created in these areas, but establishes a regulatory agency to grant franchises or licenses to promote the public convenience and necessity. As a consequence of legislative policy, no freedom of entry exists, as in competitive fields. Although franchises may be granted to competing firms, this is rarely done. Some cities have two power companies or a number of street transportation companies and even two telephone companies, but these situations are clearly exceptional when the three conditions of "natural" monopoly exist. Still, monopoly in these situations is generally the product of administrative action rather than legislative decision.

The creation by public authority of a monopoly involves an additional problem; what is to prevent the evils of monopoly? Many possibilities exist, but the two choices generally followed in the United States are government regulation or public ownership. We shall deal with the regulation of private utilities first.

The states share with the national government the responsibility for regulation of private utilities, the states acting with respect to intrastate matters under the police powers and the national government acting mainly under its power to regulate interstate commerce. State

[28] This analysis is drawn from Vernon A. Mund, *Government and Business* (New York: Harper & Bros., 1950), pp. 118-20.

supervision of utilities is often shared with cities. Street transportation and water have typically come under direct municipal control; while electric power, gas, telephone, motor carriers, railways, water, and street railways come under at least some state control in most of the states. The means of regulation is in every state by commission, but the scope and methods of regulation vary widely from state to state. Most states exercise control over entry and abandonment of service and have authority to prevent discrimination and to define adequacy of service. This may include power to expand service to unprofitable areas and to continue service that has become unprofitable as a condition of the franchise or certificate of public convenience and necessity. Commonly, regulatory authority extends to rates and prices, to safety, and occasionally to the capital structure. In one sense the purpose of regulation may be regarded as the prevention of the evils for which competition is the remedy in other areas of business.

The national government has entered the field of private utility regulation because state lines provide no natural economic boundaries from the standpoint of either production or marketing of products and services for many utilities. Railway transportation was early marked for regulation, followed by other methods of transportation and communication: motor carriers, airlines, and then radio and television (although the last two are not generally regarded as utilities). The forms of regulation correspond very much to the catalogue of state regulatory approaches including control over entry and abandonment, rates and quality of service, and to some extent capital structure. In contrast to the state organization of regulatory agencies, however, the national government has generally provided separate boards or commissions to regulate different types of utilities. Consequently, instead of one regulatory agency we find a plethora of agencies such as the Interstate Commerce Commission, Federal Power Commission, Federal Communications Commission, and the Securities Exchange Commission (usually known by the initials as ICC, FPC, FCC, and SEC) each of which has its own regulatory sphere, although the Securities Exchange Commission has some responsibility that overlaps all of them with regard to policing the investment markets. Furthermore, since most of these agencies have relations with the state utilities commissions, it is frequently useful to consider the whole process of regulating an industry at state and national levels together. The electric power industry, because it provides examples of many issues of utility regulation at these levels, will be given special attention.

Regulation of electric power and light

The quick rise of electric power industry in the last 75 years provides an interesting picture of efforts of competing and conflicting interests to control this development in accordance with their various views of the public interest. As in every other area of government action, it is these competing group interests that provide the motive, the context, and the action itself.

The most salient aspect of the electric power field is the predominance of private development, which embraces approximately 80 per cent of the firm capacity and a somewhat larger per cent of the market. This private development has been characterized by the growth of large systems with a high degree of concentration of ownership. The large systems were made possible through the holding company device; and further integration of control was accomplished through investment and financial corporations, banking affiliations, interlocking directorates, intersystem holdings, and a multitude of other financial arrangements. A second important fact is the characteristic ownership of the electric power industry by financial groups. The third is the designing of the rate structure with a view to potential competition rather than in accordance with usual utility principle of serving all equally. Thus private utilities have not provided equal service to all users; for example, industrial users of power will build their own generating capacity if utility rates are high enough to make this profitable, while residential and small commercial users do not have this alternative and are, therefore, required to pay higher rates. Each group—consumers (large and small), investors, financial control groups, management, and labor—puts forth different claims. The consumer and the investor seek protection through governmental action, while the other groups try either to prevent government policies that would protect these groups or to control the administration of government activity in the electric power field. Governmental action is the result of the interplay of these forces.

Public regulation of electric power has been marked by four well defined stages: (1) the promotional stage; (2) the state commission regulation stage; (3) the cooperative national and state commission stage; and (4) the "partnership" stage.

The promotional stage. The promotional period dates from the establishment of the first central electricity plants in 1882 to 1907. During this period, residential and street lighting was a primary function while industrial users were secondary. Utility promoters were regarded as community benefactors, the industry was believed to be risky and experimental, and utility privileges were granted by state legislation and municipalities without regard to present or potential consumer interests. The rate structure of the industry was designed to secure its income from residential and street lighting; industrial firms provided supplementary income by using day time power potential. The franchises giving these companies authority to operate were regarded by courts as contracts and protected by the Constitution from alteration. As these franchises were granted regardless of consumer interests, consumers exerted pressure for more positive regulation by state commissions.

State commission regulation. The second period of regulation was inaugurated in 1907 when New York and Wisconsin established the first regulatory commissions. This period is characterized by the absence of protection of both consumer and investor interests and by the establishment of the large utility empires already mentioned.

When the electrical utilities failed to prevent the establishment of state regulatory control, they changed their tactics and tried to frustrate the regulatory process. To accomplish this end the following methods were used: The public was saturated with publicity unfavorable to state regulation, and the cost of this campaign was charged to the rates that the consumer had to pay. This publicity had its impact on legislative votes, as did more direct lobbying efforts, with several results: Utilities commissions were typically starved for financial support to accomplish their duties. Legislation often prevented utilities commissions from exercising jurisdiction over financing and depreciation. (As late as 1934, commissions in seven states had no jurisdiction over either service or rates.) Both inadequate financing and complicated calculations of the rate base required by courts following the decision of *Smyth v. Ames*[29] made the processing of the rate cases not only time

[29] 169 U.S. 466 (1898). This case made profit of a utility an intangible property by requiring rate-making agencies to assure a rate structure that would almost always guarantee an income to all types of utility investments whether wise or foolish. The base on which income was to be calculated included the original investment, the reproduction cost, the market value of stocks and bonds, the sums required to meet operating expenses, "the probable earning capacity of the property under particular rates prescribed by statute." Each of these elements was "to be given such weight as may be right and just in each case." The Supreme Court then added that "We do not say there may not be other matters to be regarded in estimating the value of the property." This decision insured endless litigation whenever private utilities did not approve of the rates they were asked to charge. The rule of *Smyth v. Ames* was later reversed by a differently constituted Supreme Court.

consuming but often futile. Salaries of the regulators were insufficient to attract efficient commissioners; efficient commissioners were frequently tempted away from their regulatory posts by attractive job offers from the industry they were employed to regulate. Following the spread of the industry in interstate commerce through the extensive use of long-distance transmission wires, state regulatory efforts were additionally frustrated by a Supreme Court decision that the powers of state commissions did not extend to the interstate distribution of power.[30] Finally, states did not gain control of the interstate financial operations of the electric power systems, the holding companies or the control interests that lay behind the electric power industry. Although service improved gradually even under these conditions, the consumers became concerned enough to force the national government to follow a more positive regulatory program when the depression of 1929 toppled the financial empires.

National-state cooperation in regulation. Active regulation had to await the inauguration of the Roosevelt administration in 1933. This third period saw efforts by investor and consumer interests to protect themselves through both national and state regulation of the electric power industry. National power policy during this period followed a fourfold strategy: it provided a regulatory scheme for interstate transmission of electricity; it attacked the system of holding company control of the industry; it introduced national public ownership to provide a "measuring stick" for private power service and rates; and state efforts to protect the consumer were facilitated by a series of national programs. The Public Utility Holding Company Act and the Securities Exchange Act gave the national government powers to prevent many types of interstate financial manipulations that were beyond the control of the states.

The Federal Power Act of 1935 gave the national government additional authority to control waterways and hydro-electric development. This legislation rested somewhat on the experience with the Federal Water Power Act of 1920 and the Federal Power Commission. The FPC originally consisted of three Cabinet members who were responsible for licensing hydro-electric development on public lands and navigable waterways. More effective regulation was made possible when a five man independent regulatory agency replaced the busy Cabinet officers who had previously served as the Federal Power

[30] Cf. *Missouri v. Kansas Natural Gas Co.,* 265 U.S. 298 (1924); and *Public Utilities Commission of R.I. v. Attleboro Steam and Electric Co.,* 273 U.S. 83 (1927).

Commission. The New Deal administration brought to the FPC new personnel who immediately began to subject licensees to close supervision, especially on matters of cost and accounting. Under the legislation of 1935 the authority of the FPC was increased. The FPC was not only empowered to coordinate electric power development, but it was given authority to fix wholesale rates and charges, regulate security issues, mergers, sales of property, interlocking directorates, services, accounts, records and depreciation. As mentioned, this act was intended to supplement and not supersede a state regulation. State commissions were assisted by the FPC in investigating and determining the cost of transmission of electricity when such help was requested, and a national power policy was to be worked out by the FPC in consultation with the state commissions.

The basis for breaking down the holding companies' control of electric utility systems was found in an investigation by the Federal Trade Commission ordered by the U. S. Senate in 1928 which provided the factual support for pressure and proposals resulting in the Public Utilities Holding Company Act of 1935. This act gave the Securities and Exchange Commission wide discretionary authority and responsibility to stop harmful financial manipulations. This act required, on pain of being prohibited use of the mails, the registration of all holding companies including a detailed description of the structure, financing, and operations of the company. The Commission was given the duty of examining every holding company to determine how the holding company and corporate structure might be simplified so that stockholders might have equal voting power and so that the operations would be confined to a single integrated public utility system. The statute prohibits "great grandfather holding companies," that is, holding companies beyond the *second degree;* and the SEC was given power to require further corporate simplification. There were other provisions dealing with the issuance and acquisition of securities and utility assets and service, and sales and construction contracts of an intercompany character. The utilities lobby opposed this act in Congress with a campaign of synthetic letters and telegrams from investors, and, after enactment, by the refusal to register. After the Supreme Court held the registration provisions legal in 1938,[31] the companies registered and faced a conciliatory administration that recognized that the process of simplification and integration of power systems was an evolutionary process. The investor interest, in contrast to utility empire promoter

[31] *Electric Bond and Share Co. v. SEC,* 303 U.S. 419 (1938).

interest, has received great protection by this introduction of legal surveillance over corporate development.

The Tennessee Valley Authority (TVA) symbolizes the *public ownership* [32] aspect of control over the electric power industry. While the TVA represents only a portion of the nationally controlled electric power capacity, its success has become the basis of a claim by its enthusiastic supporters that it should be viewed as a measuring stick with which private power development should be compared. For this reason the private power interests have opposed further development of valley authorities systems in place of which they have advocated river development by the Departments of Army and Interior, although they prefer no government interference at all in this "private" business. Their campaigns have had impact in elections, in the halls of Congress, in the Executive Department, in the F.P.C., in the Atomic Energy Commission, and in the courts, to promote the objectives of preventing additional valley authorities and limiting the TVA. Various consumer interests have sought to oppose these groups in the same arena and with mixed effectiveness, depending on the political situation of the time.

The national ownership of large power facilities has not been the only means by which public direction has been used to reflect different consumer interests. Because private power companies were not interested in rural electrification, the Rural Electrification Administration was established to lend money to public bodies and cooperatives for the construction and operation of generating plants as well as electrical transmission systems; in this way the government has in a sense "created" the rural electricity consumer, who previously had no idea what he was missing. This subject is dealt with in greater detail in the chapter on agriculture.

The Eisenhower "partnership" program. The Eisenhower administration was elected in part on a new electric power program, which become known as the "partnership" policy. The partnership is between the national and local governments and private enterprise. Under this doctrine only those facilities that neither private enterprise nor local governments are able to provide will be built with national funds. National projects will emphasize flood control, navigation, and irrigation functions, and perhaps provide for such things as fish ladders. Power projects will be undertaken only when private enterprise is not

[32] Public ownership as such receives fuller treatment on pp. 286-88.

interested. This makes a bit more explicit the somewhat generalized statement found in the 1956 Republican Party Platform:

> We recognize that the burgeoning growth of our Nation requires a combination of Federal, State, and local water power development—a real partnership of effort by all interested parties. . . .

Some Democrats in Congress have argued that this generalized statement does not provide a clear indication of the real significance of the new power policy. They argue that the new power program is devised to permit the old financial control groups to gain control again of the whole electric power industry. They contend that the object is not to ensure that the consumers receive adequate and cheap electric power service but rather to provide that profitable electric power development be left to private interests, mainly financed by large banking houses and insurance companies. Furthermore, they argue that profitable development will be assured by easy tax writeoffs, thus providing the electric power industry with a new intangible property right. Flood control and irrigation programs, along with necessary but unprofitable power development, will continue to remain the responsibility of various government units largely to be financed out of national funds. Present public power development is to be curtailed as far as it is politically feasible, according to the opponents of the "partnership" policy.

Proponents of "partnership" argue that the New Deal—Fair Deal power program established the national government as a gigantic octopus controlling every facet of electric power development and interfering with local interests and private enterprise which could provide power more expeditiously, more cheaply and without the red tape. Proponents of "partnership" ask why the taxpayer should be required to foot the bill of electric power development in the different regions of the nation. In accordance with this view, new national power projects have been opposed by the Republican administration and old programs such as the REA and the TVA have been restricted through the device of appointing administrators friendly to the private power interests.

The Hell's Canyon controversy illustrates in part the significance of the actual power development controversy. This magnificent gorge on the Snake River offers one of the largest remaining potential sources of hydro-electric power in the nation. The Truman Administration wanted to build one high dam as part of a comprehensive federal development of the whole Columbia River basin, a development which would have been somewhat like the TVA. The Idaho Power Company wanted to build three smaller dams in the same gorge with private funds. So long as the Democratic Interior Department objected, Idaho Power could not get an FPC license. With the inauguration of a Republican administration in 1953, the Idaho Power proposal was hailed as an opportunity to show "partnership" with local private interests at work. Here private industry could show what it could do. Interior withdrew its objections, and in 1955 the FPC granted the license. A broad public power alliance, having already been formed to work on the Dixon-Yates contract, fought the proposed Idaho Power contract. Labor groups, the Farmers' Union, the American Public Power Association, and many other groups joined to support the Democratic Congressmen who were making an issue of Hell's Canyon. They argued that the private proposals were too limited to make full use of the potential, that power would be too expensive, and that there was no "local" partnership here since the Idaho Power Company actually had its headquarters in Maine.

Efforts were made to reverse the FPC license in the federal courts but without success. In 1956 the Senate Democrats attempted to pass legislation to prevent further private development in this area. This also failed; Democrats voting 39 to 8 for, Republicans 43 to 2 against. In the spring of 1957 Idaho Power was granted a rapid tax amortization certificate by the Office of Defense Mobilization. This had the effect of an interest-free loan and further heated up the controversy. Hell's Canyon was a major issue in the 1956 election, especially in the Pacific Northwest, where Douglas McKay, Eisenhower's Secretary of Interior and author of the "partnership" policy, ran in Oregon for the United States Senate seat held by Democrat Wayne Morse, a leading advocate of public power. Morse won, and in Idaho, Frank Church, Democrat, defeated a supporter of Idaho Power, incumbent Herman Welker. Elsewhere, however, public power seemed to have little appeal and Eisenhower himself carried even the Northwest States handily. None of this activity has affected the previous decision, and Idaho Power is at work building its dams.

It may be doubted whether outside the areas directly affected public power issues are of much concern to voters. It would seem so far that the farmer-labor-Democratic attempts to win elections on "giveaway" charges have had only limited and local success. Nevertheless, public power is an important issue in terms of the attention given it by the party and interest group leaders. Two other aspects of this issue should be noted: the preference clause and transmission lines.

The low-cost power from national government projects is in most cases sold at wholesale by agencies of the Interior Department. The Bonneville Power Administration, the Southwest Power Administration, and the Southeastern Administration each handle power from a group of projects while others are marketed through the Bureau of Reclamation. This power is usually sought by a number of competing customers, including municipalities, rural electrification cooperatives, and private utilities. Under the law, preference must be given "to public bodies and cooperatives," and private utilities may obtain for resale only what power is left. Private power advocates do not always oppose dam construction projects which have, as has been said, many purposes. They do oppose, however, the preference clause. Indeed they oppose federal marketing of power altogether and would prefer that private companies buy the power at the dam, or "busbar," and market it themselves. In some cases the utilities seek to buy the rights to the falling water and build their own generators as well as transmission facilities. The Army Corps of Engineers usually supports the utilities in this position, which explains why they do not and Interior does market national power. Public agencies and cooperatives contend that private utilities would force them out of business through high wholesale rates were it not for the preference clause protection.

Actually, it is not often necessary for the government to be required to dispose of power at the busbar in order to accomplish the utilities' goal. Unless the government can build transmission lines to bring the power to the municipalities and cooperatives, the small resources of these agencies may prevent them from taking advantage of the preference clause. The Interior Department is authorized by Congress to build transmission lines, but the Eisenhower Administration has not supported such construction, and there have been a number of recent instances in which private utilities have taken over the wholesale marketing of national power.

Controversies over public power, like so many political issues, are not easy to analyze objectively. The real and legitimate, but opposing, interests of many people are involved. Private utilities complain of unfair government competition and subsidies to one region at the tax expense of another. Public power advocates warn of private utility monopolies with high rates, tardy expansion to meet new demands, financial shenanigans after the fashion of Samuel Insull and Dixon and Yates, and wasteful development of precious water resources. Who is to decide which group is correct? Voters are being asked to do so in many parts of the nation. Yet in spite of the many hydro-electric installations during the third period of power development policy, water provides a considerably smaller proportion of the nation's firm capacity than it did 20 years ago. Other sources of energy have already become, or promise soon to become, primary bases of economic production. As oil, gas, atomic energy, and solar energy, perhaps, become more prominent, the disputes over water power will become less central to the political scene. Whether the Eisenhower "partnership" policy will provide the low cost electric power that it promises also remains to be seen.

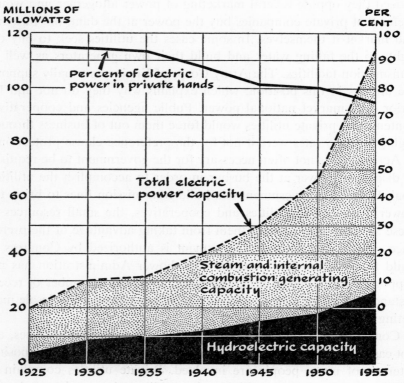

Source: STATISTICAL ABSTRACTS OF THE UNITED STATES, 1956, Fig. XXXIII, p. 526 and Table 640, p. 529.

Fig. 7.2. Total electric power capacity divided into hydroelectric steam, and other power sources, 1925–1955. Ratio of private to public capacity by per cent

Conclusions

There is an obvious contrast between the state commission type of regulation of private utilities and the organization of national regulation. In the states one commission generally covers the whole regulatory field, only occasionally dividing this responsibility with the municipalities. The national government, however, has a division of labor, the responsibility being divided among a multitude of specialized regulatory bodies. The Interstate Commerce Commission deals with rail· way, motor, and domestic water haulage; the F.P.C. with water power, electric power, and natural gas; the Civil Aeronautics Authority with transportation in the sky; the Federal Communications Commission with telephone and telegraph, as well as the ether, by licensing radio and television stations; and the Securities and Exchange Commission specializes in the regulation of both holding companies and the securities markets. Additional authorities might be mentioned, but these suggest that the coverage of specialized regulatory authorities is broad and imposes considerable restraint on some uses of property while protecting other property interests.

The methods used to regulate utilities derive largely from the monopolistic economics of these industries explained above. Although no test of industry "affected with the public interest" can be uniformly applied by the courts, the states first and the national government subsequently have found it of paramount importance to limit and regulate entry in certain areas of the economy by licenses or "certificates of public convenience and necessity." Governments have been forced by public pressure to ensure adequate service, require extension of service, regulate abandonment from service, protect the common law requirement to serve all without discrimination, and regulate rates and finances in this field of "natural" monopolies. In return for being subjected to these detailed regulations, the utilities have demanded (and generally secured) a guaranteed income on investment. Inevitably complaints have been lodged against regulatory agencies that they are manned by personnel overly friendly to utility interests.

State regulation for various reasons has been found incapable of controlling interstate commerce of utilities and interstate financing. The various interests concerned with utilities shift their focus from one level of government to another, and to both political parties in numerous elections and to the public in publicity campaigns to try to secure advantages both large and small in a multitude of contests. Occasionally, consumer groups have forced the government to engage in public ownership to secure adequate service.

PUBLIC OWNERSHIP

Public ownership, too, has become a sharply controversial issue not only because of the conscious use of this method by some interests as a yardstick by which to measure private development of electric power, but also because of the prevailing ideology of free enterprise and the challenge offered this ideology by the various mixed and socialist economies of other countries. To some extent the international controversy has obscured a long and mixed experience with public ownership in a large variety of fields. Public ownership has been practiced at local and municipal levels, and the state and national levels of government. More than two-thirds of the cities own their own water works; about 2,000 run their electric systems, almost 100 own their gas works, a growing number of cities (over 50) own their local transit systems; and all cities have their own sewage disposal systems. Public ownership is not as extensive at the state level, but North Dakota has experimented with a wide variety of state ownership projects such as banks and grain elevators. In other states one frequently finds state liquor stores, and occasionally some kinds of insurance and housing programs.

One interesting experiment in public ownership is the Port of New York Authority which was created in 1921 by means of an interstate compact between New York and New Jersey approved by Congress. Its purpose is to plan the development of the port, to construct bridges and tunnels to facilitate entry into New York City, to provide public transportation from suburban areas, and to run bus, freight, and air terminals. The national government also engages in extensive public ownership covering the postal service and banking, the Alaska Railways, the Panama Canal Company, the Inland Waterways Corporation (now in the process of liquidation), the TVA and other national hydroelectric and steam power developments, the Reconstruction Finance Corporation, and the United States Atomic Energy Authority, among others.

In many ways the Atomic Energy Commission provides a most illuminating example of public ownership combined with private development. The arguments that have compelled public ownership in this instance have been two: the development of atomic energy was paid for almost entirely from funds appropriated by Congress; and even more important, the presumed necessity of secrecy for security reasons. The Atomic Energy Act of 1946 had the serious object "of assuring the common defense and security," and in addition it provided that "the development and utilization of atomic energy shall, so far as practicable, be directed toward improving the public welfare, increasing the standard of living, strengthening free competition in private enterprise, and promoting world peace." To achieve these not always consistent objectives, a commission of five members was to be appointed by the President with the advice and consent of the Senate, and this commission was to appoint a general manager to execute its policies. To carry out its responsibilities, the Commission has nationalized all patents relating to the military applications of atomic energy and ordered that no patents should be issued for any invention "useful solely in the production of fissionable material or in the utilization of fissionable material or atomic energy for a military weapon." The principle of compulsory licensing (nationalization of the use) of other patents relating to this matter is incorporated in the law, although this provision has not been used because of the effective pressure from private industry groups. Furthermore, private development and trade (both foreign and domestic) of fissionable materials is carried on under provisions for strict licenses and contracts. The A.E.C. carries on research and production in government-owned establishments, but most of the atomic energy work today is carried on by universities and industrial concerns like General Electric and Union Carbide and Carbon under contracts with the Commission.

The law of property summarized

These various devices of public ownership, the regulation of private utilities, the protection of competition suggest that the economy of our country is much more complex than the few brief words quoted earlier from the statement of the National Association of Manufacturers could explain. One sees combined a number of different patterns of ownership and control: (1) At the base there is private property which is defined and protected by law. (2) Most of the extraction of raw materials and the manufacturing and distributive industries are operated by corporations where ownership is separated from the control of property. (3) Much of this property which is involved in production and exchange is under a variety of additional positive governmental controls. (4) Some property like the postal system is completely under government ownership and control. (5) In an earlier chapter we have observed that some property, such as the Federal Reserve System, is under private ownership but under government operation. And (6) some property is publicly owned but under private operation. This last is exemplified by portions of the Merchant Marine and by the Atomic Energy patents.

It would be hard to imagine a single theoretical standard by which all these varieties of property could be measured for their ethical or public utility. The types of property as well as the types of control are fundamentally the product of group pressures, and any method of ownership and control is only as good as the presently predominating interests wish it to be, which is merely to say again that this lack of system seems to serve a lot of different people more or less effectively depending on their particular points of view.

BIBLIOGRAPHICAL NOTE

N. J. Ware, *Wealth and Welfare,* 1949, provides a short history of the development of the U. S. economy. A. G. Papandreou and J. T. Wheeler, *Competition and Its Regulation,* 1954, carefully compares the economist's concept of competition as distinguished from the lawyer's concept of competition. Public regulations to foster competition are described, court decisions are analyzed, and recommendations are made for the improvement of the present laws.

J. R. Commons, *Legal Foundations of Capitalism,* 1924, and *The Economics of Collective Action,* 1951. The "institutional" approach to economics is well illustrated in these two volumes. The late Professor Commons views economic behavior in a context as broad as society itself and is concerned with the close relation between the activities of public officials and private groups in the economic process. B. Gross, "The Coming Revolution in Economic Thought," in *Life, Language, Law: Essays in Honor of Arthur F. Bentley,* 1957, Ch. IV, is a brilliant essay that relates the "institutional" approach to modern developments in economic theory.

J. Bauer, *Transforming Public Utility Regulations,* 1950. As well as describing modern regulation of private utilities, this volume makes recommendations for improvements.

H. C. Simons, *Economic Policy for a Free Society,* 1947, one of the best defenses of the free enterprize economy, claims that government is the chief creator of monopoly. Professor Simons argues that monopolies of both labor and business should be destroyed in order to protect and improve our economic system. W. Adams and H. M. Gray, *Monopoly in America,* 1946, agrees with Professor Simons that government has been responsible, to a large extent, for the creation of monopoly power, but argues that the protection of competition is primarily a governmental responsibility which should be pursued through more vigorous and effective regulation.

J. M. Clark, *Alternative to Serfdom*, 1948, is a modest defense of governmental planning that provides one of the most careful discussions of the issues involved in public regulation.

J. A. Schumpeter, *Capitalism, Socialism, and Democracy*, 1950. A defense of the private entrepreneur, the late Professor Schumpeter is both pessimistic about the future of capitalism and the capacity of socialist planning to achieve better results. This is must reading for defenders of "free enterprise" as well as advocates of alternative economic systems. J. K. Galbraith, *American Capitalism*, 1952 tries to show that the size of a corporation is not necessarily an index of its capacity for interfering with the competitive economy. The "countervailing power" of suppliers and purchasers is frequently sufficient to place a large corporation under adequate social control. A. A. Berle, *The Twentieth Century Capitalist Revolution*, 1954, contends that the corporate managers are replacing the politicians as the modern statesmen and that corporation law is becoming modern constitutional law.

8. JAMES M. BURNS

Government and Labor

IF we live in an era of Big Business and Big Government, surely we must talk in terms of Big Labor too. The total labor force in the United States—men and women over the age of 14 employed or seeking work —is between 67 and 70 millions. This number rises by about a million a year. Of the total labor force about one of every four workers is a member of some union. Most of these trade union members are organized in the recently merged American Federation of Labor and Congress of Industrial Organizations. "Labor" in the broadest sense dominates the American economy; and that part of labor that is organized wields tremendous economic and political power. The announcements of the AFL-CIO on a national problem reverberate in the White House and in Congress; the head of the AFL-CIO must be reckoned as one of the dozen or so most influential persons in America.

Individual unions also hold great power, especially when concentrated in particular areas. The nation's largest union, the United Auto Workers, heavily influences the politics of Michigan, and its policies and demands in bargaining with the great automobile companies influence the pattern of collective bargaining throughout the country. Pennsylvania politics would be much different without the Miners Union. Some of the craft unions, such as the Carpenters and Bricklayers, intimately affect politics in their localities. Labor as a whole is well represented in the lobbies of Washington and the state capitals.

Labor leaders like to proclaim that unions in America are "as American as America itself." To some extent this is true. The tremendous variety of labor unions reflects much of the variety of the whole economy and society. Thus we have not only unions of auto workers and carpenters, but also of radio and television actors, of bank clerks, of government workers, of Pullman porters, of tug boat operators, and of hundreds of other types of occupations. On the other hand, organized labor is not a simple mirror of the whole body of Americans employed by others. Some employees are highly organized; others—for example, farm laborers, office secretaries, department store clerks, domestic servants, college professors—are under-organized or not organized at all. Some unions are strong and independent; others are small and weak, or perhaps dominated by an employer. These distinctions and qualifications are important ones to keep in mind in considering the labor policy of government and labor's influence on it.

HISTORICAL BACKGROUND

The efforts of American workers to organize and improve their situation are part and parcel of the history of America as a whole. Trade unions in the modern sense are about as old as our system of government. The great forces that have affected America—industrialization, urbanization, wars, depressions, prosperity, and above all economic growth—have shaped the American labor movement. But the impact has not been a one-way affair. Organized labor, especially in more recent years, has significantly affected government and public policy, just as the politics and government of Washington and state, county, and local capitals have influenced labor. This situation is also true of the relation between labor and employers. Labor organization has been, to a large extent, a reaction to the organization and practices of businessmen, just as the latter have continually modified their policies one way or the other to cope with the demands of organized labor.

Hence we must visualize the development of government labor policy—including the *absence* of government policy—as in large part a response to the economic and political changes in the relation of labor and employers, this relation in turn being ceaselessly affected by basic economic, political, and social changes. For the sake of convenience we may divide the historical development of labor and labor policy into four broad periods.

The first hundred years

The first trade unions date from about the time that George Washington first took office as President. Prior to this time there had been, of course, guilds of skilled workers. But the typical organization of a small workshop was a master and a few apprentices, and such a relationship had made organization in the modern sense almost impossible. With the impact of the industrial revolution, however, important changes took place in the relations in the shop. Markets broadened, shops expanded in size, simple machinery was introduced, businessmen looked around for cheaper labor, the apprenticeship system declined, the relations between manager and worker became more impersonal, and a more distinct wage-earning class developed. The first unions were formed mainly by skilled craftsmen reacting against these new developments. By 1800 there were craft societies of carpenters, cabinetmakers, weavers, hatters, and a variety of other occupations.

It was only natural that employers would react strongly to the new organizations, and they often did so in a hostile manner. Employers formed associations of their own to deal with the workers, and they turned to the law and the courts for weapons against the workers' "illegal" organizations. The judges turned to the old English common-law doctrine of conspiracy to find journeymen shoemakers and other groups "guilty of a combination to raise wages." It was partly in protest against this alliance between the employers and the government that many workers turned to the Jeffersonian and Jacksonian political movements during the first half of the 19th century.

The first unions were often rather feeble and could be killed off by depressions or by hostile employers or judges. As the nation expanded, however, the unions took more and more secure footholds, and by the mid-19th century hitherto isolated labor groups in various cities had linked up with one another and were establishing national unions. Once established, the unions began to experiment, not always consciously, with various ways of operating. Some workers' groups used only economic weapons, such as the strike and the boycott. Others were more concerned with political action, forming workingmen's parties, even joining hands with farmers restless over economic conditions. Other unions turned to embryonic radical movements. Still others, like the notorious "Molly Maguires" resorted to terroristic tactics that led in turn to disorders, destruction, and bloodshed.

The climax of union labor's "first century" came in the form of the Knights of Labor. At first a secret organization, the Knights grew with amazing speed during the 1880's. Its importance lay in its attempt to become one great nationwide union of all types of workers and in its willingness to use political as well as economic weapons. For a time the Knights had spectacular success, increasing in size to 700,000 members and supporting some successful strikes. But its supremacy was shortlived. Disunity developed among the heterogeneous elements in the organization. Skilled workers felt that their interests were not sufficiently represented as against other workers. A number of strikes sponsored by the Knights failed badly. The leadership was often inept. By 1890 the experiment of one grand union using economic and political methods had failed.

What was government labor policy during the first hundred years? To a great extent it was non-existent, as compared with the extensive labor legislation we have today. But the *absence* of policy was in itself important. It often meant that workers and employers were left to fight out their battles without interference from the government. Lack of concern over labor and working conditions by the government in turn reflected more basic factors: the prevailing ideology of laissez-faire which, especially in the latter part of the period, emphasized the desirable operation of automatic and "natural" economic laws without intervention by the government; the emphasis in popular thinking on the Horatio Alger, Jr., "success story" of the able young man climbing the economic and social ladder; the fact that millions of workers were immigrants who could hardly speak English and who had little power to influence government; the organizational weaknesses of unions and their tendency to cave in when depressions struck.

One aspect of the negative or hostile government labor policies during this period was the role of the *courts*. In the *absence* of legislation —that is, action by the popularly elected lawmakers, who on occasion might be influenced by union pressure—judges used old, common-law doctrines against labor's "conspiracy" to combine. For example—to take a case shortly after this period—during a conflict between a union and a metal company in the metal trades, a court enjoined union leaders from boycotting the company; when the leaders persisted with the boycott, the court sentenced them to jail. In another case, a court prohibited the unionization of a coal mine without the consent of the owners.

The American Federation of Labor, 1890–1932

While the Knights of Labor were declining, a new organization of workers was gaining strength nationally. Under the leadership of a shrewd cigar-maker named Samuel Gompers, the American Federation of Labor embraced not the ambitious program of the Knights but practical, "bread-and-butter" unionism. Gompers and his associates generally believed in capitalism and strove to improve labor's lot within that system. They favored local autonomy for the A.F.L.'s member unions, emphasis on economic tactics such as the strike and picketing, and avoidance of "class warfare" and other radical ideas. The A.F.L. proved its durability when it survived the economic crises toward the end of the 19th century.[1]

The A.F.L.'s political tactics were the counterpart of its economic. In general Gompers tended to fear government—to him it was less an agency that could help labor than a distant power to be feared. His main objective was to prevent employers from using the government—legislatures, governors, judges, and officials—to thwart labor's effort to improve economic conditions. Hence for some time the A.F.L. had a limited and rather negative political program.

The government's relation to labor toward the end of the 19th century seemed to vindicate labor's suspicion of government. President Cleveland, as well as a number of state governors, used troops against strikers. Laws were passed limiting the effectiveness of strikes, picketing, the boycott, and other economic weapons. An important example of labor's difficulties with government was the Sherman Antitrust Act of 1896. Passed ostensibly to prevent illegal combinations by businessmen, the act was used against combinations of *workers*—that is, against labor unionism itself. Court injunctions, too, were often obtained by employers to thwart economic action by unions.

Disheartened by such developments, faced by the competition of more radical groups such as the "Wobblies" (Industrial Workers of the World), and impressed by the political successes of British unionists, the A.F.L. decided in the early 1900's to enter politics a bit more actively. A program was formulated demanding such reforms as sanitary inspection of shops, liability of employers for injury or loss of life, the eight-hour day, child labor laws, free schools and textbooks, and even municipal ownership of private utilities. "We have long, patiently

[1] E. E. Cummins, *The Labor Problem in the United States* (New York: D. Van Nostrand Company, Inc., 1935), p. 135.

and in vain waited for redress . . ." labor proclaimed. If government did not respond, labor threatened to appeal to the voters.[2] During the following decade the A.F.L. pursued a political tactic of trying to "help our friends and defeat our enemies."

Woodrow Wilson's election in 1912 with a Democratic Congress was hailed as a great victory for labor's heightened interest in political action. For labor, the "New Freedom" meant the Clayton Act, which seemed to exempt labor from the onerous provisions of the Sherman Act, more influence for the A.F.L. in the administration of the Labor Department and the labor policies of other government agencies, greater access to the Administration and to Congress, and passage of a bill establishing the eight-hour day for most railroad employees.[3] During World War I the Federation achieved an important place in the war administration; and the war and employment boom helped it achieve its organizational high point, until then, of almost two million members.

The next 15 years, however, brought American unionism to its lowest ebb in decades. Despite the prosperity of the 1920's, organized labor failed to augment either its economic or political power. Membership fell off, and little effort was made to organize millions of workers in the large mass-production industries such as automobiles and steel. Union strength fell off even more during the early 1930's under the impact of the Great Depression. There were few government programs to protect workers against the ravages of unemployment and wage cuts. "Men are afraid, working men are filled with fear," declared William Green, Gompers' successor as head of the A.F.L.

There were some bright spots for labor during these frustrating years. Union leaders scored an important legislative victory in 1932 with the passage of the Norris-LaGuardia Act. Sponsored by two progressive Republicans, Senator George Norris of Nebraska and Representative Fiorello LaGuardia of New York City, this act declared that, in order to protect the public interest, workers should be free to form unions without interference from employers. Recognizing that the "individual unorganized worker is commonly helpless to exercise actual liberty of contract and to protect his freedom of labor," it declared that workers may select representatives of their own choosing. It made yellow-dog contracts (contracts prohibiting workers from

---

[2] "Labor's Bill of Grievances," *American Federationist* (May 1906), pp. 293-96.

[3] Cf. A. S. Link, *Wilson: The New Freedom* (Princeton, N. J.: Princeton University Press, 1956).

joining unions) unenforceable in federal courts and drastically limited the issuance of labor injunctions in other respects. But the act established no agency to enforce its provisions.

Some states also were still taking the lead in passing laws favored by labor. For example, more than half the states by 1932 had replaced the common law with statutes prohibiting blacklisting (listing of names of union leaders and organizers so that they could be denied jobs in other companies). Some industrial states and some states run by progressive politicians (such as LaFollette in Wisconsin) had passed extensive social welfare legislation, such as minimum wage laws for various types of employees, but unfavorable court decisions on the constitutionality of such laws under the Fourteeth Amendment discouraged the states from more decisive action; moreover, there was always the problem that the more drastic the labor laws, the more businesses might threaten to leave the state.

Aside from these bright spots for labor, the 1920's and early 1930's were a period of stagnation. Long committed to the essential features of a laissez-faire economic system, the Federation seemed to be as demoralized as most businesses. Some workers tried militant economic action, such as desperate strikes, or even turned to socialist or communist movements, but nothing seemed to help much as depression tightened its grip on the American economy.

The New Deal and after

The inauguration of Franklin D. Roosevelt in 1933, like that of Woodrow Wilson 20 years before, brought a sharp change in the political climate for labor. Although the unions were not powerful enough politically to be decisive, leaders of the A.F.L. and of other unions had given far more support to Roosevelt than to President Herbert Hoover in the presidential race of 1932, and once again labor had access to the Administration and to Congress. In the very first months of the New Deal, union leaders such as Green and John L. Lewis, head of the United Mine Workers, took an active part along with representatives of employers and other groups in framing the National Industrial Recovery Act, the most important domestic legislation of the early New Deal. Under the famous Section 7a of the N.I.R.A., labor was "guaranteed" the right of collective bargaining. Benefiting from this provision and from increased employment, union membership and morale soared during 1934 and 1935. But so did divisions within labor. Restless at the continued conservative leadership of the A.F.L., eager to organize the great mass-production industries at a time that seemed ripe, and hopeful of building up a stronger labor alliance with the New Dealers, a group of unions under Lewis' leadership broke away from the A.F.L. and established the C.I.O. (then called the Committee for Industrial Organization, later changed to Congress of Industrial Organizations). Soon the rivalry between the A.F.L. and C.I.O. was dominating the world of labor organization.

In 1935 the Supreme Court declared the N.I.R.A. unconstitutional, and with it, of course, Section 7a. The court's decision, however, coincided with a leftward turn in the New Deal and helped bring the enactment of what was the most important labor legislation until that time, The National Labor Relations Act. Like Section 7a, the new act was designed to guarantee labor's right of collective bargaining, free from any employer domination or even influence, to all workers in concerns employing persons in interstate commerce or in industries substantially affecting interstate commerce. Unlike Section 7a, however, the act spelled out five types of unfair labor practices which employers were forbidden to engage in: (1) interfering with employees' rights of collective bargaining; (2) dominating or in any way influencing labor unions; (3) discriminating against union members in either hiring or firing; (4) discriminating against any employee because he took advantage of his rights under the law; and (5) refusing to bargain collectively with the properly designated representatives of the employees.[4]

Perhaps even more important than the terms of the Wagner Act was the vigor of its administration. The act provided for a National Labor Relations Board, and President Roosevelt appointed as members of the Board three men who were strongly "pro-labor" in the sense that they believed thoroughly in an act deliberately designed to improve labor's strength in collective bargaining. With the stimulus of the Wagner Act, unions gained further in membership and in economic and political power, although they were somewhat weakened by the deepening split between the A.F.L. and C.I.O.

Four other enactments during Roosevelt's first two terms that extended the government's protection of labor were:

1. *The Fair Labor Standards* (Black-Connery) *Act.* This act was passed in 1938 under President Roosevelt's leadership after a sharp

[4] For an excellent brief treatment of the Wagner Act and its administration, see Robert R. R. Brooks, *Unions of Their Own Choosing* (New Haven, Conn.: Yale University Press, 1939).

struggle within the Democratic Party between Northern and Southern members of Congress. The act excluded from interstate commerce any goods not produced in accordance with certain standards, established a 44-hour week (to be changed to 42-hours in the second year and 40-hours thereafter), a minimum wage of 25 cents an hour (after one year to be raised to 30 cents an hour, and after seven years to 40 cents an hour), and barred the use of oppressive child labor (defined as the employment of children under 16, or of children between 16 and 18 in dangerous or unhealthful occupations). Although many exemptions were written into the bill, especially for agricultural or food processing workers, the legislation served as a basis for further extension of its coverage.

2. *The Public Contracts* (Walsh-Healey) *Act*. Passed in 1936, this legislation provided that contractors with the federal government (which also meant, under the grants-in-aid system, many state agencies) must pay not less than the prevailing minimum wage for comparable work, observe the eight-hour day and 40-hour week, and meet various other requirements relating to working conditions.

3. *Settlement of labor disputes*. Amendments in 1934 strengthened the Railway Labor Act of 1926, which had established agencies for the mediation of labor disputes in the railway field. Under the terms of the original act a National Railroad Adjustment Board was created to bring representatives of railway management and labor into direct contact with each other, and the National Mediation Board, supposed to be impartial between the two sides, was set up to mediate differences between the two parties. The 1934 amendments forbade railway employers to "influence or coerce" their employees in regard to union organization.

4. *Social security*. Social security is treated separately in this volume, but it may be pointed out here that labor, as a group, traditionally exposed to economic insecurity, was especially interested in the legislation passed in 1935 for unemployment insurance and old age compensation.

As labor's organizational, economic, and legislative strength increased during the 1930's, so did its political strength. Labor groups— especially the C.I.O.—formed political action groups in support of Roosevelt in the 1936 and succeeding elections. So influential was organized labor after the 1940 election that it was given an unprecedented role in the administration of defense programs during World War II. It had an equal place with management in the National War Labor

Board, which had the job of mediating, and in effect arbitrating, wartime labor disputes. The Conciliation Service, established in 1913 in the Labor Department to aid in the settlement of labor disputes, was also expanded to handle the flock of employer-employee conflicts that rose during the war.

Following the war there was a reaction to organized labor's newly won political and economic influence. While the unions were able to help elect Harry Truman in 1948 and retain their influence with the White House, Congress was often controlled by majorities reflecting popular feeling that labor power must be checked. By far the most important legislation responsive to these developments was the Taft-Hartley Act, described in the following section of this chapter. At the state level, too, laws were passed restricting union activity; many of these were modeled after the Taft-Hartley Act on the national level. The election of Dwight Eisenhower showed the limitations of union strength in presidential elections, for most of the union leadership supported his Democratic opponent, Adlai E. Stevenson. While President Eisenhower seemed to follow a policy of "benevolent neutrality" toward labor issues, he gave generally broad support to the Taft-Hartley Act and appointed men to the National Labor Relations Board who took a far less pro-labor approach than had the earlier appointees. During Eisenhower's second term organized labor was still on the defensive in Congress, especially as a result of disclosures by a Senate committee of corruption among union leadership.

NATIONAL LABOR POLICY TODAY

The Taft-Hartley Act

The keystone of national labor policy today is the Taft-Hartley (Labor Management Relations) Act of 1947. As noted above, this legislation was a response to a decade of dissatisfaction on the part of employer, farm, and middle-class elements to what they considered to be the excesses of labor. So strong was this feeling that even though President Truman vetoed the bill, two-thirds majorities were mustered in each chamber to overturn the veto and enact the Taft-Hartley bill into law. Republican control of Congress (for the first time in a decade and a half) was the main reason for the bill's passage, but it could not have been adopted without the support of a great many Democrats, especially from the South. Technically the act was simply a series of amendments to the Wagner Act; in effect, it represented a significant departure from the 1935 act in the direction of the idea that organized labor had become such a strong force in the economic and political life of the nation that it, like business, must be more closely supervised by the national government.

The Taft-Hartley Act is really a collection of rather diverse policies grouped together in one omnibus affair.

Unfair labor practices of labor unions

The most important provisions of the Taft-Hartley Act set out unfair labor practices of *unions,* in contrast with the concern of the Wagner Act with unfair labor practices of *management.* The latter were retained, and supplemented with the following unfair labor practices:[5]

1. To restrain or coerce employees in the right to join or assist a union or to refrain from joining or assisting a union.
2. To restrain or coerce an employer in the choosing of his representatives for collective bargaining or adjusting of grievances.
3. To cause or try to cause an employer to discriminate against an employee in violation of the union-shop provisions of the Act.
4. To require, under a permitted union shop, an initiation fee for new members that the National Labor Relations Board finds "excessive or discriminatory under all circumstances."
5. To refuse to bargain collectively with an employer where the union involved is the certified bargaining agent.
6. To cause or try to cause an employer to pay a sum "in the nature of an exaction," for services which are not performed or not to be performed.
7. To engage in, or encourage employees to engage in, a strike or concerted refusal, in the course of employment, to use or otherwise handle or work on any goods or to perform any services, where the object is to force or require:
   a. any employer or self-employed person to join any labor or employer organization.
   b. any employer or other person to cease using or dealing in the products of another person or to cease doing business with any other person.
   c. another employer to recognize an uncertified union.
   d. any employer to violate a Board certification.
   e. any employer to assign particular work to employees in a particular union or trade unless that employer is failing to conform to an order or certification of the Board.

[5] Adapted from Richard A. Lester, *Labor and Industrial Relations* (New York: The Macmillan Co., 1951), p. 324.

Some of these provisions merit brief elaboration. Probably the most important of the unfair labor practices by a union (or by its agent) in the list above are the anti-boycott and anti-strike provisions under paragraph 7. After many years of almost complete immunity from the courts, secondary boycotts by unions (i.e., a boycott by a union of products of a firm dealing with another firm that might be strike-bound) were made subject to injunctions and damage suits. Moreover, the anti-boycott and anti-strike provisions of paragraph 7 are sharpened by further sections of the Taft-Hartley Act. Not only are items under paragraph 7 made illegal as well as unfair labor practices, but the National Labor Relations Board is required to give them priority of handling over all other cases.

It was obvious that such provisions as the above, while somewhat more specific than the unfair practices by employers in the Wagner Act, would require considerable interpretation by the National Labor Relations Board as specific cases came before it. Much would depend, in short, on the makeup and procedure of the Board. Believing that the Board under the Wagner Act had served unfairly as both judge and prosecutor, Congress made the NLRB's General Counsel independent of the Board and gave him supervision over all attorneys and employees in the regional offices, where cases would first be handled. Thus the General Counsel became the key figure in the agency. At the same time, the Board was enlarged from three members to five, holding overlapping terms of five years each.

Other provisions of the Taft-Hartley Act

Union shop. One of the oldest and most acute issues between labor and management has been the question of whether a union can compel employees to become members of the union. Under the *closed* shop the would-be employee must join the union before being hired. Under the *union* shop a firm may hire union or non-union workers, but after a specified period of time, usually a month, all employees must join the union. The Wagner Act had specifically authorized employers and unions to make closed shop agreements if they agreed to do so. The Taft-Hartley Act, on the other hand, made the closed shop an unfair labor practice. As for the *union* shop, the Taft-Hartley Act authorizes it only when the union is certified as the representative of the employees, when a majority of the employees eligible to vote have cast a secret ballot authorizing it, and when state laws do not prohibit it. All this "sounds complicated and is complicated. The aim is to prevent the union from using exclusion or expulsion from membership as a job penalty." [6]

Bargaining unit. A key problem under the Wagner Act has been deciding what bargaining unit an employer must (or must not) bargain with. NLRB decisions as to the bargaining unit—for example, whether office workers and skilled workers should be included in one unit along with the great number of unskilled and semi-skilled workers—had often been very difficult and controversial ones, for they not only antagonized employers but also rival union groups, such as A.F.L. craft workers. The Taft-Hartley Act made significant changes in this respect. Supervisors and foremen were removed from the definition of employee, and hence management could refuse to bargain with them if they should form unions. More important, the Board was restricted in its power to determine "appropriate bargaining units." It was prohibited from certifying as a bargaining unit any general union admitting to membership plant guards and watchmen (the latter could of course form separate unions of their own); from including professional employees in the same bargaining unit with non-professional workers unless a majority of the former voted for such inclusion; and from denying to skilled craft employees a separate bargaining unit simply because a previous NLRB decision had included such employees in a broader unit (the Board could continue to include them in the broader unit only if a majority of the craft employees so voted in a secret balloting).

Union publicity and loyalty. Unions could take advantage of the law for purposes of collective bargaining only after filing with the Secretary of Labor information on union affairs including the following: name and principal address of the union, names, titles, and salaries of the chief officers, amount of dues and initiation fees, regulations regarding membership qualifications, election of officers, calling of meetings, levying of special assessments, authorization of strikes, methods for raising union funds, participation in union benefits, and methods of and grounds for expelling members from the union. Unions were required to furnish the Secretary and their memberships a financial statement showing total assets and liabilities, amounts and sources of receipts, and information as to the purposes of the disbursements.

More controversial than the above provisions was a requirement that before a union could qualify for the benefits of the Act it must file affidavits to the effect that none of its officers was a member of the

[6] *Ibid.,* p. 323.

Communist party, or of any other organization that advocated the overthrow of government by force or by illegal or unconstitutional methods. It is to be noted that the law does not require such affidavits as such, but only if the union wishes whatever government support— such as certification as a bargaining unit—that the act might provide.

Labor-management disputes. On the grounds that the Secretary of Labor should not have control over an impartial mediation agency, the Taft-Hartley Act transferred the mediation and conciliation functions of the United States Conciliation Agency to a new, independent agency, the Federal Mediation and Conciliation Service. Important new procedures were set up for handling disputes. The parties must, as part of their duty to bargain in good faith, give 60 days' notice in advance of a proposed termination or modification of an agreement and, within 30 days thereafter, notify the Federal Mediation and Conciliation Service and any state service with jurisdiction. Under the law, the Federal Mediation and Conciliation Service may enter a case at the request of either of the parties or on its own initiative.

Whenever in the opinion of the President a threatened or actual strike or lockout will, by affecting all or a substantial part of an industry, imperil the national health or safety, he may appoint a board of inquiry. This board must report the facts of the dispute but without any recommendations. The President may then direct the Attorney General to seek a court injuction to enjoin such a strike or lockout. If the federal court finds that the situation does threaten to jeopardize the natural health or safety and issues an injunction, the board of inquiry is reconvened and, if the dispute continues, must report again to the President within 60 days with respect to the dispute, including a statement of each employer's last offer of settlement. Within the next 20 days there must be a secret ballot on the *employer's last offer* and the results certified to the Attorney General. Thereupon the injunction of the court must be dissolved and a strike becomes legal. The President then submits a full report to the Congress along with such recommendations as he may wish to make.

The act also made it unlawful for any labor organization (as well as any business corporation) to make certain political contributions or expenditures. The restriction applied to national elections (both presidential and congressional), to primary elections relating to the selection of presidential and congressional candidates, and to related political conventions and caucuses.

It was made illegal for any person employed by the federal government or by any of its agencies or corporations to take part in a strike. The penalty for striking was immediate discharge, forfeiture of civil service status, and ineligibility for reemployment for three years. Government employees were still allowed, however, to join unions and bargain with the government.

The "check-off" (an arrangement under which management assumes the job of deducting union dues and fees from the workers' pay and turning them over to the union) was restricted except upon individual written agreements with each worker.

Welfare funds were illegalized unless based upon written agreements.

The Act made unions specifically subject to suits for breach of contract, and both unions and employers were made liable for acts of their agents (although awards could not be enforced against individual union members).

Taft-Hartley's first decade

What has been the experience of labor and government during the first ten years of the Act's application? Organized labor of course greeted the Act with intense hostility, dubbing it, with considerable exaggeration, as the "slave-labor act." Many employers felt that the Act did not have enough teeth and would make little difference in curbing what they considered to be excessive labor power. Most Americans probably welcomed the Act as a desirable, if not perfect, experiment in redressing the balance between labor and management. A Gallup poll, a year after the Act went into effect, indicated that 16 per cent of those questioned favored outright repeal, while 31 per cent liked the Act as it was. Of the great middle group favoring modification rather than repeal of the Act, 14 per cent wanted liberalization of the law (in favor of labor) and 12 per cent favored a more restrictive measure.

Such reactions were somewhat ambiguous, however, because the Act included such a great diversity of separate policies. Experience with several of its specific policies has been somewhat more meaningful.

"Redressing the balance." Has the Act succeeded in achieving a "fairer" balance between management and labor? There is little agreement on this score because definition of a "fair balance" is itself a major issue. Certainly the act has not destroyed or "enslaved" organized labor as a whole. The unions have continued to grow in size, although not at the rate of a decade or so ago. Some union leaders

charge—and with considerable justification—that the Act has made far more difficult the organization of workers in the South, although "little Taft-Hartley Acts" in the states are also a roadblock to organization. The Act has had some effect in protecting individual union members and non-union members against abuses of labor power. For example, the Board has given force in certain situations to the provision that a union cannot compel an employer to discipline members for any reason other than failure to pay union dues or fees.[7] The number of charged unfair labor practices, despite the fears of union leaders, continued to be preponderantly against the employer.

Effect on labor-management peace. Here again the verdict must be less than definite, because legislation is only one of many factors affecting industrial peace. The conciliation procedure of the Act has failed to avert several serious and lengthy strikes during the past decade; on the other hand, during much of the decade the number of man-days of labor lost through strikes and lockouts has been rather low compared with the decade before (comparing two such different periods, however, is quite difficult). After a year and a half of experience under the Act the director of the Federal Mediation and Conciliation Service stated that the 80-day injunction tended to postpone collective bargaining and actually to delay dispute settlements.

Effect on union status. The Act has not had a profound effect on the union shop or the closed shop. Of the many thousands of union shop polls conducted by the Board, the workers voted overwhelmingly for the union shop. As for the *closed* shop, its prohibition has not been very effective. The closed shop is found mainly in the craft industries, where the vast majority of employees and a great many employers have lived with the system for a long time and have little wish to change it. Few employees opposed to the closed shop have the inclination or resources to file a complaint against it with the Board. Hence thousands of workers continue as members of "bootleg" closed shops.

Union loyalty. Although many union leaders attacked the loyalty provisions of the Act as unfair and discriminatory, most unions complied with them. Some of the non-complying unions were led by men who were strong foes of communism but who opposed loyalty tests in principle and who considered their unions so entrenched that government support under the Act was unnecessary. For example, John L. Lewis, a strong anti-communist, refused to sign the required affidavit.

[7] C. A. Daugherty and John B. Parrish, *The Labor Problems of American Society* (Boston: Houghton-Mifflin Co., 1952), p. 770.

Other non-complying unions were influenced or dominated by left-wing leaders—in some cases communist party members or sympathizers—and such unions suffered considerable loss of strength because of their leaders' refusal to sign the required oaths. Union leaders challenged the legality of the loyalty requirement, but the United States Supreme Court sustained the provision, holding that it did not violate freedom of speech as guaranteed by the First Amendment.[8]

Effect of limitation on political contributions. This provision of the Act has had mixed results. On the one hand, union heads, feeling that the provision was directed unfairly at labor's rightful political activity, took test cases to the courts. In 1948 the Supreme Court held that the provision could not extend to publication of editorials in union publications advising members on how to vote, but it did not pass on the constitutionality of the provision as a whole.[9] On the other hand, the provision has compelled unions to change their methods of financing political activity by setting up special funds for the purpose (rather than allotting political action funds from the general union treasury), and in this sense the provision has undoubtedly handicapped labor in its political activity.

In conclusion, it may be said that the Taft-Hartley Act has neither "destroyed free labor," as some union leaders charged it would, nor has it had as fully a "cleansing" or balancing effect as some of its proponents hoped. Some of the latter, indeed, have had second thoughts about the advisability of bringing government so much into the delicate area of labor-management relations as the Taft-Hartley Act has done. Many union members and some union leaders have come to accept—or at least to "live with"—the majority of the Act's provisions. Parts of the Act have had much of the effect expected, others have failed to have any important influence on labor behavior, and still others have important side effects that have created new and unexpected problems.

Wages and hours regulation since 1938

The standards established by the Fair Labor Standards Act on its passage in 1938 were so low that they did not have a major influence on wages except in certain industries, such as textiles. The constitutionality of the Act was upheld by the Supreme Court in 1941 after the high bench had become dominated by appointees of President

[8] *American Communication Association* v. *Douds,* 339 U.S. 382, 1950.
[9] *United States* v. *Congress of Industrial Organizations,* 335 U.S. 106 (1948).

Franklin D. Roosevelt.[10] By the time the 45 cent minimum wage went into effect in 1945 the post-World War II inflation was already getting under way and beginning to make the enforced wage limitations obsolete. After a long political struggle Congress in 1949 raised the minimum wage to 75 cents, and in 1956, after President Eisenhower had recommended an increase to 90 cents, and organized labor to $1.25, Congress set the minimum at a flat one dollar. The Act still provides no absolute limitation on the number of hours employees may work, but simply requires that time and a half be paid for all time worked beyond 40 hours a week.

Administered by the Wage and Hour and Public Contracts Division of the Labor Department, the Act provides that violators may be fined up to 10,000 dollars or, in the case of a second conviction, imprisonment up to six months, or both. Employees may also collect in court double the back wages due them plus attorneys' fees and court costs. To help in the transition to the original scales the Division was authorized to appoint industry committees composed of equal representatives of the employees, employers, and the public, and empowered to make recommendations for standards in their industries. The Act still does not extend to those millions of workers—for example, hired hands on farms, employees in such semi-agricultural activities as food processing, migratory workers, and workers in very small establishments—to whom application of the act would be administratively very difficult, even if politically feasible.

Sometimes government seeks to keep wages *down* rather than up. Such was the case during World War II and the Korean war. During World War II the National War Labor Board, composed equally of representatives of industry, labor, and the public, was established to settle disputes between unions and management and to help stabilize wages in the battle against inflation. During the Korean war Congress authorized an Economic Stabilization Agency with subsidiary wage and salary boards, again with tripartite representation, with the power to keep salaries and wages from soaring under the stimulus of war spending.

Other labor policy

The Anti-Strikebreaking (Byrnes) *Act of 1936.* This act was passed in response to widespread feeling on the part of labor and others that the importation by employers of workers to take the place of men on

[10] *United States* v. *F. W. Darby Lumber Company,* 312 U.S. 100 (1941).

strike was unfair. The Byrnes Act forbids the transportation in interstate or foreign commerce of any person with the purpose of interfering with the right of peaceful picketing in connection with a labor dispute, or the right of collective bargaining. The penalty is a fine of 5,000 dollars or imprisonment up to two years, or both. Although the law was somewhat strengthened in 1938, it has rarely if ever been invoked.

The Anti-Racketeering Act of 1946. Congress enacted a statute in 1934 making it a felony to obtain money or property through the use of threats or force, where such acts affected trade or commerce (excepting, of course, in connection with the payment of wages by a bona fide employer). The objective of the law was to prevent the "shakedown" of employers for the profit of racketeering union officials, without hurting the basic right to strike. Following a Supreme Court decision in 1942 that seemed to limit the Act's application, amendments to the 1934 law in the form of the Anti-Racketeering Act of 1946 sought to put more teeth into it. Acts of robbery or extortion that affected interstate commerce were made illegal. The definition of robbery and extortion was made somewhat clearer and more comprehensive, and the original clause exempting wages paid to bona fide employees by a bona fide employer was eliminated. The main result of this provision is to lay open to punishment unions that try, through strikes or threats of strikes, to compel employers to pay wages for work not actually performed, even when there is a bona fide employer-employee relationship.[11]

State labor policy

The great mass of national labor policy is paralleled by extensive labor legislation in the states, although there are, of course, great differences between the states, especially between industrial and rural areas. Four main objectives of state labor laws are: (1) protection of the safety and health of workers; (2) reasonable working conditions and wage scales; (3) settlement of industrial disputes; and (4) regulation of labor relations, including the power and activities of unions.

Safety and health. It was in this area that states pioneered, long ago, as the industrial revolution brought grave problems of health and safety affecting not only workers but whole urban populations. State laws prescribe minimum conditions of safety in industrial establishments; for example, active parts of machinery such as flywheels and saws must be protected, fire escapes installed, and adequate lighting

[11] Daugherty and Parrish, *op. cit.,* p. 771.

provided. Every state prohibits children from occupation in hazardous industries. Women are excluded from occupations that might endanger their health. States also require technical qualifications for such jobs as elevator operators and railroad engineers for the benefit of both the employees and the people they serve. States have long been concerned also with occupational diseases involved in occupations where workers come into contact with poisonous or deleterious substances, such as lead.

Another traditional state activity involves workmen's compensation. Years ago, whenever an accident occurred, an injured employee had to institute a lawsuit in order to recover damages; but often he might lack the necessary funds, long delays were likely, and he might have trouble proving his case. As a remedy laws were urged that would give all injured employees compensation without regard to fixing blame. Compensation laws, now found in all states, provide for payments to injured workers according to some established law; the amount usually varies with the seriousness of the injury and the amount of the employee's wages. Compensation varies widely from state to state and has tended to be low, especially in the light of inflation.

Wages and working conditions. All states have enacted some laws concerning the length of the working day. Children especially have been protected against exploitation, and almost all the states have laws restricting the hours of labor of women in specified employments. Decades ago states also began to restrict the hours of men in occupations considered especially dangerous or unhealthful. *General* hours regulation came later, and only after encountering severe constitutional challenge. In a famous case, for example, the Supreme Court vetoed a New York law limiting the hours of bakery workers to ten a day.[12] The states continued to pass legislation, however, and later laws were upheld as changes took place in the make-up of federal and state courts. A number of states today have general hours regulation; the reason the number is not greater is less a matter of constitutional power than the fear of losing industry to other states.

As for minimum wages, Massachusetts was the first state to pass a minimum wage law, in 1912. The early state laws applied only to women and children. Minimum wage legislation in Oregon was challenged on constitutional grounds and was ultimately sustained in the Supreme Court by an even vote of four to four. Later, however, the high court voided minimum wage laws in several states, only to reverse

[12] *Lochner* v. *New York,* 198 U.S. 45 (1905).

itself during the New Deal period. In the case of minimum wage laws affecting men as well, only a handful of states have passed such general legislation, partly because of the competitive position of the states, and partly because a great deal of the most important industry comes under the terms of the federal statute.

Settlement of industrial disputes. Many states have agencies of mediation and conciliation, which usually work closely with labor and management (and with federal mediation officials) in trying to bring about settlements of strikes and lockouts. Especially interesting is the attempt of one state—Kansas—to "solve" industrial disputes through compulsory means. In 1920 Kansas abolished the right to strike, lockout, picket, and boycott in certain essential industries, established a court of industrial relations with power to fix wages and set working conditions, and made decisions of this court binding on all parties concerned. The plan met strong opposition from labor and from some employers, and it was later declared unconstitutional by the Supreme Court.

Regulation of unions and collective bargaining. As noted above, for many years unions had to face hostility from courts and legislatures, which considered them combinations to restrain trade, but the legality of unionism came to be securely protected. A far more controversial question has concerned the *practices* of unionism—the closed and union shops, sympathy strikes, boycotts, and the like. State legislation, like federal, has oscillated from antipathy toward many of these practices in the 1920's, to a more favorable posture in the 1930's, to the reaction against labor of the late 1940's. Thus many states passed "little Taft-Hartley Acts" that were modelled after, or in many cases went beyond, the federal law.

As in the case of the federal Taft-Hartley Act, the most important and controversial aspect of the state legislation has involved the union shop and the closed shop. Eighteen states at the latest reckoning have passed so-called "right-to-work" laws prohibiting the union shop or any other form of compulsory union membership. The key provision in such laws is that no employer may compel a worker to join a union or remain a union member as a condition of holding a job. (Such union agreements are legal under the Taft-Hartley law, but this law gives a green light to the states to ban such agreements if they so wish.) Most of the states with such laws are Southern or rural, but the passage of a "right-to-work" law in Indiana, along with recent revelations of corruption in some unions, makes it seem likely that other industrial states might pass such legislation.

Meantime, the controversy rages on. Backers of "right-to-work" laws contend that compulsory unionism destroys individual freedom by penalizing workers economically if they do not join unions, and that by joining unions, workers become subject to union dictatorships. Opponents of such laws argue that they are passed solely to weaken the power of workers to bargain effectively with employers, and that enactment of anti-union shop legislation provides a "free ride" for employees who want all the benefits of unionism without joining the union and contributing dues and other help. Union leaders hope that by taking a strong line in favor of ethical practices in corrupt unions they can prevent public opinion from being mobilized behind further "right-to-work" legislation.

LABOR'S ORGANIZATION AND POLITICAL ACTIVITY

Roughly speaking, of the approximately 68 million total working population in the United States, about 16 million are organized in some type of union. Hence, as noted above, on the average less than one employed person out of every four is a union member. But averages, of course, are deceptive; in fact there is a great diversity in union organization from industry to industry. About two-thirds of the workers in manufacturing industries are organized, while other workers—such as farm hands and gas station attendants—are little organized, and still other types of employees are not organized at all. Union membership in the same occupation sometimes varies considerably from area to area. It is important to keep this great diversity of union membership in mind as we seek to assess the effect of labor on government and of government on labor.

The shape of union labor

The great bulk of union membership is organized in the relatively new national organization called the American Federation of Labor and Congress of Industrial Organizations. Numbering about 13.5 million members, the AFL-CIO is a federation of essentially (but not wholly) independent national unions. Dominating the AFL-CIO are some of the old, powerful craft unions that once made up the core of the original A.F.L., such as the United Brotherhood of Carpenters and Joiners of America and the International Association of Machinists, along with several "industrial" unions that came to power in the old C.I.O., such as the United Steelworkers of America and the Textile Workers Union of America. Of the 141 national unions in the AFL-CIO at the time of its beginning in 1955, 109 had been formerly affiliated with the A.F.L. and 32 with the C.I.O.[13]

We hear so much of the big international unions in the AFL-CIO, such as those mentioned above, that we tend to overlook many of the lesser ones. But these are important too, both in themselves, and in their demonstration of the great variety of occupations organized under the AFL-CIO today. They include, for example:

Air Line Pilots Association
The Journeymen Barbers, Hairdressers and Cosmetologists' International Union of America
International Alliance of Bill Posters and Billers of America
International Broom and Whisk Makers Union
American Federation of Musicians
International Association of Siderographers

In size of membership the individual unions vary widely. The auto workers number about 1,300,000, the teamsters about 1,200,000, the steelworkers about 1,200,000, the carpenters about 750,000, the machinists about 625,000, while at least a score of the small craft unions of skilled employees embrace fewer than 10,000 members each.[14]

Besides the affiliated international unions and organizing committees, the membership of the AFL-CIO also includes: (1) directly affiliated local unions; (2) state and local central bodies; and (3) trade departments. In contrast with its relation with the international unions, the AFL-CIO has considerable direct control over these three types of organizations. The first of these are usually transitional bodies that sooner or later might be embraced in an existing international union. The state and local central bodies are simply combinations of unions at the state and local level, largely for political and civic purposes. The trade departments were established in the old A.F.L. and served as a means of uniting similar types of craft unions in pursuit of common interests; for example, the Building and Construction Trades Department represented the joint interests of 19 building and construction unions. These trade departments were continued in the merged organization, and a new one—the Council of Industrial Organizations

[13] Arthur J. Goldberg, *AFL-CIO: Labor United* (New York: The McGraw-Hill Book Co., Inc., 1956), Appendix L.

[14] Florence Peterson, *American Labor Unions*, rev. ed. (New York: Harper & Bros., 1952), p. 80.

—was added to give some identity and representation to the industrial unions that had comprised the old C.I.O.

Over two million unionized American workers in about 50 unions are not affiliated with the AFL-CIO. Many of these union people are in either of two important national unions, the United Mine Workers of America and the Railroad Brotherhoods. The former of these, numbering over half a million members, has probably received more publicity, under its fiery chief John L. Lewis, than any other union, largely because of the serious strikes it has precipitated in the coal industry. The Mine Workers, under Lewis, took the lead in breaking away from the A.F.L. and forming the C.I.O., then abandoned the C.I.O. to become independent, later joined the A.F.L., and has since been independent of the big national organization.

Almost half a million railroad workers are organized into four railroad brotherhoods (trainmen, locomotive engineers, conductors, and firemen and enginemen), which never affiliated with the A.F.L. or C.I.O. Half a century old, these unions have had a special position partly because of the close governmental regulation of the railroad industry. They are fairly stable organizationally and tend to be middle-of-the-road or conservative in union political action. The Brotherhoods' lobbyists in Washington are considered highly effective and often work with AFL-CIO representatives on matters of mutual concern.

Besides the national and international unions, such as the above, there are hundreds of local unions that have declined to affiliate nationally. Such local unions range all the way from truly autonomous and vigorous organizations to associations that are secretly or even openly dominated by the employer. Most local unions are at neither of these extremes; they exist mainly to afford the workers recreational and social activities but are also able to bargain collectively more or less effectively with management.

The internal government of labor

The crucial feature of the government of the AFL-CIO is that, like that of the United States of America, it is *federal* in form. Power lies mainly in the various national and international unions that make up the AFL-CIO. But again, as in the case of the national government, important powers and functions have been delegated to the "parent" body. The Constitution of the AFL-CIO, which is somewhat longer than the Constitution of the United States, reflects both the unity and disunity of the many unions that make up the huge organization.

The AFL-CIO Constitution sets forth the principle that the integrity of each international union in the organization shall be maintained and preserved. The executive council (see below) has the authority to issue charters or certificates to new members of the organization but not in any case where there may be created a conflict with the jurisdiction of existing unions in the AFL-CIO; the rights of existing unions, in short, are fully protected. Aside from its important power to admit and expel from membership, the AFL-CIO has "no explicit controls, other than *persuasive* ones," with regard to the activities of its member unions. "Each conducts its own affairs, policies, and activities, negotiates its own contracts, collects its own dues, and expends its own money." [15] A member union may be expelled by a two-thirds vote at the national convention.

This convention is the ultimate authority of the AFL-CIO. Voting is based on the membership strength of the member unions (a "nominal" vote is granted to state and local federations). Regular conventions are to be held every two years, but special conventions may be called. Delegate strength is roughly proportional to the size of the member unions, with the smaller unions getting a little "bonus."

Between conventions the AFL-CIO is run by an Executive Council composed of the principal officers of the federation—president, secretary-treasurer, and 27 vice-presidents—elected by the convention. Members of the council are supposed to vote as individuals rather than as representatives of the member unions to which they belong. The council has power to carry out convention decisions and "to take such actions and render such decisions as are necessary and appropriate to safeguard the best interests of the federation and its affiliated unions." By far the most important position in the AFL-CIO—and one commanding prestige throughout the nation and even the world —is that of President, who serves as a full-time officer. He works with a small executive committee drawn from the Executive Council. Finally, there is a General Board, consisting of all the members of the Executive Council, the heads of all the member unions, and the heads of trade or industrial departments, which serves as a kind of "baby convention" to which the council may refer policy questions.

Since the AFL-CIO is a federation of largely independent unions, it is at the level of its member unions that we must look for the decisions that shape the day-to-day policies and activities of American unionism. Historically, these unions are amalgamations of local organizations, and hence one might expect to find the same form of federalism here as exists in the organization of the AFL-CIO. In fact, the local units had to surrender much of their autonomy in order to build a strong enough national organization to meet severe economic and political challenges from outside. Hence the national organizations usually have strong direct controls over the affairs of the local units. The supreme authority and legislative body of the national union is the convention, composed of delegates from local organizations, which can make decisions about virtually all union matters. As in the AFL-CIO, executive boards or councils make decisions between conventions. There is a "General President" who usually has considerable power and in some cases, as with Lewis in the Miners, has dictatorial powers if he wishes to wield them. The larger unions have "bureaucracies" made up of paid assistants, such as union organizers, lobbyists, publicity men, and clerical assistants.

At the great base of the AFL-CIO are the tens of thousands of local organizations. These organizations conduct the day-to-day business of unionism, such as holding meetings of workers, carrying on negotiations with employers, conducting strikes, and running a great variety of social, recreational, and political activities. Locals may be organized in many ways—on an occupational or craft basis or on a plant or multiplant basis. "The unit of organization of a local does not necessarily parallel the jurisdictional boundaries of its parent body; for example, many locals of the clothing and other industrial unions are organized on a craft basis." [16] In addition to regularly elected officers who earn their main living as regular workers, most unions have business agents, who are full-time paid employees. Serving as "contact points" between the local union and the rank and file are shop stewards, who are usually elected by union members in each department of a plant, and who handle grievances that employees have against management.

Labor in politics

With 16 million unionists and with many millions more among its members' families, organized labor might be expected to have a paramount role in the nation's politics. But in fact, labor's aims have often been divided, its methods ineffective, and its political goals unrealized.

[16] Peterson, *op. cit.*, p. 79.

As noted above, labor's political activities during the past century have been limited and intermittent, except for brief periods, such as during Franklin D. Roosevelt's administrations. Perhaps the high point of labor's political action during this period was the formation of the C.I.O.'s Political Action Committee in the early 1940's. PAC went in for practical politics in vigorous fashion. It concentrated on getting union members registered to vote, on ringing doorbells, on getting union people and their friends to the polls. PAC seemed to meet considerable success in 1944 and 1948, in the elections of Roosevelt and Truman. It seemed far less successful in the "off-year" congressional elections, when majorities were elected to Congress composed of "anti-labor" Republicans and Southern Democrats. In the 1946 election, for example, only 73 PAC-endorsed candidates won, out of 318, in contests for seats in the lower House.[17] One difficulty was that A.F.L. political committees often refused to work with PAC, and even openly opposed PAC and its candidates. Indeed, in 1948 the A.F.L. formed its own political arm, Labor's League for Political Education, as much to balance the C.I.O. effort as to advance its own interests.

The significant feature of labor's political action, however, was the fact that it had modernized but not abandoned Gompers' simple old tactic of "helping labor's friends and defeating labor's enemies." Despite urgings from some unionists and despite various experiments in other directions, as noted below, labor was on the whole content to approach politics on a piecemeal, pragmatic basis, operating through the existing two-party system and supporting or opposing individual Democratic or Republican candidates on the basis of their various records or promises.

Following merger of the A.F.L. and C.I.O., a new political action organization was formed, the Committee on Political Education, soon dubbed COPE. That COPE would represent no radical new departure in the basic political strategy of labor was made clear by George Meany, first president of AFL-CIO. Meany declared:

> The Gompers policy is very simple. You examine the candidates for public office, and on the basis of their records you decide whether they are friendly or aren't friendly . . . and you act accordingly. The failure of the Gompers policy to give us more results was in the application of the policy. . . .
>
> There's only one difference between what we're doing now and what was carried on for many years with regard to Gompers' policy. There's

[17] Hugh A. Bone, *American Politics and the Party System* (New York: The McGraw-Hill Book Co., Inc., 1955), p. 113.

no difference in regard to partisanship or nonpartisanship. We absolutely refuse to allow ourselves to be an appendage of the Democratic Party or any other party. We are absolutely nonpartisan. But what we're doing now that wasn't done before is that we're going into localities, right down to the precinct level, with our organization, and we're doing it on an educational basis.

This general approach governed the political tactics of AFL-CIO in 1956, at the time of the merged organization's first presidential election. The Executive Council endorsed Adlai E. Stevenson, the Democratic candidate, over President Eisenhower, but two heads of powerful unions broke away and openly supported the President. The AFL-CIO sponsored get-out-the-vote rallies on a closed circuit program financed by union dues. It distributed pamphlets, posters, clip-sheets, stickers, buttons, and organization manuals. It supported favored candidates in newspapers and over the radio. It publicized the records of congressional candidates and supported or opposed thousands of candidates at the state and local levels. In many areas labor worked in close unison with party headquarters, especially Democratic, but in some cases the labor and party organizations went their separate ways. The results were mixed. Eisenhower was re-elected, but with a Democratic Congress. However, many of the Democrats were, according to AFL-CIO, "anti-labor," and the AFL-CIO won in only 9 of 36 congressional districts marked for special effort.[18]

How great is organized labor's political power? A definitive answer is impossible, because its strength varies from place to place and from year to year. Certainly, labor as a whole has wielded far more political influence in the past generation than it has generally in the past century. But that influence is also very much subject to national moods and public opinion trends. For example, in a period of change and reform, such as the mid-1930's, labor had great power in Washington, despite organizational splits and weaknesses, while during the mid-1940's the national reaction against labor power gravely limited it, although in many respects its political action methods were greatly improved.

Labor's political strength is even more spotty geographically. At one end of the spectrum, it has reached peak effectiveness recently in the state of Michigan, where the auto workers are numerous and well organized. In Michigan labor has effectively entered into the Democratic party, taking control of a number of district Democratic con-

[18] *The New York Times* (December 3, 1956), p. 1.

ventions and even a state-wide one. A coalition of unionists, Reform Democrats, and a few other elements, according to a careful study, "was able to bring marked changes into the life of the Michigan Democratic party. It filled Democratic primary and convention slates. It entered liberal planks in the state Democratic platform and made the platform more binding. It governed the selection of party officers. It ejected the conservative Old Guard. It used its influence to appoint liberals to policy-determining patronage jobs and used routine patronage to strengthen its coalition. . . ." [19] Not only did labor thus show its influence, but it helped the Democrats win victory after victory, culminating in a clean sweep of statewide officers in elections in 1957.

At the center of the spectrum of labor's political power, a far more typical—and far different—example of labor in politics was in Elmira, New York. This city's politics and voting were studied shortly after the 1948 election by a group of social scientists. Elmira was chosen because it was a semi-industrial, rather small city, with considerable diversity industrially and in the size and structure of its unions. One might have expected that in such a city labor would have been fairly strong in 1948, the year that the unions hoped to counter-attack the forces responsible for the Taft-Hartley Act. On the contrary, the investigators found that the collective union efforts were ineffective, and individual unions took part in political activity only perfunctorily. Among the reasons for such limited forceful political activity, it discovered, were divisions among the labor leaders themselves, no articulate rank-and-file expression favoring political activity, jurisdictional conflicts, political inexperience of the leaders, and labor's tradition of political individualism. [20]

At the other end of the spectrum of labor power are areas in the South and other rural sections where organized labor is small in numbers, faced with strong hostile elements in the community, and divided in policies and methods. Here the political power of organized labor itself is almost nil.

MAKING AND ADMINISTERING LABOR POLICY

The making and administering of labor policy comes into focus in the nation's capital. Yet this focus is not a narrow one. A great many

[19] Fay Calkins, *The CIO and the Democratic Party* (Chicago: The University of Chicago Press, 1952), p. 145.

[20] Bernard R. Berelson, Paul F. Lazarsfeld, and William N. McPhee, *Voting* (Chicago: The University of Chicago Press, 1954), p. 53.

persons, groups, and agencies "get into the act" in labor policy making, just as in all other important areas of national policy and politics. This section treats some of the main continuing groups and agencies that shape policy, but it should be kept in mind that sudden and unexpected forces can always affect policy making. For example, a special committee set up to investigate "Improper Activities in the Labor and Management Fields" in 1957 had probably a much greater impact on public opinion and future policy making than Labor Department officials or even the regular congressional committees dealing with problems of labor.

Labor lobbies

Like all other important economic interests, organized labor maintains a formidable array of lobbyists in Washington. In a recent year, the AFL-CIO reported spending 145,181 dollars to influence legislation, more than any other group.[21] Most of the larger unions have established their headquarters in Washington; the AFL-CIO recently built its own office building a block from the White House, and some of the national unions such as the Teamsters and the Miners have spacious headquarters. The "legislative" or lobbying divisions in these headquarters are perhaps the most important activity. The head of AFL-CIO's lobbying recently has been an experienced former legislator who, as an ex-congressman, has enjoyed the right to enter the chamber of the House of Representatives and consult its members on the floor.

Usually directing the work of the lobbyists are committees on legislation that meet regularly in the various union headquarters. What does organized labor want? Individual labor unions are of course especially concerned with policies directly relating to their own industries and their role in it; for example, the Miners press for strengthened safety standards, the sailors' unions for better working conditions on the sea and for greater subsidies to the merchant marine, the government employees' unions for higher federal wages and salaries, and so on. The more general demands of organized labor as a whole are well represented in the resolutions adopted in the merger convention of the A.F.L. and C.I.O. in 1955. They may be divided into four general categories, as follows:[22]

1. *Legislation directly affecting workers and their unions.* Removal of provisions in the Taft-Hartley Act that seriously restrict the right to

[21] *Congressional Quarterly Weekly Report No. 19* (May 10, 1957), p. 568.
[22] Drawn from Goldberg, *op. cit.,* pp. 203-11.

strike, that strengthen the labor injunction, that restrict the kinds of union security agreements that unions can negotiate, that sanction "union busting" under the guise of strengthening the free speech of employers; extension of the coverage of the Fair Labor Standards Act, increasing the minimum wage to at least $1.25 an hour, and the elimination of exemptions for learners; improved occupational safety standards; broadening of the social security program; a program of national health insurance.

2. *General economic and social policy.* Assumption by government of responsibility for helping maintain full employment through public works, housing, fiscal policies, and the like; adoption of tax policies that help maintain stable economic conditions and are "fair" to the middle and low income groups; full development of natural resources with governmental participation as a yardstick for measuring the effectiveness of development by private interests; federal encouragement of a well staffed, well housed, and well equipped educational system through substantial federal aid to the states; promotion of child welfare through adequate support for government agencies concerned with this.

3. *Civil liberties and civil rights.* Condemnation of actions dangerous to civil liberties, including procedures by certain Congressional committees; establishment of a citizens' commission to recommend programs for protecting national security without depriving individuals of their rightful liberties; making illegal wiretapping a criminal offense; effective and enforceable fair employment practice laws at all levels of government; policing by unions of federal contracts to prevent discrimination; utilization of the full powers of the federal government "to frustrate and punish unlawful attempts to block implementation" of the Supreme Court's nonsegregation decree in public schools (see Chapter 10); adoption of an anti-lynching law and invalidation of poll taxes as prerequisites to voting.

4. *International policy.* To maintain the armed strength of the United States at a level consistent with a tough-minded evaluation of communist capacity for aggression; to strengthen the economic and military capacities of the free world to resist communist aggression; to invigorate the United Nations as a major instrument for achieving world peace and security; support of such specific policies as Point Four, a liberal trade policy, the use of America's influence against colonialism.

Federal policy-making and administration

The most important, but by no means the only, agency for labor policy-making and administration is the Department of Labor. This department was a culmination of many years of labor agitation for direct representation in federal administration resulting in the establishment of a Federal Bureau of Labor, then the Department of Commerce and

Labor in 1903, and finally the single Department of Labor in 1913.[23] For many years the department was headed by a man directly from the leadership of organized labor, and the agency inevitably came to be, in fact as well as law, a place for expressing labor's voice in the councils of government. Partly because of its role as representing labor, the Department has had a rather checkered history, with important functions being moved out of it on the grounds that a "pro-labor" agency should not administer them. With about 6,000 employees it is the smallest executive department (compared, for example, with the 47,000 employees in the Department of Commerce).

Among the most important units of the Department of Labor are the *Office of International Labor Affairs*, which advises on the labor aspects of foreign policy, has primary responsibility for directing United States participation in the International Labor Organization, and helps direct the work of the State Department's labor attachés in United States embassies abroad; the *Bureau of Apprenticeship and Training*, which, in cooperation with national advisory committees appointed by the Secretary, develops standards of apprenticeship for training of skilled workers in industry; the *Bureau of Labor Statistics*, a famed fact-finding agency with a staff of over 1,200 that compiles data on employment, manpower, productivity, wages, prices, cost of living, and the like; the *Wage and Hour and Public Contracts Divisions*, which administer the wage and hour and Walsh-Healey acts described above; and the Women's Bureau, which does not administer any law but formulates standards and policies for promoting the welfare of wage-earning women and advancing their opportunities for employment.

An agency outside the Department of Labor that probably outrivals it in impact on employer-employee relations is the National Labor Relations Board, which, as we have seen, administers the Wagner Act, Taft-Hartley Act, and related legislation. The Board has well over 1,000 employees, almost half of whom work in its 22 regional and seven subregional offices. Also outside the Department is the National Mediation Board (which includes the National Railroad Adjustment Board), and the Federal Mediation and Conciliation Service. Many other agencies that relate in an important way to labor are housed in other departments, such as the Bureau of Mines in the Interior Department.

[23] For a detailed account of this period, see John Lombardi, *Labor's Voice in the Cabinet* (New York: Columbia University Press, 1942).

All these agencies operate under legislation passed by Congress, or with funds appropriated by it, so that labor is ultimately concerned with the course of legislation on Capitol Hill. Both houses of Congress have committees specializing in labor legislation—the Committee on Education and Labor in the House and the Committee on Labor and Public Welfare in the Senate. It is difficult to generalize about the makeup of these committees, but it can be said that they are usually composed of a substantial number of representatives of strongly labor districts. On the other hand, southern Democrats, hostile or at least cool to union labor, often hold the balance of power in these committees between Republicans and northern Democrats. An example of the results of such a situation was the formulation of the wages and hours act in 1937–38, when southern congressmen repeatedly thwarted passage of the legislation despite President Roosevelt's strong support of it. Southerners also tend to become chairmen or ranking members of the committee because of their greater seniority.

The two labor committees are not the only committees affecting labor's interest. The appropriations committees in each house are important because they can limit or augment funds for administering laws supported by labor, such as the wages and hours act. Other substantive committees may often legislate in areas closely affecting labor matters. Finally, special investigating committees may uncover practices that affect public opinion in a direction favorable or hostile to labor's interests. For example, a House committee that investigated the National Labor Relations Board in 1940 held that its administration of the Wagner Act was biased, and this investigation undoubtedly helped create the public opinion behind the Taft-Hartley Act a few years later.

PROSPECTS—POLICY AND POLITICAL ALTERNATIVES

The future of government labor policy will turn on the outcome of a host of basic developments and tendencies. A crisis, such as a war or severe depression, would obviously produce a sharp impact on labor policy. The coming to power of a strongly left-wing or strongly right-wing government would mean a sharp change in the essentially middle-of-the-road policies of the last 20 years. Less spectacular but deep-seated forces might, in the long run, produce more significant changes than the possibilities above. For example, mechanization and automation are altering the techniques and psychology of work in such a way as to have a profound social impact on the attitudes of employees toward their work, their employers, and unions. And workers can no more than other groups escape the influence of social forces such as television, the "slick" magazines, and other of the mass media.

Indeed, even without trying to forecast the social and economic world in which labor will live, prediction of labor's role and of government labor policy turns on an estimate of its place in the quasi-competitive, quasi-regulated economy and the mixed society in which we live. To illustrate, two keen students of labor have come up with very different forecasts of the impact of labor on its economic environment. One believes that organized labor involves an inherent tendency toward monopoly, and that mass unionization means greater government intervention, increased tendency toward controlling and limiting competition, further restrictions on the powers of management, and ultimately the weakening of the competitive price system to the disadvantage of consumers (including union members themselves).[24] The other holds that the implications of labor's role in society are functionally conservative because it has served and will continue to satisfy labor's need for moral status in society, and that, instead of destroying each other, "the corporation and the union will ultimately merge in common ownership and cease to be a house divided." [25]

It is clearly impossible here to do justice either to the complex developments that will both affect and be affected by labor, nor to the varying views of students of labor. The possible combinations and permutations would require many volumes. This concluding section will seek merely to describe the various alternatives in major fields of government labor policy for the years immediately ahead, and then to describe alternatives and problems in two areas that intimately affect the course of labor policy, namely: the political methods labor uses to attain its policy goals, and the problem of labor's internal government and the relation thereto of government policy.

Choices of government policy

The key governmental policies relating to the most controversial aspect of labor will continue to be the Wagner Act as amended by the Taft-Hartley Act. While parts of this act have received considerable

[24] C. E. Lindblom, *Unions and Capitalism* (New Haven: Yale University Press, 1949).

[25] Frank Tannenbaum, *A Philosophy of Labor* (New York: Alfred A. Knopf, 1952), p. 199. Such brief mention cannot, of course, do justice to the thoughtful views and keen insights of either of the two volumes just cited.

approval from large sectors of the public, including labor and management, other sections remain highly controversial. It is likely that within the foreseeable future government policy on labor-management relations will remain at—or reach—a point of compromise somewhere between the demands of organized labor and those of organized business. The following represent the positions of spokesmen of leading labor and business organizations in recent testimony before Congress.[26]

1. *Union security.* Repeal of the provisions of the Taft-Hartley Act prohibiting a full union shop; establishment of authority to enter into full union shop agreements; elimination of the Taft-Hartley provisions that relate to internal union administration by confining enforcement of union-security provisions to collection of dues and initiation fees.

2. *Assistance to other unions.* Changes in the Taft-Hartley Act to make it legal, when a strike is going on at one plant, for employees at another plant who are asked to handle the struck work to go on strike themselves; to permit unions to picket or strike against an employer who is dealing with another employer when the other employer has refused to bargain with or recognize a certified union; full restoration of the right of free speech by according workers the right to make known their views by such means as carrying picket signs or "other peaceful means of communication."

3. *Injunctions.* Elimination of the present injunction provisions in the Taft-Hartley Act, both discretionary and mandatory, and the substitution therefore of authority for the National Labor Relations Board to expedite the hearing of cases where particular damage is threatened to the party that has filed charges.

4. *Damage suits.* Repeal of Taft-Hartley Act provisions that permit employers to sue unions for damages—specifically the sections that give a right of action for breach of contract in the federal courts and that give employers the right to sue unions for violations of the secondary boycott and the jurisdictional strike provisions of the Act.

5. *NLRB procedures and administration.* Expediting Board handling of cases by providing it with more employees and allowing it to use informal procedures, such as prehearing elections; making the General Counsel fully responsible to the Board; elimination of the requirement of non-communist affidavits; barring "strikebreakers" from

[26] Testimony of George Meany, president of the American Federation of Labor, and of George W. Armstrong, chairman of the Industrial Relations Committee of the National Association of Manufacturers, *Hearings* before the Committee on Education and Labor, House of Representatives, 83rd Congress, 1st Sess., on H. Res. 115 (February-March, 1953), Part 2.

voting in union representation elections; elimination of provisions requiring separate units for plant guards and professional workers.

6. *Other labor stands on labor-management law.* Elimination of restrictions on union administration of welfare funds; repeal of prohibition of political expenditures by unions; transfer of the Conciliation and Mediation Service back to the Department of Labor; changes in the handling of national emergency disputes to specify more clearly the conditions under which the government may intervene and to put more emphasis on settlement of disputes through conciliation and mediation.

Management representatives argue in favor of strengthening the Taft-Hartley Act and against the union amendments, such as those just listed. More specifically, management wants the law changed in the following manner:

1. Clarification and strengthening of employers' right of free speech.
2. Strengthening of the secondary boycott provisions "to carry out the original intent of Congress."
3. Discouraging or preventing strikes that do not involve legitimate disagreements between employer and employees.
4. Entire elimination of the union shop and other forms of compulsory unionism.
5. Restoration to the states of their right to regulate labor-management relations.
6. Supplementing the communist-affidavit requirement with "more realistic provisions" for dealing with communism in labor unions.
7. Prohibition of industry-wide strikes.
8. Safeguarding of the Taft-Hartley Act against such labor-sought amendments as the following, namely: redefining supervisors as to make their status uncertain (in relation to union membership); permitting welfare funds to be converted into "union slush funds"; voting in representation elections by "permanently replaced strikers"; eliminating the requirements for annual renewal of dues checkoff authority; imposing greater pressure on employers to submit to wasteful "feather-bedding" practices; relieving unions of the possibility of damage suits when they violate the law; relieving unions of the requirement to file a notice concerning the desire to terminate a contract.

What are the alternatives of government labor policy in areas outside those covered by the Wagner and Taft-Hartley Acts? The likely tendencies in some areas are more predictable than in others. It seems probable that the present minimum wage will be raised, especially if the cost of living continues to rise, but it is less certain that labor will be able to broaden the Act to include workers in presently uncovered fields. Although some unions are pressing for contracts that establish work weeks less than 40 hours, it also seems unlikely that the "hours" provisions of the Fair Labor Standards Act will soon be lowered. It does seem probable that a serious military crisis would bring about economic stabilization programs, probably with the usual machinery of tripartite representation of labor, management, and the public.

Another important policy question involves whether the federal government should police or control labor-management disputes to a far greater degree than it does now under the Taft-Hartley Act—the question, in short, of compulsory arbitration. Proponents of the notion that the government should settle emergency strikes, just as it decides other great issues between citizens or groups of citizens, contend that otherwise we leave this one area of conflict in a condition of anarchy. They can point to many strikes or lockouts that have impaired national production and to the millions of man-days of work lost every year as a result of strikes, large and small. They mention the National War Labor Board during World War II as an example of successful employment of what was in effect compulsory government arbitration of disputes. It seems doubtful, however, that there will be any trend toward compulsory arbitration in the years directly ahead. Successful collective bargaining, informal conciliation and mediation by national, state, and local agencies, and perhaps the Taft-Hartley Act's procedures for delays and "second thoughts" in severe disputes have greatly limited the severe effects of industrial conflict. Both labor and management fear, moreover, that whatever temporary advantage one side might gain would be more than offset by the likelihood that the other side would gain influence over the arbitration officials and exploit compulsory arbitration for its own ends.

Labor's choice of political tactics

Whether or not the pendulum of policy swings toward or away from union preferences will depend in part on the political influence that the unions can mobilize in government. In the late 1950's, after the great majority of union leaders had twice backed the losing presidential candidate and achieved only mixed success in Congress, the new united labor movement was busy assessing alternative political tactics in the light of experience in recent decades.

One alternative was the repudiation of political methods and a total reliance on "tried and true" methods of economic action, such as the strike. But hardly a voice in labor's ranks was raised for such a course.

It was clear to all unionists by the mid-Twentieth Century that economic action was not enough, that it had to be supplemented by political action to bring pressure on the "big government" in Washington that had such influence over unionism, including its economic weapons. The issue was not *whether* unions should use political methods, but what kind, and how much of labor's strength should be expended in this activity.

On the opposite side of the fence are the "labor militants" who call for the establishment of a separate labor party operated and manned by millions of union members and their families. Both the Republican and Democratic parties are too conservative, they argue, to give labor its due; the Republicans are dominated by employer, middle-class and conservative elements, and the Democrats unduly influenced by their southern wing. The proponents of a labor party point to the success of the Labor Party in Great Britain; they also point to the many labor parties that have been established in this country over the last century and a half.[27] Yet it seems doubtful that this appeal will attract many unionists or their leaders. The experience of labor parties has often been to isolate union membership in a separate enclave and actually to lower its influence in politics. Some labor parties have met limited success in state politics but never on a national scale.

A third political alternative is for organized labor to enter the Democratic party in force and become a highly influential if not dominant element in its composition and policies. Indeed, in a rough, unplanned sort of way, this is what labor has done in the last quarter-century, and the real question is whether this should become labor's consistent and purposeful tactic. Trade unionists who oppose this alternative hold that participation in the Democratic party means weakening labor's strength and program because of the many other elements, including some hostile to labor, that make up the Democratic party, especially in the South. Those favoring it point to the pro-labor legislation, such as the Wagner Act, won by labor in the past as a result of its support of the Democratic party and its candidates, and they contend that pushing this tactic harder and more steadfastly would lead to even greater legislative victories.

A final alternative is simply continuation of labor's traditional pol-

[27] For a recent thoughtful consideration of factors attracting labor toward a third party, see Marc Karson, "Contemporary American Labor and Politics," *The Chicago Jewish Forum* (Winter, 1956).

icy of "helping our friends and defeating our enemies," as described on page 316. Such a policy will leave labor free of commitment to either of the major parties, and able, indeed, to work with third parties or independent state or local political groups as the situation requires. The great advantage of this approach is its flexibility; since American politics varies enormously from region to region labor can adapt its specific techniques to the given political situation in any locality. It can work closely with the Democratic party where the party is strongly pro-labor, but where the party is more conservative, as in the South, labor can support the Republicans or independent parties or groups.

It seems likely that organized labor will pursue the last of the tactics described along with a tendency in some areas to become part of the Democratic party and seek to maximize influence in it. Even so, it is doubtful that labor in any area will make a full commitment to the Democratic party. Actually it has a choice of relationships with that party—it can serve in simply an *advisory* role, offering advice on party nominations, platforms, and the like; it can seek to *supplement* the efforts of the party by giving it money, votes, and workers; it can seek to establish a *balance of power* within the party, so that it can isolate and outmaneuver other interest groups within the party; or finally, it can try flatly to take over control of the party by outvoting the non-union elements in it.[28] Labor will employ each of these tactics depending on the local political situation.

Is it possible that in the long run labor will tend to lose interest in political action provided it meets its economic goals? More specifically, if union members become more "middle class" in the economic sense, will they become conservative or lethargic politically? A recent study suggests that the answer is probably in the negative. After analyzing labor voting in the Detroit area, the investigators concluded that "it is highly probable that improved socio-economic conditions and other influences will make for increasing political *interest.* . . . Both our findings and our speculative analysis lead to the conclusion that it is quite possible for wage earners to experience great social and economic gains and yet remain definitely pro-labor." [29]

[28] Each of these various relationships is drawn from the political experience of labor in recent elections, as ably described in Fay Calkins, *The CIO and the Democratic Party* (Chicago: The University of Chicago Press, 1952).

[29] Arthur Kornhauser, Harold L. Sheppard, and Albert J. Mayer, *When Labor Votes* (New York: University Books, 1956). It should be kept in mind that this study involves a particular labor union (the Auto Workers) and area, and the conclusion is suggestive rather than necessarily true of organized labor as a whole.

Problems of union self-government

As unions have increased in size and functions, popular interest has turned more and more to the question of how fairly, efficiently, and honestly unions manage their internal affairs. This matter involves government policy in at least two ways: since unions are in effect charged with a "public interest," serious failures in internal affairs will inevitably arouse public concern and lead to attempts to reform through government action; and the attitudes toward unions on the part both of members and the general public significantly influence the unity, prestige, and organizational strength of labor and hence its impact on public policy.

The spotlight has been turned on the unions' internal affairs in recent years as a result of disclosures of serious wrongdoing on the part of a number of union leaders. Handling of union welfare funds—that is, funds designed to provide life insurance, sickness pay, hospitalization, and the like—was an especially disturbing source of corruption. It was discovered that through fee-splitting arrangements, shakedowns, and kickbacks, union officials and racketeers had siphoned off millions of dollars in excessive commissions and service charges. Union officials had used welfare funds for their own profit and pleasure, had funneled insurance contracts through wives and other relatives, had steered welfare business to particular agents in return for "consultant" retainers of several hundred dollars a week. An equally grave—though perhaps less publicized—situation was the lack of democracy in some unions. Elections were held only rarely, real alternatives were seldom presented to the rank-and-file, union publicity was used for the aggrandizement of the existing leadership, and freedom of debate and dissent was stifled in one way or the other.

To be sure, the great majority of unions were largely guiltless of such failings. According to a careful study, the typical union was the scene of active and vigorous political life, of considerable compromise among competitive factions, of frequent contests among secondary officials if not for the top positions, of the right of appeal by individual members to appeals committees, of fairly modest salaries for officers. Too, most unions had responsible accounting and auditing procedures for the protection of union treasuries.[30] Still, the flagrant excesses of

[30] Philip Taft, *The Structure and Government of Labor Unions* (Cambridge, Mass.: Harvard University Press, 1954), pp. 239-46.

some union leaders inevitably arouse serious and legitimate public concern as to whether reforms should be instituted.

The main question was whether the unions would clean out their own houses or whether reforms would have to come from the outside through new government policies. This question cannot be answered yet, but it is significant that soon after some of the most serious revelations of union abuse in 1957 the AFL-CIO took drastic steps to prevent financial malpractices and to require democratic processes. In the spring of 1957 the AFL-CIO Executive Council approved a code of ethics previously drawn up by a committee of union secretary-treasurers. Among its provisions were requirements that unions keep detailed and accurate records of accounts, approve all spending through proper authorities, make at least semi-annual detailed financial reports, have the books audited at least once a year by an outside certified public accountant, and outlaw "kickbacks" to union officers. Forbidden practices included contracts bringing personal profit to union officials, personal loans to officers or members of their families to finance their private business, and investment in, or loans to, any business with which the union bargains collectively.[31]

Equally sweeping was a "code of democratic processes" adopted by the AFL-CIO Council also in the spring of 1957. Among its provisions were that each union member should have the right to "full and free participation in union self-government," including the right to vote, to run for office, and to express his views; that each union member should have the right to fair and uniform application of union rules and laws, including such essential elements of due process as notice, hearing, and judgment on the basis of the evidence; that conventions should be held at least once every four years; that elections should be fairly and frequently conducted at all levels; that local membership meetings should be held regularly; that terms of union officials should not exceed four years; and that conventions should be open to the public as far as possible.[32]

How successful these codes would be depended on many elements, including the moral and legal influence the AFL-CIO could exert over its member unions, but it was certain that widespread recurrence of abuses would swing the public gaze back toward union government, with important implications for future government labor policy.

[31] *The IUE News* (May 27, 1957), p. 3.
[32] *Ibid.*, p. 4.

BIBLIOGRAPHICAL NOTE

An extensive treatment of labor in general, with special emphasis on trade union history, internal union government and politics, and union economic and political practices, is Harry A. Millis and Royal E. Montgomery, *Organized Labor,* 1945. Robert R. R. Brooks, *When Labor Organizes,* 1937, describes graphically the problem of union organization from the vantage point of the 1930's. *The American Federationist,* journal of the A.F.L., provides insights into labor's viewpoints over several decades, and virtually all the larger international unions have journals and newspapers. Harold W. Davey, *Contemporary Collective Bargaining,* 1951, is an extensive treatment of the subject with an especially useful chapter on the impact of public policy on collective bargaining. A readable and pioneering study of the psychology of union leadership is Eli Ginzberg, *The Labor Leader,* 1948. For a recent and authoritative statement of current labor attitudes and problems from labor's viewpoint, see Arthur J. Goldberg, *AFL-CIO: Labor United,* 1956. A study of labor in politics in an industrial area but under varying political conditions is Fay Calkins, *The CIO and the Democratic Party,* 1952. C. E. Lindblom, *Unions and Capitalism,* 1949, and Frank Tannenbaum, *A Philosophy of Labor,* 1952, both offer arresting views on the future of labor in American society, although from very different vantage points. Philip Taft, *The Structure and Government of Labor Unions,* 1954, is a recent and careful treatment of the subject. Indispensable sources of views and informatin are the hearings before the labor committees of the two houses of Congress. For a concise, penetrating treatment, see John H. Leek, *Government and Labor in the United States,* 1952.

9. JACK W. PELTASON

Welfare, Health, and Housing

THE purposes of this chapter are to highlight the long-range problems that have given rise to demands for public action, to survey existing policies and their administration, and to indicate some of the continuing policy conflicts in the fields of welfare, health, and housing. We group these three areas together primarily for reasons of academic convenience rather than because of any essential relationships among them. However, these three programs do have some common features: welfare, housing to an extent, and public health in lesser part are designed to benefit in the first instance the less fortunate members of the community; all have ancient origins but their scope and significance have been expanded tremendously since the Great Depression; all are examples of what has become known as the "welfare state."

GOVERNMENT AND WELFARE

All the things our governments do are supposed to promote the national welfare. But the term "welfare" is used in a more restrictive sense to refer to assistance to those who are in need and to programs that protect us against the economic hazards flowing from old age, disability, and unemployment.

What, if anything, should be done to help those who are too old, too sick, or too young to provide for themselves? What if a man can find no job? What if he lacks the moral and mental discipline to take care of himself and his family? We could do nothing—allow them to die. This is the policy in some societies. Not so many years ago in some parts of India there was a grim but efficient and economical solution to the problem of the poor widows and orphans. A widow was compelled to throw herself on her husband's funeral pyre and her children were given to relatives. In the United States no one has ever advocated such a drastic policy, but there have been some who argue that the wisest and best policy is to let the poor perish—or at least shift for themselves. However the policy of "let them starve" is no longer, if it ever was, an alternative for the American people. There is widespread agreement that something should be done. The questions are what should be done, for whom should it be done, and who should do it?

Few deny that the family has the first responsibility, and this proposition underlies our moral and legal code. If the family is unable to help, some believe that reliance on private charity is sufficient. Others would encourage local, perhaps even state, governments to provide limited assistance financed by local taxes, but they are opposed to participation by the national government. Others believe that the central government should support welfare programs, if for no other reason than that the poorest states with the largest number of persons in need are least able to provide assistance. Some would restrict public welfare to cash handouts and limited services for those who are desperate. Others argue that the government should attack the basic causes of destitution and develop policies to reduce the chances that persons will have to seek public charity. However, before considering how contemporary welfare programs reflect responses to these views and values, it may be of some benefit to survey their historical development and note how these issues have been resolved in the past.

The Elizabethan Poor Law System

American welfare activities are an outgrowth of and, at least until the Great Depression, very much reflect the practices of Elizabethan England.[1] In 1601 the famous statute of the Queen established the

[1] The first English law concerned with the poor was passed in 1349 after the "Black Death" killed two-thirds of the people. Issued by Edward III, this statute came not from compassion for the poor but from the pressures of the landed gentry who needed workers. Edward made it a criminal offense, subject to branding or mutilation, for any able-bodied worker to refuse to accept employment from any master. In the United States the Thirteenth Amendment stands in the way of such compulsory labor, but like Edward we still consider vagrancy to be a crime.

basic public welfare system for both England and the United States which lasted with only minor alterations for the next 300 years. Under this system, public assistance was made a duty of the local units of government—the parish in England and the township or county in the United States—financed by a poor-tax collected and administered by the overseers of the poor. Each parish or township or county was responsible for all indigents born in the area or who had established residence there. (Residence requirements for relief are still common.) No person was entitled to relief unless his parents or children were unable to help—the principle of family responsibility.

Poverty was assumed to be a sign of moral and character deficiencies and paupers were treated as sinful persons. Relief was given grudgingly, and its acceptance was made sufficiently onerous that only those in desperate circumstances were inclined to seek help. Paupers had to take an "oath," their names were placed on the "poor rolls," published in the local newspapers, and exhibited in the city along with amounts received. (In 1951 the Social Security Act was amended to allow states to publicize the names of persons who were receiving federally supported relief.)

The Poor Laws divided the needy into three categories and treated them accordingly. The *able-bodied poor,* sometimes called sturdy beggars or unworthy poor—what we now call the unemployed—were sent to workhouses maintained by the parish or county. The *impotent* or *worthy poor*—those we now call "unemployables," the old, insane, feeble-minded, widows, and so on—were placed in the almshouse. Frequently the almshouse and the workhouse were merely different quarters in the same dilapidated building. Into these "human scrapheaps" often operated by unqualified persons were thrown the sick, the old, the mentally ill, petty criminals, orphans, and other destitutes without homes or friends to care for them. *Small children* were, if possible, "farmed out" to foster homes. After they reached eight, the boys were indentured to a master until they became twenty-four, and the girls did domestic work until they married or became twenty-one.

In England primary reliance was placed on "indoor," or institutional, relief; but in some parishes—and more commonly in the United States—"outdoor relief," payments in money or food and clothes, were given, especially to those who needed help to tide them over an emergency. Financial aid was carefully measured so that no person on relief received as much as could be earned by the lowest paid person not on relief. (This practice, called the principle of less-eligibility, is a feature of many present-day welfare programs.)

What was the life of a poor person like under this system? Here is how Charles Dickens in a fictional, but substantially accurate account, described the early days of Oliver Twist, who was born in a workhouse and left an orphan at birth:

> [The] parish authorities magnanimously and humanely resolved, that Oliver should be 'farmed,' or, in other words, that he should be despatched to a branch-workhouse some three miles off, where twenty or thirty other juvenile offenders against the poor-laws, rolled about the floor all day, without the inconvenience of too much food or too much clothing, under the parental superintendence of an elderly female, who received the culprits at and for the consideration of sevenpence-halfpeny per small head per week. . . . The elderly female was a woman of wisdom and experience; she knew what was good for children; and she had a very accurate perception of what was good for herself. So, she appropriated the greater part of the weekly stipend to her own use, and consigned the rising parochial generation to even a shorter allowance than was originally provided for them. . . . [At] the very moment when a child had contrived to exist upon the smallest possible portion of the weakest possible food, it did perversely happen in eight and a half cases out of ten, either that it sickened from want and cold, or fell into the fire from neglect, or got half-smothered by accident. . . .[2]

Oliver, who was made of hardy stuff, managed to survive and at the age of seven was returned to the workhouse.

> The members of this board [of overseers] were very sage, deep, philosophical men; and when they came to turn their attention to the workhouse, they found out at once, what ordinary folks would never have discovered—the poor people liked it. . . . So, they established the rule, that all poor people should have the alternative (for they would compel nobody, not they), of being starved by a gradual process in the house, or by a quick one out of it. [Here Dickens is poking fun at the principle of less-eligibility.] With this view, they contracted with the water-works to lay on an unlimited supply of water; and with a corn-factor to supply periodically small quantities of oatmeal; and issued three meals of thin gruel a day, with an onion twice a week, and a half a roll on Sundays. They made a great many other wise and humane regulations. . . . It was rather expensive at first, in consequence of the increase in the undertaker's bill, and the necessity of taking in the clothes of all the paupers. . . . But the number of workhouse inmates got thin as well as the pau-

---

[2] Charles Dickens, *The Adventures of Oliver Twist or The Parish Boy's Progress,* first published as a serial in the pages of "Bentley's Miscellany" from January, 1837, to March, 1839; quotations here taken from National Library Company edition, Vol. V, pp. 5-6.

pers; and the board were in ecstasies. [Here Dickens was attacking the "reformers" who measure public programs solely by the yardstick of "efficiency and economy." They had secured the adoption of legislation in 1834 which reduced poor relief costs by one-third.] [3]

Inadequate as poor relief was, some thought that the poor were treated too generously. For example, Francis Wayland, an influential early 19th century American economist urged abolition of the poor laws because they were "destructive of the right of property . . . they must proceed upon the concession that the rich are under obligation to the poor." [4] Others drew upon the writings of English classical economists such as T. R. Malthus who argued that poverty is unavoidable and poor relief unwise. Malthus had it figured out that population increases at a faster rate than do food supplies. Therefore, it is impossible to raise the standard of living of the great mass of the people. To feed the poor merely keeps more of them alive, wrote Malthus, and since there would be no substantial increase in the amount of food, no one would be better off than before. Furthermore, he argued, persons who are unable to provide for themselves are not fit to survive. Instead of the government taking care of the poor, he wrote, the poor should be taught "that they are themselves the causes of their own poverty; that the means of redress are in their own hands, and in the hands of no other person whatever; that the society in which they live and the government which presides over it, are without any direct power in this respect." [5]

In the last half of the 19th century, Herbert Spencer, a popular sociologist, was a leading opponent of the poor laws. Although he felt that limited private charity to reduce "superfluous suffering" was permissible, he opposed public assistance because it interfered with the natural laws of selection. If the government did not interfere, Spencer wrote, these natural laws would wipe out of existence the unemployed who were "simply good-for-nothings, who . . . live on the good-for-somethings—vagrants and sots, criminals and those who are on the way to crime. . . ." [6]

[3] *Ibid.*, pp. 14-15.
[4] Francis Wayland, *The Elements of Political Economy,* 3rd ed. (Boston: Leavitt, Lord & Co., 1840), p. 15; quoted by Sidney Fine, *Laissez-Faire and the General Welfare State* (Ann Arbor: The University of Michigan Press, 1956), p. 7.
[5] T. R. Malthus, *An Essay on the Principle of Population,* 6th ed. (London, 1826), II, pp. 287-88; quoted by Fine, *op. cit.,* p. 7.
[6] Herbert Spencer, "The Coming Slavery," *The Man versus the State* (London: Williams & Norgate, 1892), pp. 18-19; quoted by Fine, *op. cit.,* p. 38.

Reform of the Elizabethan system

During the decades following the Civil War, industrialization brought large numbers to the cities where they were exposed to the hazards of an industrial society in which illness, injury, or unemployment forced entire families on relief. Many had to live in slums, which set off a vicious circle—living in slums led to disease, and disease in turn caused poverty that forced people to continue to live in slums.

For a time the Spencerian attitude toward relief became embedded in our constitutional interpretation, but despite the writings of many eminent men and the opposition of some courts, as the century proceeded there was a gradual expansion of state and local welfare functions. Although three-fourths of all relief funds came from public sources, the essential features of the Elizabethan system were retained. There were some tentative attempts to deal with the causes of poverty, but by and large the major thrust of new programs was merely to improve relief programs.

State governments built and operated specialized institutions for the insane, deaf, blind, and delinquent. Public hospitals were established, and special wards in the almshouses were set aside for the needy ill. States began to offer financial support to local communities for certain kinds of relief—known as *categorical relief*. By 1930, 20 states had aid programs for the blind, 45 gave aid to mothers with dependent children, and 12 had old-age assistance. However, many of these programs looked better on paper than in practice. For example, by 1930 less than half of the local units authorized to give aid to mothers with dependent children were actually making payments.

In addition to expanding relief and establishing specialized institutions for the care of the needy, in some states attempts were made to deal with *causes* of poverty. Some reformers thought that alcoholism was the major cause of pauperism, and in many states they were successful in making the manufacture and sale of alcoholic beverages illegal. In this reform movement, they were joined by employers who felt that alcoholism reduced the efficiency of their employees. Many employers, however, opposed legislation to forbid child labor, to establish minimum wages, to protect workers against industrial accidents, to establish workmen's compensation, and to protect the right of workers to form trade unions. But despite employer opposition and hostility of the courts, by the 20th century such laws were gradually being enacted and strengthened in many of the industrialized states.

Any survey of pre-depression welfare programs would be deficient if it did not note the important role of the big city political organizations. The precinct captain was ready at any time of the night or day to lend a helping hand, find a job for Mr. Murphy, help Mr. Green secure a license for his pushcart, give coal to the Greenbergs, find warm clothing for the Smith family. Where there was a fire, the precinct captain was always ready to aid the distressed. These politicians had no long forms to be filled out and they asked no embarrassing questions. They gave help without making the recipient feel inferior or apologetic. True, it was a costly welfare system. The city organizations voted into office by the many grateful recipients of their favor received their *quid pro quo* in the form of graft. The politicians were unconcerned about rehabilitation or basic reforms, but they did keep people from freezing or starving to death.

What of the national government? It had an extensive program for needy veterans, a limited program for needy Indians, and specialized programs for merchant seamen, but the prevailing belief was that there was no legitimate national interest in welfare and that the national government had no constitutional authority to provide assistance. Then came the depression.

The impact of the depression

The central fact about the depression is that suddenly there were lots of poor people. By 1932 one out of four workers was unemployed. Poverty became something experienced rather than something merely read about; thousands who previously had considered relief as the recourse of the unworthy discovered that they had no choice but to join the breadlines. No longer did they argue that unemployment was produced by the individual's own failings. But whatever the theorizing, there were millions without money to buy food, clothes, or shelter.

The traditional relief structure caved in under the pressures. Local units had no machinery to process the thousands of applicants; even more critical, they did not have the money. State governments began to take emergency action, but by 1932 with even more without jobs the states too were running out of money. Many state governors, especially those of the large industrial states, made frantic appeals to the national government.

At first the national government refused to act, except to appeal to employers to continue production and to the rich to make larger contributions to charity. President Hoover was strongly opposed to federal relief. He was convinced, at first, that the depression was a temporary setback. He believed that relief was the responsibility of the local governments and he was fearful that if the national government acted, it would establish what was to him a dangerous precedent. He also believed that if the federal government gave aid to the unemployed it would deprive them of their self-reliance. However, as conditions continued to get worse and prosperity did not come around the corner, the President reluctantly approved a limited federal relief program, first in the form of loans and then gifts to the states for welfare purposes.

When Roosevelt—who did not share his predecessor's opposition to vigorous federal action—became President he sponsored a large-scale relief program administered through a variety of agencies. The initial emphasis was on getting the money as fast as possible to those in need. But in time the "dole" was replaced by putting men to work on public projects. Recipients of relief, it was hoped, would feel less deprived of their dignity since they would be working for their assistance and in turn society would gain through the schools, dams, highways, postoffices, and irrigation projects that they would build.

After the return of full employment these emergency relief programs were abandoned, but the precedent that Hoover feared had been established—in time of mass unemployment the national government would act. Perhaps of more enduring significance was the adoption in 1935 of a federal welfare program on a long-range and permanent basis. In that year Congress enacted the Social Security Act which marked the most significant development in the rise of American public welfare programs.

Patterns of welfare

The Social Security Act of 1935 combines several programs and embodies a variety of approaches. It strengthened some existing programs, added others, and since that time has been amended and supplemented by other basic statutes. It is not the purpose here to describe any particular statute, but to investigate the general scope of present-day welfare functions.

Post 1935 welfare programs are distinguishable from those which came before in several major ways. First, there is much greater reliance on social *insurance* to supplement, and it is hoped, eventually to replace public *assistance*. Insurance, unlike assistance, is not charity to the needy. There is no need to demonstrate poverty, that is no "means tests," and payments are not handouts from the taxpayers. Rather social insurance gives covered individuals a legal right to certain payments in the event of specified events that cause loss or reduction of income, for example, retirement, disability, unemployment. The insurance is financed by regular deductions from earnings, directly or indirectly. Social insurance is based on the same principle as private insurance—sharing risks, and setting money aside for rainy days. Most social insurance programs, however, differ from private insurance in major respects. They are compulsory, persons have no contractual rights to benefits but are entitled only to those which the law at the moment allows, and benefits paid out are not necessarily restricted to total funds paid into the system because additional contributions may come from the public treasury.

Social insurance has become accepted as a more systematic, less expensive, and more equitable way to meet the inevitable costs which grow out of old-age, unemployment, and disability. Old-age insurance, for example, compels people to make some provision during their working days for the time when they will be retired, and as more and more people secure this protection the percentage of the aged who have to seek public assistance should decline. Furthermore, beneficiaries of an insurance program do not suffer the loss of dignity often associated with receiving charity. Finally, there is much less opportunity for favoritism or unfair treatment, since there is no necessity to determine each applicant's need, which is so hard to define.

The second post-depression development has been the rejection of the idea that welfare policies and programs are outside the constitutional or political scope of the central government's concern. Although primary responsibility for welfare is still vested in the states and local governments, the national government operates an extensive old-age and survivors insurance program, has induced the states to establish unemployment compensation insurance, and gives generous financial grants to the states for certain kinds of relief. These grants have been instrumental in bringing about a sizeable expansion in scope of state and local welfare activity. Moreover, by attaching conditions to its grants, the national government helps support national minimum standards and has raised the level of welfare administration. The use of federal funds also helps to equalize the financial burden among the states.

The third development of recent decades might be termed the professionalization of welfare administration with a much greater emphasis upon rehabilitation and helping people become self-supporting and responsible members of the community. In the past, untrained persons passed out food, made cash payments, or placed the relief applicant into an institution. Operating in an atmosphere that made poverty a sign of the individual's own failings, and based on the assumption that "reliefers" had to be treated with severity, local overseers of poor relief had not the time, training, or inclination to be concerned with the individual's problem and his rehabilitation. Nowadays trained welfare workers attempt to diagnose each case and prescribe the proper remedy. They are not content with merely keeping the applicant alive but try to effect a "cure." For example, suppose a family applies for relief and it is discovered that the father is an alcoholic. Instead of just handing out money, an attempt is made to give the man spiritual and medical assistance that may cure his alcoholism and permit him to assume his responsibilities as a contributing member of society. This is better not only for the man and his family, but in the long run is less expensive for the community.

Finally, more use is now made of social legislation to correct the conditions leading to poverty. All levels of government have passed laws to establish minimum wages, enforce industrial health and safety standards, protect workers' right to organize so that they may bargain more effectively with their employers, and promote full employment and a prosperous economy. These and other measures it is hoped will make it less likely that persons will have to seek relief.

Turning now to specific welfare programs, what kinds of insurance and assistance are available for those whose incomes have been reduced through retirement, lack of parental support, accident or illness, unemployment, or some other disabling condition?

Old-age insurance

The main reason for loss or reduction of income is old age. Less than half the men and only one out of ten women over 65 are at work. A man of 65 may expect to live on the average 12 years longer, his wife of that age for 14 years. After a man ceases work he must maintain himself and his dependents on the resources he has been able to set aside during his working years. Not many men are able to save the 17,000 dollars it takes to provide an annuity income of 100 dollars a month for himself and his wife. Often his children help, for as Professor Sumner Slichter has pointed out, "The usual method by which men have provided for their old age has never been thrift—it has been by having plenty of children and expecting the children to help the parents." [7] When large families were common, families with their built-in social security were able to take care of the older members without too much difficulty. Nowadays it is sometimes impossible for parents and their adult children to live together in a three room apartment into which the commodious homes of the past have been divided. Although families still provide most of our old-age insurance and many persons do have private pensions, the income of the "senior citizens" is supplemented through a federally operated old-age and survivors insurance, popularly known as O.A.S.I.

Except for doctors, who are the only major occupational group not now covered, railroad workers and governmental employees, who have their own retirement systems, nine out of ten employed persons are protected by O.A.S.I. This insurance is financed by a sum equal to 4½ per cent of the first $4,200 of an employee's yearly earnings, 2¼ per cent being contributed directly from his wages, and the other 2¼ per cent being contributed by his employer. Self-employed persons pay 3⅜ per cent of their covered earnings (at the same time that they pay income taxes). These percentages are scheduled to rise gradually until they reach 8 per cent for employed persons and 6⅜ per cent for self-employed in 1975. (The fractions in each case finance disability insurance).

If a person chooses to retire at 65 (a woman may retire at 62), he is entitled to draw his insurance. A person over 65 who continues to work will receive reduced retirement insurance if he earns more each month than the law allows. At no time, however, does additional income from investments or private insurance which the worker has saved for his old age reduce his old-age insurance. After 72 there are no restrictions on the amount that may be earned. This insurance is paid to the worker as long as he or his wife lives.

O.A.S.I. retirement benefits are not handsome—the average monthly payments to a retired worker without dependents is about 60 dollars a month, for a retired worker and wife over 65 the payments are around 105 dollars a month—but combined with other resources they often make it possible for people to live with dignity and comfort in their own homes. As O.A.S.I. gradually extends its coverage to more and more older persons, a much smaller percentage of them should be required to seek relief.

[7] Sumner H. Slichter, "The Pressing Problem of Old-Age Security," *The New York Times Magazine* (October 16, 1949), p. 9.

In addition to these retirement benefits, O.A.S.I. protects a worker's family. If he dies before retirement, his family receives a lump-sum death benefit plus monthly payments that vary according to his contributions and number of dependents. The average monthly payment to a widow with two children is around 138 dollars. Moreover, since 1957 benefits have also been paid to workers over 50 who are permanently and totally disabled, a very significant development which is discussed in more detail later.

The costs to society of providing for those too old to earn their own living cannot be avoided. If the entire social security program were abolished, society would not save any money. Rather the costs of caring for the aged would merely be transferred to some other government program, to the family, or to private charity. Thus O.A.S.I., through systematic advance planning to meet these inevitable expenses, offers many advantages and has wide political support. Support for this kind of social security seems so strong that there is little possibility of the program being seriously restricted. Nevertheless, there are some who object to the national government's compelling people to participate. They are also critical of the fact that the money the national government collects is not left in the Treasury but is invested in government bonds. They charge that beneficiaries have no guarantee of receiving their benefits since they are subject to change by law at any time. They argue that future benefits will be paid in inflated dollars and beneficiaries will not receive as much in actual spending power as they have contributed.

Defenders of O.A.S.I. respond that it would be foolish to let the funds lie sterile. The government, they insist, can be trusted to make good its obligations whether it has pieces of paper on deposit called bonds or called dollars—both are government obligations, the former differing from the latter only in that they are interest paying. Benefits are not likely to be changed to the disadvantage of the 70 million citizens in the system who make a voting block large enough to scare any congressman. The possibility of inflation is an inherent risk in any insurance scheme and is an argument not against insurance but inflation.

Some critics would introduce a means test, which would change the essential nature of the program from insurance to assistance. A more likely possibility, but not probability, is to do away with all the elaborate and expensive keeping of individual records and to pay a pension out of general tax funds to all retired persons over 65. Since payments would not as directly and obviously be related to contributions, the political consequences of such a change and a person's attitude toward his "pension" might be altered.

Old-age assistance

Even with old-age insurance some persons cannot make a go of it, and there are still many elderly persons who retired before they could secure sufficient protection. Two and a half million of these *needy* aged are now receiving old-age assistance. Old-age assistance, unlike old-age insurance, is administered by state and local welfare officials; the national government's role is, however, most important. The national government supplies about half the money and as a condition of receiving these grants the states must (1) match some of the federal funds; (2) administer or supervise the program through a single stage agency; (3) adopt an acceptable merit system for the employees who administer the program; (4) provide a hearing before a state agency for all individuals whose claims for assistance are denied; (5) consider the applicant's income and other resources in establishing standards of eligibility; and (6) impose no conditions more restrictive than certain federal specifications.

At the national level, old-age assistance grants (as well as those to aid dependent children, needy blind, and the totally and permanently disabled) are administered by the Bureau of Public Assistance in the Social Security Administration which is part of the Department of Health, Education, and Welfare. It is frequently alleged that these "national bureaucrats" have too much control over state and local officials, but the occasions in which they have denied funds to a state because of violation of conditions are extremely rare. United States Senators can be depended upon to defend their respective states against "federal encroachment" and officials in the Social Security Administration are very sensitive to demands of Senators and Congressmen who appropriate the money.

Each state may grant assistance beyond the limits supported by the national government and may establish its own standards as long as they do not conflict with federal rules. Although federal money is distributed by a formula which gives more to the poorest states, these states with a large percentage of aged on relief give each of their applicants less than do the wealthy states. Among the states, there are also marked differences in the political influence of the aged, and this is reflected in the size of old-age payments. Hence, amounts and conditions of assistance and the details of the administration vary from state to state.

All states have residence requirements, some refuse aid to aliens, and some refuse to help persons convicted of a felony within the last ten years or who have failed to support their children. States have different standards to determine "need" and different procedures to recover from the estates of deceased recipients of assistance. Some states make a serious attempt to recover by making first claims on the estates after federal taxes, if any, have been paid, while others let creditors receive first with the state taking its share if there is anything left.

Applicants for relief apply first at the local welfare office where a worker investigates—perhaps emergency aid will be given—the applicant's resources and tries to locate children or other relatives. If local officials rule that the applicant is not eligible for relief, he is entitled to appeal to a state commission or board, frequently called the department of social welfare.

On a nationwide average, states pay the needy aged about $55 a month, but this varies from an average payment in Connecticut of $90.18 to $28.45 in West Virginia. These payments, although small, permit many individuals to remain at home, and with the money they receive, unrestricted as to use, they can live their own lives. This is frequently less expensive to the taxpayers than it would be to provide for them in an institution.

For those who are so poor, so alone, or so ill that money is not enough, there are only the almshouses, which are now generally being turned into nursing homes for the aged and chronically ill. Considerable progress has been made in improving these institutions. Buildings have been modernized and trained personnel have been put in charge. In many areas several counties have pooled resources in order to operate one good nursing home rather than each running an inadequate one. Those who can pay do so; those without families or their own financial resources are given tax-supported care. Although persons living in tax-supported institutions normally are not eligible for federally supported assistance, if they are receiving medical care in a nursing home they may receive old-age payments and the money can be used to help defray their expenses, an additional incentive for counties to turn almshouses into nursing homes.

Children in need

Of all who are in need, perhaps it is the children who make the strongest appeal to our charity. Even those most stoutly opposed to public assistance find it hard to argue that children are responsible for their own misfortunes and should be left without care. Nowadays the national and state governments have extensive welfare programs to promote the well-being of children, and except for the aged more money is spent on these welfare activities than any other.

O.A.S.I. provides some protection, since children of a person covered by this insurance are entitled to survivors' benefits. But for the most part, needy dependent children are cared for through assistance rather than insurance. If a child has no parents or relatives and it is impossible to secure new parents by adoption or to place him in a foster home, the only choice is an orphanage. These institutions supported by private and public sources are on the whole well-operated institutions. But however well run the institution, most students of child welfare believe that if it is at all possible children should be kept in private homes. Even if the family is broken through death, desertion, or incapacity of a parent, a mother, brother, sister, grandparent, or some other close relative can give the child more special attention and love than is possible in even the finest institution. In order to make this more likely, all states make federally supported assistance payments to dependent children.

A dependent child, defined by federal law, is one under 18 who has been deprived of parental support but who is living with the other parent or close relative. Over 600,000 families receive such support, the national average payment being around $90 per family ($25 per person) with average payments per family ranging from $27.69 in Mississippi to $144.96 in Wisconsin. Recently some states have started to restrict aid given to dependent children of unwed mothers, but others have refused to do so because it penalizes the child more than the parents. Aid to dependent children is administered through the same procedures as old-age assistance and like the other programs administered through the Bureau of Public Assistance is primarily intended to supplement the incomes of persons suffering adversity. But people in want, especially children, sometimes need advice, training, medical care, and other forms of social service. This is the responsibility of the Children's Bureau, a unit of the Social Security Administration.

The Children's Bureau, first established in 1912 as part of the Department of Labor, but now within the Department of Health, Education, and Welfare, is charged to investigate and report "upon all matters pertaining to the welfare of children and child life among all classes of people" and has the additional responsibility of administering three federal grants to the states—to extend and improve health services for mothers and children, to support state crippled children's programs, and to assist states in improving and expanding child welfare services. In the child welfare program, specialists counsel parents and children, develop community programs, and give special attention to problems of mentally retarded, emotionally disturbed, and neglected children. Some state and local welfare programs are responsible for supervision of foster care of dependent children and operate institutions for delinquent or handicapped children.

In administering the maternal and child health and crippled children programs, the Children's Bureau works with local public health officials. Among other things these grants support health supervision for expectant mothers, public nursing services after delivery, vaccination of school children for smallpox, immunization for diphtheria, and protection against poliomyelitis. The object of the crippled children's program is to locate children who require care and provide therapy and rehabilitation.

In 1921 when Congress first made grants to help states reduce the then very high maternal and infant mortality rates, public health officials—national, state, and local—argued that it was wrong to create a separate public health program for mothers and children and that its administration should be given to the Public Health Service. But the many spirited feminists, joined by spokesmen for organized labor, insisted that health officers were too conservative and unimaginative and that all federal programs concerned with children should be vested in a single agency. Since it has been in existence the Children's Bureau, staffed primarily by women, has energetically and boldly pursued its objectives. As an eminent public health authority reports, the Children's Bureau—if not rudely, at least abruptly—shattered the "smugness that existed in many state health organizations." [8]

The disabled—insurance

During the course of any single working day about 62 workers will be killed, 350 will suffer some permanent impairment, and 7,600 more

[8] Harry S. Mustard, *Government in Public Health* (New York: The Commonwealth Fund, 1945), p. 76.

will suffer injuries which will keep them from work for an average of about 18 days.[9] Occupational injuries cause more casualties than war, and even more are injured away from their jobs. When the breadwinner is injured not only is there an increased need for money to pay doctors and hospitals, but at the same time there is a decrease in earnings. If the accident results in a major injury, there may be months, perhaps years, of medical care and rehabilitation before the worker can be returned to productive employment.

What kinds of protection do Americans have against the economic loss of disability? The oldest type social insurance in the United States is *workmen's compensation,* a completely state established and operated program. Started in 1910, these programs have gradually evolved so that today all states have such insurance, but with wide extremes in coverage and protection provided.

Prior to compensation insurance, when a worker was injured the only way he could receive any reimbursement was to sue his employer and prove to a jury that the employer had been negligent. His chances of winning such a suit were slight. The common law gave the employer three practically fool-proof defenses: (1) contributory negligence—the worker could not recover if he had contributed by his own negligence to the accident, no matter how much at fault the employer had been; (2) the fellow-servant doctrine—the employer was not liable for injuries which resulted from the negligence of another employee; (3) the assumption of risk—the employer was not liable for accidents prevalent in that particular kind of job and which the common law assumed were part of the risks the worker willingly assumed when he agreed to take the job.

At first the states abolished the common law defenses of the employer, but this made no material improvement in the financial condition of injured workers. Then workmen's compensation was established, resting on a concept entirely different from a damage suit. Workmen's compensation rests on the premise that whatever the cause, workers should not be forced to bear the financial burden of industrial accidents or occupational diseases (except of course if they willfully injure themselves). Like wear and tear on machinery, these injuries are part of the costs of producing the goods and services.

The proportion of workers protected by compensation insurance

[9] Herman Miles Somers and Anne Ramsay Somers, *Workmen's Compensation* (New York: John Wiley & Sons, Inc., 1954), p. 1; most of the information in this section on workmen's compensation was taken from this excellent and comprehensive account.

varies widely among the states, but on a national basis from about two-thirds to four-fifths of all employees are protected. It is the major source of support for families of the about 16,000 workers killed at work each year and provides a large portion of the income of the two million who are injured. In most states benefits—which are supposed to compensate for loss of earning power, for doctor and hospital bills, and for rehabilitation—are financed by the employers who are required to give assurance of their ability to meet their obligations either by taking out insurance with a private company or in some states by taking out insurance with a state agency. Coverage in about half the states extends also to occupational diseases. In all but four states workers are entitled to benefits only for injuries or illness arising "out of and in the course of employment."

It was the purpose of the original promoters of workmen's compensation to keep the procedures swift and simple through automatic benefits established by a predetermined schedule and quickly paid to the injured men. However, questions as to how much compensation a worker is entitled to, whether or not the injury arose "out of and in the course of employment," and the extent of disability, often take months of litigation with appeals up through administrative agencies and the courts. Many observers believe that the system has become so fraught with litigation that it is not as much different from the old common law system as had been hoped.

What about persons who are unable to work because of *non*occupational injuries or illness? Only in four states do they have any insurance protection under workmen's compensation. Moreover, since they are unable to work, they are not entitled to unemployment compensation. Veterans with disabilities connected with their service are entitled to a pension. But until 1957, except for workmen's compensation and veterans' pensions, there was no form of social insurance to cover the economic risks of illness or accidents. In that year Congress amended O.A.S.I. to make persons over 50 eligible for benefits if they are unable to work at all and are unlikely ever to be able to work. The average payment is about 75 dollars a month. This is perhaps the first step toward general disability protection. If the history of the gradual expansion of O.A.S.I. benefits is typical, it is likely that in the years ahead the disability provisions will be slowly liberalized. If so, there will be less need for disabled persons to seek public assistance. Until that time, however, public expenditures to care for the sick and injured who are unable to work will be needed. To these programs we now turn.

Disability—assistance

The federal government supports two assistance programs for the needy disabled, one for the blind and the other for those totally and permanently disabled. These programs are administered in the same fashion as old age and dependent children assistance, although not nearly so many persons are benefited. Again like the other assistance programs they are intended primarily to supplement the incomes of those in need by making monthly grants, a national average of 57 dollars a month in the case of the permanently disabled and 60 dollars a month for the needy blind.

Disability—rehabilitation

Instead of merely making these cash payments for the rest of the disabled person's life, it is less expensive for society and more satisfactory for the individual, if it is at all possible, to rehabilitate a man so that he can earn his own living and no longer be dependent on relief. For this reason there has been a gradual expansion of vocational rehabilitation. The Veterans Administration has a well-established program. The states provided more limited services for civilians, but recently the federal government has increased its financial grants to the states to encourage them to improve and expand these activities. After a disability has become stabilized, persons who can become self-sufficient through surgical and medical care and training are eligible for a free examination. Those who can afford it are expected to pay for the necessary medical treatment, as well as for the required vocational training, but those who are unable to do so are given these services free. The costs to the taxpayer of restoring a disabled person to the wage earning category are returned manyfold in the form of his tax contributions and freedom from dependence on assistance payments.

Unemployment

Even during prosperous times, production cutbacks, shifts in plant locations, and changes in technology cause some workers to lose their jobs. Prior to the establishment of unemployment insurance, the only public source of help after savings had been exhausted was the "dole." The dismissal of a few men in one industry frequently set off a chain reaction. Those out of work could no longer buy things they needed so other men lost their jobs because their employers could no longer sell so much.

Before 1935 a few states, most notably Wisconsin, tried to establish unemployment insurance. But each state hesitated to act for fear that the additional costs would place its own industries in an economically disadvantageous position with competitors in other states. To deprive industries in states without unemployment insurance of this advantage and to induce all states to establish programs, in 1935 Congress levied a 3 per cent tax on most employers of eight or more (now four) on the first 3000 dollars paid to each employee. However, if an employer is paying a tax to a state unemployment insurance scheme which meets federal standards, he may credit all he pays to the state to cover up to 90 per cent of his federal liability. Hence, a state tax of 2.7 per cent does not increase the employer's total tax payments.

State funds are deposited in the national treasury where they are available to be used by the state to make unemployment payments. The national government gives the states the money to cover administrative costs and national officials watch to be sure federal standards are being followed, but each state has considerable freedom in shaping its own program. Unemployed workers must report in person to the state employment agency to show that they are able to work, and they must be willing to travel to secure employment. There are other questions as well—for example, does unemployment because of a strike entitle one to insurance; must a skilled worker take a job of a semi-skilled nature? After a worker's eligibility has been established, he is entitled to weekly payments; on a national average, unemployment workers receive 25 dollars a week for 26 weeks. He must continue to report periodically for employment, but since it is an insurance and not an assistance program, there are no means tests.

Summary and general assistance

To summarize—the national and state governments operate a variety of welfare programs. The national government directly provides old-age and survivors insurance to which limited disability protection has been added. Unemployment insurance is a state responsibility, but the national government uses its taxing power to establish minimum standards. Workmen's compensation is entirely state operated. In addition to these insurance schemes, the states make assistance payments and provide welfare services for the needy. The federal government through its financial support encourages the expansion and improvement of these state programs. Moreover, federal grants are a device by which the taxpayers in the wealthier states help those in the poor states to meet their welfare obligations.

Federal grants are of two kinds: (1) those to support cash payments to individuals to supplement incomes and (2) those to enable states and local governments to expand their services. Of the first kind are grants administered by Bureau of Public Assistance for old-age payments, payments to dependent children, payments to the needy blind, and payments to needy persons who are totally and permanently disabled. Of the second kind are the grants administered by the Children's Bureau to enable states to provide services for crippled children, maternal and infant health services, and child welfare programs, as well as grants to states for vocational rehabilitation.

Programs for the needy blind, needy aged, and so on are technically called *categorical assistance*. Only those who are within the defined category are eligible for assistance. Today social insurance combined with federally supported categorical assistance have provided a cushion against the major causes of destitution, but there are about 650,000 needy persons ineligible for aid under any of these programs and not covered or covered inadequately by insurance. Aid to these persons is called *general assistance*. This assistance does not receive any federal support and is still administered by local governments, although subject to some supervision by state agencies. It still follows the essential pattern and principles of the Elizabethan system. This kind of aid varies from the highest caliber of service to simple handouts by untrained local township officials.

The politics and administration of welfare

The whole field of welfare services is characterized by segmented programs and overlapping administrative organizations. For example, in the area of disability insurance and assistance, state labor departments enforce industrial safety and occupational disease regulations, workmen's compensation is administered by one state agency, vocational rehabilitation by another, and in some states aid to the blind by still another. Local health officials and local welfare agencies are involved. At the national level the Public Health Service and several bureaus of the Social Security Administration as well as units of the Department of Labor administer grants having to do with some aspect of disability. Moreover, the extent of individual protection varies. Some men have no public insurance protection whereas others are covered by both workmen's compensation and O.A.S.I. In some industries, trade unions have been able to bargain for generous welfare, disability, and old age programs, but in others there is no such protection.

Today welfare expenditures of state and local governments are among the largest, ranking only behind education and highways. Most of this expansion has taken place in recent decades, much of it in response to programs initiated by the national government. The pattern of groups supporting welfare programs is formidable. Both major political parties claim to be pioneers and champions of social security. The trade unions, which in the past were not enthusiastic about social security but preferred to rely on their own bargaining power, have become staunch supporters. Many employers have ceased to oppose. Some companies have agreed to pay their employees old-age pensions which are tied into social security insurance. The larger the benefit under social security, the less the company must pay. Hence, these employers now favor social security. Small employers who are unable to finance the welfare funds created by large unions and large employers now find that securing protection for their workers through public insurance programs presents an attractive alternative. Added to these pressures are growing proportions of older people who press their demands with considerable vigor. (Some observers have suggested that the projected increase in proportion of aged persons and the coincident increase in number of children are going to force the middle-age wage earners to choose between larger expenditures to care for their parents or larger expenditures to educate their children.) There are still a significant number of Americans who are apprehensive that the burden of supporting these welfare services is becoming too great, and who fear that these programs will undermine our sense of initiative and willingness to take risks, but the political forces now supporting these programs appear to be so considerable that they have in their grand outlines almost ceased to be items of political controversy.

However, there are still significant differences among the various groups over the details of the programs, their future development and expansion. Trade unions, employers' organizations, insurance companies, medical associations, bar associations, and organizations of welfare and health workers often have different ideas of what policies should be adopted. Each tends to be concerned with special aspects, each tends to emphasize special dangers; each is true to the national interest, in its own fashion.

Special problems of minorities

One person out of nineteen in the United States receives some form of public relief. Many of these recipients are members of minority groups who are discriminated against in education, who are forced into substandard housing, and who find it difficult to secure jobs. Traditionally, the most recently arrived immigrant groups have been subjected to this discrimination, and as a result they constituted a large portion of persons needing public relief. As soon as they became integrated into the mainstream of American society and were permitted to participate in the productive life of the economy, and perhaps even more important, as soon as they were allowed to reap the rewards of their own ability, they had less need for public assistance. Today the Negroes are given the fewest opportunities, and as a result they constitute the largest percentage of those in need.

Some persons justify discrimination because they argue that the relatively large numbers of Negroes on relief shows that they lack the initiative and self-reliance to take care of themselves. Obviously this confuses cause with effect. Discrimination leads to lack of education and opportunity, and it is opportunity that produces initiative and independence. Why should a man sacrifice to secure a college education if when he graduates the only jobs open to him are as a day laborer? As long as Negroes are denied equal opportunities, not only do they suffer, but the entire community pays in the form of high cost of relief, and we are all denied the full productive and cultural contributions of those discriminated against.

TO PROTECT THE PUBLIC HEALTH

When we think of government and protection of health we usually think of public health departments, but this is only part of the story. Government action to protect our health is not limited to the things that public health departments do. Welfare assistance and social insurance give people the money to buy food, clothing, and shelter which they need to protect their health. Highway safety officials attack one of the major hazards. Housing agencies attempt to create better environments for the care and feeding of children. In this section, however, the focus is on programs that deal more directly with threats to health caused by illness, both physical and mental in origin.

There are some highly contentious public health issues: for example, should fluorine be added to our drinking water, should social security be expanded to pay benefits in case of illness and accidents? But for the most part public health programs are routine. They seldom excite the general public, make the headlines, or cause governors and congressmen to lose sleep. Life is precious and precarious and threatened by factors that can be dealt with only by systematic social action. Only through government can we take the necessary action to prevent disease, prolong life, and promote health. There is little opposition to public regulation to provide safe water supplies and adequate sanitation facilities, to control communicable and infectious diseases, to care for the mentally ill, and to provide medical and hospital services for indigents and such special groups as veterans.

Patterns of public health—background

Epidemics and foul-smelling refuse promoted the first local health ordinances. By the beginning of the 19th century, city public health departments were common, but neither the state of medical knowledge nor the art of government had progressed sufficiently for effective programs. High death rates from plagues and childbirth and among infants were considered normal hazards beyond human control. The public became aroused only during an epidemic and interest subsided after the death rate came down.

Dr. Stephen Smith, the first President of the American Public Health Association, relates how just before the Civil War he discovered a tenement house in which there were over 100 typhus cases. "The doors and windows were broken, the cellar was filled with sewage, every room was occupied by families of Irish immigrants who had but little furniture and slept on straw scattered on the floor." [10] The city government had no authority to act and the landlord refused to correct the situation. The Board of Health, an ex-officio board of aldermen, seldom met, and when the Doctor asked the Mayor to call the Board to deal with the epidemic the Mayor replied, "I will not call the Board, for I consider it more dangerous to the city than typhus." [11] Nor were the "Health Wardens" any better. Most of them were saloonkeepers who did little more than have sulphur burned in houses if contagious diseases were called to their attention.

[10] Stephen Smith, "The History of Public Health, 1871–1921," *A Half Century of Public Health,* ed. by Mazyck P. Ravenel (New York: American Public Health Association, 1921), pp. 4-5.
[11] *Ibid.,* p. 7.

By the end of the 19th century considerable progress had been made. Medical science was making spectacular advances in understanding the causes of communicable diseases and developing vaccines and antitoxins to immunize against them. After the Civil War state health departments were established and the American Public Health Association provided the leadership of medical men and other specialists to put pressure on city councils, state legislators, and congressmen to establish porfessionalized public health services.

State health departments

Nowadays within a single state there may be as many as 18 different state agencies concerned in some way with some aspect of public health. But all states have a public health department, usually headed by a board, often with an executive officer in charge of administration. State health departments supervise local programs, distribute the sizeable federal grants to the local health departments, operate laboratories to service local departments, provide health services in areas where there are not local health facilities, and in many states are responsible for the operation of mental and tuberculosis hospitals.

Local health departments

Local health officers provide most of the services directly for the public. City health departments, although subject to state supervision, normally function as self-contained and practically autonomous units. In rural areas, public health is usually a county function, but public health officials have successfully sponsored the establishment of public health districts consisting of several counties containing a sufficiently large population to support a more adequate health program than each county could afford. In order to be eligible for federal grants, public health employees must operate under a merit system. Heads of the departments are almost always medical men, and where available are specialists in the public health field.

What do public health officials do? One Saturday night in a "gritty little first-floor office at the New York City Health Department," the phone rang in the office of the night emergency inspector. An interne at Roosevelt Hospital was on the line. "What," he asked, "were the ingredients of CN and how should it be treated?" He had to know fast because he had a five-year-old boy whose mother had accidentally fed him a teaspoonful of this disinfectant an hour or so ago. The night inspector searched through his card file which contained the ingredients of and the remedies for the thousands of household commercial products used in American homes. He quickly identified CN as a carbolic and prescribed the standard remedy.[12]

Before the operation of Poison Control Centers by our large metropolitan health departments, doctors had no way of knowing how to treat children who swallowed various substances—from shoe polish to car cleaning fluid—since the poisoning agents are not always identified on labels. The long-distance telephone makes it unnecessary for smaller city and county departments to provide such specialized services, but all health departments are active in the following fields: vital statistics, control of communicable diseases, environmental sanitation, laboratory services, hygiene of maternity, infancy, and childhood, and general health education. Protection against communicable and infectious diseases is one of the oldest and most successful public health duties. By enforcing quarantine regulations, encouraging immunization, and regular health supervision of school children, the death rates from these diseases have been brought way down.

Protection of water and milk supply is another well established public health duty. Milk, so vital to the physical development of children, is a potentially dangerous drink. Health regulations, backed by vigorous inspection of the production and distribution of milk from cow to consumer, have largely licked this menace. Likewise we drink water with assurance that the health department has guaranteed its safety for human consumption. Although drinking water has been made safe and sanitary, water pollution is still a vexing problem. Polluted water annually destroys thousands of dollars' worth of wildlife, creates offensive odors, and defaces the landscape.

Recently public health officers have become concerned with air pollution which aggravates respiratory conditions, may cause or contribute to lung cancer, and may even lead to fatal poisoning. Some cities—Philadelphia, Pittsburgh, and St. Louis, for example—have been able to purify the air their citizens breathe by requiring residential and industrial fuel users to burn only certain kinds of fuels and to use purifying devices. Although there are still some unsolved technical problems, the knowledge is now available to reduce drastically the pollution of the atmosphere. However, in many cities there is insuffi-

[12] Paraphrase of materials taken from Berton Roueché, "Annals of Medicine," *The New Yorker* (May 4, 1957), pp. 144 ff.

cient political pressure to secure the adoption of the sometimes costly remedies.

Public health departments concentrate on the prevention of disease and, except in special circumstances, leave to private practitioners the major responsibility for treatment. In line with this tradition, in 47 states health officials have been persuaded by medical and dental science that we could reduce substantially the number of dental cavities if controlled amounts of fluorine were added to drinking water. Although over 1,000 communities have acted on this advice, the question has lead to many intense community political battles.

Certain groups object to fluoridation because of religious reasons, and their opposition was not unexpected. In view of the long accepted and standard practice of adding chlorine to our drinking water, the intensity and violence of the objections of others, however, was both unexpected and difficult to explain. Opponents of fluoridation have argued that the statistics of health officials are incomplete and misleading. They caution that it is too soon to determine the harmful affects of adding fluorine, a poison, to drinking water, even if it is added in small amounts. Some have argued that fluoridation smacks of socialism and undermines individual liberty. Some have even accused the sponsors of these proposals, usually the local dental and medical associations and public health officials, of wanting to weaken the population so that the Communists can more readily take over. In many cities so intense have been the battles between the pro and anti-fluoridation groups that they have made the regular partisan campaigns between Democrats and Republicans look tame.

The federal government and public health

The central, but not the only, public health agency of the national government is the Public Health Service headed by the Surgeon General, now a constituent part of the Department of Health, Education, and Welfare. One of the oldest federal agencies, it was created in 1798 as the Marine Hospital Service to provide prepaid medical and hospital care for American merchant seamen.

The service now *provides medical services and operates hospitals* where seamen employed on American vessels, Coast Guard personnel, and certain other groups receive free hospitalization, medical and dental care and preventive health services. It also administers medical and hospital facilities for Indians and supervises Freedmen's Hospital in the District of Columbia, a general hospital for the treatment of serious conditions which also furnishes teaching facilities for medical students of Howard University. It is responsible for the medical services for persons in federal penal institutions and operates hospitals for drug addicts.

The service enforces foreign *quarantine regulations,* inspects sea, land, and air traffic, and *conducts medical examinations of immigrants.* It also has the authority to prevent the spread of diseases through interstate commerce but rarely exercises this power and routinely advises and assists the state health authorities in these matters.

The service *licenses the manufacture and interstate sale of biological products* such as serums, toxins, and vaccines, to guarantee their potency and freedom from dangerous extraneous ingredients. (However, the inspection of food and drugs sold in interstate commerce is the duty of the Food and Drug Administration, now also housed in the Department of Health, Education, and Welfare, which also enforces the federal labelling laws. Food and Drug officials attempt to prevent the sale of impure food and dangerous drugs, and enforce the laws against making false claims for drug products. Still another agency, the Federal Trade Commission, regulates the interstate advertising of these products to prevent misleading and false statements. And still another agency, the Bureau of Narcotics in the Treasury Department, enforces federal tax regulations against illegal sale of narcotics.)

The Public Health Service *engages in and sponsors research* through its National Institutes of Health. These institutions operate their own research hospitals and administer grant programs to other scientists searching for ways to treat and cure cancer, heart disease, mental illness, and other specified diseases.

The Public Health Service also administers *grants to the states* to aid them in improving their general services along with special grants to improve particular programs. Among the larger of these is the federal aid program to promote the construction of hospitals, nursing homes, diagnostic centers, and rehabilitation and other medical facilities. Federal money has been used to aid in the construction of over 3,000 projects that will add 133,239 hospital beds, 2,259 nursing home beds, and 648 health units, many of which are located in areas that formerly had no such services. For each federal dollar spent, the states and local governments have put up two. Even so, there is still a deficiency in hospital facilities, and it is likely that this aid program, due to expire in 1958, will be extended by Congress.

Public health officials in action

Since the spread of diseases recognizes no man-made governmental boundaries, cooperative action of international, national, and local officials is required. This can be dramatically illustrated by the action taken to combat the 1957 influenza pandemic (a pandemic refers to a worldwide epidemic). Severe influenza pandemics have occurred about four times every hundred years. The pandemic prior to the one in 1957 had occurred in 1918–19 and had killed more than 300,000 people in the United States alone.

During the summer of 1957 an epidemic suddenly struck in the Orient, and its rapid spread alerted public officials to the possibility that it marked the early stages of a pandemic. The World Health Organization, a specialized UN agency, operates a World Influenza Center in London which is the center of a network of over 50 laboratories all over the world. The United States Public Health Service Influenza Information Center is tied into this network, which provides for the immediate exchange of information and transmission of knowledge about the nature of particular influenza viruses. Although vaccines can be used, it is necessary constantly to develop new ones because influenza viruses are always changing. A vaccine successful in previous epidemics is not effective against the new strains.

As soon as the 1957 epidemic started, Public Health Officials working with those in World Health Organization isolated the new strain of virus and distributed specimens to commercial vaccine manufacturers so that production could be immediately started. Although influenza is not a quarantinable disease, the Division of Foreign Quarantine of the Public Health Service inaugurated a more vigorous examination of all travelers from the epidemic areas. The Public Health Service worked out arrangements with state health departments for an exchange of information and for development of procedures to prevent the spread of the disease within the United States. Plans were made for the stockpiling of antibiotics to take care of secondary infections. Priorities in the distribution of vaccine were determined and the Civil Defense Administration was alerted to the possibility that it might have to be prepared to maintain essential services in communities where the disease might strike hard and fast.[13]

[13] Information in this section is taken from David D. Rutstein, M.D., "The Influenza Epidemic," *Harper's Magazine,* Vol. 215, No. 1287 (August, 1957), pp. 23-28.

The special problems of the mentally ill

Over half of all hospital beds in the United States are occupied by the mentally ill. Persons physically sick are treated with compassion and consideration, but until recently those suffering from mental illness were chained and treated as a public danger. Even today concern for the mentally ill, especially if the illness causes antisocial behavior, is colored by implications of moral condemnation not placed upon those suffering from other disabilities.

Governments have always assumed a much greater role in providing direct medical and hospital services for the mentally ill than for those suffering from physically based illness for the following reasons: (1) The original purpose of public action was to protect the society from what were then thought to be dangerous evil spirits. Just as government incarcerated criminals, so it chained up the mentally sick. (2) The high cost of medical and hospital care, which often takes months or even years, is beyond the means of all except the very well to do. Hence, tax supported institutions have become the general pattern.

State governments operate mental hospitals, although a few states continue to use county institutions. State policy in the administration and operation of these institutions defies classification. In some states, each hospital is administered independently by its own board and officers; in others, the state mental health departments run all hospitals; in some, the state public health department operates them; in others, it is the department of welfare; and in others, a single department of public institutions operates mental hospitals, prisons, and reformatories.

Some states offer minimal services, others have a more liberal program. Dr. George S. Stevenson, noted authority in this field, has classified the scope of state programs as follows: "The state may intend: (1) To hospitalize the patient if he is a danger to himself or others— a police function. (2) To hospitalize the indigent—essentially a welfare function. (3) To offer hospital service to all who need it, charging according to financial capacity. (4) To provide all types of psychiatric service in the community as well as in the hospital for all who need it." [14]

The quality of treatment also varies from those states that provide little more than a hospital bed to those that make a serious attempt

[14] George S. Stevenson, *Mental Health Planning for Social Action* (New York: The McGraw-Hill Book Co., Inc., 1956), pp. 50-51.

to treat patients. It is doubtful if any state hospital has the financial support or staff to give its patients the best treatment that medical and psychiatric knowledge makes possible. Despite major increases in financial support, the states still spend from a third to a fifth as much per mental patient as the best federal or private hospitals.

Legislators, governors, and others who must slice up the state's expenditures respond to the demands of the electorate. Groups interested in better schools, better highways, and better welfare have more political power than do those interested in improving the care for the mentally ill. Hence, appropriations for these hospitals tend to be what is left after the other more powerful political demands have been assuaged. Mental institutions are often geographically and socially isolated from the rest of the community. Despite the fact that about one in every 17 Americans is suffering from some form of mental illness, there is an apparent reluctance on the part of the electorate to recognize that mental hospitals may be of service to them or their families.

But even if the hospitals had more money, they would still have difficulty in providing the best possible medical service because of a shortage of attendants, nurses, and doctors. Although advances in developing cures for mental diseases have lagged behind some other medical developments, even with the existing knowledge, more cures could be produced if resources, finances, and manpower, were devoted to the effort.

By and large public health officers have been slow in developing preventive mental health programs. Mental hygiene is relatively less developed scientifically than is the case with respect to organically based diseases, but part of the explanation for its lack of attention is that public health personnel are primarily trained in the nonpsychiatric phases of medicine. However, after World War II with the encouragement of the Public Health Services, state and local departments have started preventive programs. Perhaps the most important action has been the establishment, often in cooperation with local volunteer groups, of community mental health clinics. These clinics provide psychiatric services either free or at a price that most people can afford, and through these clinics it is hoped that potentially dangerous cases can be identified and, if treated in their early stages, arrested before hospitalization is required.

The national government operates a large number of mental hospitals. Nearly 10 per cent of the hospitalized psychiatric patients in the United States are in Veterans Administration hospitals. The Public Health Service also provides psychiatric care in its hospitals, which—although limited in terms of numbers treated—have had a disproportionate significance, their high quality service having set standards for the rest of the nation.

How to pay the bills?

As we have seen, all levels of government play a significant role in promoting and protecting health, but except for certain special groups governments do not provide medical services. This is left to private practitioners with the patients financing the costs. Although our governments build and operate many hospitals and provide care for more people than is sometimes realized—men in armed services, Indians, veterans, mentally ill, merchant seamen—most patients have to pay their own hospital bills without public support.

As we have also noted, the major hazard to loss of income for which there is at present no public insurance protection is nonoccupational illness and accident. Nor is there any social insurance scheme that covers costs of illness in a worker's *family*. If a 40-year-old man suffers a heart attack or has an automobile accident and cannot work, he has to rely on his own savings and such private health insurance as Blue Cross. If his union or company has a welfare fund, he can turn to these. When these are exhausted, he has to depend on family, friends, and charity. If he sells most of his property and is reduced to pauperism, he is eligible for public assistance. Perhaps the hospital will treat him as a "charity" patient, and his doctors may contribute their time and skill without charge. If he is a veteran and willing to swear that he is unable to pay, he may be admitted to a V.A. hospital, provided there are no patients with higher priorities—those with service connected casualties.

In the average year 92 per cent of the nation's families need some kind of medical care, 12 per cent of the population become patients in a general hospital. About 11 per cent of all families pay medical bills of 500 dollars or more each year and 4 per cent of the population are faced with hospital charges of more than 500 dollars. Thus, although each year a large number of people have medical and hospital bills, only a small proportion of the families have very large bills.[15]

[15] From a study of the Health Information Foundation of New York published in *U.S. News & World Report*, "Do Doctors Charge Too Much or Not Enough?" (July 5, 1957), p. 36.

No single family can predict whether or not it will be faced in any year with large bills, but if all families made periodic small payments there would be enough to finance the medical and hospital costs of those who do require these services. Hence, there are many people who urge some form of health and hospitalization insurance. Should it be private or public, compulsory or elective?

Advocates of public insurance argue that large numbers of low income families are endangering their health by not seeking medical care because of fear of its expense. Even middle income families, they argue, are sometimes unable to bear the financial burden of sustained illness and may be forced into long and burdensome debt. Private health insurance, they argue, does not protect the lowest income families who cannot afford it. Moreover, this insurance usually does not cover all the costs. One study, for example, showed that patients had to pay on the average 21 per cent of hospital and 55 per cent of surgical costs out of their own pockets, over and above the cost of the insurance.[16] Mental illness is not covered, nor do private insurance policies usually provide money to supplement loss of income. Moreover, they argue, since private insurance covers only a select portion of the population, its per-person cost is higher than if all were covered and there were a wider sharing of risks. Advocates of public insurance insist that such a program would provide the least expensive and most sensible way to meet the inevitable costs of illness and spread the benefits of medical science to the largest number of people. They deny that it is or would lead to "socialized medicine." Although there would have to be some kind of advance agreement about fees, doctors and patients would continue in their present relation, the only difference being that insurance would make for prepaid and preplanned financing.

On the other hand, opponents of compulsory public health insurance argue that its supporters exaggerate the existing needs, and they insist that most people are willing and able to finance their own medical and hospital costs. Our present system, they argue, has given us the world's best medical practice. Although it is proper for the government to support research, help finance the construction of hospitals, and give relief to those in need, it should not attempt to compete with private insurance. Public insurance, they argue, would lead to regimentation since the government would fix the doctors' fees, require them to fill out elaborate forms, and police them in their practice. Such a program,

[16] *Ibid.*

they argue, would destroy the existing confidential relationship between doctor and patient. They also insist that since persons would no longer be restrained by the immediate costs of medical care, many would rush to the doctors on the slightest provocation and would so swamp the profession and the hospitals that the whole level of American medical practice would be endangered.

Support for some kind of public health insurance has come from a variety of liberal and labor organizations, such as the American Federation of Labor and Congress of Industrial Organizations, National Farmers Union, and American Veterans Committee, and it was also championed by the Truman Administration. The details of various proposals vary. Some would expand O.A.S.I. by increasing contributions into the fund to finance benefits in case of illness. Some would restrict benefits to cover actual cost of medical, surgical, and hospital care, whereas others propose that contributions should be increased sufficiently to finance payments for loss of income also. Others have proposed that the federal government levy taxes and establish national standards but return the money to the states and let each state establish and administer its own program. Either one of these schemes would make workmen's compensation and existing disability provisions less necessary and would also reduce the expenditures of relief funds.

The American Medical Association and insurance companies have opposed public health insurance proposals. When President Truman was unexpectedly re-elected in 1948, the AMA was moved to intensify its opposition and mobilize its political resources. The Association assessed each of its members 25 dollars and hired an experienced public relations firm to direct a full-scale assault on public health insurance. A National Education Campaign headquarters was established and all kinds of techniques were adopted. Organizations were lined up to go on record against what the AMA insisted upon calling "socialized medicine." Spot announcements were made on television, and newspaper ads were sponsored. Doctors were encouraged to discuss the matter with their patients and indicate their opposition. Candidates who had gone on record in favor of public health insurance were opposed in campaigns. The doctors showed their political talents by putting on a most astute and effective political program.[17]

The election of President Eisenhower assuaged the AMA's fears,

[17] For a detailed account see Stanley Kelley, Jr., *Professional Public Relations and Political Power* (Baltimore: The Johns Hopkins Press, 1956), Chap. 3.

since he opposes public health insurance. The President did suggest, however, that the national government might use its credit facilities to guarantee private insurance companies against loss, and, therefore, make it possible for them to sell their insurance at lower costs. But this too was opposed by both the American Medical Association and spokesmen for the insurance industry, and the President did not press vigorously for it. Unless the President or some major political group makes the adoption of public health insurance a high priority, it is unlikely that such a scheme will be adopted in the near future. A more likely development is the expansion of tax supported medical care through the Veterans Administration progressively relaxing the "means" tests and expanding the category of veterans eligible for care and, as noted, through an expansion of the disability provisions of O.A.S.I. to cover more groups.

CREATION OF THE DEPARTMENT OF HEALTH, EDUCATION, AND WELFARE

A case study

The gradual extension of federal health and welfare programs has, by and large, been an outgrowth of the industrialization and urbanization of the United States. It is not surprising, therefore, to learn that our Presidents, who are more likely to be responsive to values of urban voters than are the leaders of Congress, have generally been more vigorous in backing social legislation than have congressional spokesmen. One phase in this struggle between the President and Congress has been the presidential attempts to create a department with cabinet status to administer federal health and welfare functions.

President Harding was the first to recommend a department of education and welfare. Following Presidents made similar proposals, but those in the Senate and House opposed to "the welfare state" blocked approval. By 1939 the Social Security Administration, Children's Bureau, Public Health Service, Food and Drug Administration, and United States Office of Education were administering related programs, but without central direction. In that year President Roosevelt persuaded Congress to approve the establishment of a Federal Security Agency to coordinate the programs and policies of all these agencies. However, each unit retained considerable independence and the Agency was not given cabinet rank.

President Truman recommended five times that the FSA be elevated to departmental status. In 1949 he proposed that it be called the Department of Welfare. The Senate vetoed. Organizations especially concerned with health and education objected because they were afraid that these two programs would not receive adequate support in a department where welfare loomed as the largest function. Again in 1950 President Truman recommended the creation of a Department of Health, Education and Security, but this time with safeguards to insure the independence of the several constituent units. The American Medical Association very actively opposed this proposal, as it had the other attempts to establish such a department. At the time, Mr. Oscar Ewing was the head of FSA and slated to become head of the new department. He had sponsored a study of the nation's health and on the basis of this report had recommended an expansion of social security to provide state administered but nationally financed compulsory sickness insurance. Congressional opponents of such schemes contended that to elevate this official to a cabinet status would considerably increase the prestige of his position and authority toward advancement of a program to which they objected.[18]

One of President Eisenhower's first reorganization recommendations was to create a Department of Health, Education, and Welfare. However, before submitting his proposal to Congress, he conferred with leaders of the AMA. The President agreed to create a special assistant to the new Secretary to advise the Secretary on medical matters. This special assistant was to be a doctor "widely recognized in the medical field with wide nongovernmental experience," that is, he was to be a man agreeable to the American Medical Association and representing their point of view. With this understanding, the AMA withdrew its objection.

Spokesmen for organized labor and proponents of sickness insurance charged that the President had sold out to the "special interest." But the Joint Committee of the House and Senate that held hearings on the proposal recommended favorable action after first making clear that the special assistant to the Secretary was not to undertake "comprehensive studies of all aspects of medical care for the American people," but to limit his advice and assistance to the scope of the functions vested in the Department.[19]

[18] Senate Reprint No. 128, 83rd Cong., 1st Sess. (March 23, 1953), from *U.S. Code: Congressional and Administrative News;* 83, 1st, Vol. 2, p. 1332.

[19] *Ibid.,* p. 1338. See also *Hearings on Reorganization Plan No. 1,* Subcommittee on Reorganization of Senate Committee on Government Operations, 83, 1st (March 23, 1953).

Thus we have an example of the common pattern of interrelations among organized interest, public officials and Congress that characterizes the shaping and administration of our public policy. Organizations especially concerned with programs may be expected both to support and restrain public officials. The rest of the electorate, not immediately affected, pays little attention.

HOUSING

Americans live in better houses than do most of the people in the world. Electricity, indoor plumbing, and mechanical refrigeration are standard. Human "needs," however, are measured by what is available. If all live in mud huts, those without bathtubs are not likely to be considered wanting in the necessities of life, but in a nation as rich as the United States a family of four or five living in two or three rooms without decent sanitation *needs* better housing. And despite our wealth, we have slums. In fact there is some evidence that we are creating slums faster than we are getting rid of them. One-third of our urban dwellings are over 30 years old, and many people live in blighted areas. Dirty, crowded tenement houses and rural shanties are evident to any who would make a casual investigation.

Inadequate housing is more acute in some portions of the nation and for some groups than for others. In one southern state, 60 per cent of the total dwellings are dilapidated or lack running water. Certain minority groups—Negroes in most places; Latin Americans, Puerto Ricans, and Orientals in some areas—have difficulty in finding clean and modern living quarters. Many Negroes who have the least opportunities for education and remunerative employment cannot afford to buy or rent good homes. But even if they can afford to do so, they are forced to live in "Jim Crow" areas which, to say the least, are not located in the most desirable parts of the city and do not contain the nicest homes. In the rural areas, tenant farmers and migratory workers are crowded together in work camps or forced to live in shanties that have no heat or electricity.

Other Americans live much better. They have invested their savings in good homes, and they hope to preserve the value of their property. They want to be sure that the apartments they rent or the houses they buy are safe and the neighborhoods they live in are conducive to the "good life."

Our governments are involved in helping all of us enjoy better housing. Government housing programs may be characterized as falling into three general categories: (1) programs, such as building and zoning regulations, that preserve property values, protect health and safety, and guide community development; (2) programs, such as insured mortgages, that indirectly create a demand for homes and supply a market for private builders; (3) programs, such as public housing and slum clearance, that directly increase the supply of houses and make is possible for low income groups to have better homes.

Building codes, zoning, and city planning

In the country a person can do almost whatever he wishes with the land he owns. He may build almost any kind of structure on his land. But when he moves to the city, where his actions affect the health and well-being of others, he discovers a host of regulations restricting his use of his own property. Building codes, electrical codes, plumbing codes, and fire codes establish minimum standards for construction, lighting, ventilation, sanitation, and fire protection. These codes apply to new construction of all kinds, and in the case of public buildings and those that accommodate the public—apartment houses, stores, theaters—there are periodic checks to insure compliance with the standards.

Building codes are supposed to protect the public against buildings falling or burning down. Their actual writing reflects the combined pressures of manufacturers of building materials, builders, real-estate people, insurance companies, apartment owners, and building-trade unions. It has been alleged that some of these codes keep up the cost of construction and give special advantages to builders and workers. Some were written years ago and do not allow the use of modern and economic means of building such as prefabrication and dry-wall construction. Some prevent the use of new labor-saving techniques. On the other hand, others have alleged that building codes are not stringent enough to protect the public. Most complaints are directed at enforcement. Often inspectors are untrained patronage appointees. Only after a disastrous fire in which flammable materials and blocked exits cause unnecessary deaths or after a building collapses does the general public become aroused. But the subject is so technical that sensible public discussion is difficult.

Most cities have elaborate regulations requiring landlords to maintain their properties and keep their buildings in safe and sanitary condition. But in the decaying parts of some of our cities these regulations are not vigorously enforced. Tenants lack the knowledge or are afraid of eviction, and there are not enough city inspectors to go around. By crowding many families into small space and by spending no money to keep the buildings in repair, these slums return rich rewards. A few cities—for example, Milwaukee and Baltimore—however, have adopted ordinances which permit the city to repair properties if the owner fails to do so after he has been properly warned, and the costs are then assessed against the property.

During the post-war building boom many subdividers moved outside the city to escape building codes. Others who could not afford to build a house that would meet city standards went to the surrounding country. Some of these hastily built tract homes and cheaply constructed buildings may deteriorate so rapidly that in the not too distant future slums may no longer be limited to the central core of the city.

Most American cities, especially those over 25,000, also have zoning restrictions concerning the use of buildings, their height, and their location on lots. The city is divided into zones—for example, a single-family zone, a light industry zone, a heavy industry zone, and so on. There are also regulations requiring structures to be set back so many feet from the street, and specified distances must be maintained between adjoining lots.

Comprehensive zoning ordinances date from the end of World War I and were not imposed until after the uses of the land and the location of the buildings had already been determined through the dictates of the market and the desires of each individual owner. In most states, the courts would object to retroactive application of zoning requirements so all that the regulations can do is prevent future unplanned development. However, ordinances which give 30 or 40 years advance notice for the termination of noncomplying uses are permissible.

Zoning boards are subject to intense pressures to make exceptions. This "spot zoning"—the classification of a single lot or a few lots to permit a grocery store or filling station in a residential area means, as Charles Adrian has pointed out, "a loss in the total value of the community. Because this loss is socialized among many persons who individually have less incentive to pressure the council than does the single profiteer, such practices take place with considerable regularity in some cities." [20] Once an exception is made for one store it is hard, perhaps illegal, to hold the line against others.

[20] Charles R. Adrian, *Governing Urban America* (New York: The McGraw-Hill Book Co., Inc., 1955), p. 413.

Unless the county has introduced zoning outside of the city limits, the only protection property owners have against having a factory located next door is if there are deed restrictions covering the entire area. To enforce these provisions it is necessary to bring a civil action against the violator, an expensive and time-consuming practice. Hence many city fringe developments are still largely uncontrolled as to land use.

Building codes and zoning ordinances are techniques to bring about ordered development of living areas. In order to use these techniques to achieve desired goals there must be a plan. Today all our large cities have some kind of planning agency, usually consisting of from five to seven members, some city officials and some private citizens, and aided by a professional staff. The planning board is responsible for considering all the human and material resources and developing long-range and integrated programs covering parks, housing, slum clearance, traffic, parking, public health, utilities, zoning, building codes, and other elements that make up city life.

After a comprehensive plan has been adopted, and constantly revised, it is supposed to guide the various decision-making agencies. However, frequently the plan is adopted by the city council as a statement of policy, only to have everyone proceed as before without much consideration of the beautiful maps and glowing descriptions of the future. Furthermore, planning is complicated by the fact that many of our metropolitan urban areas consist of a dozen or so cities, unincorporated areas, and a mixture of special districts. These suburban governments are not bound by the planning programs of the central city. To overcome this, metropolitan planning commissions consisting of representatives of all the governments in the area have drawn up advisory plans to coordinate programs. So far these plans have had little impact upon city development. The federal government has tried to strengthen city planning by making matching grants to help cities of less than 25,000 as well as large metropolitan areas to develop their planning programs. It is too early to determine if these grants-in-aid will have any major effect.

Indirect governmental action to increase the demand for houses

Although the cumulative costs for all the automobiles that each American feels he must buy during the course of his life may exceed all other expenditures, for most people buying a home is the single largest purchase. Until the Depression only those with enough money to make a substantial down payment and good enough credit to borrow the rest were able to build or buy a home. Today the national government through the Federal Housing Administration in the Housing and Home Finance Agency and the Veterans Administration has made it possible for middle-income groups to buy their own homes.

The Federal Housing Administration and the Veterans Administration do not, as is sometimes thought, lend the money. Rather the F.H.A. insures lending institutions that in the event the home buyer defaults and the lender suffers a loss the F.H.A. will make it good. Thus private lenders are encouraged to lend at a lower rate and for longer periods of time than would be the case if the creditor had to assume the entire risk. F.H.A. insurance is financed by collecting a small premium from each person who has an F.H.A. insured mortgage. F.H.A. also insures loans to allow repair and improvement of homes and loans to builders to permit them to borrow the capital to build rental units.

The Veterans Administration guarantees rather than insures mortgages, which gives lenders slightly more protection, but the effect is the same as the F.H.A. program. Would-be home owners still must find a lender willing to lend the money at the rates allowed by the laws. The homes purchased must meet standards of the V.A. or F.H.A. Recently, some lenders have been unwilling to make V.A. or F.H.A. loans except by charging large discounts, which means that home builders have been paying considerably more to borrow the money than is sometimes apparent at first glance.

To assist members of minority groups who are sometimes discriminated against in securing mortgages and persons living in remote areas and small communities where lending institutions are scarce, the Voluntary Home Mortgage Credit Program was established This is a joint industry-government program in which applicants who have made at least two unsuccessful attempts to obtain F.H.A.-insured and V.A.-guaranteed loans may apply. The VHMCP brings these applicants together with life insurance companies, and if they are qualified and their homes meet standards they may thus obtain benefits of F.H.A. and V.A. home mortgage credits.

The national government also increases the supply of home-buying credit through chartering savings and loan institutions and insuring those who place their savings on deposit with these institutions that they will suffer no loss. (Each account is insured up to 10,000 dollars.) Thus many private individuals are encouraged to make their savings available to supply credit for those who wish to build or buy homes. The national government further encourages the flow of credit for homes through the Federal National Mortgage Association—popularly known as "Fanny May"—which by purchasing mortgages creates a secondary market for these investments and introduces a liquidity into the market and increases the supply of mortgage money. Thus even persons who do not use F.H.A. or V.A. mortgages and buy their homes with what are called conventional mortgages benefit from the federal government's credit-supplying activities.

Public housing, urban redevelopment and renewal

It is the ambition of most Americans to own a home out where there are grass yards, playgrounds, and sunshine. Whenever they can afford to do so, they rush to the periphery. The central core of the city is allowed to run down. Decay sets in and old homes are turned into apartments. Into these low-rent quarters move those who cannot afford anything better. Large numbers are crowded into small apartments and little is spent to keep them in repair, only what the city health and sanitation officials insist on. Before long, the area becomes a slum.

Should our governments clear these slums? What about persons who would be displaced, should the government provide subsidized rental units for them? Should public housing be located on vacant sites or should it be limited to slum clearance? Should governments encourage private builders to turn their efforts from the more profitable construction of homes for upper and middle-income groups to building low-rent housing? These are just a few of the highly charged political issues which find insurance companies and the well-organized real estate and building groups opposed to any form of public housing. Private builders have no objection to the use of governmental funds to increase the number of buyers for the homes they build, but they are stoutly opposed to the government itself building homes or directly increasing their supply. Against this opposition, supporters of public housing have been able to secure a limited federal-state-local program based on the Federal Housing Act of 1937.

The Federal Housing Act of 1937, supplemented by Housing Acts of 1949 and 1954, provides for federal assistance to local communities "to remedy the unsafe and insanitary housing conditions and acute shortage of decent, safe, and sanitary dwellings for families of low income." If state laws so authorize, the Act calls for the establishment of local housing authorities, most commonly made up of city officials. If the local housing authority submits a program to the Public Housing Administration which meets federal specifications, PHA lends it most of the money to initiate the program. The local housing authority then sells bonds to finance the project over a longer time and pays back the federal government, the bondholders being indemnified through rents. The federal government also makes an annual subsidy to bridge the gap between the actual costs of the project and the rent charged the tenants. As a condition of this federal assistance, except if there is an acute housing shortage, local governments have to agree to eliminate unsafe dwelling units equal in number to the new units constructed and to furnish municipal services free or for a small charge. Only persons whose incomes are under specified limits are eligible to rent one of these apartments and if a person's income exceeds the limits he has to move.

This public housing program was interrupted during World War II and the federal government directly built and encouraged others to build homes for war workers some of which were after the war turned over to local public housing authorities. Although Congress approved an extension of the public housing program in the Act of 1949, opponents of public housing have been able to restrict the annual appropriations so that the number of yearly starts are considerably less than the 1949 Act calls for. Furthermore, in 1953 Congress prohibited any new public housing units, even if already under construction, if the governing body of a municipality or a public referendum rejected such a proposal. Numerous other restrictions have been imposed. However, there are now 900 local authorities administering 40,000 units in which 1,500,000 persons live. Although most of these public housing units have been built and are operated with help of federal funds, some states and cities have undertaken their own programs without federal grants, loans, or subsidies.

Public housing has been criticized because it is said to stifle the ambition of the occupants into bettering themselves by the requirement that they move out if they raise their incomes beyond prevailing limits. It is also contended that public housing projects constitute unfair competition for private builders and landlords. On the other hand, there is the fact that many people cannot afford decent housing, and without some form of subsidy they have to live in slums or near slums.

Not only is this bad for the individuals who have to live under these conditions, but slums are also costly to the community. Slum property pays little in taxes but demands much in terms of police, fire, and health services.

In addition to public housing—and not to be confused with it— are federal-state-local *urban redevelopment* and *urban renewal* projects. Experience has indicated that it is not sufficient to tear down a few slums. If razing is all that is done, frequently "slums creep back" and blight the new project. Thus it is necessary to plan the redevelopment of entire areas. In addition, the blight could be stopped in certain sections that are beginning to run down, if attention were given in time.

In order to encourage cities to engage in comprehensive planning and to attack energetically the whole program of urban renewal, the federal government makes outright grants and loans to cities that have developed "workable programs." The Urban Renewal Administration administers these grants, which can be used to acquire, clear, and prepare blighted areas for the construction of new dwellings. The cleared land can then be used either for public housing projects or for resale to private builders for redevelopment. The F.H.A. is authorized to insure mortgages to aid private industry in the redevelopment or rehabilitation of residential structures on this land. By this cooperative effort of national-state-local government and private industry, it is hoped that private builders will be encouraged to invest in these redevelopment projects, since they can secure the land at relatively low cost and borrow their capital at relatively low rates.

BIBLIOGRAPHICAL NOTE

W. A. Friedlander, *Introduction to Social Welfare,* a standard text, provides comprehensive coverage. *Annual Report* of the Department of Health, Education, and Welfare is most useful for information about current programs. *The Social Welfare Year Book,* published yearly by the National Association of Social Workers, contains excellent articles. Harry S. Mustard, *Government in Public Health,* 1945, by a noted public health expert is a short and amusingly written description of problems. Wilson G. Smillie, *Public Health, Its Promise for the Future,* 1955, is a detailed history of the development of public health programs in the United States up to 1914. Oscar R. Ewing, *The Nation's Health,* 1948, contains findings and recommendations for public action; this is the report which moved leadership of AMA into active opposition. The President's Commission on the Health Needs of the Nation, *Building America's Health,*

1951, the report and recommendations of Commission appointed by President Truman, much of which is also opposed by the AMA. The best source for position of the AMA is in editorials of the *Journal of the American Medical Association*. James H. Means, *Doctors, People, and Government,* 1953, written by a doctor who dissents from official position of AMA and is generally critical of that Association's political position but who does not support compulsory health insurance presents a balanced general account.

Martin Meyerson and Edward C. Banfield in *Politics, Planning and the Public Interest,* 1955, present an excellent account of the development of public housing policy in Chicago which shows the complexity and interrelations of issues. *Annual Report* of the Housing and Home Finance Agency contains valuable factual data.

10. LAWRENCE J. R. HERSON

Government and Civil Rights

CIVIL rights in America is the product of many hands, a blending of the legacy of the past with decisions of the moment. Constitutional framers, legislators, judges, policemen and private citizens have all helped shape our liberties and freedoms; accordingly, this present chapter will treat civil rights from several corresponding vantage points: (1) the relationship of civil rights to democracy itself; (2) the connection between civil rights and the pattern of American constitutions; (3) the impact upon civil rights of legislative, judicial, and police processes of government; and (4) an examination of contemporary civil rights issues.[1]

Through the use of these perspectives some total understanding of civil rights is sought, but before moving to these vantage points, there is one bit of prior ground that must now be covered: We must make clear the dual nature of civil rights within our system of government.

[1] "Civil rights" will be used here to include those freedoms often subsumed, short-hand style, under the term "civil liberties." Technically speaking, civil liberties generally refers to such rights as are included in the first three amendments to the Federal Constitution, while civil rights generally refers to the equality requirements of the Thirteenth, Fourteenth, and Fifteenth Amendments and to "fair trial" requirements such as those contained in Amendments Four to Eight.

CIVIL RIGHTS AND DEMOCRACY

Like the other subjects considered in this book, civil rights can be viewed as a product of the governmental process, an emergent of the governmental will. Thus, when the legislature passes a law forbidding discrimination in public housing, the ensuing right emerges as a product of government and is subject, therefore, to all the pressures, conflict, and politics inherent in any governmental decision. But civil rights are more than a product of government. They are also an essential characteristic of democracy and in this sense they are an *attribute* of democracy, one of its identifying hallmarks.

To make this attributive aspect of civil rights clearer, it would be useful to stretch our imagination to an epoch where government is not much concerned with things such as old age pensions, housing, economic regulation and the like. Such, indeed, approximates the actual state of governmental affairs in the United States not more than three or four decades ago. And yet, if we assume that democracy, roughly put, is a system of government that acts upon the demands of the greatest portion of society; and if we further assume that society is not much concerned with social security or housing, then it is perfectly valid to conclude that lack of government action in these areas is perfectly consistent with democracy. Or, conversely put, a democratic government need not concern itself with housing, pensions, and the like.

Now take by way of contrast this matter of civil rights. Let us suppose an instance in which the government, again responding to the wishes of its citizens, decides to repress freedom of speech. There would be in many minds grave doubts as to the democratic qualities of that government for in those minds free speech is an essential characteristic of democracy. Without free speech, it can well be argued, democracy is no more.

It may be, of course, that repression of one right or freedom might not constitute sufficient grounds for reading a government out of the democratic ranks. But, at the same time, there is little doubt that if a government proceeded systematically to destroy all freedoms, then that government would cease to operate as a democracy. Thus the point to be made here is simply that civil rights constitute both a product of democratic government and also one of its essential characteristics. Accordingly, our first concern in making this canvass of civil rights will be with the attributive phase of the civil-rights duality: the relationship between these rights and democracy.

THE COMPONENTS OF DEMOCRACY

Metaphorically speaking, it is almost as easy to fell an elephant with a slingshot as it is to define democracy with a single sentence. Lincoln, perhaps, came closest to accomplishing this feat in the sonorous closing line of his Gettysburg Address. But even there, the idea of a "government of the people, by the people and for the people" does not so much define democracy as it sums up its underlying ideas and calls attention to the fact that, in the last say, democracy involves a *process,* a method of governmental action.

Process, of course, invokes activity and operation, and when we look to the center of the democratic operation, we find that its motive force is provided by a single social commitment: that the activities of government shall reflect the wishes and desires of the greatest number in the society. But for government to reflect and carry out these wishes there must also exist some device for determining what these wishes are and for determining what constitutes the greatest number in the society. And at this point, we become aware of two very remarkable social inventions that constitute the vital linkages of democracy. The first of these inventions is the election, for it is the show of hands and the counting of ballots that give the society a device for scheduling and measuring the preferences of its members. And the second of these inventions is a formula for ascertaining with some precision the wishes of the greatest number. This formula is expressed in terms of the *majority* (one half plus one, of the total number voting); and with these parts in place it thus becomes possible to speak of democracy as a system of government that operates according to the principle of majority rule.

But democracy involves ingredients other than majority rule and their presence serves not only to thicken the democratic broth but to complicate the definitional process. Briefly put, civil rights are these other ingredients of democracy and to explain their importance to democracy it is necessary to look, first, to the purposes of majority rule and second, to democracy's historic growth.

The purposes of majority rule

As to the purposes of majority rule, it might first be noted that majority rule is not an end in itself, but merely a device for achieving more important purposes: that of permitting the members of a democratic society to control their government, to bend governmental power to their demands, to create governmental decisions in their own image. In a word, majority rule is a technique through which the members of a society decide what government is to do about each one of a never-ending series of social questions and problems. As each new problem is solved, as each new social demand is met, it is majority rule that determines the form of the solution, and consequently, the majority rules, not once, but through a never-ending series of vote tallies. In these terms, there is not one majority and its rule, but a new majority created for every vote taken and for every problem to be solved. Thus, democracy might be described as a system of majorities in flux, and it is in the protection of the process by which new majorities are constructed that civil rights assume their true importance.

To understand this importance, it is necessary to speak briefly about the ideas and premises that underlie majority rule itself. For a society to commit itself to rule by the greatest number implies, first of all, that the society has faith in the collective wisdom of its members. This faith, in turn, rests upon the idea that men will have knowledge of the issues before them. And if men are to have this knowledge, upon which they will base their judgment and eventually their vote, then it is necessary that they have access to information about those issues.

Second, if majority rule is to prevail, it must be understood that all men have equal access to the voting out of which a majority will be tallied. Anything other than equality of voting will produce rule by less than the majority (that is, by a *minority*) thus breaking the system, even before it begins.

And third, if men are to participate equally in voting and if they are to bring their best judgment to bear upon the issue at hand, they must be free from being punished for their vote or for expressing their ideas upon the issue with which they are concerned.

Now, when we reassemble this chain of premises we find that civil rights constitute its welding force. For men to acquire the knowledge upon which their vote will rest, it is necessary that all men have the right to communicate freely about the problems that confront the society. Free speech, free press, free conscience—these are the liberties that the individual must enjoy if majority rule is to achieve its own ultimate purposes. For men to have equal access to the vote, it is necessary that liberty of the ballot be guaranteed; and for the individual to be free from the threat of punishment for his voting and communication, it is necessary that the government's powers of punishment be carefully confined to acts outside the realm of political participation. And for this purpose, it is necessary that there be established a Code of Law and Justice that specifies most carefully the nature of crime, punishment, and the process by which guilt is established, for if this Code is not established then it becomes possible to stretch the meaning of crime, to increase the degree of punishment, and to relax the standards of establishing guilt in a fashion so as to intimidate those who join in the process of unseating old majorities and bringing new ones in to rule.

Thus, it is civil rights that provide the motive force behind democracy's basic process of majority rule. They make it possible for the society to remedy an unsolved problem or a previously solved problem for which a new majority creates a new solution. The importance of these remedial rights cannot be overemphasized, but to see them in fuller perspective, it is necessary to turn briefly to democracy's historic development.

Civil rights in historic perspective

Although we have approached democracy by first stressing its majority-rule component, in terms of historical fact, Anglo-Saxon democracy developed in quite the reverse fashion. First there came the guarantee of individual rights and only later came the operation of majority rule. Beginning, perhaps in 1215 with the wresting of certain rights from King John through the Magna Carta, there developed in England the idea and tradition of the "Rights of Englishmen" whereby government respected the right of each man to be secure in his person and possessions, to be free from arbitrary arrest and punishment, and to be punished if at all only through the regularized procedures of the law ("due process of law"). Then out of the governmental conflicts of the 17th century there grew up first as tradition, and then as rights that might not be abridged, the freedoms of speech, press, and conscience. And finally with the extension of full suffrage (over a period from 1835 to 1928) majority rule became a reality, and democracy came to England full blown.

In the United States the same process also took place, in almost parallel fashion. At the time of the Revolution, the Rights of Englishmen were already incorporated into the "Law of the Land," and it was partly in a quarrel over the denial of these rights to the colonists that the War of Independence was waged. Freedom of communication and conscience was the growing pattern in all the states at the time of the Declaration of Independence, and both state and the federal constitutions incorporated the principle of majority rule even as the movement toward universal suffrage got under way.

This summary presentation, of course, cannot canvass the full range of historic relationships between majority rule and civil rights, but it does suggest two significant conclusions: First, the fact that Anglo-Saxon democracy has grown historically not out of one, but out of both its twin components, and second, the idea that this historic growth came as the result of an interplay between these components. That is to say, our democracy might not have arisen at all if civil rights had not provided the seed bed in which majority rule was eventually to grow.

Thus, out of this and the previous discussion, it becomes possible to broaden our definition of democracy to denote a system that provides for both civil rights and majority rule. And at this point, we have reinforced our original contention that civil rights constitute a significant characteristic, or attribute, of democracy. But before we can lay to rest our definition, there is one further problem that needs to be explored. This is one of democracy's thorniest problems. It concerns still another aspect of the relationship between majority rule and civil rights, and out of this relationship, in fact, has come the constitutional structure that we are soon to examine.

THE CONFLICT BETWEEN MAJORITY RULE AND CIVIL RIGHTS

Although civil rights and majority rule are the building blocks of democracy, these elements are not easily bound within a single system. In logic and practice, these principles are not harmonious, and every democratic system exhibits the stresses and strains that result from fusing these elements into a single whole.

Majority rule as an example

To illustrate this disharmony, take the principle that governmental power is to rest in the hands of the majority. Suppose, for example, that the majority were to decide that the "best interests of the nation" required that advocacy of communism be punished as a criminal act and that persons accused of this advocacy be denied the right to trial by jury. Those affected by this majority ruling (call them for the moment, a minority) would accordingly be stripped of two of democracy's fundamental freedoms: the right to communicate freely concerning beliefs that they espouse, and the right to trial procedures within the meaning of "due process of law." At this moment, and for this minority, democracy would cease to exist.

Picture, by way of contrast, another ending to this conflict between majority demands and minority rights. Suppose the hand of the majority were stayed from action and the rights of the minority were upheld. At this moment, the minority would triumph over the demands of the majority, resulting in a situation of rule by the minority—presumably, and once again, the antithesis of democratic government.

Examples of this conflict of principles stud the history of our government; they include the sedition acts of 1798, the sedition and criminal-anarchy statutes passed both by Congress and several state legislatures during World War I, and the more recent anti-communist laws, which (among other things) make it a crime to advocate knowingly the overthrow of government by force or violence, or to aid any organization engaged in such advocacy.

Included in these examples of conflicting principles is the bundling off to concentration camps during World War II of some 112,000 Japanese of whom 70,000 were American citizens. These people were accused of no crime and were guilty of nothing other than the fact that their heritage constituted a supposed threat to the nation's wartime safety. Also included in the examples are the various acts of local majorities in our southern states whose total effect has been to deny Negroes access to the ballot box.

In each of these instances (and the list is merely illustrative, not exhaustive) majority demands have been pressed home and civil rights (minority rights) have been lost. And yet however one may disagree with these majority demands, it is difficult to deny that the problem the majority was attempting to solve was, in the majority's eyes, a crucial one. The survival of a nation, of a culture, a way of life, is the justification that threads these acts together, and those who side with the majority must realize that however justified, each of these acts buries democracy by burying its civil-rights principle.

Those who oppose the majority, however, are also in difficult straits, for they lay themselves open to a series of sharp challenges: Is majority rule that smothers civil rights never justified? If it is justified in instances involving the survival of the community, who is better qualified than the majority to define the steps necessary for that survival?

Is it better to "protect a right" or to lose the system? And, if the answer is, "lose the system," should not the majority be the judge of so momentous a question?

No easy answer can be given these questions, for any answer reveals that when majority-rule and civil rights conflict, one of democracy's basic principles must be elevated to a position of superiority over the other. Ideally, of course, the way to avoid this elevation is to prevent any clash between these principles. But sooner or later, given a truly significant issue, and given the disharmony of these principles, conflict is bound to arise.

Majoritarians vs. libertarians

To help our society thread its way through such conflict, a series of writers have dissected and sought solutions to this basic problem. In situations of conflict, one group of political theorists (the majoritarians) would have us abide by the wishes of the majority; for these writers generally argue that the ultimate function of a government is to solve society's problems and that in a democracy any resulting action must accord with the preferences of the majority. These writers recognize the importance of civil rights and they further recognize that the healthier the democracy, the greater its concern for those rights. But, say these writers, the majority must be supreme and the freedoms accorded the individual must be regarded not as rights that are immune from majority control, but rather as privileges that the majority bestows upon the members of the society, in order to further the goals of the society—as the majority defines those goals.

An opposing group (the libertarians) generally recognizes that in the history of democracy, determined majorities nearly always get their way. Such success, however, does not clothe majority action with moral correctness; for the defenders of civil rights argue that though the function of government is to act, the highest duty of democratic government is to preserve democracy. If necessary, non-action is preferable to government action, for democracy cannot be preserved when basic freedoms are suppressed. Moreover, if democracy is to be true to its principles, such freedoms must be regarded as rights and not as privileges that can be bestowed or destroyed by majority action.

But however much these writers divide on their solution, each camp links itself to our constitutional tradition, for the American constitutions, both federal and state, were created in large measure to solve this very problem of clashing democratic principles. What the constitution-framers did, in fact, was to recognize the necessity for majority rule; but in order to prevent that rule from smothering liberty and freedom, they weighted the scales of government in favor of civil rights. Basically, majorities were to be permitted to rule, but only after hurdling a series of barriers that afforded special protections for civil rights. By building these special protections into our constitutions, the framers hoped to solve the problem of clashing principles; and in so doing, they established civil rights as a basic fixture (an attribute) of our governmental system.

CIVIL RIGHTS AND THE AMERICAN CONSTITUTIONS

Although the forty-nine American constitutions are complex documents, their over-all purpose is fairly simple to define; for their basic goal is to place permanent limitations upon the powers of government. And, since government in the American system belongs to whatever majority can capture it, our constitutions may be defined as a system of permanent limitations upon majority action, a hobble affixed to majority rule.

Basically, these constitutions construct their network of limitations on two levels. On the first level, through outright prohibition, they attempt to place a great range of affairs forever beyond majority reach. For example, in the national constitution, state governments (that is, state majorities) are denied the power to raise armies, to lay and collect import duties, etc. More important to this discussion is the list of prohibitions upon the national government pertaining to civil rights: Congress shall pass no law abridging free speech, press, and so forth.

On the second level, the limitations upon majorities are not direct, but indirect; for the limitations placed upon majority rule are constructed out of the groups into which the constitutions divide the body politic. Through the twin principles of separation of power and check and balance, groups are set apart, and played off, each against the others. In order to catch hold of governmental power, these divided, separated groups must overcome their division and fuse into a majority. Such fusion generally involves caution, compromise, and bargaining between interested groups. As a result, majority-sway over contentious issues is made difficult, and in this fashion additional safeguards are built around such protected areas as civil rights. But to see more clearly these civil rights protections, it is now necessary to treat more fully these two levels of constitutional limitations.

Civil rights and constitutional prohibitions

Fortunately for the student of American politics, the broad pattern of both state and federal government is much the same. In part, this sameness arises out of the shared belief system of the American people, and in part this sameness can be traced to the similarity of the 49 American constitutions. Each constitution is built around the principle of separation of powers, and each constitution has a similar declaration of civil rights. Thus, for simplicity's sake, the following analysis will be drawn largely from the Federal Constitution.

In providing for civil rights, the 49 constitutions have sought to wall out the majority by building an injunctive fence around each of a series of liberties and freedoms. But where most state constitutions set their prohibitions upon majority action *within* the body of the constitution, the Federal Constitution is distinguished by the fact that most of its civil rights protections are contained in the *amendments* to the original document. One explanation for this placement is that the framers of the Constitution thought they were building a government of specified, enumerated powers; and since the Constitution did not authorize the central government to abridge civil rights, no further statement of protections for these rights were thought to be needed. Opposition to the omission of these protections was so great, however, that they were appended to the Constitution within two years of its ratification. This appended statement of civil rights comprises the first ten Amendments to the Constitution, the national government's Bill of Rights. In these ten Amendments, in four others (Thirteenth, Fourteenth, Fifteenth, and Nineteenth amendments), and in a few short sentences in the original document, are contained the basic constitutional prohibitions against an abridgement of civil rights.

These prohibitions group themselves into the categories of democracy's essential freedoms: freedom of thought and communication, equal access to the ballot box, and the freedoms gained through a rigidly defined code of justice. Basically, the Constitution's prohibitions take the form of a denial of power to the chief instrument of majority rule, Congress, constitutionally the architect of public policy. Thus, in the First Amendment, whose very priority is an indication of its essentiality, comes the denial to government of the power to make any law "respecting an establishment of religion, or prohibiting the free exercise thereof; or abridging the freedom of speech, or of the press, or the right of the people peaceably to assemble, and to petition the Government for a redress of grievances."

In the Fourth through the Eighth amendments come requirements for a system of justice. The Fourth Amendment forbids "unreasonable searches and seizures" and speaks of the "right of the people to be secure in their persons, house, papers and effects." The Fifth Amendment lays down the rights that shall be accorded those accused of crime: no call to trial without a prior indictment by a Grand Jury, no "double jeopardy," no denial of the traditional procedures of the law ("due process of law"), and no self-incrimination. The Sixth Amendment extends these rights to a "speedy and public trial, by an impartial jury" and gives the accused the right to know the charges being brought against him, the right to confront the witnesses against him, and the right to "a compulsory process for obtaining witnesses in his favor." The Seventh Amendment states that "Excessive bail shall not be required, nor excessive fines imposed, nor cruel and unusual punishments inflicted. "And the foregoing rights are augmented by two provisions in the original Constitution (Article III, Section 9) that forbid the suspension of the Writ of Habeas Corpus, except in circumstances of rebellion or invasion; and that forbid the legislature to take onto itself the powers and duties of a court, or to punish vengefully. ("No bill of attainder or ex post facto law shall be passed.")

In the Thirteenth, Fourteenth, Fifteenth, and Nineteenth amendments are stated constitutional injunctions against inequality: the Thirteenth Amendment abolishes slavery and other forms of peonage; the Fourteenth Amendment removes from states ("sectional majorities") the power to abridge citizenship or any of the "privileges and immunities of citizens of the United States," including the right to "life, liberty and property" and "equal protection of the laws"; the Fifteenth Amendment forbids any abridgement of voting rights on account of "race, color or previous condition of servitude"; and the Nineteenth Amendment rounds out these injunctions against inequality by extending the vote to women.

Thus, through these enjoinders, the Constitution attempts to keep from the majority the power to abridge democracy's essential freedoms.

Civil rights and the dilution of the majority

Although the American constitutions attempt to guarantee civil rights by wrapping majorities in a net of prohibitions, these guarantees are also reinforced by the structure of government that these constitutions create. In all 49 constitutions, the governmental process revolves around the principle of separation of powers. Governmental power is apportioned among the executive, legislative and judicial branches in order to guard against the possibility that any branch will take onto itself power of such magnitude as to become tyrannical. Concern for the possible tyranny of one branch of government is thus one purpose of separation of powers and its attendant principle of check and balance. A concern for the tyranny of the majority is a second such purpose; for as a result of separation of powers majority action is discouraged and made difficult. As a consequence, the likelihood is lessened that a majority will overstep the bounds of civil rights enumerated in the Constitution.

This relationship between separated powers and majority restraints proceeds in at least two ways. First, as a result of the separation of powers, the body politic is divided into a patchwork of electing bodies —constituencies—each of which has a representative who answers to the majority within that constituency. Thus, in the national government, the constituency of the President is the country as a whole. (Technically speaking, because of the electoral college, his constituency is a composite of 48 state-constituencies, and the majority to whom he must eventually answer is fused out of the majority within each state.) The people of his state are the constituency of each senator, and that of the representative a still smaller unit, the congressional district. Each of these constituencies, varying as it does in size, economic activity, traditions, party affiliation, and population characteristics, tends to demand different things of its representative. These demands, in fact, are made still more diffuse by the varying times in which they are put forward, for each "class" of representative seeks his mandate at a different calendar interval: the President every four years, the Senator every six years, and the Representative every two years. Thus, the Constitution breaks the society up into a series of separated and often competing "majorities." It permits not one majority, but only a patchwork of groups competing for political power.

Now the essential connection between the protection of civil rights and this atomization of power is simply this: For public policy to get made, representatives of these competing groups must fuse themselves into an effective whole. Enough of them must band together in common cause to constitute a majority, the requisite for a capture of governmental power. But for these representatives to weld themselves into a majority, they must compromise and mediate their conflicting demands and, in fact, search out the area of greatest common agreement. This area of greatest agreement is not always readily found, or, more precisely, it is generally found only by watering down a program of action, sometimes to a point of inoffensiveness. In this fashion, majority rule is blunted; and given the concern of a great part of our society for the rights spelled out in the Constitution, and given further their concern not to offend against these rights, a stout yoke is thus fastened upon any potential majority that seeks to destroy these rights.

Checks and balances

The force of the majority is yoked, however, by more than the creation of competing constituencies. For the constitutions (once again, through the device of separation of powers) do not permit any sort of *direct* majority rule on the part of the society's political representatives. That is, governmental policy is not created merely by forging a majority out of the total membership of the House, Senate, and the Presidency. (Fifty per cent plus one of 365, plus 96, plus one do not constitute a policy-making majority.) Instead, as is well known, senators, representatives, and the Presidency are grouped into fixed institutions; and for public policy to be made, a majority *within* each of these institutions must concur with a majority within each of the other two. (The President, so to speak, in himself constitutes a majority within his office.) And because each institution has its own traditions, its own outlook, and its own view of what is useful and wise for our society, the resulting inability of these institutions to agree readily upon a course of governmental action constitutes another check against encroachments upon civil rights. And should majorities within these institutions find an area of common agreement, there is still the Supreme Court to be reckoned with. For the constituency of the Court, like that of the President, is the nation as a whole. But unlike the President, its responsibility to the nation is not defined through elections, but (given the life tenure of the justices) through the conscience of the judge. Thus the power of the court to disallow legislation through judicial review constitutes still another check upon majority rule, and it takes its place as one of a series of institutional hurdles over which any encroachment of civil rights must pass.

To sum up, separation of powers—as a separation of constituencies and institutions—creates a series of barriers that stand between any majority and the abridgement of civil rights. In fashioning these barriers, our constitutions work to establish civil rights as an essential element of our governmental system. And thus, having reinforced the proposition that civil rights are an attribute of our governmental system, our discussion may now move to its second phase, that of viewing these rights as a *product* of that system. But before moving to this discussion, some last comments need to be made about the relative success of separation of powers and the consequences of that success for democratic government.

Separation of powers, to state the obvious, is no sure formula for the suppression of majority tyranny. One test of this proposition is the varying performance of this formula from the federal to the state governments and among the states themselves. For in viewing the incidence of affronts to civil rights in this country, it is difficult not to conclude that the traditional enemy of these rights has been, not the federal government, but the states. Witness the disabling and punitive statutes directed at Orientals by the Western states, the legal jostling of the Hispano in the Southwest, the treatment of evangelical religious sects in states such as West Virginia, and, of course, the treatment afforded Negroes in the South.

Majority tyranny that rests upon prejudice is a complex problem, not easily analyzed. But in terms of the present discussion, it seems significant to note first, the obvious conclusion that constitutional patterns have been incapable of blunting the thrusts of determined state majorities; and second, a suggestive hypothesis: that the creation, through separation of powers, of separated constituencies within the state governments does not create the same degree of check and balance as is found in the federal system, perhaps because such check and balance works best when the separated constituencies are marked by a wide measure of heterogeneity. Heterogeneity, in short, creates the competing demands that result in compromise and restraint. In the states, given their limited geographic area, heterogeneity does not exist so markedly as it does in the federal system. And, in fact, the states that are characterized by the majority tyranny referred to above may be the very ones that are generally the most homogeneous.

But if separation of powers seems to have given civil rights a surer protection on the level of the federal government, this same separation has also created grave problems for that government. To paraphrase Emerson, every gain has its debit side, and the need to search out an area of greatest agreement between representatives of competing constituencies often renders the federal government impotent to act in the face of pressing problems. Too much compromise produces not protection, but impotence. Moreover, the contrasting and rival constituencies of the President and Congressmen are one source of a fundamental antagonism between these two branches of government. Out of this antagonism comes a quarreling that is often crippling to the creation of governmental policy, and thus one of the questions being asked of the proponents of separation of powers in these recent, crisis-laden years, is whether protection for rights is not too great a price to pay, if that price is reckoned in rivalry and inaction rather than governmental policy.

A final perspective

This question, however, may be more rhetorical than sound, not only because it is unlikely that our society will ever scrap its basic design of government, but also because the question is too narrow of perspective. Separation of powers, it is true, aids in the protection of civil rights; but separation of powers purchases other benefits for our society as well: It helps infuse *wisdom* into majority rule, an infusion that is vital for any democratic society.

Earlier in this chapter, democracy was defined as a process of majority rule that seeks to accommodate civil rights; and our constitutional system (built upon separation of powers) has been viewed as a device for easing the tension that exists between these twin components. In larger perspective, however, democracy may also be viewed as a system that seeks to implant wisdom in the rule of the greatest number. Between these elements of wisdom and majority rule, there exists a tension similar to that described above; and once again, it is separation of powers that aids in easing this latter tension.

Briefly put, it is often argued that though democracy proceeds by majority rule, no guarantee exists that what the majority may want will result in wise or prudent policy. Indeed, common sense has it that truth is not necessarily found in numbers, that numerical might (a majority) does not make right. Every democracy is confronted with the problem of infusing wisdom into the rule of the majority, and it is at this problematic juncture that both civil rights and separation of powers may be built into our final calculus.

First, regarding the interplay between civil rights and majority wisdom, it might be noted that freedom of communication not only provides the channels by which new majorities may be formed, but it also affords society some measure of assurance that the new majority will have the benefit of a wide range of arguments and that, in the interchange and conflict of ideas, wisdom will have an opportunity to be heard. To use the celebrated metaphor of John Stuart Mill, freedom of speech creates a market place of ideas in which the society may freely choose the wisest and best ideas, so that ultimately good ideas may have full opportunity to banish unsound ones from the public domain. In these terms, and in harness with the basic proposition of this chapter, civil liberties become a necessary attribute of democracy's pursuit of wisdom.

But free speech and its attendant market place of ideas by themselves may not be sufficient to afford the wisdom necessary to majority rule. Further to assure this wisdom, democratic societies create for themselves legislative bodies that serve as the crucible from which majority demands may emerge as public policy. By providing a formal arena for discussion and debate and by removing the making of public policy from any direct show of hands in the body politic, the legislature functions not merely to mirror and reflect majority demands, but to reflect upon them in a way that will provide the broadest possible opportunity for wise counsel to prevail. And it is in this reflective process that separation of powers comes into play, for our constitutions (by dividing between the great branches of government the responsibility for creating public policy) create a system that maximizes the opportunities for conflict-laden discussion. In this division, the constitutions hold out the hope that wisdom will not only be heard, but also ultimately prevail.

Thus, to put this scattering of ideas into a final perspective, it may be said that civil rights not only keep open the remedial channels of democracy, but also that they help wise counsel to enter the stream of public demands. And separation of powers, by forcing extended discussion and political compromise, works not only to protect civil rights, but to safeguard political wisdom, including the portion of wisdom that restrains the majority from shortening democracy's civil rights dimension.

CIVIL RIGHTS AS A PRODUCT OF GOVERNMENT

Having examined civil rights in relation to the pattern of American constitutions, we turn now to a second important relationship, that between civil rights and the policy-making and policy-enforcing organs of government. Here, we view civil rights as a product of government, for the specific content of these rights is created by legislatures, courts and executive agencies (especially local police departments). Metaphorically speaking, the constitutions provide a foundation for civil rights, but the usable edifice of these rights is created by the political organs of government. Thus, what we do here is examine the ways in which the operating branches of government build civil rights upon constitutional foundations; more specifically, our concern is with three basic activities that shape civil rights: first, the ways in which government agencies attempt to give precise meaning to the general constitutional provisions for civil rights; second, the ways in which these agencies sometimes attempt to extend civil rights clearly beyond those provided for in a constitution; and third, the ways in which government agencies clothe with civil rights the individual members of our society.

Defining civil rights

Although nearly every constitution is constructed out of the most precise words available to its framers, every constitution, nevertheless, is a bundle of ambiguities. Words have a way of defying precision of meaning—more accurately put, men will differ in the meaning that they impute to words—and hence one of the most common characteristics of the American system of governments is a never ending debate over the meaning (and therefore, power) of the various provisions of the several constitutions.

For those who assign meaning to constitutions, the range of definitions is almost as broad as man's skill in manipulating words. Certain constitutional provisions, more than others, attract intense argument over meaning. Generally speaking, these are provisions that cut to the heart of the political process and affect the way in which the government is to be carried on or the control that government is to have over its citizenry. Debate upon such matters is sharp, for the groups that win such debate do more than read their own meaning into the constitution: They ultimately come to bend governmental power to their own ends.

As might be expected, civil rights fall within this category of the controversial provision, and to illustrate the range of definitions available to those who interpret constitutions—mainly, legislatures and courts—let us take the First Amendment to the national Constitution, which reads in part that Congress shall make no law abridging the freedom of speech. Here is forthright expression, and yet even to the casual reader certain difficulties of definition come forward. What things are included in the word speech, and what is meant by "abridging"? To take a simple example: Are the words used in radio broadcasting a form of speech? If so, may radio messages be sent without regulation? Logically, both these questions might be answered in the affirmative; but as Congress and the courts have defined speech, their definition has not included speech that is sent out over the airwaves. No man may build and operate a radio station without express governmental consent, and once that consent is given, he is severely restricted as to what he may say over the air. Thus, as Congress and the courts have dealt with radio broadcasting, they have defined one aspect of speech and one aspect of "abridgement"; accordingly, they have turned general constitutional language into a more precise statement of rights and privileges.

Broadly speaking, the opportunities for choice in defining constitutional terms proceed on two levels. On the first level exists the opportunity for expanding or contracting the coverage of constitutional words. Thus, in the radio illustration used above, Congress might have expanded the category of speech to include radio broadcasting. As it happened, Congress shrank the category to exclude that particular form of communication, and in so doing, was able to subject that communication to rigorous control. To take another example of categorical manipulation, what is meant by the federal Constitution's protection against "unreasonable searches and seizures"? Does a tape recording of a telephone conversation made without the speakers' knowledge constitute an unreasonable search and seizure? Should the recording be admitted as evidence in criminal prosecution? More than this (and here we move to another constitutional concept) would use of the recording constitute a situation in which the accused is being compelled to give testimony against himself?

For the most part, federal courts have expanded these categories of unreasonable search and seizure and evidence against oneself so as to preclude the use of "wire-tapped" evidence in criminal trials. But several state courts, interpreting similar terms in state constitutions, have defined these categories so as to exclude wiretapping from the roster of forbidden activity; accordingly, wire-tapped conversations are admitted as valid trial evidence.

Now, the second level of choice-through-definition is woven out of an American tradition of constitutional interpretation which holds that no provision of a constitution stands completely free. Any statement of a right or power must harmonize with other sections of a constitution. Thus, in legislating on radio transmission, Congress felt free to regulate to the point of extinction, because the federal Constitution also provides that Congress may regulate interstate commerce. By expanding its definition of commerce to include electronic transmission, Congress was thus able to regulate radio messages on grounds other than the privileges of speech. What occurred here was a bringing of two constitutional provisions (commerce and speech) into a kind of harmony. More pointedly, by expanding one category of constitutional provision, Congress was able to deflate a rival category.

In most instances of fixing meaning to civil rights the rivalry of categories is not so specific. All constitutions, either by direct statement or by implication (that is, by interpretation) require that the government provide for the safety, health, and welfare of its citizens. These provisions constitute categories of governmental power susceptible to the broadest sort expansion: For what, after all, may not be attempted in the interest of public safety? By regarding these categories as rivals of constitutional provisions for civil rights, and by expanding these categories, legislatures and courts have often squeezed to the wall and deflated the scope of civil rights. Through this process, for example, the right to free speech in wartime has been curtailed in the interests of national survival. Again, in the interests of public safety and morals, southern legislatures and courts have required the segregation of the races.

But the process of controlling civil rights through competing categories can also work in the other direction. Categories of public safety and morals have also been deflated to expand the scope of civil rights. In recent years, for example, the Supreme Court has been setting aside arguments that protection of public morals and safety require a segregation of races, and segregated schools have been declared to be a violation of the Fourteenth Amendment's requirement of equality before the law. The significance of competing categories is thus not that they inevitably curtail civil rights, but that in conjunction with defining constitutional terms, they afford vast discretion to the arms of government that decide upon the precise meaning and coverage of civil rights.

Thus, to sum up, constitutional provisions for the protection of civil rights are flasks into which legislatures and courts pour definitional content. In doing so, two further characteristics are given these rights. First, because of the legislative role in defining civil rights, these rights are affected by majority action within legislative bodies, and accordingly, they are tied back once again into the problem of majority-minority relations and the attendant problem of possible majority tyranny. Second, given the number of courts and legislatures in our federal system and given the principle of check and balance by which these bodies are often pitted one against the others, civil rights are in constant flux, always awaiting some newer legislation or court decision that will, for the moment, redefine those rights, and accordingly, tell the citizen the precise nature of his freedoms.

Extending civil rights

Although the greatest portion of civil rights is cut directly from constitutional cloth, another portion has come into existence out of *legislative* supplements to our constitutions. Constitutional provisions for civil rights, it will be recalled, are cast largely in the form of prohibitions upon government action. But there is generally thought to be no provision in any American constitution that prevents the legislature from extending the scope of liberty and freedom. Thus what has happened in this country, largely since the turn of the present century, is the growth of an additional body of guarantees, concerned mainly with the rights in the *social* and *economic* realms.

Some of these supplemental rights border, of course, upon the provision of the Fourteenth Amendment that no person be denied equal protection of the law nor any of the privileges and immunities of citizens of the United States. Acting upon these clauses, Congress has passed legislation designed to insure social equality in such matters as hotel accommodations, public conveyances, and so forth, regardless of race and color. For many years the Supreme Court refused to bring this legislation (the Civil Rights Acts of 1866 and 1875) to bear upon the actions of private persons, but beginning in the late 1940's the scope of this legislation has been expanded outward through judicial enforcement, especially in the direction of nonsegregated housing and public transportation.

An example of rights that are more clearly supplemental to the Constitution consists of the Fair Employment Practices Acts now in effect in several of the states. Under the terms of this legislation, employers, labor unions, and employment agencies are generally forbidden to discriminate against employees as regards race, creed or national origin.

Supplemental civil rights may be an inapt phrase for these outward extensions, for many persons regard them as requisites to the enjoyment of the more ordinary (politically oriented) civil rights: How may a man participate, such persons ask, in the process of politics, make meaningful decisions with his ballot, or even retain the legal counsel necessary for fullest trial protections if he can find no employment because of his race or social background? And again, of what use is political equality if a man be treated as a second-class citizen in the ordinary affairs of life? And finally, how free is free speech if those who hold unpopular views are punished for their ideas by finding the doors of employment closed?

But while our legislatures show an increasing concern for the creation of social and economic rights, legislation in this realm is filled with noteworthy difficulties. First, establishing rights in this realm constitutes a marked departure from the quality and style of the more ordinary civil rights. Those rights, it will be recalled, are established by throwing around the citizen a wall of protection against the government. Such civil rights are hence maintained by forbidding governmental action, but in this newer realm of rights, the protections are afforded the citizen against his *fellow citizens.* As opposed to the older style of rights, government here is not to be inactive; instead it must act in positive fashion. This positivistic feature in itself invokes caution on the part of legislatures, for positivistic government not only involves complex problems of enforcement, but also a problem as to whether freedom shall be used to nullify freedom.

What is meant by this last problem is simply this: Shall one man's freedom be guaranteed by foreclosing another man's freedom to act? Shall an employer lose his right to hire and fire whom he chooses in order to guarantee equal access to employment for all? Shall persons of one racial, religious, or ethnic group be forced to admit to their neighborhood persons with whom they do not desire to associate in order that all men may have equal access to opportunities for housing? Shall a man who professes disturbing ideas be forced upon unwilling co-workers in order that freedom of conscience be given its fullest extent?

These questions admit of no simple answer, for the issue of freedom, in some measure, lies on both sides of the argument. These questions do, however, point up an aspect of the accommodation between majority rule and civil rights that many critics of our society see as crucial: majority pressure that acts not through government, but through community sentiment. More than a half century ago, for example, Lord Bryce in his *The American Commonwealth* noted the presence in our society of what he termed the "fatalism of the multitude." By this term he designated so great an attachment to the principle of majority rule that the bulk of our society had become convinced that majority action is clothed with moral correctness and that, accordingly, it is useless (and perhaps improper) for the citizen to swim against the tide of community sentiment. This being so, the pressure for conformity weighs heavily upon the citizen, and even though he is guaranteed the right to speak freely without fear of government reprisal, he who does speak freely may find himself elbowed into silence by the pressures of a community that seeks conformity, not dissent.

Thus, the issue of supplemental civil rights catches very neatly this problem of the smothering blanket of conformity and community pressure; and whenever supplementary civil rights legislation has been enacted, we find the majority voting, in effect, to curb itself and offering various minority groups (social, racial, and intellectual) a reassurance of democracy's basic premises of equality and free communication.

Enforcing civil rights

Basically, the *enforcement* of civil rights is a transaction in the realities of political life. For no matter how broad the scope of legislative and court protections, these rights amount to nothing if officers of law enforcement are unwilling to act within the spirit of the law. When police are lax, when jurors are prejudiced, when prosecuting attorneys fear to protect the unpopular, the guarantees of civil rights are lost, for they are simply not enforceable.

Civil rights are created by the democratic society as a buffer that protects the citizen from the jostlings of his government and, to a degree, from the abuse of his fellow men. Paradoxically, enforcement of these rights rests with officers of that government; equally important, enforcement rests largely with *elected* officials, who by virtue of their office are especially sensitive to the currents of community pressure. Thus, the basic problem of civil rights enforcement is how shall respect for civil rights be forced upon those who, in turn, enforce these rights? As Seneca once asked: Who guards the guardians?

In some instances—when, for example, civil rights are lost through a failure to observe the requirements for a fair trial—a remedy may be found in the provisions our society has made for successive court appeals through successive levels of the judiciary. In other instances—when, for example, community prejudice conspires to deprive a racial or ethnic minority of its rights, say of voting—the remedy may be found by the lifting up of responsibility for the enforcement of civil rights to another level of government: By lifting this responsibility from county to state or from state to federal government, it is sometimes possible to dilute the prejudices of local government through the infusion of a larger, more distant, and hence, more dispassionate majority.

But in many instances of faulty civil rights enforcement, no such remedies are available. A police force that seeks to avoid the frustrations of careful crime detection by utilizing "third-degree" interrogations violates the guarantees of civil rights in a way that no subsequent court of appeals can ever overcome. A sheriff who abandons his prisoner to the brutality of a lynch mob violates the guarantees of a fair trial in a final, irreparable act. A police officer who yanks a nettlesome speaker from his soapbox, rather than defending his right to speak, may some day let him return to his rostrum: by that time, however, the occasion for speaking may have slipped by and nothing will serve to right that particular wrong.

Basically, the enforcement of civil rights is a transaction between the individual citizen and the officers of his government. In this transaction the citizen either stands alone and is, therefore, relatively helpless, or he stands with the force of community sentiment behind him. Such sentiment is never easily marshalled; most often, it is never forthcoming. The gathering of such sentiment depends upon the seriousness with which the citizenry takes its democratic obligations; for in the ideal democracy, the rights of one man are the concern of the entire society. Where civil rights are at issue, no man should stand alone. As Jefferson might have phrased it, eternal vigilance is the price of civil rights.

CIVIL RIGHTS IN TRANSITION

Thus far, we have strung our lines of inquiry so as to capture some idea of the forces that mold civil rights and some idea of the general pattern of these rights. But general patterns by themselves cannot fully convey the dynamics of civil rights formation, nor can they indicate the directions in which these rights are now being carried. Therefore, as a final task we will canvass two of the most important issues of present-day civil rights: the reconciliation of the fourteenth and fifteenth amendments with the treatment afforded Negroes in the South, and the confronting of free speech with the requirements of national security.

The issue of racial equality

With the possible exception of the American Indian, no group in this country has suffered more at the hands of the majority than the Negro. Despite the requirements of the Fifteenth Amendment that race constitutes no bar to suffrage and despite the requirements of the Fourteenth Amendment that no state deprive any citizen of due process of law or equal protection of the law, the American Negro has enjoyed far less than a full measure of basic civil rights. He has been forced to live in segregated housing in nearly all areas of the United States, but his deprivations have been especially acute in the South. There, he has been forced to attend segregated schools, ride segregated conveyances, use segregated facilities in public buildings, and more, he has been denied both access to the ballot box and the full guarantees of fair trial.

As little as three decades ago the Negro seemed frozen in his status as a "second-class citizen," and the lack of civil rights that attended that status was a source of despair both to the Negro and to all who took seriously democracy's basic premise of equality. But even during this period of discouragement, beneath the surface of events, there were forces at work that were eventually to thaw the civil rights glacier. For one thing, the increasing migrations of Negroes to the North, following the industrial demands of World War I, made the Negro an important element in northern politics, and set his congressional representatives to demanding federal intervention in behalf of civil rights. For another thing, the increasing concentration of Negroes in the great northern cities, coupled with the importance of those cities to presidential elections, has made the "Negro vote" an important factor in presidential politics and has worked to make the presidential office especially sensitive to Negro demands. For a third thing, the growing power of labor unions, accompanied by an increasing Negro membership in many of those unions—as for example, the United Auto Workers—has given the Negroes an important set of non-Negro, pressure group spokesmen. And fourth, an era of economic prosperity has enabled the Negro to divert an increasing portion of his earnings in support of pressure groups directly concerned with his welfare. The National Association for the Advancement of Colored People (NAACP) is one such organization, and among its many activities has been the underwriting of litigation designed to force the courts into reconsidering their approval of such state laws as those which require segregated schools and segregation of passengers in public conveyances.

Challenging the constitutional validity of such laws is generally a costly process. To carry a case through successive judicial levels until at last the Supreme Court is reached requires that lawyers be hired, that witnesses be found, that court reporters be retained and that legal briefs be printed. Successful litigation is expensive, and especially so if it is part of a program of recurring challenges to the validity of not one law but a whole series of laws in each of several states. Litigation of widespread proportions has been one of the programs of the NAACP, and as its membership and its treasury have swelled, its courtroom activities have likewise increased.

But parties, pressure groups, and litigation are not the only factors working to thaw the glacial barriers to Negro rights. This country's struggle against totalitarianism in World War II and the Korean War and our clash with international communism after each of these wars have made our society increasingly conscious of democracy's basic precepts. Reacting to this awareness, a growing sector of the citizenry has found it increasingly difficult to reconcile the treatment afforded Negroes with the second paragraph of the Declaration of Independence.

Thus, even before the end of World War II, the tides of change were running. In 1941 President Roosevelt, by virtue of his wartime-emergency powers, ordered all federal agencies to include in their war-production contracts a requirement forbidding discrimination against persons of any race, color, or creed in the matter of employment; and even though Congress refused to enact this requirement into peacetime law, several of the states carried forward this wartime policy and enacted the Fair Employment Practices legislation referred to earlier in this chapter. In 1946 the Supreme Court ordered an end to segregation on motor-vehicle carriers moving in interstate commerce, and in 1950 the court forbade the railroads to segregate dining accommodations on interstate trains.[2] In 1948 President Truman took the first of a series of steps designed to end segregation in the armed forces, and in that same year the Supreme Court declared illegal and non-enforceable all real-estate contracts designed to prevent Negroes from acquiring property in so-called restricted (for example, all-white) communities.[3]

[2] *Morgan* v. *Virginia,* 328 U.S. 373, and *Henderson* v. *United States,* 339 U.S. 816.
[3] *Shelley* v. *Kramer,* 334 U.S. 1.

Still other examples might be cited of this changing pattern of civil rights, but because the most dramatic of these changes are in the areas of segregated schools and equal access to the ballot, it is to these that we now turn.

The demise of segregated education

Although the school segregation issue may be reduced to a single question, packed within that question are nearly all of civil rights' many dimensions. Basically, this issue asks whether it is constitutionally valid that Negro and white children be required to attend separate public schools. But within this question come such issues as formed our earlier discussion: the potential disharmony between majority rule and civil rights; the utility of constitutional limitations; the possibility that the federal government, reflecting larger majorities, may dilute the tyranny of local majorities; and the need to pour definitional content into constitutional clauses. In these terms, the segregation issue is macrocosmic, and to see its several dimensions, some historic perspective is now necessary.

The Fourteenth Amendment, it will be recalled, requires (among other things) that no state shall deprive any citizen of the equal protection of the laws nor any of the privileges and immunities belonging to a citizen of the United States. Adopted in 1868, this amendment was designed to afford the newly freed Negro a legal status equal to that of white citizens, but despite the wording and intent of the Amendment, the states of the South later put upon their statute books laws requiring a segregation of races in places of public gathering, in public conveyances, and most important for this discussion, in the public schools.[4]

For about 50 years, the validity of these statutes—particularly as they applied to school segregation—was upheld by the United States

[4] "The South" is a geographic, political, and social term, not a legal one. As such, it does not have precise meaning, but is often spoken of as "a state of mind" common to those states that are marked by allegiance to the Democratic party, a discriminatory treatment of the Negro, and a high concentration of Negroes whose presence makes especially acute the problems arising out of such discrimination.

Here, we use the term "Solid South" to include the 11 states that seceded from the Union to form the Confederacy: Alabama, Arkansas, Florida, Georgia, Louisiana, Mississippi, North Carolina, South Carolina, Tennessee, Texas, and Virginia. More generally speaking, the South also includes the "border states" of Kentucky, Oklahoma, Missouri, Maryland, and Delaware.

On this problem of definition see V. O. Key, Jr., *Southern Politics* (New York: Alfred A. Knopf, 1950), chap. 1; and Austin Ranney and Willmoore Kendall, *Democracy and the American Party System* (New York: Harcourt, Brace, and Co., Inc., 1956), chap. 8.

Supreme Court, following a line of reasoning made famous in the case of Plessy v. Ferguson, (1896).[5] In that case, the issue turned around the legality of enforcing segregated railroad accommodations upon Negro and white passengers and the Supreme Court decided that a separation of races did not violate the requirements of the Fourteenth Amendment if *equal accommodations* were provided for both races. "Separate but equal" thus became the judicial formula that put the stamp of constitutionality upon segregation, and it was not until late in the 1930's, in the instance of school segregation, that this formula was successfully challenged.

In 1938, the State of Missouri, having no law school for Negroes, and having rejected a Negro's application for admission to the law school of the state university, offered to pay the applicant's expenses at any of the law schools in neighboring states that were open to Negroes. But the rejected applicant, not satisfied at going elsewhere for legal training, appealed to the Supreme Court to force his admission to the University of Missouri. The Supreme Court accepted the applicant's argument that the doctrine of separate but equal facilities was violated by Missouri's failure to provide a law school for Negroes, and the Court went on to say that the state's offer to send the student elsewhere did not overcome this violation. In this case, the "separate but equal" formula was held to be constitutional, but under the terms of the Court's ruling, the student could not be "separated" beyond the borders of the state. The Court had thus begun the first of a long series of steps leading to the contraction of a constitutional category.[6]

Then, in 1950 came another important case also dealing with separated legal education. In *Sweatt* v. *Painter,* the Supreme Court refused to admit that a newly established law school for Negroes could satisfy the demands of the equal protection clause.[7] Sweatt had come before the Court asking that the State of Texas be forced to admit him to the University of Texas Law School. Prior to appealing to the Supreme Court, he had petitioned the courts of Texas to enter him at the University of Texas but the answer of Texas judiciary had been to require the state to establish a law school for Negroes inasmuch as none was then in existence. Sweatt, however, refused to enter the newly-created school, claiming that its establishment had created separation *without* equality, inasmuch as the Negro law school was a small college with few faculty and a minimal library, in contrast to the law school of the

[5] 163 U.S. 537.
[6] *Missouri ex. rel. Gains* v. *Canada,* 305 U.S. 337.
[7] 339 U.S. 629.

state university which was built around an excellent library and a faculty of renown.

The members of the Supreme Court, as lawyers and former law teachers themselves, accepted the merits of Sweatt's argument and stressed the idea that the quality of legal training is determined not merely by courses of instruction, but by such intangible factors as a university's intellectual climate, its traditions, prestige, and the social status of its alumni. Segregation in the law schools of Texas was thus declared to be a violation of the equal protection clause of the Fourteenth Amendment and in handing down this decision, the Supreme Court served notice that it had begun to look at the *realities* that lay behind the "separate but equal" doctrine.

On the same day as the Sweatt case was decided, came another inquiry into these realities. In *McLaurin* v. *Oklahoma,* the Court decided that education equality was violated in the instance of a Negro graduate student, newly admitted to the University of Oklahoma, who was forced to sit in a special section in his classroom, use a segregated desk in the library, and eat at a special table in the university dining hall. These restrictions, said the Court, impaired the student's "ability to study, to engage in discussions and exchange views with other students," and generally handicapped him in his pursuit of education. As a result, said the Court, his educational opportunities were separated from, but hardly equal to those afforded white students.[8]

In the three cases cited above, the Supreme Court had looked at segregated education on the college level and had found it wanting in equality, but the Court had not as yet disturbed segregation in the *primary* and *secondary public school* systems. However, the pattern of the Court's approach to segregation was becoming increasingly clear, and for many southerners the consequences were profoundly disturbing. In the words of many southern leaders, racial segregation of the young was so completely the basis of the South's social structure that they were prepared to defend this segregation by force if necessary.

But the Supreme Court, if it heard these angry words, did not depart from its pattern of subjecting segregation to an ever closer scrutiny, and in 1954 the capstone of this pattern was firmly set in place: For in that year the Court handed down a decision, declaring primary and secondary school segregation to be a violation of the Fourteenth

[8] *McLaurin* v. *Oklahoma State Regents,* 339 U.S. 637.

Amendment; and in so declaring, the Court ordered an end to segregation in public schools.[9]

To arrive at its decision, the Court chose to go once again behind the existence of two school systems (one for Negroes and one for whites) to inquire into the effects of segregation upon the learning process. In looking to these effects, the Court took its lead from a carefully prepared brief drawn up by lawyers for the NAACP. In that brief were set down sociological and psychological evidence as to the effects of segregation upon learning and social adjustment; and stress was placed upon the psychic sufferings of Negro children who were forced by segregation to wear the badges of a "second-class citizenship." School segregation, this brief argued, by its very nature creates a condition of inequality, and in so doing, violates the meaning and intent of the Fourteenth Amendment.

With these arguments the Supreme Court concurred; and it placed in the hands of the various federal district judges responsibility for enforcing desegregation (for example, integration) upon the school systems of the several states.

By 1957 desegregation had taken place quite readily in those states just north of the Mason-Dixon line (in school districts of Southern Illinois, for example). The northern tier of southern states had also accomplished desegregation largely without untoward incident, but in some parts of the deeper South desegregation met with outraged protest and open violence. In South Carolina, for example, the governor and state legislature talked of closing down the state's school system rather than submit it to desegregation. In several communities in the South, school officials delayed integration because of threatened violence, and in still other communities, violence flared openly as Negro students, seeking to enter previously all-white schools, were stoned and pushed aside.

Thus far, the integration of southern schools is still far from completed, and many southerners remain deeply convinced that commingling of races is morally wrong. But despite the force of southern sentiment and the anti-segregation strategies that have been adopted in many communities, segregation is under heavy siege. Opponents of segregation are busy seeking court relief in scores of communities in the South; and following an outright defiance of federal court orders in Little Rock, Arkansas, the federal government ordered troops to a

[9] *Brown* v. *Board of Education,* 347 U.S. 483, and *Bolling* v. *Sharp,* 347 U.S. 497.

newly-integrated high school to quell disorder and to protect Negro students who sought to enter there. The presence of the army in Little Rock, dispatched to that spot by President Eisenhower, served notice that the powers of the President and the force of the federal government stand behind the decisions of federal courts. Thus supported, it seems that desegregated education will come eventually to the South. The question in the minds of most observers, however, is: With what speed?

EXTENDING NEGRO SUFFRAGE

Much like the issues of segregation, the problem of Negro suffrage has revolved largely around the Constitution's Civil War amendments and the attempts of the southern states to thwart those amendments. Legal and extra-legal barriers have long blocked the path of Negro voting, and it is only in recent years that the federal government, through courts and Congress, has made serious attempts to haul the barricades down. Negro suffrage, in fact, is almost a twice-told tale; for as we shall presently see, the drama of Negro voting has unfolded in a fashion similar to that of segregation.

Suffrage and the courts

In the aftermath of the Civil War, with control of Congress firmly in the hands of abolitionist and anti-southern groups, the national legislature in 1870 and 1871 passed a series of laws designed to ensure Negro suffrage, by placing congressional elections directly under federal supervision and by providing severe penalties for any persons found guilty of intimidating or using force against any voter. On the surface, these laws would appear to have been constitutional inasmuch as the fourteenth and fifteenth amendments provide Congress with the power to enforce the rights of citizenship "by appropriate legislation," while the Fifteenth Amendment directly states that "The right of citizens . . . to vote shall not be denied or abridged . . . by any state on account of race, color, or previous condition of servitude." But the Supreme Court, in *United States* v. *Reese* (1876) and in *United States* v. *Harris* (1883), destroyed the force of the congressional voting acts by declaring (1) that neither the Fourteenth nor the Fifteenth Amendment was designed to take from the states their control over elections, and (2) that these amendments forbade only state action, not the action of private individuals such as those who might bar the Negro from approaching the polling place.[10]

With these decisions, control over elections was returned to state hands, but seemingly on condition that the state governments take no discriminatory action against the Negro voter. Negroes, of course, might be kept from the polls by mob action (for the Court forbade only *state* interference with voting, not interference by private individuals) but neither violence nor public disorder was to the liking of most southerners. As a consequence, they began a search for legal devices that would bar the Negro from voting but remain, at the same time, within the Court's admonition that the *state governments* practice no discrimination. Eventually, three such devices were found, and they were adopted almost universally by the eleven states constituting the former Confederacy, and in part by several of the states bordering the "Solid South."

Voting barriers

The poll tax. The first of these devices, the poll tax, has required the payment of an individual voting fee (generally one or two dollars per year) as a prerequisite for admission to the voting rolls. To cloak this tax with constitutionality and thus smuggle it past the courts, it has been made applicable to whites and Negroes alike. The logic of the tax has it, however, that it will discourage the poorer citizen from voting, and given the greater incidence of poverty among Negroes, it will cut most heavily against that race. Logic and practice, however, do not always go hand in hand, for as the Negro has been disenfranchised by other devices, the poll tax has fallen upon those who do succeed in voting—the white citizenry. As a consequence of this, several of the states once using the poll tax have repealed it, and other states show signs of following suit.

The literacy test. The second of these devices for disenfranchising the Negro also cuts both ways—at least in the logic required to obtain court approval. In principle, the literacy test is no more than a device for assuring that those who participate in the elective process can understand the purpose and importance of their vote. Under the terms of such tests the prospective voter is generally required to give to voting officials evidence of his capacity to read and write and understand the general terms of his state's constitution. In principle, the literacy test should cut against the illiterate voter, both Negro and white. But

[10] 924 U.S. 214, and 106 U.S. 629.

in practice, the test has been rarely applied to whites, whereas the standards of literacy applied to Negroes have been such that few, no matter how well educated, have been able to pass these tests. As one careful student of southern politics has phrased it: "No matter from what direction one looks at it, the southern literacy test is a fraud and nothing more." [11]

But where the poll tax and literacy test have remained largely immune from judicial interference, the third of these devices, the *white primary,* has not. And so important has this device been for disenfranchising the Negro, that its disallowance by the Supreme Court in 1944 is marked as another of the turning points in the extension of Negro civil rights.

Briefly put, the significance of the white primary lies in the fact that the politics of the deeper South have been one-party politics. Partly out of resentment against the Republican party which prosecuted the Civil War against the South and governed it in the Reconstruction era, the South, since those times, has been firmly committed to the Democratic party. As a result of the citizenry's allegiance to this party, nearly all who secure its nomination for office are assured of being elected to that office in the general elections. With election thus assured to the Democratic party's nominees, the truly important political contests in the South have been those that choose the various candidates to be the party's standard bearers in the general elections. In short, *effective* political participation is confined to the primary elections within the Democratic party, and to keep the Negro from that participation it has been necessary only to exclude him from participation in the primaries.

End of the white primary?

As might be expected, the course of the white primary has left a great deal of litigation in its wake. In the 1920's and 1930's these elections were given Supreme Court sanction on the grounds that the choice of party candidates was not an election within the *meaning* of the Fourteenth and Fifteenth Amendments. Briefly put, the argument accepted by the Court was that political parties were *private* associations and not agents of the state. As such, elections *within* parties (as opposed to elections between parties) involved no state action, and any resulting racial discrimination did not, therefore, violate the terms of the

[11] V. O. Key, Jr., *op. cit.,* p. 576.

suffrage amendments, which spoke not of private discrimination but only of discrimination by the state government.

But in the 1940's, following its general pattern of looking into the realities of Negro rights, the Supreme Court came to recognize that primary elections were tantamount to ultimate elections, and thus part of the general election machinery of the states. In 1944, in the case of *Smith v. Allwright,* the Supreme Court declared that the choosing of party candidates, whether by primary elections or by party convention was part of the state-controlled election process.[12] As such, it lay within the meaning of the suffrage amendments and could not, therefore, be closed to Negro voters.

With the outlawing of the white primary, the South's chief bastion against Negro suffrage has been destroyed; and several sections of the South are now moving to other mechanisms of defense, including the arbitrary operation of the literacy test, intimidation of Negroes seeking to vote, and an outright denial of Negro petitions for voter's registration.[13] But in holding the color line of suffrage, the South must henceforth contend with Congress and the President as well as the federal courts, for in 1957 Congress passed a law designed to throw a greater degree of federal power behind the drive for Negro suffrage. As a result, the South may now be standing upon the threshold of a changed political system.

The Civil Rights Act of 1957

Although the Act of 1957 marks the first civil rights legislation to have passed Congress in 85 years, the stage has been set for this legislation for more than a decade. In 1946 President Truman appointed a Committee on Civil Rights, which spent a year inquiring into the condition of civil rights in the United States.[14] Following the Committee's recommendations, the President in 1948 sent a special message to Congress, urging upon that body the passage of legislation that would outlaw the poll tax as a franchise requirement in federal elections; extend federal protections against lynching; and establish a na-

[12] 321 U.S. 649.

[13] The Supreme Court has recently shown increased concern for the realities behind the literacy test. In 1949, for example, it put the stamp of illegality on an amendment to the Alabama Constitution that placed unlimited discretion in the hands of local officials for purposes of determining the literacy of voter registrants; *Schnell* v. *Davis,* 336 U.S. 933.

[14] The Report of the President's Committee, *To Secure These Rights* (Washington, D.C.: U.S. Government Printing Office, 1947).

tional Fair Employment Practices Commission endowed with enforcement powers.

But for all the debate that attended the President's message, the resulting bill was doomed to failure: in part, because of the threat of a southern filibuster in the Senate; in part, because of the fear of many Democrats that a determined effort to force civil rights upon the South would smash the Democratic party; and in part, because of the fear in many quarters that a forced civil rights bill might make worse, rather than better, race relations in the South. The failure of the bill, however, could not erase the publicity that surrounded it, and the pledges made by the bill's supporters in behalf of civil rights were transferred out of Congress into the arena of national politics. In both the 1952 and 1956 presidential campaigns, both parties included in their platforms a pledge to strengthen civil rights; and the 1957 legislation represents, at least in part, a redemption of those pledges.

Briefly put, the 1957 legislation provides for four things. (1) It creates a permanent Civil Rights Commission, charged with investigating civil rights abuses and with suggesting to Congress remedial legislation for those abuses. (2) The act creates within the Justice Department a special civil rights division, whose lawyers are charged with seeking court protection for persons whose rights have been abridged. (3) The law expressly forbids interference with or denial of the voting rights of persons legally qualified to vote in any election (both general or primary) involving the selection of federal officials. And (4) the act bestows upon federal judges the power to enforce suffrage rights through the use of restraining orders (injunctions), fines, and jail sentences.

It is this last provision especially that constitutes the vital center of the law, for under this provision it is expected that federal judges will have at their disposal power to force Negro suffrage upon recalcitrant election officials and to punish those who seek to bar the path to the polls. In past times, for example, Negroes seeking to vote have been turned away from registration and voting booths on the excuse that the proper forms had been lost, that the hours of voting (or registration) had been changed, or that the election officials had been called suddenly away. In other instances, Negroes have simply found the doors to places of election blocked by a wedge of determined whites. But under the new law, Negroes who have been unable to penetrate the procedures of registration may appeal to a federal judge to force that registration, and under the broad sweep of court order, the judge might very well require that election officials bring their records to court and perform the act of registration right in the court. Moreover, should any person suspect that the election door will be barred to him at some future date, he may seek from the court a restraining order that makes liable to punishment for *contempt of court* any person subsequently barring his vote.[15]

As is usual with any piece of major legislation, this law represents a compromise on many sides, but here, the greatest compromise has been between the northern Congressmen and their opponents from the South. Given the South's previous intransigence on civil rights legislation, and given the power bestowed on the South by the filibuster threat, its yielding in 1957 raises an intriguing question: How did the bill survive? The answer, in part, may lie in the threat offered by northern senators of both parties to move for the abolition of those rules that make the filibuster possible, thus stripping the South of its protections against future legislation, and in part the answer may lie in the fact that some southern Congressmen as Democrats may have wished to aid their party colleagues from the North in wooing the Negro vote. When the Democrats are a majority in Congress, southern Congressmen, by virtue of seniority, take over a large share of committee chairmanships. But in order for the Democratic party to gain that majority, the party's northern wing must capture a sizable portion of the northern Negro vote. Thus, southern Congressmen may have been willing to see a civil rights bill pass Congress, to help assure their party's future control over Congress.

It is, of course, still too early to measure the results of the 1957 Act, but if it does succeed in extending Negro suffrage in the South, the law will have telling effects upon the entire pattern of civil rights in that section of the country. For as the Negro gains the vote, officeholders will be forced to compete for his support. And in seeking that support, they will be forced to promise the Negro whatever it is that government can do to improve his status. Thus, if this pattern of prediction is borne out in fact, the Act of 1957 will have unleashed in the South a powerfully explosive force. At this moment, however, we can only await the first "shock waves."

[15] Technically speaking, the 1957 Act only supplements post Civil War laws that are still on the statute books (see Title 8, U.S. Code). The suffrage requirements of those laws, however, were largely nullified by judicial interpretation and by congressional failure to provide sufficient appropriations for Justice Department activities in behalf of civil rights enforcement. The new legislation implies a congressional commitment to increased appropriations, and the wording of the law, coupled with a rights-conscious Supreme Court, gives promise of a more effective enforcement.

NATIONAL SECURITY AND THE FIRST AMENDMENT

In the issues that center on national security, we come again to a problem of familiar dimensions. Basically, the problem springs from majority determination to protect our government from communist subversion even if the price of protection be an undercutting of democracy's requirement of free speech and conscience. Where the ultimate principles of democracy might require (in the words of Oliver Wendell Holmes) that we protect even those "opinions that we loathe and believe to be fraught with death," we have stopped short of ultimate principles and have chosen, instead, to deny free speech to those who would carry us into communism. In the recurring tension between majority rule and civil rights, the majority here has won.

But to state the problem so baldly is to strip it of the complexities and justification that have determined the course of majority action. For one thing, those who advocate communism are no ordinary political minority who, having once achieved control of government, would be content to be *displaced* by a succeeding political majority. With the accession of communists to power, the remedial processes of democracy might be forever closed. And for another thing, the speech that the majority now seeks to suppress is no ordinary political advocacy: strong evidence supports the fact that communist groups intermingle ordinary political agitation with plans to overthrow the government by force and violence. Thus, the choice for government has been a hard one, and because a majority in Congress has not thought it possible to reconcile the demands of unfettered speech with those of national security, Congress has opted for security.

Congress and national security

Briefly, the most important federal legislation upon this subject is contained in three laws. The first of these is the Smith Act of 1940 which forbids any person to advocate the violent overthrow of the government, to organize or be associated with any group having that intent, or to teach or encourage such violence. The second of these laws is the Internal Security Act of 1950 (the McCarran Act) which provides, among other things: fine and punishment for anyone who contributes substantially to the "establishment within the United States of a totalitarian dictatorship, the direction and control of which is to be vested in . . . any foreign government, foreign organization, or foreign individual." And beyond these provisions, the McCarran Act attempts to cripple communist activity generally by forbidding communists to secure passports, to work in defense plants, or to hold non-elective federal offices, and by further requiring every communist organization to register with the Attorney General and to reveal to his office the names of all members and the source and disposition of the organization's finances.

And third, the Communist Control Act of 1954 declares the Communist Party of the United States to constitute a "conspiracy to overthrow the government of the United States" and that "its role as the agency of a hostile power" makes it a danger to the security of the United States. Accordingly, the Act denies to the Communist Party all of the rights and privileges generally possessed by political parties under federal and state law. And beyond this, the Act declares any willful or knowing member of that party to be subject to the punishments and penalties of the McCarran Act.

From the language of these laws, it is clear that their basic purpose is not that of punishing sabotage, espionage, or an armed uprising against the government. Such acts are clearly within the category of the criminal endeavor and Congress has provided other laws for their suppression. Instead, the three laws cited above are concerned first, with preventing the accession of communists to political office even through ordinary, legal channels (for example, elections), and second, these laws seek to crush communist activity in general, on the grounds that such activity can lay the basis of later acts of violence, sabotage, and espionage. The argument here is that in an age of atomic warfare, for government to wait until the first blows are struck before bringing the offenders to justice is openly to invite disaster. Thus, these laws look more to the prevention of communist successes than to punishment for achieved success. But in seeking these goals, they have crowded the requirements of the First Amendment.

The place of the First Amendment

The First Amendment, it will be recalled, requires among other things that Congress shall make no law "abridging the freedom of speech, or of the press, or the right of the people peaceably to assemble, and to petition the Government for a redress of grievances." But under the terms of these anti-subversion laws, communist groups are forbidden such peaceful assembly; moreover, by outlawing the communists as a political party, their right to petition for redress of grievances is also abridged; and further, by making a crime out of the *advocacy* and *teaching* of communist doctrines (such as those that call for over-throw of government) these laws have spelled an end to free-speech in certain areas of discussion.

Taken as a group, these laws do not rest easily among the liberties of the First Amendment, but to understand their present relationship to that amendment, it is necessary to recall the object of an earlier discussion, namely: that few, if any, of the Constitution's clauses are self-defining; and that, as a consequence, constitutional requirements are in a state of constant transition, evolving in accordance with the meanings poured into that document by the political and judicial organs of government. Accordingly, as Congress has come to apply the First Amendment to the treatment accorded communist groups, the congressional position, broadly put, is that liberties are never abso-lute, that free speech and freedom of political association are always subject to governmental control in the interests of a secure and orderly society, and that the communist presence requires precisely such con-trol.

Thus, to reduce the communist threat, Congress has deflated certain of the First Amendment's liberties, and though there are few who would question the need for suppressing communism, there are many who rest uneasy at the thought of defining to the point of extinction any aspect either of free speech or freedom of political association.

Security and the Supreme Court

Congress, of course, does not bear sole responsibility for giving mean-ing to the Constitution. The definitional process is also the responsi-bility of both the President and the courts, and the Supreme Court, especially, is the linchpin in this endeavor. Like Congress and the President, the Court has its own bag of formulae for defining the Con-stitution and for testing statutes against the requirements of that docu-ment. But in many ways, it is the Court that is the chief conveyor of changing meaning, for in each successive piece of litigation, the Court has an opportunity not only to redefine the Constitution, but to deter-mine the meaning (and scope) of the relevant congressional statutes. As a result, even though Congress has defined (and constricted) First Amendment liberties as they apply to communist action, the Supreme Court has begun a definitional spiral of its own: first following the congressional pattern; more recently moving away from it.

When the appeal of 11 communist leaders, convicted under the Smith Act, came before the Court in 1951 (*Dennis* v. *United States*), the Court agreed with Congress that freedom of speech and association were never so absolute as to be exempt from regulation.[16] Our society, said the Court, is confronted with "an apparatus designed and dedicated to the overthrow of the government, in the context of world crisis after crisis." In the face of such grave and probable danger, speech is permissibly constricted, and accordingly, the Court upheld the conviction of the communist leaders and sustained the constitutionality of the Smith Act as well.

But in making these decisions, the Court aroused criticism, both inside the judicial chambers and out. Justice Frankfurter, although supporting the Court's majority, warned that "in sustaining the conviction before us we can hardly escape restriction on the interchange of ideas . . . without open minds there can be no open society." And Justice Black, dissenting from the majority, labelled the Smith Act "unconstitutional on its face," and the conviction "a virulent form of prior censorship of speech and press which . . . the First Amendment forbids."

And outside the Court as well there was criticism of the formula that had been used to sustain both the conviction and the Smith Act. Prior to this case, the Clear and Present Danger Rule had long been regarded as a bulwark in the cause of free speech. This phrase (coined by Mr. Justice Holmes in Schenk v. United States, 1919) admits that speech is never absolutely free, but seeks to determine the need for curtailing speech by proposing that it may be fettered only when words "are of such a nature as to create a clear and present danger that they will bring about . . . substantive evils." [17] And in an extension at the hands of Mr. Justice Brandeis (Whitney v. California, 1927) the Rule was said to require that "no danger flowing from speech can be deemed clear and present unless the incidence of the evil is so imminent that it may befall before there is opportunity for full discussion." [18] Thus, as employed by Holmes and Brandeis, the Clear and Present Danger Rule required that danger or evil be imminent, that cause and effect be clearly seen before speech could be curtailed.

But in the Dennis case, the Court was no longer concerned with clear and present danger. The communist leaders, in fact, had not been indicted on a charge of actually conspiring to overthrow the gov-

[16] 341 U.S. 494.
[17] 249 U.S. 47.
[18] 247 U.S. 357.

ernment by force or violence, but merely on a charge that they had conspired to form groups advocating such overthrow and had conspired to form groups that taught this same overthrow. In these terms, the test of clear and present danger did not apply to their actions; therefore, in sustaining their conviction the Court invoked another formula, that of grave and probable danger. Technically speaking, the Court continued to invoke the clear and present danger formula, expanding it however, so that its meaning became practically coterminus with that of grave and probable danger. To understand this expansion, the reader must further understand that courts often inflate and deflate the formulae used in interpreting constitutional passages, in much the same fashion as constitutional categories themselves are expanded and contracted. As a test of speech that may be restrained, the grave and probable danger formula is far looser than a test of clear and present danger, for under the Grave Danger Rule, speech may be forbidden even though its effects are beyond the horizon. As a result, there were many critics in 1951 who felt that the Court had collapsed the First Amendment beyond the point called for by the communist threat.

But change and adjustment are the hallmarks of the Supreme Court's operation. New justices bring to the Court a new outlook as to the needs of society and the formulae that can be used to fill those needs. Accordingly, in the summer of 1957, when the Court re-examined the Smith Act, it *overturned* the conviction of another group of communist leaders.[19] In this case, the Court showed itself to be returning to the clear and present danger rule, for it stated that in order for advocacy of communism to be a crime, "those to whom the advocacy is addressed must be urged to do something now or in the future, rather than merely to believe in something." In short, the Court has now *modified the Smith Act* so that its penalties will not apply to those who engage merely in "abstract preaching" or "advocacy in the realm of ideas," but only to those who advocate a concrete course of illegal action.

Not all in our society would agree that the Court has acted here in the best interests of national security, and many will disagree as to what results, if any, this recent decision will have upon the course of our struggle against communism. Nearly all, however, would agree that the Court serves us well when it reminds us that in cutting free

19 *Oleta Yates et al.* v. *U.S.* 354 U.S. 298.

speech, no matter how good the cause, we risk slashing the jugular of democracy.

BIBLIOGRAPHICAL NOTE

On the general dimensions of American democracy see Robert M. Mac-Iver, *The Ramparts We Guard,* 1950; Carl L. Becker, *Freedom and Responsibility in the American Way of Life,* 2nd ed., 1955; Robert A. Dahl, *A Preface to Democratic Theory,* 1956.

For a universal argument on behalf of civil rights (for example, liberty) see John Stuart Mill, *On Liberty,* 1859 (in several subsequent editions); and for a treatment of civil rights in the American context see Robert K. Carr, ed., *Civil Rights in America, Annals,* May, 1951; Zechariah Chafee, *Free Speech in the United States,* 1941; Milton R. Konvitz, *Bill of Rights Reader,* 1954.

On the relationship between American constitutional patterns and civil rights, *The Federalist,* 1787–1788 (in several editions) remains a basic exposition, especially papers numbered 9, 10, 31, 35, 51. On the (constitutional) interpretive powers of the courts see Edward Levi, *An Introduction to Legal Reasoning,* 1948; and on the interpretive powers of the President, see Edward S. Corwin, *The President,* 1948, Chapter IV.

On specific civil rights issues and on contemporary civil rights patterns see: U.S. President's Committee on Civil Rights, *To Secure These Rights,* 1947; Morton Grodzins, *Americans Betrayed: Politics and the Japanese Evacuation,* 1949; Albert P. Blaustein and Clarence C. Ferguson, Jr., *Desegregation and the Law,* 1957; V. O. Key, Jr., *Southern Politics,* 1949, especially Part IV, "Southern Voters"; Henry S. Commager, *Freedom, Loyalty, Dissent,* 1954; and David Spitz, "On the Abuses of Power in Democratic States," *Midwest Journal of Political Science,* Vol. I, Nov. 1957.

11. JAMES M. BURNS

Some Conclusions On the Study of Public Policy

ONE obvious conclusion stands out in any survey of the major policies and functions of American government—the amazing scope and complexity of governmental activity in America as this nation moves deeper into the second half of the Twentieth Century. The scope of governmental activity hardly needs elaboration here, as all the foregoing pages furnish extensive documentation. One little fact not noted above, however, offers a striking demonstration of the contrast between Big Government today and the scope of government only a few decades ago. At the turn of the century one of the Vanderbilts employed more men and spent more money in experimental work in agriculture and forestry than did the Department of Agriculture itself.[1] In 1957 the Agriculture Department's Agricultural Research Service employed 18,847—and this did not include the research personnel of the Forest Service.

Along with the increase in size has gone an enormous increase in complexity. Government policy surrounds almost every flicker of activity in our industrial, urbanized society. A century ago Henry Thoreau retreated to his hut on the shores of Lake Walden to escape from civilization, including sheriffs and constables with their laws and

[1] Frederick Lewis Allen, *The Big Change* (New York: Harper & Bros., 1952), p. 30.

rules. If he were to do so today, he could not get away from the ear-splitting roar of jet planes from a nearby Air Force base, nor could he avoid seeing improvements made by the local government for the sake of public use of the lake. Again, it is hardly necessary to document the fact that government function and policy are all around us; the foregoing pages attest to this.

Obviously, many influences bring about the final policy. A political scientist, summing-up a most astute study of one public policy—the Employment Act of 1946—suggests forces that have appeared again and again in our own study of many other policies. Speaking in this case of *legislative* policy making, Professor Stephen K. Bailey concluded that the process was "unbelievably complex." He continued:

> Legislative policy-making appears to be the result of a confluence of factors streaming from an almost endless number of tributaries: national experience, the contributions of social theorists, the clash of powerful economic interests, the quality of Presidential leadership, other institutional and personal ambitions and administrative arrangements in the Executive Branch, the initiative, effort, and ambitions of individual legislators and their governmental and nongovernmental staffs, the policy commitments of political parties, and the predominant culture symbols in the minds both of leaders and followers in the Congress.[2]

When one considers that this account involved essentially only the national government and that many policies, as depicted above, involve at least two other layers of government, the full dimension of complexity is suggested.

It is the task of the student, however, to try to make sense out of all the confusion by finding similarities among the forces affecting the making of policy. What generalizations are permissible? What common factors seem to shape most policies at all levels of government?

THE GROUP APPROACH TO POLICY-MAKING

In the first chapter of this volume politics was viewed essentially as interest group—as the product of the conflict and combinations of literally millions of groups coalescing around particular problems for the solution of which they seek government action (or inaction). It was suggested that we do not need to view interest groups—or "pressure groups," as they are often called—as being "bad" or "good"; it was suggested that politics is not just a battle between the good guys

[2] Stephen K. Bailey, *Congress Makes a Law* (New York: Columbia University Press, 1950), p. 236.

and the bad guys. The struggle among interests is a traditional, normal and desirable—even indispensable—attribute of a free society and a democratic political system. Without such group struggles we would have the cold, gray, dead society that might be produced in a totalitarian country only after decades of systematic and successful brainwashing.

On this score, too, one can conclude that the chapters on specific policies and functions have well documented the vital and central role of the group struggle. All government policy seems mainly and directly the product of group politics. Businessmen want subsidies; workers want protective legislation; farmers want government aid; minorities suffering discrimination want enforcement of civil rights statutes or the passage of new legislation, as in the case of the Civil Rights Act (voting rights) of 1957; teachers want government aid to education; city groups want heavier taxation on rural groups; automobile drivers want better roads; parents want more playground equipment; and so it goes.

Intra-group conflicts make policies

All this is obvious to anyone who merely glances at the front page of the newspaper; less obvious but often more important are the clashes that take place within or between groups. Tussles between business and labor, between middlemen and farmers, between consumers and producers, are obvious—but what are we to say of issues that arise *within* the ranks of business itself, *between* different wings of the labor movement, *among* various farm groups? Yet as we look back on the multifarious policies of government, it seems to be such intramural conflicts that give shape and character to government policy.

One of the major influences on labor policy, for example, has been the split between labor groups—for example, between craft unions and industrial unions, or between leftist, "ideological" labor groups and those, such as Gompers' A.F.L., more concerned with "bread-and-butter" unionism, more hopeful of gaining what it wanted by working within, rather than against, the capitalistic system. Or consider transportation policy. Chapter 5 suggests again and again that the history of transportation policy in the United States is the history of elements in the transportation industry fighting among themselves. To be sure, outside forces are not to be dismissed, as in the case of Granger protest against railway rates and the ensuing laws establishing state supervision of railway rates and services. But since the rise of intensive competition within the industry, as in the case of the tremendous development of trucking, the shape of government transportation policy has been largely forged between the hammer and anvil of the transportation groups striking for advantage.

Indeed, the point can be pressed further, for there is some political combat even within the *same* transportation industry. For example, not only are truckers as a whole arrayed against their railroad and water competition; but within the trucking industry one finds some competition (though of course muted, for the sake of putting up a somewhat united front against the common opposition) between the large truckers with a hundred or more vehicles, and the small operators with one or two trucks. Many examples can be found in other areas—for example, there is a discernible, though not major, lack of identity of interest between doctors with private practices and doctors employed in large hospitals, clinics, and government agencies. Again, the "sugar interests" would seem to be a small enough group to allow for solidarity in politics, but in fact one finds disunity between beet sugar producers in this country and importers of cane sugar from Cuba and other countries.

It may be noted parenthetically that such intra-group differences are the bane of the politician's life. He would much prefer to take a stand for a large group with the certainty that its members stand foursquare behind him; but he is constantly discovering, to his chagrin, that the group lacks unity, that by taking some stand he has opened up a Pandora's box of differences within the group, and these intramural clashes are often more ticklish and unpredictable than those between the whole group and some "out-group." The politician discovers, in short, that "cross-pressures" are at work among and within his groups, and the art of compromising among all these factions is not easily come by. No wonder the typical candidate would prefer to seize on some issue that might win support from the whole group—wrapping himself in the flag, denouncing foreigners, attacking subversives, favoring peace, and so forth—than get involved in the tricky specific issues of policy that divide interest groups.

Policies make groups

It would be a mistake, however, to think of public policy and function as merely products of the group struggle, whether external or internal. Government not only reflects groups—it creates them. The foregoing pages are studded with examples of new groups that have sprung up around activities of local, state, and national governments. The TVA is an example. This enterprise, whatever its merits or demerits in the eyes of the public as a whole, has brought great benefits to the Tennessee River valley; its directors were politically astute enough to capitalize on this fact and to establish close ties with Senators, Governors, state resource, agricultural, and conservation chiefs, and with other leaders and interest groups throughout the area benefitting from the program. Here is a new and powerful interest group that springs into militant action when the interests of the TVA—and hence of themselves—are challenged.

Other examples of government-created interest groups are those enjoying public power at low rates from the Rural Electrification Administration or from government dams; farmers benefiting from agricultural programs; teacher lobbying for better salaries and more federal aid to education; highway users; and the myriad associations of government officials and employees, organized either in professional groups such as the Municipal Finance Officers Association, or in unions under the AFL-CIO or independent auspices.

To be sure, the precise relation of cause and effect must be traced out in individual cases. If government creates groups, it is also true that in some cases a small group might have brought about in the first instance a government policy that in turn nourished the group and contributed ultimately to a powerful interest operating through a "pressure group." What we clearly have is a complex system of interaction, or reciprocal cause and effect, in which group and government become hopelessly entangled, each nurturing the other. The end product of this process, as Chapter 1 suggests, is that there is no sharp line between the group and the government—group leaders are *in* government, or to express the same matter differently, government is made up of concentric and overlapping circles of group leaders. Hence it is not surprising that in the study cited above, Professor Bailey concluded that it was not so much pressure *on* government as pressure *in* government that basically affected the makeup of the Employment Act of 1946.

Such a view of government is a worrisome one, for it raises the question whether government officials are merely puppets of powerful and perhaps sinister forces—indeed, that government officials *are* these forces. The saving fact is that no one group is large enough or powerful enough to exert such influence in a systematic and decisive fashion. Our society is heterogeneous and pluralistic. Government officials are members of many groups—they must be in order to get elected or appointed in the first place. A huge variety of groups press their claims on, in, and through government. Not only are officials themselves subject to a great cross-hatching and patchwork of attitudes and loyalties, but groups leaders outside government are subject to the same forces. No man, no group, is an island. The effective group leader must keep in mind the claims of other groups even as he presses his own. It is this vast give-and-take, this mutual accommodation, this sensitivity to competing group interests on the part of group leaders both inside and outside government that maintains moderation and balance in our policy. To be sure, an occasional group leader like John L. Lewis of the United Mine Workers seems to ignore the claims of other groups, but usually government and society are able to summon countervailing forces that prevent any one group, no matter how powerfully organized and militantly led, from upsetting the balance of interests.

The recognition of this balance is not an invitation to smugness over the American political system. For one thing, certain groups—consumers, migratory farmers, certain white collar groups—have far less influence over public policy than their numbers in a democracy should provide. For another, groups have long taken advantage of peculiar aspects of our system in order to maximize their power. This is not surprising, since the framers of the Constitution deliberately erected a balanced system that would, for example, provide special representation to rural and agricultural interests in the Senate, and to urban (or at least more thickly settled) areas in the House of Representatives. The division of power between the national and state governments was designed in part to break the power of "faction", whether majority or minority, as Madison suggested.[3] The previous chapters raise questions, however, as to whether modern "factions" do not benefit unduly from our joint system of division of power and separation of powers. Madison was thinking mainly of preventing one faction from tyrannizing over another; we can ponder today the problem of a specially favored group systematically exploiting government for more than is its due.

OTHER APPROACHES TO POLICY-MAKING

Is the group approach to policy-making, in the light of the above considerations, an *all-inclusive* approach? Can all policies be studied and

[3] *Federalist Paper, No. 10.*

understood in terms of the vast and complex ferment of group struggle? The answer is yes *if* the concept of group is broadened enough. If the concept of "group" is viewed as including *potential* groups that might spring into existence if a certain policy were followed (for example, a special and heavy tax on all redheaded men would doubtless produce a militant League of Redheaded Men far different from the fictional one concocted by A. Conan Doyle); if the concept of group is viewed as including groups that mediate between the symbols, values, and expectations of the American people on the one hand and the policy-making mechanism on the other hand; if the group concept is used— as it sometimes is—to differentiate between the passive rank and file of groups and their group leaders; if the group concept is broad enough to cover these and other elements of the political process— *then* the group concept can be used as virtually a total explanation.[4]

Some students of politics and policy-making, however, believe that to use the group concept in so broad a fashion is to make it a less effective device for thinking about the role of other elements in the political process. They feel, in short, that the group approach is necessary but not adequate. Two other ways of evaluating the forces behind government policy and function are worth noting.

The total environment

By total environment we mean the totality of values, expectations, traditions, customs, usages, and beliefs that form the psychological context within which the group struggle takes place (and which it reflects and reshapes). These are the ideas and expectations in the minds of men—voters, group leaders, governmental officials—long before they turn to the job of voting on, discussing, or drawing up a particular policy. The idea may be so vague or implicit that it is hard to define—"inarticulate major premises," as Justice Oliver Wendell Holmes once termed them. Or it may be, on occasion, as explicit as a code of law, especially in such areas as morals. Most basic values are neither very explicit nor very vague—they do have some meaning that can be applied in deciding among alternative policies. Examples of fundamental values have been well phrased by a sociologist:[5]

Achievement and success: These are indispensable values in a mixed

---

[4] For an able development of this problem, see David B. Truman, *The Governmental Process* (New York: Alfred A. Knopf, 1951), chap. 3.

[5] Adapted from Robin M. Williams, Jr., *American Society* (New York: Alfred A. Knopf, 1951), pp. 374-84, 388-440.

private enterprise, "pecuniary" society such as ours, which measures success largely in terms of money, status, and prestige.

Efficiency: Americans usually emphasize practicality and "hard-headedness" at the expense of aesthetic, reflective, or theoretical approaches or preoccupations.

Progress: The idea of progress has been one of the vital and dynamic factors in the immense material and technical advances of Western civilization. Most things—at least material things—of the past are now outdated and outmoded. Progress often means bigness. Despite much nostalgic talk for the way we lived decades ago, most Americans have little use today for that way of life.

External conformity: We should be like other people, not be "different," not "rock the boat." Business mores pervade the whole culture, according to some observers, and especially the corporate, middle- and upper-class world.[6] Despite our professions of individualism, we increasingly tend to conform to the opinions, manners, dress, housing, speech, and ideas of others.

Such values as these have implications for many areas of study, but especially for that of policy-making. Our concern with efficiency leads us often to test government policies and functions in simple, efficient terms—"the most bang for a buck," to take an example from recent military policy. Our tendency toward conformity is closely related to our attitudes toward the specific application of such liberties as those embraced in the Bill of Rights. Other major value orientations, such as humanitarianism, egalitarianism, freedom, and democracy, have even more direct relation to policy-making. These values are, to be sure, very vague and inchoate—but this is precisely why they are so powerful and durable. "Individualism" as a basic value may come to have varying specific implications and applications as the years pass, but it is a concept not to be discounted at any one time in the policy-making process. Changes in the meaning and intensity of values are precisely the factors to be considered by the student of policy-making, not to be ignored as indicating the meaninglessness of the values or the fickleness of the people.

It is useful to keep in mind that a belief-system embraces not only values prized by a people but includes also their *expectations*. For example, people may prize material welfare—they may want to have two houses and several cars for each person—but this want will not be an actual factor in their political behavior because they realize that

---

[6] William H. Whyte, Jr., *The Organization Man* (New York: Simon & Schuster, 1956).

it is impossible. What *is* important politically is what they *expect* to have—what they think is rightfully theirs. In an environment dominated by inegalitarian ideas the expectations of the working class might be quite low, and this would have a profound impact on policy-making; but in another society, such as ours, expectations are raised high by our value system (and by certain great documents) stressing considerable equality for all men. These expectations are sharpened by the media—the slick magazines, television, movies—which proclaim in advertising that *everyone* can and should have a freezer, dishwasher, and perhaps even a second car.

Two examples in history point up the impact of expectations on policy-making. In 1787 the framers of the Constitution at Philadelphia produced a Constitution bristling with features—indirect election of Senators, checks and balances, and so on—ably contrived to prevent government from falling into the hands of popular majorities intent on converting their beliefs into law. The anti-Federalists of the day mainly objected to the new Constitution because it seemed to give too much power to the national government and perhaps too much power to the executive. From our vantage point today this seems strange—why, we ask, did not the less propertied groups attack the new charter on the ground that it was well designed to keep them from getting control of the government, to keep them from mobilizing a majority from the ranks of the discontented? Why did they not, in other words, press for a Constitution that would more readily translate popular demands into public policy? The answer, in part, is that the "ordinary" people of the day did not look on government as a source of good—they did not expect of government that it could be used extensively to help the common man; what they wanted from government was hands-off. Their best hope was not that government should be given power that could be used to help them, but that it would be hemmed in so as not to hurt them.

More recent developments show an equally close relation between expectations and public policy. During the depression there was not widespread demand for strong national action, at least for the first two or three years. Americans in general did not *expect* the national government to cope with the kind of economic crisis that faced the nation; many Americans, indeed, felt that the depression would lift as quickly as government further disentangled itself from the economy. Notice the shift in expectations today. The Employment Act of 1946 reflected new expectations of most Americans, bred in the depression conditions of the 1930's, the reformist period of the New Deal, and the full employment conditions of wartime, that government should be responsible for working with management, labor, and other groups to prevent depression or relieve it quickly if it comes. So strong has this expectation become that national party leaders today are aware that inability to cope with a depression or major recession by either party would mean not only its repudiation at the polls in the next election but a long period of wandering in the political wilderness.

Leadership and policy

All those affected by, or ultimately involved in, a public policy do not have the same role in creating it. In the example of the Redheaded League mentioned previously, a punitive tax on redheads would not produce an equal reaction on the part of all those favored with such hair. Some would rush to see their legislator, write letters to the President, or issue a call for a protest meeting—but many others would not do anything, and still others would lend only passive support to the zealots. Some redheads would not be nearly as active as some blondes, brunettes, and grayheads who simply disapproved of such arbitrary government action or who had daughters, or cousins, or friends who were caught in the meshes of the Redheaded Tax. The mainspring of action, in short, would consist of *leaders* inside and outside the group immediately involved.

As in the use of the group approach, the leadership concept should be employed as a generality.[7] There are many kinds of leaders—leaders in government, such as Presidents, Congressmen, mayors, and state attorney generals; leaders in groups ranging from the official councils or officers that may run a huge group such as the AFL-CIO to the thousands of formal local leaders, like union shop stewards and commanders of local Legion posts, and ranging still further to the tens of thousands of *informal* local group leaders—the "active minorities" that dominate the affairs of local groups whether through the formally chosen officers or not.

As noted, just as we can regard group memberships as cutting across government officials and "ordinary" voters, so we must think of leadership both inside and outside the government. Leadership is not some quality that is automatically granted to some person simply because

[7] For an excellent example of how the group concept can be used to embrace a concept such as leadership, see Truman, *op. cit.*, pp. 139 ff., where he employs the term "active minority" in generalizing about the roles of leaders within groups.

he holds some formal position or power; nor is it a trait or quality that some people are gifted with at birth, or somehow learn from a book. Leadership is always a function of such factors as time and place and the interaction of varied personalities in ever-changing contexts. Its exercise depends on its relation to all the other elements—groups politics, the environment, the policy-making process itself, and so on— that make up the total political process. Leadership, in short, is an ingredient of policy-making, not a total explanation of it.[8]

Still, it is the *politician* in office—the politician who has won election or appointment—who is at the end of the policy-making process, at the crucial point where environmental forces, group pressures and vacuums, and the long decision-making process come to a final focus before policies take their literal form on statute books. As the first chapter suggests, he is the "vital link" in two senses—he mediates among the groups concerned in the policy, and he *reflects* what his constituents (both group and electoral) want and in turn *influences* what his constituents want—or at least will accept.

The central role of the politician (as decision-maker) in serving as a link between inchoate and unfocused popular attitudes and expectations and ultimate public policy is well illustrated in a recent study of responses to the televised Kefauver Committee hearings.[9] It will be recalled that these hearings on local bribery and corruption in New York City a few years ago had a sensational impact on public attention —taxis were hard to get, the routine of city life was altered as New Yorkers watched the parade of local wrong-doing exposed on their television screens. People were aroused. Indignation ran high. But what did the aroused people actually *do* in a constructive way? According to the study, the main result was indignation combined with a feeling of impotence—a situation characterized by "concern with a common problem; impulses compounded of undirected energy, power fantasies, disassociation, and some impulses toward problem-solving behavior; much talking . . . but little actual behavior directed toward the solution of the problem; and finally, the strong tendency to reject even the problem-solving behavior as hopeless." What was clearly lacking here (among other things) was electoral or group political

[8] For a thoughtful introduction to aspects of leadership, see Lester G. Seligman, "The Study of Political Leadership," *The American Political Science Review,* Vol. XLIV, No. 4 (December, 1950), pp. 908-9. For a comparative study of leadership in different contexts, see Elmer E. Cornwell, Jr., "Lloyd George: A Study in Political Leadership," (Ph.D. dissertation, Harvard University, 1954).

[9] G. D. Wiebe, "Responses to the Televised Kefauver Hearings: Some Social Psychological Implications," *Public Opinion Quarterly,* Vol. 16 (Summer, 1952), pp. 179-200.

leadership to translate these intense but unfocused responses into clear sets of alternatives and finally into public policy. The politician's role would have been both *activist* and *mediatory*—he would have both translated opinions into policy and at the same time, in framing alternative policies, in debating them, he would have in turn re-shaped and crystallized the opinions of those wanting something done about local corruption.

How much power should the leader have over policy-making—how much discretion or leeway? No flat answer to the question is possible even for a single polity like that of the United States, much less for the great variety of other systems throughout the world. Perhaps the best that we can ask is that the political system allow leadership initiative and flexibility when these may be necessary—for example, in severe military and economic crisis—while allowing or requiring a shifting of powers away from leaders, and a re-diffusing of powers among various power points (such as courts) and interest groups, after the crisis has been met. To a great extent the American system has met this test. Much of the policy described in previous chapters found its inauguration or modernization in the 1930's, when a magnetic presidential leader was able to operate the federal system to move ahead rapidly on many policy fronts, making up in a few years for decades of inertia in those fields. Whether we can depend on our system to operate in time of crisis, especially when a gifted leader may not be available, is one of the leading problems of political science.

THE INEVITABILITY OF POLICY

In the light of the emphasis throughout this volume on the role of government or other positive agencies in the fashioning of policy, it might be well to conclude by reminding ourselves that policy, as broadly defined, is formed whether or not government takes positive action. By "policy as broadly defined" we mean privately (nongovernmentally) framed policy, and we mean that the absence of public policy may be as important as the existence of policy as far as major interests are concerned.

Many of the foregoing pages have stressed that in the absence of public policy a host of private policies were important enough to have impact far outside the boundaries of a particular economic or social enterprise. For example, in the absence of public regulation of prices, output, quality, and the like, private industries may cooperate to set up an internal system of self-government to make decisions on these matters and even to police them. In short, where public government is not present, private government may exist. Since the decisions of such private governments may—and usually do—significantly affect the public interest, it is idle to talk about the absence of policy—policy exists, but is not shaped or necessarily sanctioned by government responsible to the voters.

On occasion, as in the Sherman Anti-Trust Act of 1890, the "public" government may decide to illegalize any self-government (called "monopoly") within certain "private" sectors of business and industry. Does this mean the absence of policy? Again we would say no. In the absence of central public or centralized private decision-making this sector of the economy is being left to the interplay of tens of thousands of local, private, and separate decisions (or policies) on the part of the businessmen involved in the marketplace. These policies may be obscure, fugitive, and unpredictable—but they exist, and they touch on the interests of many groups (labor, suppliers, exporters, dealers) outside the immediate marketplace.

This notion of the inevitability of policy also has implications for policy-making between different branches or levels of government. Consider the case of civil rights. For many decades Congress refused to make new public decisions involving civil rights because a dominant element in Congress was satisfied with the *private* policies of white groups in southern communities and with the *public* policies of state and local officials in the South. Presidents of the United States took some action, as noted in Chapter 10, but Presidents lacked the constitutional power to make their public policies very extensive or durable. One might have thought that, assuming no drastic change in the outlook or power organization of Congress, no national public policy of importance would be forthcoming. But then in 1954 came one of the epochal policy announcements of this century—that of school integration. The author of this policy was not the President nor Congress, but the Supreme Court. The forces that had been piling up for years in favor of broadened civil rights in education had at last found response in—ironically enough—the least "popular" (directly representative) branch of the national government. Policy cannot be endlessly dammed up—it must find outlet either in altered sets of private arrangements or in new public decisions.

Another example of the inevitability of policy involves the division of power between the national and state governments. The chapters on business, labor, transportation, welfare, and other policy areas show that again and again the forces behind policies have turned to the layer of government most responsive to the new public decisions wanted, meantime desperately hunting for the necessary constitutional authority (which shrewd lawyers have usually been able to find) to authorize action at one level as against the other. Perhaps for a time both levels of government have remained impervious to the forces behind new public policies, but ultimately, as one would expect and hope in a free society, part of the barrier (perhaps a state such as Wisconsin or a branch of the national government such as the Executive) gives way and public policies come to be altered.

The stream of policy sweeps ever on. Sometimes—as in the 1930's —it rises to flood stage; at other times it dwindles; and all the time it follows a confused course, backing up, bursting over old levees, eddying and swirling, pursuing subterranean courses. But it is always there, and always in motion. We need not deplore it; we need not seek to stop it; we need only study it and channel it in the light of experience, intelligence, and the processes and principles of a free society.

Index

433

C